The Law of Capi
in the E

C000079757

Konstantinos Sergakis
University of Glasgow, UK

The Law of Capital Markets in the EU

Disclosure and Enforcement

First published 2018 by
PALGRAVE

Palgrave in the UK is an imprint of Macmillan Publishers Limited,
registered in England, company number 785998, of 4 Crinan Street,
London, N1 9XW.

Palgrave® and Macmillan® are registered trademarks in the United States,
the United Kingdom, Europe and other countries.

ISBN 978–1–137–51846–0 paperback

This book is printed on paper suitable for recycling and made from fully
managed and sustained forest sources. Logging, pulping and manufacturing
processes are expected to conform to the environmental regulations of
the country of origin.

A catalogue record for this book is available from the British Library.

A catalog record for this book is available from the Library of Congress.

Printed and bound by CPI Group (UK) Ltd, Croydon, CR0 4YY

To P. and to the promising years ahead

CONTENTS

PREFACE

This book is the culmination of thirteen years of research, since I embarked on the study of the fascinating area of capital markets law back in 2004. The main driving force behind my ongoing research in this field is the delicate task of attempting to decipher the EU policy-making agenda aimed at making capital markets attractive, both to issuers and to (retail and institutional) investors, while at the same time trying to challenge and propose ways to overcome the various obstacles related to national idiosyncrasies (rooted in legal, economic, cultural and social traditions) that continue to impede meaningful market integration. The legislative and regulatory drive at harmonization and convergence at the EU level has undoubtedly been a very complicated task. EU capital markets law has been subject to profound changes and developments, especially after the global financial crisis, which, while more related to deficiencies in the wider area of financial markets, inevitably fuelled a political need to ensure market integrity and stability in capital markets as well.

Capital markets are trading venues that allow issuers to raise capital by issuing bonds, shares and other financial instruments that are publicly traded. They are further divided into regulated and unregulated markets. This book focuses exclusively on regulated markets since they are the ones that attract the most regulatory attention in the form of weighty legal obligations and a series of requirements (such as disclosure requirements and operating standards), as well as numerous prohibitions. Among the numerous financial instruments in capital markets (including transferable securities, money market instruments, units in collective investment undertakings, derivative contracts and so forth), my approach focuses exclusively on transferable securities – predominantly shares. This is because I want to target only the relationship between publicly traded companies and other market actors in equity finance – a relationship that continues to be poorly understood and highly complex, raising challenges for all affected parties in the investment chain. The arguments developed in this book will, I hope, allow for a better understanding of the ongoing challenges and move the academic and policy-making debates forward in a more fruitful direction for the overall efficiency of capital markets law in the EU.

Maintaining the attractiveness of these markets on a steady basis is a goal that has been achieved through extensive disclosure obligations. Information provided to the various market actors has been a key regulatory tool to foster confidence and trust in capital markets. My approach considers this regulatory agenda to be the most visible one in this area of law – and hence open to prolific constructive criticism – and therefore concentrates predominantly on the various aspects of disclosure, their merits and shortfalls, as well as the enforcement methods that are present to ensure that the applicable rules are respected. One of the central arguments of this book is that investor protection, which has repeatedly been praised in various pieces of EU legislation as one of the main pillars for reform, is mostly seen in the spectrum of issuer disclosure obligations. In other words, investor protection is translated into a need to provide the investor community with information *ex ante* so that it can make informed decisions, and much less as something that needs to be strengthened *ex post* within the enforcement framework. I firmly believe that in order for investor protection to take on a more holistic, trustworthy and efficient dimension, both the *ex ante* and *ex post* facets of regulatory intervention need to be developed at a similar (if not equal) pace. As we shall see in various chapters of this book, issuers are subject to potential enforcement mechanisms that have not yet attained optimal levels of deterrence. This book therefore aims to highlight the discrepancy between these two prerogatives and to propose their recalibration at the EU level.

I would like to thank several colleagues who have contributed, directly or indirectly, to this piece of work. First of all, Dr Marc Moore, who entrusted me with this task and gave me *carte blanche* to shape this topic in the way I always desired. His continuous support and flexibility all these years are greatly appreciated. Secondly, I would like to thank Professor Iris Chiu for her invaluable advice during the various stages of writing this book, as well as for her continuous support in my academic endeavours and our stimulating discussions. Both Dr Moore and Professor Chiu have been great colleagues and excellent editors of this Palgrave series throughout this period. Professor Charlotte Villiers was also a great supporter of this project and strongly encouraged me to join this new Palgrave initiative; most importantly, she was an extremely supportive mentor to me during my two years at the University of Bristol, for which I am truly grateful.

Thirdly, I had the pleasure and great honour to discuss parts of the book (or related research ideas) with Professors Emilios Avgouleas, Blanaid Clarke, Pierre Henri Conac, James Chalmers, Christoph Van der Elst, Iain MacNeil, Jennifer Payne and Takis Tridimas, as well as with CONSOB Commissioner Carmine Di Noia. Their insightful comments are greatly appreciated. Of course, it should not be assumed that they necessarily endorse the views in this book.

My gratitude also goes out to my colleague and friend Professor Hanne Søndergaard Birkmose, who has been a source of constant encouragement. Her outstanding leadership as Principal Investigator in our Research Project entitled 'Shareholder Duties', funded by the Danish Ministry of Education (2014–2017), not only meant that I had very generous and continuous funding for three years, enabling me to travel around the world for my research, but also that I had the opportunity to participate in numerous activities with extremely inspiring and esteemed colleagues. I am grateful as ever for our discussions and her understanding with regard to the time I dedicated to this book while being part of this great project.

I am also greatly indebted to Professor Iain MacNeil, the Head of the School of Law at the University of Glasgow, for his inspiring scholarship, unconditional support and constant availability. Our continuous exchange of ideas about various aspects of my career aspirations (and concerns) have inculcated me with sound foundations for the future. Most importantly, I am thankful for his valuable mentorship and headship at Glasgow, a place that has proven to be the most stimulating and exciting working environment in my career.

During the various stages of this book, I have been greatly assisted by various individuals: Rob Gibson (formerly of Palgrave Macmillan), Aléta Bezuidenhout and Helen Bugler at Palgrave; their advice, flexibility and understanding of my various needs over these years are testimonies to their dedication and professionalism. Christopher Mobley provided excellent proofreading assistance with great efficiency and responsiveness to pressing deadlines. I am also truly thankful to the anonymous reviewers for their constructive comments on the various aspects of this book. Their valuable comments and vital assistance made it possible to complete this work in the most satisfactory way.

A special word of thanks is due to my memorable students in France, Germany and the UK, who have always nurtured my desire to teach capital markets law with a truly EU dimension in mind, while attaching importance to these three national frameworks that represent, in my view, important references for any capital markets law scholar. The analysis of this book focuses on these three jurisdictions on an ad hoc basis, depicting these stimulating discussions (during and after class), as well as my own passion for advocating the enhancement of harmonization and convergence at the EU level in this area of law. I do hope that this book will be the testimony of my students' engagement in my courses, as well as a reliable guide to the fascinating area of capital markets law to many more students in the future.

This work is dedicated to my precious Emma for her unconditional love, support and encouragement all these years.

Konstantinos Sergakis,
22 October 2017,
Glasgow

PART I

Introduction to the Law of Capital Markets in the EU

CHAPTER 1

The Foundations of the Law of Capital Markets in the EU

1.1 INTRODUCTION

This chapter aims to provide an overall analysis of the historical foundations of capital markets legislative initiatives at the EU level, bringing us up to the most recent legislative initiatives. By following the evolution of the EU legal framework in this area, the analysis will touch on the market, political and legislative landmarks that were crucial to shaping the current regulatory spectrum. After a brief explanation of the first legislative approach at the EU level (1979–1999), this chapter will analyse the Financial Services Action Plan (FSAP) (1999), as well as the Lamfalussy report (2000), which gave birth to the most crucial EU (minimum and maximum) harmonization trends with a series of Directives and Regulations coming out in the following years.

The chapter will then present and explain regulatory decisions with regard to the outcomes of the global financial crisis, and will attempt to show the responsiveness of EU law and its aspects as a 'financial scandal-driven' regulation. This will aim to highlight not only the historical background of the first developments in capital markets but, most importantly, the driving forces behind the evolution of the legislative framework which has shaped and continues to influence the regulatory agenda.[1]

At the same time, the chapter will provide a brief overview of the regulatory rationales for the creation and the continuous development of rules in the area of capital markets law and will also seek to challenge the choice of minimum or maximum harmonization as regulatory tools in various areas subject to EU rules. This analysis will shed light on the outcomes of both harmonization levels and will aim to propose overarching guidelines for the future shaping of EU capital markets rules.

---

[1] For an overview, see T. Tridimas, 'EU Financial Regulation: Federalization, Crisis Management, and Law Reform' in P. Craig and G. De Búrca (eds), *The Evolution of EU Law* (2nd edn, Oxford University Press, 2011), 783.

1.2 A Short History

1.2.1 The Embryonic Stages

The Segré report launched the first sign of the creation of an EU capital market by recommending, *inter alia*, the use of disclosure, not only at the prospectus stage but also as a 'continuous flow of information' at the service of investors so as to familiarize them with issuers and the functioning of capital markets.[2] The report was considerably lengthy and provided various rationales for the creation of an EU capital market, mainly deriving its arguments from the apparent deficiencies and gaps observed during the past, notably in terms of market integration, harmonization of disclosed information and enforcement.

It is important to note that one of the main driving forces for such integration was – and remains – the attractiveness of capital markets for retail investors. Indeed, EU retail investors have traditionally been reluctant to invest their savings in capital markets, in the absence of a truly integrated regulatory and enforcement framework that inspires confidence in the markets and provides reassurance of appropriate compensation mechanisms in the event of investor losses. It therefore became vital to the success of any EU regulatory initiative to foster such confidence in the functioning of capital markets via the introduction of rules that strengthened the harmonization of informational requirements.[3]

Following the Segré report's recommendations for setting rules for admission of securities to trading as well as for disclosure requirements in prospectuses, EU law attempted to draw a first picture of what EU capital markets should look like, at least at the entry level of securities, with the enactment of Directives 79/279/EEC[4] and 80/390/EEC.[5] Then came another Directive (82/121/EEC),[6] introducing some common rules regarding information that would have to be disclosed to the market on a regular basis. These three Directives aimed to shape the applicable framework for the first time, by respecting the various differences among national laws and by opting for minimum harmonization of admission and disclosure requirements. Indeed, maximum harmonization at the embryonic stage was considered overly ambitious and unfeasible on a practical level.

---

[2] C. Segré, 'The Development of a European Capital Market. Report of a Group of Experts Appointed by the EEC Commission' (1966), 30, at http://aei.pitt.edu/31823/. For an analysis of this first regulatory era, see N. Moloney, *EU Securities and Financial Markets Regulation* (3rd edn, Oxford University Press, 2014), 22.

[3] The same willingness has not been observed with regard to enforcement mechanisms, which will be dealt with later in this chapter.

[4] Council Directive 79/279/EEC of 5 March 1979 coordinating the conditions for the admission of securities to official stock exchange listing [1979] OJ L 066/21.

[5] Council Directive 80/390/EEC of 17 March 1980 coordinating the requirements for the drawing up, scrutiny and distribution of the listing particulars to be published for the admission of securities to official stock exchange listing [1980] OJ L 100/1.

[6] Council Directive 82/121/EEC of 15 February 1982 on information to be published on a regular basis by companies the shares of which have been admitted to official stock-exchange listing [1982] OJ L 48/26.

1.2.2 The Decisive Steps Towards Harmonization

Following the publication of a White Paper entitled 'Completing the Internal Market',[7] whose main aim, in relation to capital markets, was to highlight the existence of barriers between stock exchanges and the need to create an EU trading system for securities, EU law responded more drastically by gradually increasing the level of harmonization in the areas of disclosure of major shareholdings,[8] prospectuses,[9] insider dealing[10] and investment services.[11] These Directives offered a strengthened regulatory framework in critical sectors of capital markets and aimed to convey the message of further integration to investors. Nevertheless, various differences among Member States persisted.

The Commission responded to the increasing need for modernization of capital markets law with the FSAP[12] in 1999. The FSAP, benefiting from the introduction of the euro that same year, had a Commission mandate for the elimination of the remaining capital market fragmentation, so as to reduce the cost of capital raised on EU markets; the free exploitation of opportunities offered by a single financial market for both users and suppliers of financial services; the closer coordination of supervisory authorities; and the development of an integrated EU infrastructure for retail and wholesale financial transactions.[13] The FSAP therefore decided to recommend major changes to enable issuers to raise capital on competitive terms at the EU level; to provide investors and intermediaries with access to all markets from a single point of entry; to allow investment service providers to offer their services on a cross-border basis by eliminating administrative or legal obstacles; to establish a sophisticated prudential framework that asset managers can use effectively; and to create legal certainty in the area of security trade and settlement.[14]

These new objectives required revisions to existing Directives and Regulations (related to prospectus and ongoing information requirements, as well as

---

[7] Commission, 'Completing the Internal Market: White Paper from the Commission to the European Council (1985) Brussels, COM(85) 310 final, at http://europa.eu/documents/comm/white_papers/pdf/com1985_0310_f_en.pdf.

[8] Council Directive 88/627/EEC of 12 December 1988 on the information to be published when a major holding in a listed company is acquired or disposed of [1988] OJ L 348/62.

[9] Council Directive 89/298/EEC of 17 April 1989 coordinating the requirements for the drawing-up, scrutiny and distribution of the prospectus to be published when transferable securities are offered to the public [1989] OJ L 124/8.

[10] Council Directive 89/592/EEC of 13 November 1989 coordinating regulations on insider dealing [1989] OJ L 334/30.

[11] Council Directive 93/22/EEC of 10 May 1993 on investment services in the securities field [1993] OJ L 141/27.

[12] Communication from the Commission, 'Implementing the Framework for Financial Markets: Action Plan' (1999) COM(1999) 232 final, at http://eur-lex.europa.eu/legal-content/EN/TXT/PDF/?uri=CELEX:51999DC0232&from=EN.

[13] Communication from the Commission, 'Financial Services: Building a Framework for Action' (1998) COM (98) 625 final, at http://ec.europa.eu/internal_market/finances/docs/actionplan/index/fs_en.pdf.

[14] FSAP, above n. 12, 17.

accounting issues), along with the introduction of new measures (related, *inter alia*, to market manipulation and takeover bids). EU law was ready to modernize various areas of capital markets law but, admittedly, the problem was not the content of rules but the method of their design and the speed at which they were implemented, interpreted and effectively applied at national level. This was especially relevant in capital markets due to the constantly changing market trends and challenges that required quickly adaptable and sophisticated rules.

The next decisive step was made by the Lamfalussy Group, which focused on these problematic issues and proposed an alternative process for the enactment and implementation of EU legislation.[15] The so-called 'Lamfalussy process'[16] introduced a four-level comitology approach for faster, more efficient law-making.

> Level 1 refers to the enactment of Directives or Regulations that contain the main and broadly formulated rules in a specific area of capital markets law and that have been shaped by the Commission after an extensive consultation process, with the involvement of the European Parliament and the Council.
>
> Level 2 refers to implementing measures that aim to further specify technical details to make the general Level 1 rules more concrete. Level 2 was therefore conceived to offer a more adaptable and quick regulatory response to new market challenges that would be able to trigger new rules in due time. The Lamfalussy Group also proposed the creation of two new Committees: the European Securities Committee (ESC), which would assume both regulatory and advisory capacities, and the Committee of European Securities Regulators (CESR),[17] which was to assume a purely advisory capacity and would assist in the preparation of such implementing measures. The European Securities and Markets Authority (ESMA)[18] has now absorbed CESR's role and considerably expanded its own presence within this framework.
>
> Level 3 deals with ESMA's role in issuing guidelines and recommendations to ensure the uniform application of the Level 1 and Level 2 rules by national competent authorities (NCAs) or market participants. It must be noted that Level 3 tools do not have any binding force (these are soft law rules), but the sole aim to assist concerned parties in interpreting the

---

[15] The Committee of Wise Men, 'Final Report of the Committee of Wise Men on the Regulation of European Securities Markets' (2001), at http://ec.europa.eu/internal_market/securities/docs/lamfalussy/wisemen/final-report-wise-men_en.pdf; for a critical approach, see G. Hertig and R. Lee, 'Four Predictions about the Future of EU Securities Regulation' (2003) 3(2) *Journal of Corporate Law Studies* 359.

[16] Moloney, above n. 2, 862.

[17] CESR served as the basis for the creation of the European Securities Markets Authority (ESMA).

[18] See 3.2.2. P-H. Conac and V. Caillat, 'De CESR à l'ESMA: le Rubicon est franchi' (2010) 6 *Bulletin Joly Bourse* 500.

applicable rules uniformly. A notion of indirect harmonization emerges at Level 3, aiming to further accentuate the creation of a level playing field among national frameworks.

Level 4 deals with the supervision of national laws in terms of enforcement of the applicable rules. The Commission retains the right to take the necessary measures if national laws have not complied with EU law.

ESMA has a key role to play in this framework in terms of the supervisory convergence that needs to be ensured among NCAs. This is undoubtedly a delicate task since, notwithstanding the ongoing efforts at the EU level, national differences still remain.[19]

The Lamfalussy process was – and remains – a very popular method that has received considerable political support. It has also managed to involve stakeholders since the initial stage of the comitology at Level 1 via extensive consultation processes, as well as at Level 2 with various stakeholder groups[20] assisting ESMA in an advisory capacity. ESMA in particular has a key role to play in the success of the existing and future regulatory initiatives, since it has been granted significant powers that enable it to accentuate harmonization among national frameworks.

Following the launch of the Lamfalussy process, and before the creation of ESMA, EU law benefited from the comitology framework by further modernizing disclosure obligations. The Prospectus Directive,[21] the Market Abuse Directive[22] and the Transparency Directive[23] are the most notable examples of such reforms that allowed EU capital markets law to reach a more concrete operational framework. At the same time, EU law made a decisive step towards framing investment firms' activities with Directive 2004/39/EC.[24] Another achievement of that period, albeit a more modest one, was the enactment of the Takeover Directive, which introduced a harmonized disclosure framework

---

[19] For an early critical assessment of the FSAP and ESMA's predecessor CESR within the Lamfalussy process, see L. Enriques and M. Gatti, 'Is There a Uniform EU Securities Law After the Financial Services Action Plan?' (2008) 14(1) *Stanford Journal of Law Business and Finance* 43.

[20] For example, the Securities and Markets Stakeholder Group (SMSG).

[21] Directive 2003/71/EC of the European Parliament and the Council of 4 November 2003 on the prospectus to be published when securities are offered to the public or admitted to trading and amending Directive 2001/34/EC [2003] OJ L 345/64 (hereinafter PD).

[22] Directive 2004/109/EC of the European Parliament and of the Council of 15 December 2004 on the harmonization of transparency requirements in relation to information about issuers whose securities are admitted to trading on a regulated market and amending Directive 2001/34/EC [2004] OJ L 390/38.

[23] Directive 2003/6/EC of the European Parliament and of the Council of 28 January 2003 on insider dealing and market manipulation [2003] OJ L 96/16 (hereinafter 2003 MAD).

[24] Directive 2004/39/EC of the European Parliament and of the Council of 21 April 2004 on markets in financial instruments amending Council Directives 85/611/EEC and 93/6/EEC and Directive 2000/12/EC of the European Parliament and of the Council and repealing Council Directive 93/22/EEC [2004] OJ L 145/1 (hereinafter MiFID I).

for takeovers as well as the well-known and largely debated board neutrality and breakthrough rules.[25]

What can be already deduced from this second phase of EU capital markets law is the drastic shift from minimum harmonization to a much more increased harmonization and the steady removal of barriers among jurisdictions so as to facilitate access to capital markets for issuers and to achieve true market integration. At the same time, cooperation among national regulators was seen as crucial to resolve enforcement issues, a regulatory choice that has not yet resolved persisting discrepancies at the national level.

1.2.3 The Refinement of EU Regulation

After the completion of these decisive regulatory steps, EU law stood at a good level with a series of successes in terms of both the creation of a legal framework adaptable to market needs and increasing attempts to boost the responsiveness of rules to new market challenges. Nevertheless, the global financial crisis alarmed regulators as to the deficient levels of supervision of financial products and of enforcement, the latter being an area that has yet to be developed sufficiently in the EU. The *de Larosière* report[26] highlighted these deficiencies and proposed, among many things, more harmonization in enforcement mechanisms as well as a reorganization of the law-making process system within the EU, namely the strengthening of the Level 3 committees in the Lamfalussy framework in terms of resources, upgrading their quality and impact of their peer review processes and, most importantly, their legal transformation into European authorities (for example, CESR became ESMA). These new authorities would of course maintain all powers awarded to their predecessors while, at the same time, receiving a significant amount of new powers within the Lamfalussy process and with regard to the coordination of supervisory mechanisms at the national level.[27] The *de Larosière* report therefore did not fundamentally challenge the previous steps that had been achieved at the EU level, the majority of which were beneficial, but principally aimed at refining law-making processes and supervisory systems.

Of course, the global financial crisis also triggered specific concerns with regard to certain industries that were either involved in deficient market practices (such as Credit Rating Agencies, hereinafter CRAs) or had further exacerbated the crisis's already catastrophic consequences, by threatening market stability (for example, short selling practices). New regulatory measures in such areas were therefore inevitable.

---

[25] Directive 2004/25/EC of the European Parliament and of the Council of 21 April 2004 on takeover bids [2004] OJ L 142/12.

[26] The High-Level Group on Financial Supervision in the EU Report, Brussels, 25 February 2009, at http://ec.europa.eu/internal_market/finances/docs/de_larosiere_report_en.pdf.

[27] Ibid., 52.

The political and social framework was very receptive for a much more interventionist approach on behalf of the Commission, which adopted in 2009 Regulation (EC) No 1060/2009.[28] The message was clear: the EU was ready to set higher and more stringent regulatory standards. ESMA's significant empowerment with regard to the registration, supervision and sanctioning of CRAs followed, surprisingly quickly, with the adoption of Regulation (EU) No 513/2011.[29] The last important reform in the CRA agenda was adopted in 2013 via Regulation (EU) No 462/2013.[30] This regulatory intervention was aimed at controlling even more subtle issues related to market risks, such as, among others, the reduction of regulatory dependence on ratings, specific issues on conflicts of interest and rotation of CRAs. Most importantly, this Regulation created a civil liability regime for CRAs, aiming to enhance investor and issuer confidence in their activities.

Short selling also became subject to a stringent EU regulatory framework in 2012,[31] following the well-known and widely publicized incidents related to sovereign credit default swaps, combined with the collapse of major financial services firms. Regulatory bodies intervened due to market stability concerns, reflecting the popular (mis)conception of short selling's detrimental effects on market functioning and stability.[32]

At the same time, EU law endeavoured to improve further the pillars of EU capital markets law, such as Prospectus,[33] Transparency[34] and Market Abuse[35]

---

[28] Regulation (EC) No 1060/2009 of the European Parliament and of the Council of 16 September 2009 on credit rating agencies [2009] OJ L 302/1.

[29] Regulation (EU) No 513/2011 the European Parliament and of the Council of 11 May 2011 amending Regulation (EC) No 1060/2009 on credit rating agencies [2011] OJ L 145/30.

[30] Regulation (EU) No 462/2013 the European Parliament and of the Council of 21 May 2013 amending Regulation (EC) No 1060/2009 on credit rating agencies [2013] OJ L 146/1.

[31] Regulation (EU) 236/2012 of the European Parliament and of the Council of 14 March 2012 on short selling and certain aspects of credit default swaps [2012] OJ L 86/1.

[32] See Chapter 10.

[33] Regulation (EU) 2017/1129 of the European Parliament and of the Council of 14 June 2017 on the prospectus to be published when securities are offered to the public or admitted to trading on a regulated market, and repealing Directive 2003/71/EC [2017] OJ L 168/12 (hereinafter PR).

[34] Directive 2013/50/EU of the European Parliament and of the Council of 22 October 2013 amending Directive 2004/109/EC of the European Parliament and of the Council on the harmonization of transparency requirements in relation to information about issuers whose securities are admitted to trading on a regulated market, Directive 2003/71/EC of the European Parliament and of the Council on the prospectus to be published when securities are offered to the public or admitted to trading, and Commission Directive 2007/14/EC laying down detailed rules for the implementation of certain provisions of Directive 2004/109/EC [2013] OJ L 294/13.

[35] Regulation (EU) No 596/2014 of the European Parliament and of the Council of 16 April 2014 on market abuse (market abuse regulation) and repealing Directive 2003/6/EC of the European Parliament and of the Council and Commission Directives 2003/124/EC, 2003/125/EC and 2004/72/EC OJ L 173/1 (hereinafter 2014 MAR); Directive 2014/57/EU of the European Parliament and of the Council of April 16, 2014 on criminal sanctions for insider dealing and market manipulation [2014] OJ L 173/179 (hereinafter 2014 MAD).

rules, so as to provide rules updated to meet the new challenges that emerged after the global financial crisis. Similar efforts were made with regard to investment firms and, more specifically, with the replacement of MiFID I by Directive 2014/65/EU[36] and Regulation 600/2014/EU.[37] What is observed in this crucial regulatory era is the multiplication of Regulations that replace Directives, since they do not require enactment into national law and accelerate the removal of barriers among jurisdictions. Conversely, Directives require transposition into national law by Member States and are thus less quick in facilitating the elimination of national specificities.

Another critical step has been more recently initiated and relates to the ambitious plan of achieving a truly integrated EU capital market. The Capital Markets Union Action Plan (CMU)[38] was launched in 2015 and aspires to unlocking more investment from the EU and the rest of the world, better connecting financing to various investment projects, stabilizing the financial system and deepening financial integration, as well as increasing competition. It is apparent that the CMU mainly aims to make capital markets more attractive to SMEs, by reducing lowering regulatory barriers,[39] as well as to retail investors while at the same time eliminating cross-border barriers across the EU that can still impede investment opportunities and raising capital operations. Should that political agenda go even further and centralize certain powers more at the EU level that have traditionally been awarded to NCAs, thus leading to an unprecedented reshaping of capital markets regulation as we know it today?[40] There is no doubt that the CMU has offered a prolific field for further reflection upon what kind of regulatory framework we want to have in the future to simplify EU capital markets and boost their efficiency and appeal. The CMU also focuses on crowdfunding opportunities, seen as one new way of making capital markets more attractive and accessible to a broader swathe of retail investors. The overall CMU agenda is highly promising, but it remains to

---

[36] Directive 2014/65/EU of the European Parliament and of the Council of 15 May 2014 on markets in financial instruments and amending Directive 2002/92/EC and Directive 2011/61/EU Text with EEA relevance [2014] OJ L 173/349 (hereinafter MiFID II).

[37] Regulation 600/2014/EU of the European Parliament and of the Council of 15 May 2014 on markets in financial instruments and amending Regulation 648/2012/EU [2014] OJ L 173/84 (hereinafter MiFIR).

[38] Communication from the Commission to the European Parliament, the Council, the European Economic and Social Committee and the Committee of the Regions: Action Plan on Building a Capital Markets Union' (2015) COM(2015) 468 final, at http://eur-lex. europa.eu/legal-content/EN/TXT/PDF/?uri=CELEX:52015DC0468&from=EN.

[39] For a critical approach and a series of interesting proposals, see M. Bianchi, C. Di Noia and M. Gargantini, 'The EU Securities Law Framework for SMEs: Can Firms and Investors Meet?' in Colin Mayer, Stefano Micossi, Marco Onado, Marco Pagano and Andrea Polo (eds), *Finance and Investment: The European Case* (Oxford University Press, 2018) 253.

[40] See, for example, the study of Avgouleas and Ferrarini examining the feasibility of a centralized system of scrutiny and approval of public offers of securities or of listing: E. Avgouleas and G. Ferrarini, 'The Future of ESMA and a Single Listing Authority and Securities Regulator for the CMU' in E. Avgouleas, D. Busch and G. Ferrarini (eds), *European Capital Markets Union* (Oxford University Press, 2018).

be seen whether the Commission will take tangible, realistic action to achieve all these high-level goals.

What can be deduced from the era of refinement of EU regulation is that there is a certain political will to constantly revise applicable rules to make them responsive to market and technological challenges. At the same time, EU law has not avoided some regulatory *faux pas*,[41] showing a preference for more apparent than substantial regulatory choices, especially taking into account the reprioritization of regulatory objectives after the global financial crisis and the inevitable importance of visible regulatory responses so as to convey a quick message to market actors about market stability and investor protection.

Capital markets are constantly changing and the regulatory response is – to a certain extent – inherently experimental. This should not become a traditional excuse for regulatory deficiencies since EU law has already built considerable 'know-how' in tackling market challenges. Moreover, we must bear in mind that EU capital markets law has been particularly sensitive to facilitating capital-raising operations and maintaining market actor and investor confidence, but less prone to intervening into equally important topics that could act as a counterbalance to various infringements. Indeed, there are areas that have not yet received the same amount of attention and progress, notwithstanding their vital importance for the safeguarding of capital markets. A notable example is the area of sanctions mechanisms that, notwithstanding some modest but laudable efforts in the area of administrative sanctions, are still at an embryonic stage and mostly dependent on national idiosyncrasies.[42]

1.3 REGULATORY RATIONALES

Having briefly touched upon the history of EU capital markets law, a brief overview of the rationales that have been influential in the shaping of the EU regulatory agenda is also crucial as an introduction to the regulatory mindset that drives reforms in this area. This analysis will also aim to shed light on the more – and less – visible motives for regulatory action and to explain why some areas have been constantly revised and kept updated, whereas others remain perfectible, if not marginalized. Of the many regulatory tools used in EU capital markets law, the main ones are disclosure obligations (for example, prospectus, periodic and episodic disclosure requirements) and restrictive measures to certain activities (for example, market abuse practices). Disclosure obligations aim to enable market actors to make informed decisions, deriving from the information available on the market, and restrictive measures aim to safeguard the market integrity that can be destabilized by various infringements.[43]

---

[41] For example, the Short Selling Regulation, above n. 31; see Chapter 10.

[42] For more details, see Chapter 3.

[43] For a comprehensive analysis of disclosure policy rationales and drawbacks, see L. Enriques and S. Gilotta, 'Disclosure and Financial Market Regulation' in N. Moloney, E. Ferran and J. Payne (eds), *The Oxford Handbook on Financial Regulation* (Oxford University Press, 2015), 511.

1.3.1 Market Integrity

The orderly functioning and integrity of markets became a prominent rationale for the adoption of interventionist rules after the financial crisis, which presented clear threats for the entire financial system. Various pieces of EU legislation testify to the willingness to safeguard markets from systemic and other risks. The most notable examples are the Short Selling Regulation[44] and the CRA Regulation[45] as well as the latest developments in the Market Abuse Regulation.[46] At the same time, rules aiming to regulate investment firms (MiFID II/MiFIR) also serve market integrity rationales,[47] in the presence of important risks arising in this area of activities.

Supervisory authorities, at both the national and EU levels, have also been given additional powers after the financial crisis to be able to intervene in critical moments and to safeguard market integrity.[48] EU law has not defined in tangible terms what could threaten financial stability so as to trigger such intervention. This conceptual broadness is explained in the light of constantly evolving practices that cannot always be anticipated by rules, and regulators need to be able to exercise the power to intervene within a considerably large discretionary framework.

1.3.2 Efficient Allocation of Resources and Economic Growth

EU law has traditionally viewed its own role as the driving and facilitating force that enables issuers to raise capital in public markets. This has driven the shaping of business-friendly rules that make capital market accessible to issuers and to investors. It is expected to multiply financing operations and to allow the promising ones to attract capital so as to give the opportunity to issuers to expand their businesses, offer employment and contribute to national economic growth. At the same time, investors are able to allocate their resources efficiently and, by increasing the chances of making their investment portfolios more profitable, they personally benefit from their decisions and also contribute to the financing of promising businesses. Reduction of costs for raising capital is a natural consequence of the efficient allocation of resources that further enhances entrepreneurship and growth.[49] In order for market actors to believe in such benefits and in the efficient allocation of resources, confidence in capital markets is crucial.

---

[44] Recital 1, Regulation (EU) 236/2012.

[45] Recital 11, Regulation (EU) No 513/2011.

[46] Recital 2, 3 and 23 (among many), Regulation (EU) No 596/2014.

[47] Recital 53, 54 and 68 (among many), Directive 2014/65/EU and Recital 29, Regulation 600/2014/EU.

[48] For example, see Sections 9.5 and 10.5.1.

[49] J.N. Gordon and L.A. Kornhauser, 'Efficient Markets, Costly Information, and Securities Research' (1985) 60 *New York University Law Review* 761.

1.3.3 Investor Confidence and Investor Protection

Investor confidence is a recurrent concept in almost every piece of EU capital markets legislation and one of the main regulatory rationales for reforms. Confidence in capital markets is the driving force of investment and market liquidity. Lack of confidence in the functioning of markets results in the fall of share prices, market illiquidity and, more generally, economic downturn. In order to maintain confidence, applicable rules must be intrusive enough to constrain issuers and financial intermediaries to perform their functions in a way that aligns their interests with those of the investor community. Disclosure obligations are one example of such rules that aim to enable investors to make informed decisions and inspire confidence through the availability of a wide range of information in the market. At the same time, various prohibitions of certain practices, such as market abuse, convey the message of market equality and investor protection against unfair tactics in the markets.

Even if empowering investors with information secures (to a certain extent) a better and more sophisticated investment environment, disclosure obligations may also have the countereffect of creating over-optimistic investors who tend to rely primarily on the disclosed information and less on their own assessment skills for making investment decisions.[50] The disclosure mantra has nevertheless proven so popular with the Commission that it is unlikely to witness a retreat in the use of this regulatory tool (notwithstanding its obvious merits).

As we will see throughout this book, the main focus so far has been the praising of investor confidence as the 'Holy Grail' of regulatory reforms, but little has been done to convey an equally important message to the investor community that can sustain the long-term confidence in the market, namely the need to provide a reliable and multi-layered framework for investor education.[51] Some laudable efforts have taken place at the national level, but coordination and convergence of these practices at the EU level is long overdue. In parallel, assuming that all investors (both retail and institutional) are capable and financially literate to absorb, understand and evaluate available information is simply a fallacious interpretation of the everyday life in capital markets: retail investors inevitably turn to financial intermediaries who can present and offer them a wide range of financial products,[52] and financial analysts who produce reports about issuers.[53] Most of them may feel more comfortable in forming part of institutional investment schemes, by being their ultimate beneficiaries, and by thus contributing to the ongoing increase in importance and size of

---

[50] D.C. Langevoort, 'Taming the Animal Spirits of the Stock Markets: A Behavioral Approach to Securities Regulation' (2002) 97 *Northwestern University Law Review* 135.

[51] On investor education, see N. Moloney, *How to Protect Investors: Lessons from the EC and the UK* (CUP, 2010) 374.

[52] For example, see the analysis in Chapter 11 on investment firms. On the important role and various facets of financial intermediation more generally, see I. MacNeil, *An Introduction to the Law on Financial Investment* (2nd edn, Hart Publishing, 2012), 7.

[53] See Chapter 12.

institutional investors whose role is to invest the capital provided by individuals on a massive scale.[54] Their capital will be managed by asset owners who can also delegate management functions to asset managers. The multiplication of financial intermediaries standing between the ultimate beneficiaries and investee companies further exacerbates the investor educational gap.[55]

Instead, another regulatory aim, namely investor protection, needs to be strengthened considerably in EU capital markets law. Although it has been used frequently in various pieces of EU legislation, investor protection has mainly been conceived under the spectrum of safeguarding operational and governance standards across a wide area of actors (issuers, investment firms and institutional shareholders) so as to ensure reduction of agency costs or, more generally, the avoidance of practices that may trigger investor losses.

Unfortunately, investor confidence has not been seen as a corollary of enforcement and, more specifically, of sanctions related to infringement of applicable rules. For example, civil liability regimes, which are supposed to be the epitome of *ex post* investor protection and can ensure investor compensation (and therefore confidence), have not been developed sufficiently and remain largely tied to national frameworks. The disparate level of investor protection from one Member State to the next is as yet unable to ensure an appropriate regulatory response at the EU level. The same observation could be made with regard to other types of sanctions, such as administrative and criminal ones, that can also be seen as indirect parts of investor protection, in the sense that they can function as a 'safety valve' against further infringements that ultimately affect investors. The whole spectrum of sanctions is still in need of further development and harmonization among national laws. This observation leads us to the conclusion that investor protection is a concept constantly used for the legitimation of certain regulatory choices but not fully explored as an overarching concept that should have a more profound impact upon the shaping of applicable rules.

1.3.4 Harmonization and Convergence

Harmonization has been one of the main regulatory aims since the very first stages of the creation of an EU single market. It can be distinguished, with many variations, in minimum and maximum harmonization. Minimum harmonization ensures the introduction of minimum requirements, while leaving Member States the option of introducing additional ones in their national laws.[56] Maximum harmonization provides for a uniform framework without the possibility of deviating from the set rules. Directives and Regulations are used

---

[54] See Section 2.4.2.1 for a detailed analysis. On the various institutional investor organizations in the UK, see MacNeil, above n. 52, 189.

[55] See, more generally, K. Sergakis, 'The UK Stewardship Code: Bridging the Gap Between Companies and Institutional Investors' (2013) 47 *Revue Juridique Thémis* 109.

[56] M. Dougan, 'Minimum Harmonization and the Internal Market' (2000) 37(4) *Common Market Law Review* 853.

as the main tools for legislation, the former requiring enactment into national law and the latter being directly applicable. Both Directives and Regulations may contain minimum and maximum harmonization provisions, depending on the content of each rule and the underlying rationales for such regulatory choice. It should be also noted that minimum and maximum harmonization can include certain limitations or exceptions for Member States, thus offering mixed solutions in terms of the discretionary space that national laws can use to comply with EU law.

Examining the merits and shortfalls of both minimum and maximum harmonization, it is difficult to draw a definitive conclusion on the eventual supremacy of one of these two models. The gradual removal of barriers among jurisdictions and markets gives issuers incentives to access capital markets on a cross-border basis and also makes these markets more attractive to investors from various Member States. The levels of harmonization may vary according to the delicate (i.e. market sensitive) character of certain activities, to the variable legal, economic and cultural national traditions and to the considerations that need to be made on a case-by-case basis and that will determine the 'cost–benefit' factor for regulatory forms.[57]

It is therefore not a question of making certain activities easier or more difficult, but of carefully choosing the level of harmonization depending on the inherent nature of each regulated activity that may require different regulatory approaches. For example, it has been a particularly straightforward exercise to enhance harmonization of rules related to facilitating capital-raising operations and issuers at large. Nevertheless, the same assessment cannot be made with regard to sanctioning rules for infringements that have been mainly left to Member States due to their considerable differences at the national level and – admittedly – the less favourable perception markets have regarding the effects of their harmonization that will significantly increase the levels of accountability.

Minimum harmonization presents the considerable advantage of adaptability of rules to national contexts and of a discretionary space for regulatory innovation and constant evolution. This also enables regulatory competition and national laws to function as points of attractiveness for issuers.[58] Nevertheless, these advantages may be seen under a more critical light in the sense that they may hamper EU market integration, drive national laws into a regulatory 'race to the bottom', and also create legal uncertainty and additional costs to market actors who operate on a cross-border basis. Indeed, such risks are avoided with maximum harmonization since there is no space for regulatory

---

[57] On the merits of minimum and maximum harmonization as well as on a measured approach in deciding about harmonization levels, see C. Gerner-Beuerle, 'United in Diversity: Maximum vs. Minimum Harmonization in EU Securities Regulation' (2012) 7(3) *Capital Markets Law Journal* 317.

[58] For the merits of such competition, see R. Romano, 'Empowering Investors: A Market Approach to Securities Regulation' (1998) 107 *Yale Law Journal* 2359.

competition and it is easier for market actors to develop their activities within a less costly framework given the uniformity of rules across the EU.[59]

Although the debate between minimum and maximum harmonization can arise in various areas of law, as far as capital markets are concerned, experience has shown that a gradual advancement of rules towards maximum harmonization (or at least increased minimum harmonization) is the preferred option. Both issuers and investors benefit from accessible, comparable, understandable and less costly standards and procedures. Understanding the benefits of maximum harmonization in this framework has not always been straightforward.

Minimum harmonization marked the first era of EU capital markets law via the introduction of minimum standards for entry to capital markets (prospectus requirements), as well as ongoing disclosure obligations for issuers. At that time, minimum harmonization was considered to be the preferred regulatory method for the gradual advancement of a common regulatory framework in its infancy. That choice was objectively the right one since a drastic shift to maximum harmonization would have risked triggering uncontrollable compliance costs and confusion to the investor community (at least for an initial period). The critical shift towards a higher level of harmonization arrived later on and went hand in hand with the understanding of the economic benefits arising from abandonment of barriers and further market integration.

Nowadays, the EU law of capital markets testifies to a clear preference for more harmonization[60] – either through maximum harmonization Directives or through Regulations – and increased cooperation among Member States in the areas that have been left behind, due to national idiosyncrasies. At the same time, ESMA has taken on a prominent role in ensuring further convergence among national frameworks.

Contrary to harmonization that is mostly identified with the need to respect national differences (minimum standards) or strictly enforce similar rules across national frameworks (maximum standards), the concept of convergence has a slightly different connotation: that of raising the standards to a higher level for all parties involved (regulators and national laws among others), notwithstanding some minor differences that may still exist.[61] Convergence aims to ensure the common attainment of widely accepted and welcomed outcomes, and it is ultimately the most vital aspect of regulatory design since it focuses on the actual dimension that rules or supervisory practices yield on an everyday

---

[59] H. Fleischer and K.U. Schmolke, 'The Reform of the Transparency Directive: Minimum or Full Harmonization of Ownership Disclosure?' (2011) 12 *European Business Organization Law Review* 121.

[60] More generally on the use of mutual recognition, equivalence and harmonization, see E. Ferran, 'EU Financial Supervision in the Context of Global Financial Governance' in D. Mügge (ed.), *Europe's Place in Global Financial Governance* (Oxford University Press, 2014), 16.

[61] Bearing in mind that full convergence may be unfeasible (if not unrealistic) in some circumstances. On these differences, see E. Ferran and L.C. Ho, *Principles of Corporate Finance Law* (2nd edn, Oxford University Press, 2014), 416.

basis.[62] Specifically for rules, convergence may also refer to the gradual abandonment of different rules for the adoption of a new one of a higher standard; this process necessarily implies the abolition of pre-existing differences.

1.3.5 Regulatory Visibility

Another regulatory rationale that has not been sufficiently developed in academic literature relates to regulators' need to become visible and be seen as active, especially during financial crises.[63] During tumultuous times for institutions and markets, regulators inherently experiment with various solutions to convey the message to the public that an unpredictable and highly complicated situation is being taking care of. Although some of these reforms may not be justified economically or, even worse, if empirical data clearly show their limited efficiency,[64] political expediency and regulatory concerns about institutional public image and media exposure to the public at large may well justify initiatives that may serve, during that critical period, the purpose of safeguarding the legitimacy and the *raison d'être* of such institutions.[65] At the same time, such drastic and timely reforms may also preserve investor confidence and maintain a natural flow of investment in the markets.

The importance for regulators to convey the message to the public that they are actually dealing with a major crisis is intertwined with their natural propensity to fix only the immediately (and more) visible deficiencies that are the root of a scandal or a crisis. Such an approach may be reasonable, since it targets blatant regulatory loopholes and safeguards markets from the occurrence of the same problems, but it also shows a particularly single-minded view of the merits of reforms that neglects the long-term effects on the market as well as their efficiency for the avoidance of new crises. Measured and more holistic regulatory responses, especially in critical times, may not be useful for public consumption purposes but they may well be the starting point for a gradual overhaul of certain market *acquis* that are at the heart of repetitive scandals as it will be shown below.

1.3.6 Regulatory Responsiveness

The regulatory rationales that pertain to the regulators' view of the markets and the considerable difficulties they face when attempting to tackle non-compliant behaviour[66] also relate to the concept of 'regulatory responsiveness'. Regulatory

---

[62] A notable example is the current effort to achieve convergence in supervisory practices among national regulators in EU capital markets law.

[63] For the initial development of this idea, see L. Enriques, 'Regulators' Response to the Current Crisis and the Upcoming Reregulation of Financial Markets: One Reluctant Regulator's View' (2009) 30(4) *University of Pennsylvania Journal of International Law* 1147.

[64] For example, see some aspects of the Short Selling Regulation, analysed in Chapter 10.

[65] Enriques, above n. 63, 1149–1150.

[66] More generally, see R. Baldwin and M. Cave, *Understanding Regulation: Theory, Strategy, and Practice* (Oxford University Press, 1999).

responsiveness refers to the way in which regulatory frameworks respond to various challenges in the markets. It is a crucial concept for the design of an appropriate regulatory framework. Indeed, in the presence of highly complex market systems, one regulatory method has been the 'principles-based' approach,[67] which allows market actors to develop their own strategies and overall compliance stance within broadly formulated rules so as not to impede their operational flexibility, competitiveness and 'know-how'. This regulatory model has been subject to criticism given the risk of low-quality compliance by concerned parties that may be tempted to take advantage of the fact that the rules are quite general in nature.[68]

Another regulatory trend in this context has been 'risk-based regulation',[69] reflected in the regulators' prioritization of strategies based on a risk assessment of non-compliance by the concerned market actors, as well as of the impact of such non-compliance. This 'risk-based regulation' inevitably focuses, *inter alia*, on enforcement mechanisms that aim to rebalance market stability after violations of the applicable rules have occurred. Nevertheless, experience has shown that this regulatory approach may be deficient in certain respects since it fails to adopt a more holistic stance towards market failures, highly complex situations or many other risks. As mentioned above, by focusing on what is immediately threatening or socially reprehensible, regulators may lose sight of more overarching and important challenges that they will be called upon to face in the future.

In response to these shortcomings, Black and Baldwin have developed the concept of 'really responsible risk-based regulation', whereby regulators need to be responsive in relation to the following five elements: (1) the firm's behaviour, attitude and culture, (2) the institutional environment, (3) the interactions of different regulatory methods, (4) the regulatory performance in practice, and (5) the eventual changes that inevitably take place in regulatory strategies.[70] This framework undoubtedly presents a much more convincing regulatory approach, despite the complexity, costs and time needed for fruitful implementation across regulators. This is because it allows for a constant re-evaluation of the regulatory approach while taking into account the affected market actors, their specificities and the complex interactions among themselves and with regulators.

Given the risks of low-quality compliance and the above-mentioned difficulty in deciphering future regulatory steps following the emergence of regulatory deficiencies, 'regulatory responsiveness' becomes central to any regulatory

---

[67] J. Black, 'The Rise, Fall and Fate of Principles Based Regulation' (2010) LSE Law, Society and Economy Working Papers 17/2010, at http://eprints.lse.ac.uk/32892/1/WPS2010-17_Black.pdf. For some examples, see Chapter 11.

[68] J. Black, 'Paradoxes and Failures: '"New Governance" Techniques and the Financial Crisis' (2012) 75 *Modern Law Review* 1037.

[69] J. Black and R. Baldwin, 'Really Responsive Risk-Based Regulation' (2010) 32(2) *Law & Policy* 181.

[70] Ibid.

design since it also focuses on the regulators' capacity to anticipate market crises and potentially destabilizing effects on the overall economy. It would be utopic to envisage a perfect regulatory approach that would enable States to safeguard markets from further crises. Nevertheless, the lack of political determination and support for the strengthening of regulatory approaches is something tangible and incrementally manageable at both national and EU levels, and it requires coordinated efforts and compromises among different constituencies so as to enable the regulatory framework to reach a more reliable stance when faced with the above-mentioned challenges.

1.4 CONCLUSION

This chapter aimed to highlight the foundations of capital markets law in the EU by providing a brief overview of the history of the applicable EU legal framework and by explaining the underlying regulatory rationales that have been decisive at various stages of the long path towards the shaping of sophisticated, responsive and harmonized rules.

The history of capital markets law testifies to a gradual evolution from mutual recognition and equivalence to minimum harmonization of access to capital markets, disclosure and prohibitive rules that, in their totality, frame a legal spectrum that facilitates capital-raising operations while safeguarding markets from illegal practices. The minimum harmonization mindset has more recently been subject to a transformation towards maximum harmonization, in some areas, and to the increasingly popular view that the removal of barriers will contribute to the sustained growth of markets and the broader EU economy. Notwithstanding the willingness to further harmonize facilitating rules, other equally important components of capital markets law, such as sanction rules, have not received the same level of regulatory attention and have been left to national laws or have been harmonized to a modest and minimum level.

EU capital markets law has traditionally been driven by a series of regulatory aims that coincide with efficient allocation of resources and economic growth, investor confidence, market integrity and also regulatory visibility. As we will see in later chapters, although these rationales are eminently portrayed in various pieces of EU legislation, the overall approach towards their realization is, if not formalistic, incomplete. This is because the enhancement of accountability regimes in capital markets is still seen as an insurmountable task, even though it can serve all these regulatory rationales. It is argued that investor confidence, market integrity – as well as (less substantial) regulatory visibility concerns – can be considerably strengthened via the concomitant harmonization of enforcement mechanisms in EU capital markets law. The furtherance of reforms and the gradual increase of harmonization in the single-minded perspective of access to the market or disclosure rules are welcomed, but they cannot, on their own, function as a reliable safety valve for sustainable capital markets.

In this chapter, we have seen that the overarching priority of EU capital markets law is to ensure the security of an integrated single EU market while facilitating issuer operations and investment flows; we will now focus on the various profiles and characteristics of market actors. This analysis will shed light on various actors' importance in designing rules, as well as on the financial instruments that are envisaged in this area.

CHAPTER 2

Markets, Participants and Financial Instruments

2.1 INTRODUCTION

Capital markets bring together different types of market participants, such as listed companies, individual investors, institutional investors, financial intermediaries and others. Our analysis aims to give a holistic view of the coexistence of capital markets and the various actors and available financial instruments for trading. Moreover, we will explain the basic components of market choices made by listed companies (admission to trading of their shares, as well as market exit strategies), investors (growing reliance on institutional investor schemes) and financial intermediaries (asset owners, asset managers, etc.) in today's markets. This analysis will highlight participants' incentives and explain how their agenda seeks to minimize incidents of market failure.

This chapter will also cover some corporate governance issues that are crucial for the understanding of the investment chain in capital markets, such as stewardship trends in financial intermediation, as well as the recent regulatory interest in the proxy advisory industry and the services that it offers to investors. This more general analysis focused on corporate governance will provide insights into the general operational framework to which capital market law rules apply so as to offer a more holistic view of the usefulness, feasibility and adaptability of rules to the realities of markets themselves.

2.2 MARKETS

Capital markets are trading venues that allow issuers to raise capital by issuing bonds, shares and other financial instruments that are publicly traded. Trading venues, in turn, comprise regulated markets[1] (the main focus of this book),

---

[1] These are multilateral systems operated and/or managed by a market operator, which bring together or facilitate the bringing together of multiple third-party buying and selling interests in financial instruments in a way that results in a contract, in respect of the financial instruments admitted to trading under its rules and/or systems: Article 4(1)(21) of the Directive 2014/65/EU of the European Parliament and of the Council of 15 May 2014 on markets in financial instruments and amending Directive 2002/92/EC and Directive 2011/61/EU Text with EEA relevance [2014] OJ L 173/349 (hereinafter MiFID II).

multilateral trading facilities (MTFs)[2] and organized trading facilities (OTFs).[3] Regulated markets attract most of the regulatory attention in the form of considerable legal obligations and a series of requirements, such as disclosure requirements, operational standards and numerous prohibitions.[4] It should also be noted that some regulated markets are further divided into different segments. This allows for additional layers of requirements (for example, corporate governance ones) that go beyond the EU legal rules and aim to create even more attractive trading venues by increasing prestige and quality. This extra level of requirements is regarded by the market as issuer willingness to engage even more in achieving a better image for capital-raising purposes, and inevitably influences the attractiveness of shares.[5]

The other (unregulated) markets are subject to a much lighter regulatory framework (for example, considerably less disclosure requirements), which makes them more attractive to issuers that may not be in a position or simply are not willing to subject their activities to a burdensome and more rigorous legal framework.

A further distinction must be made with regard to primary and secondary markets. Primary markets deal with issuers offering new shares, in the ambit of what is commonly called initial public offerings (IPOs), and with investors who purchase these shares for the first time. Issuers will most probably use underwriting services. Secondary markets are the trading spectrum among investors that buy or sell shares that have already been issued, following the initial purchase on the primary markets.

2.3 FINANCIAL INSTRUMENTS

Financial instruments are a broad term, including transferable securities as well as money market instruments, units in collective investment undertakings, derivative contracts and others.[6] This book focuses exclusively on transferable securities and, predominantly, shares.[7] Transferable securities are classes of

---

[2] These are multilateral systems, operated by an investment firm or a market operator, which bring together multiple third-party buying and selling interests in financial instruments in a way that results in a contract: Article 4(1)(22), ibid.

[3] These are multilateral systems which are not a regulated market or an MTF and in which multiple third-party buying and selling interests in bonds, structured finance products, emission allowances or derivatives are able to interact in the system in a way that results in a contract: Article 4(1)(23), ibid.

[4] For a complete list, see the European Securities and Markets Authority (ESMA) Register, at https://registers.esma.europa.eu/publication/searchRegister?core=esma_registers_mifid_rma. On trading markets more generally, see Iain MacNeil, *An Introduction to the Law on Financial Investment* (2nd edn, Hart Publishing, 2012), 381.

[5] See, for example, the different segments of the London Stock Exchange's (LSE) Main Market: High Growth Segment, Specialist Fund Segment, Standard Segment and Premium Segment.

[6] For a complete list, see Article 4(1)(15) and Annex I Section C, MiFID II.

[7] Article 4(1)(44), ibid.

securities negotiable on a capital market, with the exception of instruments of payment; they include shares in companies, bonds or other forms of securitized debt, and other types of securities giving the right to acquire or sell any such transferable securities or giving rise to a cash settlement determined by reference to transferable securities, currencies, interest rates or yields, commodities or other indices or measures.

2.4 MARKET ACTORS

2.4.1 Issuers

Issuers[8] have different profiles, sizes and capital-raising needs. EU law defines them, at the entry stage to capital markets, as legal entities issuing or proposing to issue securities[9] and, for the ongoing obligations they have in these markets, as natural persons, or legal entities governed by private or public law, including a State, whose securities are admitted to trading on a regulated market.[10] EU law has demonstrated particular sensitivity to the facilitation of capital-raising operations and issuer needs regarding a predictable, flexible and understandable legal framework. Indeed, in various recitals of pieces of EU legislation, and most notably in the Prospectus Regulation,[11] it is clearly stated that the aim of the Capital Markets Union is to help businesses access more diverse sources of capital from anywhere within the EU.

The facilitation of issuers and capital-raising operations may also be seen under a more critical approach in the sense that EU law nurtures a more 'market friendly' approach by aiming to maintain the attractiveness of capital markets. This approach may convey the message that market liquidity and integrity are the utmost priorities of capital markets law, compared to other hotly debated issues, such as investor protection through enforcement mechanisms. More

---

[8] Throughout this book, issuers and companies will be used interchangeably, denoting publicly traded companies.

[9] Article 2(h), Regulation (EU) 2017/1129 of the European Parliament and of the Council of 14 June 2017 on the prospectus to be published when securities are offered to the public or admitted to trading on a regulated market, and repealing Directive 2003/71/EC [2017] OJ L 168/12.

[10] Article 2(1)(d), Directive 2013/50/EU of the European Parliament and of the Council of 22 October 2013 amending Directive 2004/109/EC of the European Parliament and of the Council on the harmonisation of transparency requirements in relation to information about issuers whose securities are admitted to trading on a regulated market, Directive 2003/71/EC of the European Parliament and of the Council on the prospectus to be published when securities are offered to the public or admitted to trading, and Commission Directive 2007/14/EC laying down detailed rules for the implementation of certain provisions of Directive 2004/109/EC [2013] OJ L 294/13. In the case of depository receipts admitted to trading on a regulated market, the issuer means the issuer of the securities represented, whether or not those securities are admitted to trading on a regulated market.

[11] Recital 1, above n. 9. For more provisions aiming to facilitate issuers and to demonstrate the necessary amount of flexibility so as to maintain the attractiveness of capital markets, see Chapter 5.

specifically, investor protection has repeatedly been praised in various pieces of EU legislation as one of the main rationales for reform,[12] but it is mostly viewed in terms of issuer disclosure obligations. In other words, investor protection is translated into the need to provide information to the investor community *ex ante* so that investors can make informed decisions, and much less as something that needs to be strengthened *ex post* within the enforcement framework.

We firmly believe that in order for investor protection to take on a more holistic, trustworthy and efficient dimension, both *ex ante* and *ex post* facets of regulatory intervention need to be developed at a similar (if not equal) pace. As we will see in various chapters of this book, issuers are subject to potential enforcement mechanisms that have not yet attained optimal levels of deterrence.

At a parallel level, issuers have traditionally been criticized for pursuing short-term goals and for disregarding the long-term consequences of management decisions on the company itself, its employees and other stakeholders. Notwithstanding some viable arguments that correlate director remuneration schemes with agency problems[13] and short-termism,[14] it would be an erroneous assumption to exclusively link distorted managerial incentives to the pathological phenomena in contemporary management practices. Indeed, while it may be true that corporate managers may pursue their own agendas at the expense of the issuer, shareholders and stakeholders, it should be borne in mind that they may also operate under constant pressure to generate positive news to continue to boost a company's share price. Issuers are thus compelled to keep on showing a positive profile for current and prospective investors.

The overall 'dependence of markets on constant company-relevant data streams as a basis for stock allocation decisions and associated professional communications' has been described as an 'informational centricity' phenomenon that creates a 'compelling pressure on corporate managers to generate fresh "news" indicative of perceived business "progress", in an effort to influence future share price movements'.[15] Trying therefore to impose onerous obligations upon issuers so as to efficiently protect shareholders, stakeholders and the market at large is a laudable regulatory task but may risk missing an important piece of the puzzle: that of shareholder demands that may drive issuers into a single-minded and short-term operational tunnel.

---

[12] See, more generally, M. Siems, *Convergence in Shareholder Law* (CUP 2008); J. Mukwiri and M. Siems, 'The Financial Crisis: A Reason to Improve Shareholder Protection in the EU?' (2014) 41(1) *Journal of Law and Society* 51.

[13] See, more generally, L.A. Bebchuk and J.M. Fried, 'Executive Compensation as an Agency Problem' (2003) 17 *Journal of Economic Perspectives* 71.

[14] J.C. Coffee Jr, 'What Caused Enron – A Capsule Social and Economic History of the 1990s' (2003) 89 *Cornell Law Review* 269; For a more general analysis of directors' remuneration schemes, see G. Ferrarini, N. Moloney and M.C. Ungureanu, 'Understanding Directors' Pay in Europe: A Comparative and Empirical Analysis' (2009) ECGI – Law Working Paper No 126/2009, at https://ssrn.com/abstract=1418463.

[15] M.T. Moore and E. Walker-Arnott, 'A Fresh Look at Stock Market Short-Termism' (2014) 41(3) *Journal of Law and Society* 416, 418.

Indeed, shareholders' unquestionable importance for managerial decision-making may also be seen if we pay particular attention to issuer ownership structures. These structures play a major role in understanding corporate culture, management strategies and also the furtherance of legal reforms,[16] since they are quite indicative of the way that issuers interact with their shareholders.

It is generally believed that in companies with dispersed shareholding, management will be much more focused on short-term objectives. This is because the shareholding base is so diverse that the level of communication and overall engagement with management will be rather low or because majority shareholders (mainly institutional ones) will inevitably try to impose their own agendas, without being interested in the long-term consequences of their needs for the issuer, since they may have a short-term investment strategy.

Nevertheless, in family-owned businesses that have concentrated ownership, the management board is much more closely associated with the company's identity and tends to pay more attention to longer-term plans, as it strives to secure the company's continuous existence and prosperous development. Although generalized arguments can be perceived to be less reliable in this area, the depth of relationship between management and shareholders, as well as the frequency of communication and quality of engagement, on both sides, may be highly indicative of the choices in the short or long term regarding the issuers' future. Indeed, managing a variety of shareholders with different shareholdings (minority versus majority), priorities and needs is a highly complex task for issuers. It is therefore crucial to start shifting the regulatory attention to shareholders, so as to ensure that their communication with issuers becomes more productive, in-depth and engaging.

2.4.2 Investors

2.4.2.1 Various Investor Profiles
Broadly speaking, investors can be classified as retail (individual) or institutional investors. Retail investors have frequently been seen as a priority for EU policymaking since capital markets have a clear interest in becoming more accessible to household investment and not to rely exclusively on institutional investors. The accentuation of disclosure obligations upon issuers and the excessive regulatory focus on the importance of well-informed and independent investors may seem single-minded and potentially incomplete. This is particularly true if we take into consideration that disclosure – on its own – is not sufficient to ensure optimal decision-making. Investors may be influenced by myriad reasons in making their decisions. Moreover, bounded rationality[17] in the markets and the lack of financial literacy are inevitable and need to be

---

[16] More generally on this topic, see: B.R. Cheffins, *Corporate Ownership and Control: British Business Transformed* (Oxford University Press, 2008).

[17] E. Avgouleas, 'Cognitive Biases and Investor Protection Regulation an Evolutionary Approach' (2006), at https://ssrn.com/abstract=1133214.

addressed by a multi-layered regulatory response that goes beyond the informational transparency concept. EU law has gradually broadened the concept of investor, by including that of the consumer, thus making the regulatory framework more interventionist with regard to the provision of financial services, the product regulation and relevant regulatory safeguards that aim to protect investors/consumers from various deficiencies.[18]

Institutional investors present different characteristics from their retail counterparts, since they are grouped and entrust their assets to a series of intermediaries, such as asset owners and managers. These intermediaries make investment decisions as to which investee company represents a good investment opportunity for the large number of portfolios they manage, representing the interests of the ultimate beneficiaries of the group who are their clients. In theory, this multi-layered investment chain is justified thanks to the presence of experienced intermediaries that are supposed to act in the best interests of their clients and, with the assistance of financial analysts and proxy advisors, are able to evaluate issuers, fulfil their duties towards their clients and contribute to the success of capital markets worldwide. Intermediation represents the advantage of allowing the ultimate beneficiaries to participate in investment groups, by delegating the decision-making function to experts.

Nevertheless, agency problems that are well known in company law[19] can be reproduced in this framework since asset owners and asset managers may have distorted incentives in executing their roles and may not act in the best interests of their clients. A notable example relates to their remuneration schemes of asset managers: these schemes are based on a purely short-term evaluation (a quarterly benchmark), which focuses on their capacity to generate short-term returns by exercising adequate pressure on investee companies towards that objective. In this case, it is highly unlikely that asset managers will be willing to engage with companies to build up a better understanding of the long-term priorities and objectives that will eventually lead to better financial performance for the benefit of all actors engaged in this procedure. The quarterly benchmark triggers a collateral effect on the short-termism with which asset managers and companies interact in order for both of them to capture profits to satisfy their mandates according to the predominant trading rules and methods of evaluation.

To ensure a more efficient investment chain and constructive shareholder engagement with investee companies, there are other broader and equally important factors that must be taken into consideration in any kind of debate aimed at improving such engagement. As stated in the Kay Report, the distance between companies and investors continues to become lengthier and

---

[18] N. Moloney, 'The Investor Model Underlying the EU's Investor Protection Regime: Consumers or Investors?' (2012) 13 *European Business Organization Law Review* 169.

[19] Directors (agents) with misaligned interests creating 'agency costs' for shareholders (principals) when they do not act in their best interests: M.C. Jensen and W.H. Meckling, 'Theory of the Firm: Managerial Behaviour, Agency Costs and Ownership Structure' (1976) 3 *Journal of Financial Economics* 305.

more complicated due to a series of factors that characterize modern investment and trading techniques.[20] The number of financial intermediaries continues to increase, which does not facilitate the establishment of a true dialogue between a company and shareholders. Moreover, the tendency to diversify investment portfolios does not encourage shareholders to commit themselves to a long-term relationship with investee companies.

More generally, academic literature has developed the debate surrounding the usefulness of institutional investors, reaching controversial conclusions. Some views support the idea that investor groups are beneficial to capital markets since they prefer long-term investment, loyalty to the investee company and serious engagement with the latter in order to improve corporate governance strategies.[21] This is especially the case with ethically or environmentally driven institutional investor groups, but not necessarily with all such groups. Others consider institutional investors to be potentially harmful to the stability of companies and markets in general, since they are deemed to act with an excessive focus on short-term returns and the achievement of a specific set of goals that are not compatible with the true progression of the company and its overall perspectives and objectives.[22]

The debate continues on the existence of empirical proof of the benefits of shareholder engagement and on the overall benefits of engagement, especially considering that engagement may nurture more pressure for short-term profits – when shareholders have short-term agendas – or for the adoption of potentially counterproductive decisions in the long term. The empirical studies conducted in the past are not conclusive as to whether shareholder activism is crucial to improving companies' performance or simply irrelevant. Regardless of the negative or positive effect of this kind of activism, it could be said that in theory it is always better to have a certain amount of indirect pressure from asset managers or asset owners of the shares, which will possibly alert the company's management in order to avert certain deficiencies in conducting business,[23] if of course such engagement and pressure aim to improve corporate

---

[20] The UK government, following a call for evidence, 'A Long-term Focus for Corporate Britain', published in October 2010, asked Professor John Kay in 2011 to launch a report examining to what extent equity markets are achieving their core purposes. After a respective call for evidence and an Interim Report, the Final Report was published: J. Kay, 'The Kay Review of UK Equity Markets and Long-Term Decision Making' (2012), at http://www.bis.gov.uk/ assets/biscore/business-law/docs/k/12-917-kay-review-of-equity-markets-final-report.pdf.

[21] S.L. Gillan and L.T. Starks, 'The Evolution of Shareholder Activism in the United States' (2007) 19 *Journal of Applied Corporate Finance* 55.

[22] J. Winter, 'Shareholder Engagement and Stewardship: The Realities and Illusions of Institutional Share Ownership' (2011), at http://papers.ssrn.com/sol3/papers.cfm?abstract_id=1867564; B.W. Heineman Jr., 'A "Stewardship Code" for institutional investors', Harvard Business Review blog, 18 January 2010, 24, at http://blogs.hbr.org/cs/2010/01/a_stewardship_code_for_institu.html.

[23] R. Romano, 'Less is More: Making Institutional Shareholder Activism a Valuable Mechanism of Corporate Governance' (2001) 18 *Yale Journal on Regulation* 174.

governance systems and are not simply seen as an excuse for exercising more pressure with distorted incentives that go against the company's and shareholders' interests.

Current investment strategies and the very nature of institutional ownership have become extremely complicated and interrelated to a series of other investment priorities that need closer examination. There is a range of issues that will continue to be a preoccupation despite regulatory reform aimed at changing the market's investment mentality. Recent regulatory attempts to tackle those issues have given rise to the 'stewardship' concept, to which our attention will now turn.

2.4.2.2 The Concepts of Stewardship and Shareholder Engagement

Stewardship is a relatively recent phenomenon that has been indirectly associated with the heavily criticized image and identity of capital markets and short-term mentality at large. It has been portrayed as one of the remedies for avoiding crises in the future, as it purports to trigger more active engagement of market participants in various critical issues. Its core notion refers to the responsibility of taking care of assets that belong to other parties, and more specifically, as far as institutional investors are concerned, the stewardship responsibilities are bestowed upon the trustees of the investor group, as well as on the asset managers in charge of monitoring and developing their portfolios.[24]

In an ideal scenario, a good steward is someone who truly understands the needs of the ultimate beneficiaries of her actions and is able to engage effectively with the latter in order to establish a trustful relationship and to manage their financial interests in an optimal way. According to another definition, 'stewardship is responsible and thoughtful ownership. It is synonymous with an ownership mindset and adopts a long-term perspective, but with a focus on value creation.'[25]

Trust in the capital markets has been eroded, and several regulatory reforms across the globe are currently aimed at restoring confidence in the ever-lengthening investment chain that separates final investors from companies. One of those initiatives was initially the UK Stewardship Code,[26] which set a target of increasing awareness of the problematic issues involved in the vicious circle of investment and probably to change the current mentality of market participants in exercising different powers and rights involved in this

---

[24] More generally, see I. H-Y. Chiu, 'Turning Institutional Investors into "Stewards": Exploring the Meaning and Objectives of "Stewardship"' (2013) 66 *Current Legal Problems* 443.

[25] Foundation for Governance Research and Education, 'An Investigation into Stewardship: Engagement between Investors and Public Companies: Impediments and their Resolution' (2011), 12, at http://www.foundationgre.com/Stewardship%20 Report%20Final%20-%20 22.6.11.pdf.

[26] Financial Reporting Council (FRC), 'The UK Stewardship Code' (2012), at http://www. frc. org.uk/getattachment/e2db042e-120b-4e4e-bdc7-d540923533a6/UK-Stewardship-Code-September-2012.aspx.

chain. The notion of stewardship itself has proven crucial to the viability of the modern financial system. Indeed, a generation of active and informed investors exercising a beneficial amount of pressure on companies' managers can in theory help avert numerous short-term and high-risk management decisions.

Nevertheless, as mentioned above, investors tend to have different priorities, needs, expectations and resources. The purpose, underlying motivations and quality of engagement with issuers cannot be predicted with precision, given the heterogeneity of shareholder profiles and the short- or long-term goals they are seeking to realize. It thus becomes extremely difficult for issuers to be constantly receptive to potentially diametrically opposed demands for the future of the company, and the content of decisions that need to be made in the overall direction that they need to follow. Respectively, the shaping of legal rules aiming to address these underlying dynamics in capital markets becomes an equally delicate task. It is no surprise that corporate governance has been predominantly subject to soft law measures (at least in the EU) whereas capital markets law has been heavily regulated, with the former touching on the various dynamics among issuers, shareholders and stakeholders, while the latter aim to preserve market integrity and informational investor protection.

Moreover, the main problem with the current generation of investors lies in the fact that 'educational efforts' stemming from regulatory initiatives have not ramped up strongly enough for this generation to become increasingly or even adequately aware of its rights. Moreover, it is crucial for investors to understand the broader challenges they have to face and the responsibilities arising from the fact that they invest in issuers.[27] Having a fair view of their rights and responsibilities, they need to move forward to a more active position with regard to the rest of the market, express their views and require different market practice plans that respect their investment decisions.

Therefore, the main contribution and intention of the Stewardship Code was firstly to play an educational role to the benefit of fund managers and various groups of investors, and, secondly, to make them engage in a more demanding disclosure framework on how they view their role and how they are prepared to exercise it in the UK corporate landscape. Apart from some inherent difficulties since the inception of the Code itself,[28] the main problem that emerged over time lies with deficient enforceability, the triviality of some of its principles and the lack of responsiveness and meaningful engagement from market actors.[29]

---

[27] For the emergent concept of shareholder duties, see H. Søndergaard Birkmose (ed.), *Shareholders' Duties* (Kluwer Law International, 2017).

[28] B.R. Cheffins, 'The Stewardship Code's Achilles' Heel' (2010) 73 *Modern Law Review* 1004.

[29] A. Reisberg, 'The UK Stewardship Code: On the Road to Nowhere?' (2015) 15(2) *Journal of Corporate Law Studies* 217. For an interesting proposal of a new decentralized form of 'meetings of and with shareholders' see C. Van der Elst and A. Lafarre, 'Bringing the AGM to the 21st Century: Blockchain and Smart Contracting Tech for Shareholder Involvement' (2017) ECGI – Law Working Paper No. 358/2017, at https://ssrn.com/abstract=2992804.

The stewardship and shareholder engagement concepts continued to gain momentum across the EU[30] and, influenced by this trend while trying to address market deficiencies arising from short-termism, the Commission proposed an amendment to the Shareholder Rights Directive with the aim of encouraging long-term shareholder engagement and certain elements of the corporate governance statement.[31]

Aiming to increase transparency in financial intermediation, Article 3(g) of the amended Shareholder Rights Directive requires Member States to ensure that institutional investors and asset managers will develop an 'engagement policy' that will define the general way they will exercise their activities with regard to the integration of shareholder engagement into their strategy, the monitoring of and dialogue with investee companies, the exercise of voting rights, the use of proxy advisory services and cooperation with other shareholders.[32] Most importantly, this engagement policy shall describe how they manage actual or potential conflicts of interest that may arise in this framework. They are also expected to describe in this policy how they monitor investee companies with regard to non-financial performance and social and environmental impact, as well as how they communicate with relevant stakeholders of these companies.

The enlargement of the engagement spectrum is – in theory – welcome, but it may prove to be problematic in practice since non-financial elements and stakeholders may be difficult to evaluate, disclose and describe in a meaningful way.[33] EU law has undoubtedly taken this into account, which is why such disclosure obligations will function in accordance with the 'comply or explain' principle;[34] institutional investors and asset managers will either declare

---

[30] B. Clarke, 'The EU's Shareholder Empowerment Model in the Context of the Sustainable Companies Agenda' (2014) 11(2) *European Company Law* 103; F. Möslein and K. Engsig Sørensen, 'Nudging for Corporate Long-Termism and Sustainability? Regulatory Instruments from a Comparative and Functional Perspective' (2017), at https://ssrn.com/abstract=2987734.

[31] Directive (EU) 2017/828 of the European Parliament and of the Council of 17 May 2017 amending Directive 2007/36/EC as regards the encouragement of long-term shareholder engagement [2017] OJ L 132/1.

[32] Article 3(g), ibid.

[33] Article 3(h) also aims to frame the investment strategy of institutional investors and their arrangements with asset managers by introducing a series of disclosure obligations. Institutional investors shall publicly disclose, among other things, how the investment strategy they adopt is in line with the profile and duration of their liabilities and how it contributes to the medium- to long-term performance of their assets. Asset managers are also expected to disclose on an annual basis to institutional investors, with which they have arrangements, how their investment strategy complies with such arrangements and contributes to the medium and long-term performance of the assets of the institutional investor: Article 3(i), ibid.

[34] On the various aspects of this principle in this area, see I. MacNeil and X. Li, 'Comply or Explain: Market Discipline and Non-Compliance with the Combined Code' (2006) 14(5) *Corporate Governance: An International Review* 486; A.R. Keay, 'Comply or Explain in Corporate Governance Codes: In Need of Greater Regulatory Oversight?' (2014) 34(2) *Legal Studies* 279; K. Sergakis, 'Deconstruction and Reconstruction of the "Comply or Explain" Principle in EU Capital Markets' (2015) 5(3) *Accounting, Economics and Law: A Convivium* 233.

compliance with these requirements or publicly disclose an explanation as to why they have chosen not to comply with one or more requirements. The flexibility given to investors in this framework is considerable since they can disregard certain or all requirements, being nevertheless expected to explain in a clear and reasoned way their stance. The experience from the function of the same principle in corporate governance statements issued by companies in various jurisdictions has shown that the explanatory part is not meaningful most of the time;[35] such reservations with regard to the efficiency of the same principle in this new emerging area thus still hold true.

From the above-mentioned the disclosure obligations, we can observe a shift of attention from a purely private company law agenda (enabling and flexible nature among shareholders and companies) towards a top-down capital markets law agenda (stricter and based on increased disclosure obligations for all market actors in the investment chain).[36] Institutional investors and asset managers are now expected to make public various facets of their engagement with companies, shareholders and stakeholders. Such widely applicable disclosure obligations reflect EU law's vision about the future role that such investors are expected to play with regard to a wider range of actors in capital markets. Chiu and Katelouzou have opined that we are witnessing a legalization of stewardship via the introduction of a duty to demonstrate engagement, which is based upon public interests that aim to re-regulate this area.[37]

But is disclosure enough on its own to ensure engagement and long-termism in capital markets? Indeed, these new obligations may be seen under a more critical light; Birkmose has noted that disclosure in this area will not necessarily increase the low levels of engagement since it does not create any financial incentives for investors towards the accomplishment of such role. At a parallel level, it may increase the costs of engagement if the ultimate beneficiaries start exerting pressure upon institutional investors for more engagement.[38]

Questions also may arise with regard to the enforcement methods of these shareholders' duties, as it will prove particularly difficult to achieve a meaningful respect of these broadly formulated provisions that are also based on the 'comply or explain' principle. Moreover, legal sanctions potentially imposed in this area, given the legalization of stewardship as previously mentioned, may be subject to criticism given the lack of clarity of the duties themselves, the

---

[35] M.T. Moore, '"Whispering Sweet Nothings": The Limitations of Informal Conformance in UK Corporate Governance' (2009) 9 *Journal of Corporate Law Studies* 95.

[36] On the more general distinction between the private or facilitative law and public or regulatory law, see M.T. Moore, *Corporate Governance in the Shadow of the State* (Hart Publishing, 2013).

[37] I. H-Y. Chiu and D. Katelouzou, 'From Shareholder Stewardship to Shareholder Duties: Is the Time Ripe?' in Birkmose, above n. 27, 143.

[38] H. Søndergaard Birkmose, 'European Challenges for Institutional Investor Engagement – Is Mandatory Disclosure the Way Forward' (2014) 2 *European Company and Financial Law Review* 214, 236.

difficulty in deciphering the expected outcome of such duties and the embryonic stage of their understanding by courts and national competent authorities (NCAs).[39]

2.4.3 Financial Intermediaries

Financial intermediaries are an essential component of capital markets as they offer a series of invaluable services to investors and they also function as gatekeepers – directly or indirectly – by analysing, evaluating and channelling the available information to the markets. In this book, our focus will be on the three following categories of financial intermediaries: investment firms, financial analysts and credit rating agencies (CRAs).

Investment firms are legal persons 'whose regular occupation or business is the provision of one or more investment services to third parties and/or the performance of one or more investment activities on a professional basis'.[40] They offer, among many things, access to financial products (by trading on behalf of their clients) and advisory services to investors. They are therefore well placed to offer high-quality services to their clients so as to enable them to make informed decisions and to have access to various products. By performing their role in an efficient way, they are able to channel investment towards issuers by safeguarding the efficient allocation of resources and market liquidity. It is their unique position between investors and issuers that grants them a gatekeeping function and places them under a strict regulatory framework that aims to protect investors from unqualified, inefficient or fraudulent investment firms. Investors do not have a homogeneous level of understanding, knowledge and capacity to buy or sell shares and will inevitably make use of investment firms' services for their actions.

Financial analysts gather and analyse information related to issuers and assist market actors in their future investment decisions.[41] Their presence and importance in the market is undoubtedly due to the fact that market actors are not in a position to decipher the plethora of available information and will need to rely – to some extent – on financial analysts. Financial analysts can be categorized in the following way: buy-side, sell-side and independent financial analysts.[42] Buy-side analysts are usually employed by institutional investors and aim to increase the performance of their various investment portfolios. Sell-side analysts are employed by brokerage firms, whose role is to sell financial instruments, while

---

[39] On the enforcement issues, see K. Sergakis, 'Legal Versus Social Enforcement' in H. Søndergaard Birkmose and K. Sergakis (eds), *Enforcing Shareholder Duties* (Edward Elgar, 2018).

[40] Article 4(1)(1), MiFID II.

[41] S.J. Choi, 'Framework for the Regulation of Securities Market Intermediaries' (2004) 1(1) *Berkeley Business Law Journal* 45.

[42] On these and further categories of analysts, see Forum Group, 'Financial Analysts: Best Practices in an Integrated European Financial Market', 4 September 2003, 18, at http://euroirp.com/wp-content/uploads/2016/10/EU_Forum_Group_Report_04-09-03.pdf.

at the same time providing other services to issuers, such as underwriting services. Independent analysts generally work for market actors, who want to receive financial analyst services either by hiring the analysts directly or by subscribing to these services together with other market actors. In doing so, they work for sell-side firms who are not engaged in the concomitant provision of investment banking services, offering thus a more 'independent' operational framework from potential conflicts of interest.

CRAs have become undoubtedly key players in capital and financial markets due to the pivotal role of their activities in relation to the creditworthiness of the various entities (companies, States, etc.) whose debt is subject to their evaluation.[43] A rating is an 'opinion regarding the creditworthiness of an entity, a debt or financial obligation, debt security, preferred share or other financial instrument, or of an issuer of such a debt or financial obligation, debt security, preferred share or other financial instrument, issued using an established and defined ranking system of rating categories'.[44] Ratings are usually the result of a contract between an issuer and a CRA in order for the latter to evaluate its credit quality, in whichever form it may arise as seen above, or they may also be the result of a unilateral decision made by the CRA.

The information CRAs provide has clearly shown its impact on various market actors since they function as informational intermediaries between the rated entities and the rest of the market that is interested in deciphering the quality of their debt. To highlight even further their importance, it should be borne in mind that they have also functioned in the past decades as providers of 'regulatory licences'[45] due to the ever-growing regulatory reliance upon their ratings. Regulators chose indeed to issue a series of criteria in order to recognize certain CRAs for regulatory purposes in an effort to discharge an inevitably complex task of constant verification of the quality of ratings which are used by various market actors. This regulatory over-reliance made credit ratings even more important since the main focus shifted (unfortunately) to their regulatory accreditation – and their ensuing prestige – rather than their quality *in se*.

The role played by financial intermediaries is also complemented by other market actors, such as proxy advisors, who assist shareholders in the exercise of their rights (for example, voting rights) and also provide evaluation services of corporate resolutions so as to enable them to exercise those rights in an informed way. Their role is increasingly important as the level of reliance on their services is considerable. Evaluating the legal framework applicable to their activities becomes therefore an indispensable task for the completion of the 'market participants' spectrum covered in this book.

---

[43] J.C. Coffee Jr., *Gatekeepers: The Professions and Corporate Governance* (Oxford University Press, 2006), 287.

[44] Article 3(1), ibid.

[45] F. Partnoy, 'The Siskel and Ebert of Financial Markets? Two Thumbs Down for the Credit Rating Agencies' (1999) 77 *Washington University Law Quarterly* 619, 624.

2.5 CONCLUSION

This chapter endeavoured to introduce the reader to the complex world of capital markets. Issuers, shareholders and stakeholders form – together with various market actors in the investment chain that provide a wide range of services – a fascinating mosaic of various contracts, arrangements, communication channels and incentives (or disincentives) for engagement. All these actors have different incentives, prerogatives, levels of sophistication and needs. Yet they interact with each other in a unique fashion on an everyday basis. The distance between investee companies and investors has considerably lengthened, thus making it impracticable for all market participants to engage efficiently. Stewardship has moved and will remain at the centre of debate in order to introduce and strengthen a better coexistence in the same investment chain of different and various participants. Even if we cannot expect an ongoing communication among all these constituencies of capital markets, the inculcation of a sound capital-raising (for issuers) and investment (for other market actors) mentality needs to be promoted by the legal order in the most efficient way.

More recently, the Shareholder Rights Directive has envisaged an educational role for all actors, by encouraging disclosure of information with regard to the ultimate objectives in the agendas of groups or other asset managers, as well as the conception of their role. As we have seen, disclosure has been called on to play a critical role in this emerging framework, by offering the public a series of information and expecting demonstration of engagement for some market actors.

Even if the entire investment chain needs to be fully transparent – and open to criticism when decision-making methods are subject to different interpretations and generate excessive risk levels – how disclosure will be used by other constituencies cannot be predicted. At the current stage, disclosure seems to be the only preferred way by EU law to foster engagement in capital markets. We firmly believe that disclosure can only be one of the main pillars for such a strategy to succeed. The concomitant provision of financial incentives and the avoidance of inconsistencies, as well as of unduly burdensome and inconsistent rules, may prove to be a reasonable auxiliary component for the success of this ambitious EU agenda.

Improvement in the investment philosophy will not be accomplished immediately since educating investors and their asset managers will be a long and arduous process. Nevertheless, enabling investors to be properly informed about other market actors' activities is currently a reasonable regulatory tool, given that if investors start changing their demands towards companies, institutional investors and asset managers, the cycle currently driven by short-term objectives will start functioning around a whole new series of priorities that have thus far been dissociated from long-term targets.

CHAPTER 3

Supervision and Enforcement

3.1 Introduction

Driven by the ramifications of the global financial crisis,[1] EU capital markets law has made important progress in enriching and increasing the sophistication of supervision mechanisms for the safeguard of market integrity, as well as the prompt detection of irregularities or infringements of the applicable legal framework. This chapter gives an overview of the European financial supervisory scheme, tracing its roots back to the global financial crisis. It will then focus on the current EU supervisory model in capital markets, namely the European Securities and Markets Authority (ESMA) and its relationship with national competent authorities (NCAs). Particular importance will be given to the powers acknowledged to ESMA under a series of arguments that prevailed after the financial crisis broke out, and which justify the regulatory and political choice to create ESMA. NCAs are still the key players in supervision, under ESMA's overall coordination, but ESMA has also been given direct and centralized supervisory powers at the EU level in certain specific cases, such as the supervision of credit rating agencies.[2] Our analysis will also touch on the cooperation between NCAs themselves and with ESMA, not to mention the relevant provisions in EU legislative texts that seek to make the supervisory system and overall EU cooperation more efficient.

In parallel, EU capital markets law has considerably strengthened – at least in theory – sanction mechanisms to increase deterrence and credibly punish various types of violations. Nevertheless, considerable differences remain at the national level, creating discrepancies between jurisdictions and opening space for regulatory competition. Institutional weaknesses, lack of sophistication and lack of cooperation in the area of enforcement[3] need to be addressed

---

[1] E. Ferran, N. Moloney, J.G. Hill and J.C. Coffee Jr., *The Regulatory Aftermath of the Global Financial Crisis* (Cambridge University Press, 2012).

[2] See Chapter 13.

[3] 'Enforcement' is a broad concept that deals with the overall regulatory mechanisms that aim to ensure the compliance of market actors with the applicable rules. It can be broken down into formal and informal enforcement. Informal enforcement involves both public and private actors, and has functioned as a substitute or a complementary mechanism to drive legal or natural persons towards a more compliant stance in the light of previously committed violations: I. MacNeil, 'Enforcement and Sanctioning' in E. Ferran, N. Moloney and J. Payne (eds), *The Oxford Handbook on Financial Regulation* (Oxford University Press, 2015), 280. 'Sanctions' form part of the enforcement agenda, being exclusively the *ex post* regulatory

and improved since they weaken the attractiveness and threaten the viability of the EU internal market against illegal practices that harm, in turn, its reputation and credibility.

3.2 SUPERVISION OF CAPITAL MARKETS

3.2.1 The New EU Financial Supervision Architecture

The global financial crisis raised concerns not only in respect to highly complex and very sophisticated practices that were not sufficiently targeted by the regulatory framework, but also in respect to the appropriate supervisory mechanisms that needed to be introduced to tackle new challenges in financial and capital markets.[4] In a surprisingly prompt fashion, and under considerable political pressure to calm market actors so that trading venues could regain their reliability, EU law proceeded with a major overhaul of the supervisory system.[5]

ESMA,[6] the European Banking Authority (EBA)[7] and the European Insurance and Occupational Pensions Authority (EIOPA)[8] are the three European Supervisory Authorities (ESAs) that have now become the key reference for financial and capital markets supervision of their respective sectors. They exercise supervision of the concerned market participants at a micro-prudential level.

The European Systemic Risk Board (ESRB)[9] is also an essential component of this architecture; its role is to oversee the financial system, as well as to

---

reaction to infringements of rules. They break down into legal (civil liability, administrative and criminal sanctions) and social ('name and shame', reputational sanctions) sanctions.

[4] E. Avgouleas, *Governance of Global Financial Markets: The Law, the Economics, the Politics* (Cambridge University Press, 2012).

[5] E. Ferran, 'Understanding the New Institutional Architecture of EU Financial Market Supervision' in G. Ferrarini, K.J. Hopt and E. Wymeersch (eds), *Rethinking Financial Regulation and Supervision in Times of Crisis* (Oxford University Press, 2012); N. Moloney, 'Resetting the Location of Regulatory and Supervisory Control Over EU Financial Markets: Lessons from Five Years on' (2013) 62(4) *International and Comparative Law Quarterly* 955.

[6] Regulation 1095/2010/EU of the European Parliament and of the Council of 24 November 2010 establishing a European Supervisory Authority (European Securities and Markets Authority), amending Decision No 716/2009/EC and repealing Commission Decision 2009/77/EC [2010] OJ L 331/84. For a complete overview, see N. Moloney, 'The European Securities and Markets Authority and Institutional Design for the EU Financial Market – A Tale of Two Competences: Part (1) Rule-Making', (2011) 12 *European Business Organization Law Review* 41; N. Moloney, 'Part (2) Rules in Action' (2011) 12 *European Business Organization Law Review* 177.

[7] Regulation (EU) No 1093/2010 of the European Parliament and of the Council of 24 November 2010 establishing a European Supervisory Authority (European Banking Authority) [2010] OJ L331/12; E. Ferran, 'The Existential Search of the European Banking Authority' (2016) 17 *European Business Organization Law Review* 285.

[8] Regulation 1094/2010/EU of the European Parliament and of the Council of 24 November 2010 establishing a European Supervisory Authority (European Insurance and Occupational Pensions Authority), amending Decision No 716/2009/EC and repealing Commission Decision 2009/79/EC [2010] OJ L 331/48.

[9] Regulation (EU) No 1092/2010 of the European Parliament and of the Council of 24 November 2010 on European Union macro-prudential oversight of the financial system and establishing a European Systemic Risk Board [2010] OJ L 331/1.

prevent or at least mitigate systemic risks. It functions as a soft law[10] coopera-tion mechanism between the SEAs, the NCAs, the Commission and, lastly, the European Central Bank (ECB), which is responsible, together with national banking supervisory authorities, for the supervision of banks operating in the euro zone. Both ESRB and ECB operate upon a macro-prudential supervisory task, dealing with overarching systemic risks, and form part of the European Banking Union that has three main components: the Single Supervisory Mech-anism (SSM), the single resolution mechanism (SRM) and a euro zone deposit guarantee scheme.

All EU authorities are constantly trying to respond to ever-changing and highly complex market strategies that may raise concerns for the credibility and integrity of financial and capital markets. There is no doubt that there is no magic solution to the constant challenges that regulators face, and legal reforms have not escaped from experimental, crisis-driven solutions. Such solu-tions may prove to be perfectible, but regulatory decisions should be evaluated within the context in which they were taken and, with this factor in mind, the overall post-crisis EU financial supervision architecture has at least offered a sound starting point for further regulatory refinements in the future.[11]

As far as micro-prudential supervision is concerned, ESAs play an increas-ingly important role also in guiding NCAs and market actors towards a more compliant stance. They do this by issuing instructions directly and by using a series of convergence tools.[12] Turning to supervisory mechanisms, the sole focus of our book will be the relevant NCAs for the supervision of capital markets and ESMA.

3.2.2 The European Securities and Markets Authority (ESMA)

ESMA was created in 2010[13] as the successor to the Committee of European Securities Regulators (CESR), while considerably expanding its own opera-tional ambit within the wider EU financial architecture. Its core function is to protect market integrity, while ensuring a high, effective and consistent level of regulation and supervision across the EU; by doing so, it is expected to take into account the various interests of Member States and market actors. Other key parts of its functions are to ensure a level playing field, together with pre-venting regulatory arbitrage (competition)[14] and strengthening international

---

[10] E. Ferran and K. Alexander, 'Can Soft Law Bodies Be Effective? The Special Case of the European Systemic Risk Board' (2010) 6 *European Law Review* 751.

[11] E. Ferran, 'European Banking Union: Imperfect, But It Can Work' in D. Busch and G. Ferrarini (eds), *European Banking Union* (Oxford University Press, 2015).

[12] See M. Scholten and A. Ottow, 'Institutional Design of Enforcement in the EU: The Case of Financial Markets' (2014) 10(5) *Utrecht Law Review* 80.

[13] Regulation 1095/2010/EU, above n. 6.

[14] Regulatory arbitrage (competition) refers to the potential opportunities for jurisdictions, in the absence of maximum harmonization, to attract market actors given their advantageous provisions compared to other jurisdictions. See, more generally, J. Armour, 'Who Should Make Corporate Law? EC Legislation versus Regulatory Competition' (2005) 48 *Current Legal Problems* 369. This

supervisory coordination. The ongoing guidance to NCAs through the provision of advice is another important function that will continue to gain
momentum in the future, given the similar powers that NCAs have and the
need to ensure convergence in their exercise.[15]

This coordination function between NCAs is also seen as a necessary tool
for avoiding adverse situations that could disrupt the orderly functioning,
integrity and stability of markets and of the financial system at large. ESMA is
therefore expected to:

- facilitate the exchange of information between NCAs
- determine the scope and verify the reliability of all information that
  should be made available to all NCAs
- carry out non-binding mediation (requested by NCAs or on its own initiative)
- notify the ESRB of any potential emergency situations without delay
- take all appropriate measures in case of developments that could potentially jeopardize the functioning of financial markets
- centralize information received from NCAs.[16]

ESMA has not been given centralized powers in the area of supervision and
intervention, except in very few cases,[17] since its main role is to coordinate
NCAs and promote convergence between them. It would also be quite complicated and burdensome for ESMA to regulate issuers and other market
actors across the EU. Its main role is therefore to create a common supervisory culture by providing opinions to NCAs, promoting effective bilateral
and multilateral exchange of information between NCAs, contributing to the
development of high-quality and uniform supervisory standards, reviewing the
application of implementing technical standards adopted by the Commission
and, lastly, establishing training programmes.[18] The issuance of guidelines and
recommendations has proven to be very successful.[19]

ESMA is also expected to conduct peer reviews of NCAs to strengthen consistency in supervisory outcomes. More specifically, such a review will include

---

situation may drive jurisdictions towards a 'race to the bottom' so as to continue offering
a flexible – and potentially less rigorous – regulatory environment to market actors who are
interested in choosing a jurisdiction with the same mindset; alternatively, jurisdictions can be part
of a regulatory 'race to the top' to attract market actors who are willing and ready to be associated
with a more stringent legal environment and to enjoy a good collective reputation for their stance.
This situation has been coined by Coffee as 'bonding theory', with its negative (for the former
category) and positive (for the latter category) connotations: J. C. Coffee Jr., 'Racing Towards the
Top? The Impact of Cross-Listings and Stock Market Competition on International Corporate
Governance' (2002) 102 *Columbia Law Review* 1757.

[15] Recital 11, Regulation 1095/2010/EU, above n. 6.

[16] Article 31, ibid.

[17] See, for example, its centralized role in the area of credit rating agencies (Chapter 13).
ESMA is also directly involved in the supervision of trade repositories.

[18] Article 29, ibid.

[19] Article 16, ibid.

the adequacy of resources and governance arrangements of NCAs; the degree of convergence reached in the application of EU law and in supervisory practice; and the best practices developed by some NCAs that can function as an example to follow for other NCAs and that enhance the effectiveness and degree of convergence in the area of enforcement.[20] At a slightly higher level of intervention, ESMA has the power to request all necessary information from NCAs to carry out its own duties. NCAs also request information from ESMA for the exercise of their own duties.[21]

In the presence of certain serious circumstances, ESMA can take appropriate action with regard to NCAs or even market actors.

The first category relates to a breach of EU law by NCAs; ESMA may investigate the alleged breach or non-application of EU law, and the NCA is expected to provide ESMA, without delay, with all the information necessary for the investigation. Within two months from the initiation of such an investigation, ESMA can send the NCA a recommendation describing the action required for compliance with EU law. In turn, the NCA is expected to inform ESMA, within ten working days, of the steps it has taken or intends to take to ensure such compliance.[22] If the NCA has not complied with EU law within one month of receiving ESMA's recommendation, the Commission has the right to issue a formal opinion requiring the NCA to take the requisite action for compliance, and the NCA must report back to the Commission and ESMA, within ten working days, with the steps it has taken or intends to take to comply with that opinion.[23] If the NCA does not comply with the formal opinion and it is deemed necessary to rectify this non-compliance in order to protect market integrity, ESMA can adopt an individual decision addressed directly to a financial market practice event and require necessary actions for compliance with EU law (including the cessation of any practice).[24]

The second category relates to intervention powers recognized to ESMA in the presence of 'emergency situations'. These situations are defined as developments that may seriously jeopardize market integrity and the ordinary functioning of markets, as well as the stability of the EU financial system. ESMA is expected to facilitate and coordinate any actions taken by NCAs in this framework. It must be informed of any relevant developments, as well as invited to participate as an observer in any meetings between NCAs.[25] Where the Council has decided that an emergency situation exists, as well as in exceptional cases where coordinated action by national authorities is necessary to respond to adverse developments that could seriously jeopardize market integrity or the financial system stability,[26] ESMA has the right to adopt individual decisions

---

[20] Article 30, ibid.
[21] Article 35, ibid.
[22] Article 17(1)(2)(3), ibid.
[23] Article 17(4), ibid.
[24] Article 17(6), ibid.
[25] Article 18, ibid.
[26] Article 18(3), ibid.

requiring NCAs to take any necessary action to address emergency situations by safeguarding the compliance of market actors and NCAs with EU law.[27] If an NCA does not comply with this decision, ESMA can make an individual decision addressed directly to a market actor requiring necessary action to be taken for compliance with EU law (including the cessation of any practice).[28]

The third category relates to the settlement of disagreements between NCAs in cross-border situations; ESMA can assist them in reaching an agreement upon the condition that such a request has been formulated by one or more NCAs, although it can also act on its own initiative if it can objectively determine the existence of such disagreement.[29] ESMA must set a time limit for conciliation between NCAs and, if they fail to reach an agreement within that period, it can make a decision requiring them to take specific action or to refrain from action so as to settle the matter and comply with EU law.[30] The above-mentioned possibilities for direct intervention powers addressed to market actors also exist in this framework in cases of non-compliance by an NCA.[31]

The EU regulatory agenda for promoting financial stability and supervisory convergence was most recently elaborated in the Capital Markets Union Action Plan.[32] It is therefore crucial to ensure an optimal use of new and indirect convergence regulatory means by proposing efficient operating models at the EU level. Supervisory convergence is definitely ESMA's greatest challenge for the future.

3.2.3 The Role of NCAs

Various pieces of EU legislation provide for a supervision system articulated around NCAs and ESMA, including a series of powers, cooperation arrangements with ESMA and cooperation with the NCAs of other Member States and third countries. The wide range of powers enables NCAs to monitor compliance with the applicable rules. These powers refer, *inter alia*, to the right to have access to any document and data, to demand information and to carry out on-site inspections and investigations. NCAs are expected to cooperate with each other and with ESMA in all areas deemed necessary, and they shall exchange information without undue delay, as well as cooperate in investigation, supervision and enforcement activities.

Cooperation with third countries is also a valuable part of the supervisory chain, and the conclusion of cooperation arrangements is vital for the exchange

---

[27] Article 18(3), ibid.
[28] Article 18(4), ibid.
[29] Article 19(1), ibid.
[30] Article 19(2)(3), ibid.
[31] Article 19(4), ibid.
[32] Commission, 'Communication from the Commission to the European Parliament, the Council, the European Economic and Social Committee and the Committee of the Regions: Action Plan on Building a Capital Markets Union' (2015) COM(2015) 468 final, at http://eur-lex.europa.eu/legal-content/EN/TXT/PDF/?uri=CELEX:52015DC0468&from=EN.

of information between supervisory authorities, especially since their arrangements are also facilitated by guidance provided by ESMA. Notwithstanding these types of provisions in various EU texts, the main challenge for an effective monitoring framework will be the gradual convergence of regulatory best practices in order to eliminate (to a certain extent) the current divergent interpretations of the broadly formulated EU rules.[33]

Going beyond the interpretational issues that inevitably arise among NCAs, the crucial issue for any further regulatory development is the gradual convergence in terms of sophistication, regulatory 'know-how', staffing and resources. We firmly believe that this 'top-down' approach adopted in various EU legislative texts with the general empowerment of NCAs will not, on its own, suffice to ensure an efficient supervisory framework. NCAs need to be given the appropriate tools and resources also at the national level so that they can evolve into a more sophisticated and responsive 'reference point' in capital markets for all actors.

As things stand, notwithstanding ESMA's aegis, differences remain, not least because national specificities, legal traditions and cultural patterns may impede NCAs from converging with other NCAs at the EU level. ESMA will undoubtedly contribute to these efforts by coordinating related activities not only via its guidelines and technical standards but, most importantly, by providing guidance to national NCAs as and when requested. Nevertheless, a wider consensus needs to be reached among Member States about the actions that should be taken, with the same rigour and efficiency, as to enable NCAs to converge in the way that they perform their tasks.

3.3 ENFORCEMENT IN CAPITAL MARKETS LAW

3.3.1 Background

Legal sanction strategies in capital markets law have traditionally relied on two main operational pillars: public enforcement, which refers to criminal or administrative proceedings, and private enforcement, which consists of civil claims by harmed parties due to violations of the applicable legal rules. In parallel, social sanctions also play an important role, at least in theory; these refer to the reaction stemming from market actors with regard to the infringement of applicable rules. Such reaction may have a considerable effect on the reputation of the concerned persons (both natural and legal), as well as clear financial implications for their activities.

Driven by the ramifications of the global financial crisis, national laws have considerably strengthened – at least on paper – their formal sanction

---

[33] For example, on the interpretational difficulties among market actors and national regulators surrounding the notion of 'inside information', see J. Lau Hansen and D. Moalem, 'The MAD Disclosure Regime and the Twofold Notion of Inside Information: The Available Solution' (2009) 4(3) *Capital Markets Law Journal* 323. See also C. Di Noia and M. Gargantini, 'Issuers at Midstream: Disclosure of Multistage Events in the Current and in the Proposed EU Market Abuse Regime' (2012) 9(4) *European Company and Financial Law Review* 484, 510.

mechanisms to increase deterrence and to punish various types of violations more severely. Nevertheless, the imposition of sanctions has proven in practice to be a particularly complex task. Historically, legislation in various countries has treated several violations differently, undoubtedly reflecting countries' cultural, political and legal traditions and related, among other factors, to the political willingness to tackle illegal behaviour efficiently; to the regulators' sophistication with regard to deciphering complex market practices; and to 'regulatory capture' issues. Choosing enforcement practices that are commensurate with and efficiently targeted to the distinctive features of each rule-breaking incident can prove to be quite an arduous task. This is due not only to the particulars of each case of reprehensible behaviour, which inevitably vary across different types of market actors and different markets at large, but also to the different symbolic connotations that each enforcement mechanism conveys.

The creation of the EU internal market and the risks associated with national legal practices have triggered a series of initiatives aimed at harmonizing enforcement measures at the EU level. Overall, these initiatives show some accomplishments. For example, a common understanding has gradually emerged that similar breaches of legal rules in different jurisdictions must be sanctioned with equal severity at the EU level. Nevertheless, considerable differences persist at the national level, creating discrepancies between national laws and opening space for regulatory competition. Sanction strategies in various legal systems have therefore failed to demonstrate their effectiveness in terms of punishment and dissuasion, either because the applicable framework is not stringent enough or because its implementation lacks consistency, frequency and rigour.

Sanctions are crucial to the viability of capital markets, as they are best placed to punish, deter, compensate and inculcate a sound culture and market practices to legal and natural persons. The distinctive merits of such mechanisms in ensuring accountability, restoring justice and shifting social norms make them worthy of more extensive research and greater attention from policymakers to ensure their efficiency and their impact upon various market actors.

Public and private enforcement approaches currently coexist as part of a wider EU and international trend towards deterrence, dissuasion and compensation. Academic literature has not conclusively determined which enforcement means is preferable; various authors have opined in different ways on the importance and usefulness of various types of enforcement mechanisms. On the one hand, there is a doctrinal trend which favours the efficiency of 'private enforcement', based on the argument that private parties have more incentives to bring a civil claim against non-compliant behaviour.[34] On the other hand, a more holistic conception of enforcement mechanisms has been advanced, which can secure the protection of financial markets from defective strategies,

---

[34] R. La Porta, F. Lopez-de-Silanes and A. Shleifer, 'What Works in Securities Laws?' (2006) 61 *Journal of Finance* 1.

namely that 'public enforcement' has an important role to play.[35] The EU legislature has aimed to reinforce harmonization trends in various areas of capital markets law with regard to enforcement mechanisms, but the steps taken are perfectible since they leave considerable space for the persistence of national idiosyncrasies. Indeed, the difference between national legal provisions is striking despite these harmonization trends.

One of the central ideas of this book is that investor protection – which has repeatedly been praised in various pieces of EU legislation as one of the main pillars for reform – is mostly seen under the spectrum of issuer disclosure obligations. In other words, investor protection is translated into the need to provide information to the investor community *ex ante* so as to make informed decisions, and much less as something that needs to be strengthened *ex post* within the enforcement framework. I firmly believe that in order for investor protection to obtain a more holistic, trustworthy and efficient dimension, both *ex ante* and *ex post* facets of regulatory intervention need to be developed at a similar (if not equal) pace. As we will show in various chapters of this book, issuers are subject to potential enforcement mechanisms that have not yet attained optimal levels of deterrence.

3.3.2 Civil Liability

Civil liability is a characteristic example of an enforcement scheme that has not yet made a convincing case for its own merits. Market actors harmed by infringements committed by natural or legal persons need to receive appropriate compensation for their loss; the compensatory function also serves deterrence objectives to prevent similar infringements from recurring in the future, as well as accountability at large for the concerned persons. Nevertheless, the discrepancies among national laws are striking. Some Member States have traditionally been more receptive to the implementation of civil liability regimes in capital markets law violations, contrary to others that continue to have highly complex or less protective civil liability provisions. Moreover, there are continuous obstacles to the establishment of individual responsibility across the EU (for example, in the area of issuer disclosure obligations)[36] and some jurisdictions' current efforts to accentuate individual responsibility lack efficiency due to ambiguous wording or the absence of a common understanding of the contours of such responsibility.

---

[35] B.S. Black, 'The Legal and Institutional Preconditions for Strong Securities Markets' (2001) 48 *UCLA Law Review* 781; M. Welsh and V. Morabito, 'Public vs Private Enforcement of Securities Laws: An Australian Empirical Study' (2014) 14(1) *Journal of Corporate Law Studies* 39. On the coexistence and the distinctive features of private and public enforcement, see G. Ferrarini and P. Giudici, 'Financial Scandals and the Role of Private Enforcement: The Parmalat Case' (2005) ECGI – Law Working Paper No. 40/2005, 42, at http://ssrn.com/abstract=730403.

[36] See Sections 4.7.1 and 5.4.1.

Going beyond the mere existence of different civil liability provisions across the EU, national courts also apply civil liability rules in different ways, depending on their legal traditions; the discrepancies both in terms of content of the provisions and in terms of applicability by the courts result in different levels of investor protection across the EU. The persistent uncertainty around this issue does not favour the creation of a rigorous accountability framework for issuers, as the risks of liability arbitrage among different jurisdictions will certainly continue to play a major role for issuers or market actors when choosing capital markets for their activities in the EU.

In some (but very few) areas of capital markets law,[37] the EU has attempted to provide a common framework that establishes an obligation for national laws to include civil liability provisions, while leaving it up to Member States to determine the *modus operandi* of such provisions. Consequently, it has not yet offered a convincing liability regime at the EU level but has only shown, in an experimental way, the first steps towards a broader and more harmonized future civil liability regime under the condition that political willingness allows such developments to take place. Adding to these concerns, investors across the EU do not benefit from a facilitated procedural framework that would allow them to bring an action to court without being forced to face dissuasive cost, resource and time constraints. As a result, they feel less incentivized to perform this role and to seek compensation for the harm suffered. It also seems surprising that EU law has shown a timid evolution towards the acceptance of private enforcement in some areas – therefore asking indirectly for market actors to assume a sanctioning role in capital markets[38] – while at the same time refraining from convincing national laws to ease the exercise of civil claims.

Although legal transplants of US-style class actions to the EU would not necessarily be the preferred way forward,[39] given the numerous market, legal and cultural specificities and constraints of EU Member States, the question remains open: do investors deserve a facilitated path to launching a civil action given the interconnectivity of capital markets and the need to offer the same level of protection across the EU? If the answer is yes and if EU law is unable to harmonize this field further given the above-mentioned constraints, then national laws need to offer concrete and convincing solutions for an efficient and facilitated access to civil procedures.

Harmonization of civil liability regimes in capital markets law not only corresponds to a legitimate need for protection and compensation, but also goes hand in hand with an ever-growing cross-border operational framework for issuers and firms, whose deficiencies may impact various investors in different

---

[37] See, for example, civil liability for infringements related to prospectus disclosure obligations (Section 4.7.1) and to credit rating agencies (Section 13.5.4).

[38] Indeed, although compensation should be distinguished from deterrence, as private enforcement serves primarily the first function, compensatory schemes should also be seen as indirect deterrence mechanisms given their dissuasive function for the repetition of infringements by defendants.

[39] R. Veil (ed.), *European Capital Markets Law* (2nd edn, Hart Publishing, 2017), 178.

jurisdictions. It therefore remains to be seen whether the political willingness at the EU level will in the future be decisive in overcoming the barriers of different legal traditions and reluctance from issuers or other concerned entities whose financial exposure would significantly increase in a stricter civil liability regime.

3.3.3 Criminal Sanctions

Adding to these concerns, criminal proceedings have been largely marginalized across the EU. Criminal courts have traditionally shown a certain degree of reluctance in imposing criminal sanctions due to the high level of proof required in this framework. Their rarity has regrettably acted as a weakening factor for their presence in EU legislative texts. Moreover, the lack of harmonization among national frameworks has not helped in entrusting these types of sanctions to create an efficient counterbalance to violations in capital markets. The various discrepancies among national frameworks for the duration of imprisonment, the maximum pecuniary sanctions and the rules surrounding criminal provisions are notable problems that need further reflection and reforms.

EU law is considerate of such discrepancies as well as the difficulty in achieving a commonly accepted framework among Member States; this is why, as we will see throughout this book, for almost all infringements in capital markets law, EU legislative texts leave it up to the Member States to provide for such sanctions and to define their features. The three criteria that EU law require within this flexible framework are effectiveness, dissuasiveness and proportionality. Although these criteria are pertinent and useful for national developments, it is also true that they largely depend on national mentalities and legal traditions; they cannot therefore, on their own, function as a reliable guide for further harmonization. The inevitable result is that criminal provisions remain an unexplored field of public intervention in capital markets, notwithstanding their potential contribution to the combat of illegal practices.

Nevertheless, new criminal provisions, especially in the area of market abuse,[40] are emerging to denote a political willingness either to tackle illegal behaviour efficiently or to convey a stronger message to the public about governmental responsiveness to socially unacceptable market practices. Criminal courts have been particularly reluctant to impose criminal sanctions due to the requirement of intent, which makes these enforcement mechanisms very difficult – if not impossible – to apply. The latest EU reforms in the area of market abuse[41] have not managed to clarify the contours of criminal provisions to ensure their efficiency; these reforms convey a – more symbolic than realistic – message about their harmonization at the EU level.[42]

---

[40] See, for example, Sections 8.5.2 and 9.6.3.

[41] Directive 2014/57/EU of the European Parliament and of the Council of 16 April 2014 on criminal sanctions for insider dealing and market manipulation [2014] OJ L 173/179 (hereinafter 2014 MAD).

[42] M. Luchtman and J. Vervaele, 'Enforcing the Market Abuse Regime: Towards an Integrated Model of Criminal and Administrative Law Enforcement in the European Union?' (2014) 5(2) *New Journal of European Criminal Law* 192.

3.3.4 Administrative Sanctions and Measures

Administrative sanctions and measures have probably been the only sanctions framework that has been promoted with such certainty at the EU level. The reason behind this legislative choice is undoubtedly the NCA status and structure; NCAs are nowadays the focal point in capital markets regulation given their 'know-how' and their ongoing contact with markets and market actors. They are considered to be the most suitable sources for sanctions also because they are considerably faster than civil or criminal courts in investigating and imposition sanctions. Various EU legislative texts provide for both sanctions and measures, the former being mainly handled through pecuniary sanctions that are now subject to minimum harmonization rules[43] and the latter aiming to serve other objectives, such as the safeguarding of market integrity and investor protection.[44] Minimum harmonization in this area is welcome but undoubtedly more is needed for national rules to achieve the same levels of deterrence. The current EU efforts to bring national laws closer should be seen as the first phase of a long-term strategy that will aim to achieve higher levels of harmonization.

A new regulatory trend in the area of administrative sanctions is related to the provision of a useful guide to NCAs as to the elements that they must take into account when determining the type and level of such sanctions.[45] These factors continue to multiply in various EU legislative texts,[46] showing a clear preference for harmonizing the regulatory reaction in an indirect way. Administrative sanctions are thus expected to converge, namely to go beyond the minimum and maximum of each national legal framework (that will continue to vary) and to reach similar levels of efficiency, while operating in their own national contexts. This is definitely an encouraging step towards gradual convergence of the *modus operandi* of NCAs. It may prove even more useful than formal harmonization measures that deal with minimal penalties, insofar as it could accustom authorities to a new way of thinking about and calculating the

---

[43] National laws are expected to provide for 'minimum maximums' so as to increase their maximum sanctions and accentuate their dissuasiveness. Of course, an even more efficient solution would be for EU law to reach an agreement among national laws and introduce 'minimums' for all infringements; such a revolution would improve the efficiency of sanctions since no trivial minimums would be allowed for the sanctioning of infringements.

[44] Measures typically include, among others, the issuance of a public statement indicating the nature of the infringement and the identity of the (legal or natural) person concerned, as well as the publication of an order requiring the concerned persons to cease the conduct constituting an infringement and to avoid repetition of similar activities. They may also refer to the withdrawal or suspension of the authorization of an institution (for example, an investment firm, market operator or regulated market), temporary or permanent ban of investment firms or any member of their management body.

[45] The gravity of the duration of the breach, the degree of responsibility and the financial strength of the natural or legal person, the magnitude of profits and losses suffered by third parties due to the breach, the level of cooperation with the competent authority, any eventual former breaches and any measures taken to prevent the breach from recurring.

[46] See, for example, Sections 4.7.2, 5.4.2, 6.4.2, 7.2.2.2, 11.8.1 and 12.7.1.

severity of sanctions, prompting them to adopt a much more holistic approach that may not necessarily coincide with traditional approaches.

It is also interesting to note that Member States have the discretion not to introduce rules for administrative sanctions when the infringements concerned are already subject to criminal sanctions. This is undoubtedly due to the complex relationship between these two types of sanctions, especially in the light of the case *Grande Stevens and others* v. *Italy*,[47] in which the European Court of Human Rights (ECHR) confirmed that administrative sanctions are in substance criminal sanctions. The characterization of administrative sanctions as criminal means that Articles 6(2) and 6(3) of the European Convention of Human Rights are therefore applicable, rendering administrative proceedings – subject to the Conventions – protective provisions for all affected parties. Moreover, national laws that allow the potential application of both types of sanctions may violate the principle of *ne bis in idem*, which forbids the imposition of sanctions twice for the same facts.

3.3.5 Social Sanctions

Along with formal enforcement mechanisms, EU law appears to be opting for an approximation of legal sanctions to informal enforcement strategies, such as 'naming and shaming', via the disclosure not only of the violations themselves (e.g. public warning instead of the imposition of pecuniary sanctions) but also of formal sanctions imposed (e.g. pecuniary sanctions).[48] This particular focus on enhancing the dynamics of social sanctions, based on the unpredictable cascading effects on investors, third parties and stakeholders at large, is entering an entirely new phase given the current discrepancies across jurisdictions, with some regulators currently adopting these practices with positive results and others who are reluctant to do so, citing concerns about disproportionality and unpredictable market reactions.

The discreet reinforcement of social sanctions through the use of disclosure as an exposure tool towards other market actors is a welcome revolution in EU law, but its ultimate efficiency will depend on the behavioural patterns of these actors. For social sanctions to take on a meaningful dimension and to act as a counterbalance to various infringements, market actors need to already have the necessary education and evaluation skills to act responsibly upon receiving any information related to infringements. Education is the key here, as it will prove critical for market actors that must reprioritize their strategies and not focus exclusively on the financial implications of infringements.

In other words, if these actors are solely concerned about avoiding the losses arising from such infringements, and sanction at the social level the concerned persons (by retracting from agreements, selling securities, etc.) only when they

---

[47] Application Nos. 18640/10, 18647/10, 18663/10, 18668/10 and 18698/10 ECHR, 4 March 2014.
[48] See, for example, Sections 4.7.2, 5.4.2, 11.8.1 and 13.5.3.

are financially harmed, they will be unlikely to react when they learn about such infringements but are not themselves affected. The reprioritization of their strategies lies therefore in understanding the need to react to all infringements, even when they are not directly harmed, and to avoid adopting a single-minded vision of such violations. Disregarding infringements when there is no personal damage or, as is usually the case, when the concerned persons continue to be profitable for their own interests, has created a general apathy in the markets. It is therefore hoped that these new disclosure tools will, together with educational efforts, inculcate market actors with a different mentality so as to enhance the functioning of social sanctions.

3.4 CONCLUSION

This chapter introduced the main and overarching supervision and sanction themes of EU capital markets law. The ramifications of the global financial crisis for both supervision and sanction have been made clear in the area of financial and capital markets.

Focusing solely on capital markets, we examined the wide range of powers and regulatory tools granted to ESMA since its creation. We emphasized ESMA's regulatory tools to coordinate NCAs and promote convergence in some areas, as well as to supervise and enforce rules directly in others. ESMA has also been given a series of intervention powers in the presence of important situations that may jeopardize the orderly functioning of the market and the stability of the financial system. NCAs have received reinforced and harmonized powers as well as cooperation methods, both between themselves and with ESMA. Notwithstanding these harmonization efforts, persistent differences and discrepancies – in the way these powers are conceived, evaluated and ultimately exercised at the national level – continue to impede convergence in supervision of capital markets and a holistic regulatory spectrum that could safeguard market integrity. The crucial question is for NCAs to be given more resources and guidance so as to have further incentives and tools to converge with other NCAs. ESMA's role is also crucial in this area as it has at its disposal a series of convergence tools and provides ongoing support.

Sanctioning regimes have received different levels of attention from the EU legislature. Civil liability seems to be left up to national laws given the great variety of such national regimes, with some of them maintaining a general framework applicable to any type of infringement and others opting for specific and more protective provisions in this area. The well-known difficulties related to the proof of a causal link between the loss suffered and the infringement, as well as to the identification of the loss itself, make it more difficult to enhance and coordinate such sanctions at the EU level. Even in areas where civil liability regimes have been subject to a sort of coordination, the general framework in which courts will be asked to exercise their functions deprives the legal system of a possibility to develop and apply more targeted enforcement tools against infringements that have caused harm to claimants.

The same conclusion can be reached for criminal sanctions, which are used unfrequently and are largely unpopular despite their social connotation and deterrence function. The high level of proof with regard to the element of intent in an infringement continue to constitute, among many other elements, important obstacles towards further harmonization of this sanctioning method. A more positive assessment can be formulated in relation to administrative sanctions and measures that show increasing steps towards further harmonization and convergence. The introduction of 'minimum maximums' in administrative pecuniary sanctions, as well as the provision of administrative measures for all NCAs, are the first steps of convergence in this area. This is accentuated by the current provisions of indirect harmonization that is expressed via the factors that NCAs have to take into consideration when they sanction various infringements.

PART II

Listed Companies and Disclosure Obligations

CHAPTER 4

Prospectus Disclosure Obligations

4.1 INTRODUCTION

Prospectus disclosure obligations are the first cornerstone for the regulatory framework for listed companies. When shares are admitted for trading on a regulated market for the first time (or additional new shares are issued),[1] an important 'informational contact' is triggered with underwriters,[2] analysts[3] and (mostly institutional) investors. At this stage of entry to the primary market,[4] transparency and accessibility of information are necessary so that investors can make informed investment decisions. This contact involves the publication of a prospectus. As the main informational vehicle, a prospectus includes various types of information related to the issuer's financial situation, its prospects and any other element that may be relevant to the investment decision-making process.

The primary function of disclosure obligations is to minimize the informational asymmetry that exists between the various market actors and issuers seeking to enter the capital markets for the first time (or to issue new shares). A new investment opportunity inevitably holds appeal for market actors, but they must also understand its main features in order to make an informed decision. EU law has endeavoured to make information more accessible and comparable in an ever-growing cross-border investment landscape that justifies

---

[1] What is commonly identified as initial public offerings (IPOs).

[2] 'Underwriting' is a contract that secures, in the absence of market interest, the purchase of securities either by the underwriters directly (investment banks) or by other parties that the underwriters will find. A slightly different technique, 'bookbuilding' denotes the market research conducted by underwriters prior to the IPO – by contacting institutional investors – so as to understand which would be a realistically attractive price for investors and assist the issuer in entering the capital markets with an approximate prediction of market demand: on the merits and costs of both practices, see I. MacNeil, *An Introduction to the Law on Financial Investment* (2nd edn, Hart Publishing, 2012), 261.

[3] See Chapter 12.

[4] Namely the market where investors will purchase for the first time the shares from issuers. Primary markets need to be distinguished from secondary markets that are identified as the trading spectrum among investors that buy or sell shares, following the initial purchase in the primary markets.

the 'necessity'[5] to incentivize actors to participate in the capital markets, as well as to maintain their confidence in the reliability of IPOs.

Under an increased FSAP-driven harmonization wave, prospectus disclosure obligations were first laid out in 2003 in the Prospectus Directive,[6] which served as the first meaningful EU framework for the harmonization of rules applicable to issuers seeking to attract capital market investment. However, the EU's priority was not harmonization *per se*, but rather the simplification and increased competitiveness of EU capital markets that could be ensured by creating a uniform informational framework. Bearing in mind that the driving force behind the Prospectus Directive (PD) was to simplify capital issues and encourage capital market investment across borders, through identical informational requirements allowing comparability and accessibility from the investor community,[7] the EU policy agenda inevitably focused on accelerating the harmonization of informational requirements. This aim was indeed obvious given the maximum harmonization level provided in the Directive.[8]

Other parts of EU law are equally important for the study of prospectus disclosure obligations, such as the powers that EU law gives NCAs so that they can perform their gatekeeping function for new investment proposals entering the market. Nowadays, the applicable legal framework provides for a harmonized approval process, as well as specific monitoring powers for NCAs to further strengthen capital market entry standards, while maintaining their reliability in the eyes of an ever-growing and cross-border investor community. In parallel, the EU passport system allows issuers to use the same prospectus in other Member States, thus further facilitating cross-border securities offers and making EU capital markets more fluid and vibrant.

Nevertheless, the Directive left other aspects – notably sanctions – up to the Member States to decide the optimal framework for providing investor protection in cases of disclosure obligation breaches.[9] This striking differ-

---

[5] Nevertheless, it should also be observed that an excessive focus on the necessity to widen disclosure obligations raises the risk of creating and further nurturing a new generation of overconfident investors who may rely on an irrational belief that disclosure itself empowers them to make optimal investment decisions. For a more general discussion on investor overconfidence and the perils of disclosure, see D.C. Langervoort, 'Taming the Animal Spirits of the Stock Markets: A Behavioral Approach to Securities Regulation' (2002) 97 *Northwestern University Law Review* 135.

[6] Directive 2003/71/EC of the European Parliament and the Council of 4 November 2003 on the prospectus to be published when securities are offered to the public or admitted to trading and amending Directive 2001/34/EC [2003] OJ L 345/64 (hereinafter PD); N. Moloney, *EU Securities and Financial Markets Regulation* (3rd edn, Oxford University Press, 2014), 73.

[7] M. Pellegrini, 'Critical Analysis of the Prospectus Directive' (2006) 17 *European Business Law Review* 1679, 1681.

[8] With some minor exceptions related to the possibility for Member States to impose additional informational requirements based on an investor protection rationale: Article 32(1)(a), PR (below n. 11). See also recital 8, PR (below n. 11) for a similar possibility related to, *inter alia*, corporate governance requirements.

[9] More generally, this regulatory choice is in line with broader EU financial regulation policy.

ence between maximum harmonization of informational requirements and flexibility on sanctions imposed at the national level was undoubtedly due to the realization that progress could not realistically be achieved on all levels from the very outset of the PD. Facilitating access to capital and creating truly integrated EU capital markets were a matter of pivotal importance and sanctions should be – at that time – left mostly under national frameworks to delineate their scope, especially taking into consideration the very strict time limits.[10]

The Prospectus Regulation (PR)[11] is the latest development in this area. It aims to eliminate persistent differences in the implementation of the PD at the national level, while also facilitating capital-raising operations so as to further enhance the Capital Markets Union (CMU).[12] This new piece of EU legislation shows some signs of further laudable efforts and allows for some optimism, nevertheless leaving considerable space for further improvement.

Beyond legislative acts, the applicable EU framework is also complemented by a lengthy series of administrative acts (Delegated Regulations), as well as by various convergence initiatives (by CESR and nowadays ESMA) such as Q&As, Recommendations and Opinions.

4.2 THE REGULATORY SCOPE OF PROSPECTUS DISCLOSURE OBLIGATIONS

4.2.1 Public Offers and Listing

Prospectuses must be prepared by the issuer, approved by the NCA and published when securities are offered to the public[13] or when they are admitted to trading on a regulated market[14] (what is commonly called listing).[15] Distinguishing between these two categories in capital markets is essential for understanding the operational framework of prospectuses, as well as of the necessity to protect investors in both regulated and unregulated markets.

Beginning with the notion 'offers to the public', such offers are not necessarily linked to trading on a regulated market since they most frequently take place in unregulated markets tailored for smaller companies with stronger

---

[10] P. Schammo, *EU Prospectus Law: New Perspectives on Regulatory Competition in Securities Markets* (Cambridge University Press, 2011), 243.

[11] Regulation (EU) 2017/1129 of the European Parliament and of the Council of 14 June 2017 on the prospectus to be published when securities are offered to the public or admitted to trading on a regulated market, and repealing Directive 2003/71/EC [2017] OJ L 168/12 (hereinafter PR).

[12] See Section 1.2.3.

[13] By an offeror, namely a legal entity or individual proceeding with such an offer: Article 2(i), PR.

[14] By an issuer, namely a legal entity which issues or proposes to issue securities: Article 2(h), ibid.

[15] Article 3(3), ibid.

growth prospects.[16] However, different Member States have interpreted the concept of public offers in different ways. The persistent discrepancies in understanding, interpreting and applying this concept may create a diversified operational spectrum in the EU, with some activities being qualified as 'public offers' in some jurisdictions – and hence subject to a series of rules – and others not. The PR attempts to take into account national discrepancies by broadly defining public offers as 'communication to persons in any form and by any means, presenting sufficient information on the terms of the offer and the securities to be offered, so as to enable an investor to decide to purchase or subscribe to these securities'.[17] This definition aims to foster a common perception of a capital-raising operation involving the public, as well as the disclosure obligations that flow naturally from such an operation. This broad definition has been successful in gradually eliminating major discrepancies among Member States,[18] but it may need to be further refined as there may still be room for manoeuvre at the national level.[19]

Continuing with the notion of 'trading on a regulated market', this type of operation does not necessarily involve an offer to the public, as admission to listing is a distinct operation. The need to ensure access to adequate information in regulated markets is nonetheless much greater (compared to unregulated ones), as the making of informed investment decisions is synonymous with investor protection concerns in IPOs where larger-sized and more well-known and prestigious companies participate. Minimizing the informational asymmetry is key to investor confidence; therefore, capital-raising operations in regulated markets must comply with particularly onerous requirements.

The PR also provides a series of cases that justify its non-applicability.[20] It opts for an optional disclosure framework for securities included in an offer where the total consideration for the offer is less than €1 million (calculated over a period of 12 months). Indeed, in such cases, issuers are simply entitled

---

[16] Nevertheless, they may be combined with trading on a regulated market so as to satisfy the requirement that, at the time of admission to trading, at least 25% of each class of listed shares must be in the hands of the public in States belonging to the EEA. Issuers aiming for listing may therefore proceed concomitantly to a public offer.

[17] Article 2(d), ibid.

[18] See, for example, the abolishment of the French notion '*appel public à l'épargne*' in 2009 and the adoption of the duopoly 'public offer–listing': *Ordonnance n° 2009-80 du 22 janvier 2009*, JO, 23 January 2009, 1431. More generally, before the PD in 2003, public offers were not conceived in the same way at a national level. For example, certain issuers were obliged to publish a prospectus and others were exempt from such obligation for the same type of operation that was perceived to be a private placement in another country.

[19] See, for example, the traditional German (*Mitteilung an das Publikum*) and Portuguese (*comunicação ao público*) versions of the PD, which represent a slightly less adaptable version of the notion of 'persons' used in the English version of the PD: L. Enriques and M. Gatti, 'Is There a Uniform EU Securities Law After the Financial Services Action Plan?' (2008–2009) 14 *Stanford Journal of Law, Business and Finance* 43, 54. It could thus be argued that further convergence may be needed in this area so as to avoid variable treatment of same type of operations.

[20] Article 1(2), PR.

and not obliged to draw up a prospectus in the case of a public offer or listing. Member States retain the right to require other disclosure items without creating a disproportionate or unnecessary burden.[21]

4.2.2 Exemptions from Prospectus Requirements

The EU framework lays out various possible exemptions from the requirement to publish a prospectus. These exemptions fall into different categories, pertaining to situations that can legitimately justify a lower level of investor protection given investors' identity, financial position and exposure to a particular investment or certain capital-raising operations' features.

The first category of exemptions covers offers targeting investors that do not fit into the classic retail investor framework (therefore justifying a lower degree of disclosure): for example, securities offers targeting only qualified investors, a small number of persons (fewer than 150), to persons who individually acquire securities for an amount of at least €100,000, and offers of securities whose denomination per unit amounts to at least €100,000 or that have a total consideration of less than €100,000.[22]

The second category refers specifically to offers to the public and exempts the following types of securities from a prospectus publication: issuance of shares in substitution for already issued shares (without any capital increase), takeovers (when the offer is an exchange offer) or merger/division scenarios. In all three cases, these offers must be accompanied by a document containing information equivalent to that of a prospectus, dividends paid out to existing shareholders and the securities offered or allotted to existing or former directors or employees.[23]

The third category refers specifically to trading on a regulated market and exempts the following types of securities from a prospectus publication: shares that represent less than 20% of the already listed shares, shares issued in substitution of already listed shares (without any capital increase), takeovers (when the offer is an exchange offer) or merger/division scenarios.[24]

Under the PR, a Member State may also exempt offers of securities from the prospectus requirement if the offer is only made in its territory and its total consideration is below €8 million (compared to €5 million under the PD).[25]

---

[21] Article 1(3), ibid.

[22] Article 1(4), ibid.

[23] Article 1(4), ibid. Provided that a document containing information on this operation is available.

[24] Article 1(5), ibid. Provided that a document containing information on this operation is available. It is important to note that 20% is the new PR threshold, which is considerably higher than the one established under the (now replaced) PD (10%): this reform reflects the Commission's willingness to increase the attractiveness of capital markets to issuers and to further facilitate new IPOs.

[25] Article 3(2), ibid. Member States also need to notify ESMA of the exercise of this option. It should be also borne in mind that this threshold is not harmonized across the EU, a regrettable fact that needs further reflection in the future.

The PR is therefore aiming to facilitate and attract more offers to the public by raising this threshold.

4.3 THE SINGLE PASSPORT MECHANISM AND HARMONIZATION ISSUES

If there is one provision of the PR that has come to embody the entire Regulation, it is the 'single passport'. This mechanism is the PR's most important *acquis*, marking considerable progress towards creating a new EU framework to facilitate cross-border listings (which were rare under the previous regime).[26] Under the single passport, when a prospectus has been approved by one Member State's NCA, the issuer can use the same prospectus in other Member States within a period of 12 months, without having to provide other types of information. This mechanism gives the prospectus a pan-European status and opens up access to all other regulated markets without any further intervention. All the information in the prospectus is identical across the EU; this enhances investors' ability to compare various prospectuses from different issuers in a harmonized, simplified and cross-border framework.[27] As previously mentioned,[28] Member States still have the option to impose additional requirements, but such requirements cannot restrict, either directly or indirectly, the content or dissemination of a prospectus that has been already approved by another NCA.[29]

The harmonization introduced in prospectus disclosure obligations has been subject to extensive debate given the various advantages but also the perils that may result from the current legal framework. The main benefits of increased harmonization relate to increased investor confidence in evaluating various prospectuses and adopting a more cross-border mindset.[30] It is obvious from the various EU texts that the main objective of these reforms was to incentivize a new generation of investors to contribute to EU capital markets on a massive and lasting basis. Prior to these reforms, the national mechanisms that were supposed to perform this function proved unable to sustain the investment 'safety valve' that is vital to creating liquidity and prosperity in the markets. This was mainly because they were not perceived as components of a

---

[26] The previous system was characterized by mutual recognition which, notwithstanding its usefulness, left considerable leeway to Member States to impose additional and burdensome requirements to issuers. For an interesting discussion regarding difficulties that issuers faced prior to the adoption of the PD, see K. Lanoo, 'The Emerging Framework for Disclosure in the EU' (2003) 3 *Journal of Corporate Law Studies* 329, 340.

[27] N. Moloney, 'Confidence and Competence: The Conundrum of EC Capital Markets Law' (2004) 4 *Journal of Corporate Law Studies* 1.

[28] See above n. 8.

[29] Recital 8, PR.

[30] See, more generally, J.C. Coffee Jr., 'Racing Towards the Top? The Impact of Cross-Listings and Stock Market Competition on International Corporate Governance' (2002) 102 *Columbia Law Review* 1757.

wider transnational context, but as vital mechanisms for maintaining liquidity in the national capital markets.

Aside from the above-mentioned benefits, maximum harmonization measures could also be seen as impeding some Member States from maintaining a more efficient informational framework. Indeed, these measures may be seen as a regulatory overreaction.[31] Under this line of interpretation, it could also be argued that an alternative system – whereby Member States could impose more stringent disclosure requirements only upon issuers in their own territory[32] – would be more efficient.[33] In fact, maximum harmonization prevents some jurisdictions from imposing additional safeguards and thereby creating a much more competitive capital market that could attract issuers willing to comply with more stringent requirements in order to become identified with a more rigorous and prestigious market. It could be also suggested that Member States would not risk imposing excessive and unreasonably onerous requirements in order not to become too stringent and less attractive to other issuers.

While these arguments are quite relevant in this context and undoubtedly portray a series of advantages for capital markets, the EU law's priority was to ensure uniformity and accessibility to the same amount of information so as to facilitate cross-border listings. Under this political agenda, it would seem unrealistic to allow Member States a greater level of freedom regarding prospectus disclosure obligations that constitute the entry-level stage for issuers and investors in capital markets. The risk of creating a variable level of disclosure across the various national jurisdictions was seen as a serious impediment to strengthening investment incentives and accessibility mechanisms.

Transposing the harmonization debate onto a more general discussion of the overall benefits of these policy strategies, disclosure obligations could also be seen as an optimal way to educate retail investors and create a new generation (currently largely absent due to reliance on underwriters and analysts, as well as on institutional investment schemes) that has been accustomed to having access to the same amount of information across the EU, is able to compare various prospectuses and has confidence in EU capital markets. Opening up investment and equity finance operations to a broader public required, during the enactment of the PD in 2003, a political choice of compromising more sophisticated and advanced requirements by some national capital markets for the sake of a more holistic and unifying approach at the EU level.

It should be also borne in mind that the EU has always lacked a unified 'investment culture',[34] and transparency in capital markets could act as a vehicle for the creation of an 'EU investor identity' akin to the concept of 'EU citizenship'. It is argued that disclosure has a key role to play in creating widely shared

---

[31] E. Ferran, 'Cross-border Offers of Securities in the EU' (2007) 4(4) *European Company and Financial Law Review* 470.

[32] But not upon issuers with prior prospectus approval from another NCA, for which mutual recognition would apply and no additional requirements could be imposed.

[33] E. Ferran, *Building an EU Securities Market* (Cambridge University Press, 2004), 144.

[34] In contrast to other regions, such as the USA.

confidence in capital markets by shaping a widely shared vision of an 'EU investor identity'. Maximum harmonization was and remains relevant for achieving this aim: the choice of the (directly applicable) PR as the new legislative framework attests to this objective. Moreover, a potential future reform reintroducing minimum harmonization in prospectus disclosure obligations could be beneficial provided that a new generation of EU investors would already have grown accustomed to operating in a truly transnational framework and absorbing some legitimate informational divergences among jurisdictions.

4.4 THE INFORMATIONAL SCOPE OF PROSPECTUS DISCLOSURE OBLIGATIONS

4.4.1 Required Prospectus Content

The PR is based on a pedagogical mindset that aims to make prospectuses the main informational vehicle for assisting investors in making informed investment decisions. Prospectuses must contain all information which is material to enable investors to make an informed assessment of the assets and liabilities, financial position, profit and losses, and prospects of the issuer and of any guarantor, of the rights attaching to such securities on the reasons for the issuance and its impact on the issuer. The PR also specifies that the information disclosed may vary depending on the nature of the issuer, the type of securities and the circumstances of the issuer.[35]

It is also fairly straightforward to understand the PR's (potential) pedagogical framework, aiming to incentivize investors by introducing a legal framework whereby information is presented 'in an easily analysable, concise and comprehensible form',[36] is 'appropriate, taking into account the information needs of the investors concerned',[37] and adopts a 'key information'-oriented[38] and 'consistent' approach[39] as to its presentation methods.

The PR aims for a certain degree of flexibility as to information that can be omitted from the prospectus without endangering investors' decision-making and market reliability. First of all, if the final offer price and/or number of securities offered to the public cannot be included in the prospectus, issuers must disclose the valuation methods and criteria, and/or conditions, in accordance with which the final offer price is to be determined and an explanation of any valuation methods used.[40] Alternatively, issuers must guarantee investors the right to withdraw their agreement to purchase or subscribe to securities within no less than two working days after the final offer price and number

---

[35] Article 6(1), PR.
[36] Article 6(2), ibid.
[37] Article 13(1), ibid.
[38] Article 7(1), ibid.
[39] Article 7(2), ibid.
[40] Article 17(1)(b), ibid.

of securities offered to the public have been filed.[41] The final offer price and number of securities must be filed with the NCA of the home Member State.[42]

Under a subtler perspective, the home NCA may authorize an issuer to omit certain information from a prospectus provided that the following criteria are satisfied: the disclosure of the information would be contrary to the public interest or seriously detrimental to the issuer (and its omission would be unlikely to mislead the public) or it is of minor importance only for a specific offer or an admission to trading on a regulated market (and it cannot influence the issuer's or guarantor's financial position and prospects assessment).[43]

Although the notion of public interest is a legitimate one in this area (given the fact that investors are not always in a position to evaluate information in a neutral way, let alone information whose disclosure could be contrary to the public interest and further destabilize the market), it is also important to note that NCAs may interpret this notion in various ways. Indeed, the perception of public interest may be associated with national capital markets' capacity to absorb high levels of volatility or with investors' familiarity with certain types of information that may be considered riskier or more sensitive to public interest concerns in other markets.

The same critical approach must be adopted with regard to the flexibility shown for the disclosure of information that would be seriously detrimental to the issuer, but whose omission would be unlikely to mislead the public. This criterion may appear to be a contradiction in terms, for any information whose disclosure would be detrimental to the issuer would inevitably be of some significance, and omitting such information could also mislead the public given its potential importance for the formation of investment decisions. The same concerns could be raised with regard to informational elements of minor importance, as explained above. While they may not influence investment decision-making, it is difficult to decipher *ex ante* their prospective importance for future developments that may lead to more significant events. Indeed, some events may remain insignificant (and their omission from the prospectus would be justifiable) but NCAs will not be in a position to understand eventual developments related with this type of information and they also adopt a slightly different method when they interpret the notion of information of 'minor importance'.

It could be argued that the PR implies that informational asymmetry cannot be dealt with in its entirety in the presence of risks that issuers may be faced with. The PR therefore opts for flexibility to allow issuers to raise capital notwithstanding the partial informational spectrum offered to investors. While legitimate competition and confidentiality concerns should be protected at all times and excessive transparency should not risk compromising capital-raising operations (due to increased costs or excessive regulatory burdens), it is also

---

[41] Article 17(1)(a), ibid.

[42] Article 17(2), ibid.

[43] Article 18, ibid.

important to note that investors should be more sophisticated and better prepared to absorb the entire range of disclosed information. In fact, notwithstanding the previously formulated critiques related to the regulatory flexibility for omitting certain informational elements, the EU's stance on this matter can also be seen as the provision of flexibility for any issuer inevitably faced with an extremely variable and highly demanding (but not homogeneously sophisticated) investor community. Future reforms must address the delicate balance between issuer priorities and ways to better prepare investors to make good use even of information that can currently be omitted from prospectuses.

The PR also provides another layer of flexibility related to certain required information that may not be appropriate for the issuer's area of activity or its legal form, or for the securities to which the prospectus relates. In the presence of such difficulties, the prospectus must contain information equivalent to that which is usually required.[44] This last layer of flexibility seems able to balance issuer needs and transparency concerns more effectively, since it would result in equivalent information being given to the readers of a prospectus.

4.4.2 Disclosure of Critically Important Information: The Case of Risk Factors

The PR pays particular attention to critically important information so as to protect investors and facilitate informed investment decisions. For the purposes of this chapter, we will focus on the notion of risk factors that can be present at the levels of both the issuer and the securities admitted to trading or offered. They also refer to risks that are material for taking investment decisions.[45] The notion of risk should not be identified as 'uncertainty' since risks are always identifiable and quantifiable from the issuer *ex ante*, as events that are known to a certain extent. Uncertainty could eventually be identifiable but not quantifiable since it would constitute an unpredictable situation for issuers. In other words, an uncertainty could eventually evolve into a risk and would then – only then – be subject to a disclosure obligation. Notwithstanding the obvious benefits of such a disclosure requirement, it needs to be underlined that the perception of risk factors in this area varies across the EU.[46] Inevitably, issuers may treat certain events differently for prospectus disclosure purposes and the informational protection of investors cannot be secured in a harmonized way across the EU.

If such divergences were inevitable, up to a certain extent, an adequate solution could be the introduction of a requirement for the prospectus to disclose

---

[44] Article 18(2), ibid.

[45] Regulation (EC) No 809/2004 of 29 April 2004 implementing Directive 2003/71/EC of the European Parliament and of the Council as regards information contained in prospectuses as well as the format, incorporation by reference and publication of such prospectuses and dissemination of advertisements [2004] OJ L 149/1: Article 2(3), Annexes I and III.

[46] M. Van Daelen, 'Risk Management Solutions in Business Law: Prospectus Disclosure Requirements' (2008), at http://ssrn.com/abstract=1287624.

the method that the issuer has chosen to evaluate such material risks. Issuers could thus inform the market that they have identified such risks and that they have decided to disclose them following a classification of their impact and a calculation of the probability that they will actually occur. Investors would therefore be in a better position to understand the issuer's underlying rationale for such disclosure. Even though such a proposal could appear to be very restrictive and time-consuming for issuers, it should be borne in mind that listing rules[47] and corporate governance codes[48] across the EU already refer to risk management systems in financial reporting. Adopting such information, contained in the annual report, for risk factors and integrating it into the prospectus would then be a less onerous requirement than expected. This would also be in line with the requirement for the provision in the prospectus of a statement as to whether or not the issuer complies with the corporate governance regime of its country of incorporation.[49]

The latest developments in the area of risk factors focus on simplifying this part of the prospectus, reducing its length – due to the fact that issuers opt for very broadly formulated statements on risk factors, aiming effectively to turn them into disclaimers – and targeting information useful for investment decision-making. Indeed, the PR provides that the risk factors shall be allocated across a limited number of categories defined by issuers' assessment of the probability of their occurrence and the expected magnitude of their anticipated impact.[50] ESMA is also expected to develop guidelines on the assessment by NCAs of the allocation of risk factors across categories as well as of their specificity and materiality.[51] This is a positive step towards convergence among NCAs but our above-mentioned proposal retains its relevance, by offering a realistic solution for a better understanding of risk factors.

4.4.3 Voluntary Prospectus Content

Going beyond the disclosure of the required information in prospectuses, many issuers may also decide to disclose additional information on a purely voluntary basis. The reasons behind such a decision may be various: openness to other markets, willingness to profit from a larger reduction in underpricing, desire to attract more investors, especially in the case of start-up companies. All these

---

[47] See, for example, Disclosure and Transparency Rules 7.2.5 R under UK law: '[t]he corporate governance statement must contain a description of the main features of the issuer's internal control and risk management systems in relation to the financial reporting process.'
[48] See, for example, Provision C.2.1 of the UK Corporate Governance Code: 'the directors should confirm that they have carried out a robust assessment of the principal risks facing the company – including those that would threaten its business model, future performance, solvency or liquidity. The directors should describe those risks and explain how they are being managed or mitigated.'
[49] Annex I, 16.4, Regulation (EC) No 809/2004.
[50] Article 16(1), PR.
[51] Article 16(4), ibid.

incentives are related to a strategy of reducing informational asymmetry with the investor community.[52] It should be noted that IPOs function as the first informational contact point for investors regarding issuers who may either have a short history or are simply less known to capital markets. Reinforcing the informational content of prospectuses therefore aims to reassure and further incentivize market actors during the IPO. These incentives are nevertheless not exempt from risks related to the truthfulness of the disclosed information. Indeed, issuers need to ensure, on the one hand, the drafting of a highly informative and attractive prospectus and, on the other hand, the maintenance of informational equilibrium between attractiveness and their true situation.

Such a balance may not always be achieved in a straightforward way, especially when issuers seek to attract more investors by including additional forward-looking information regarding business plans that may not materialize in the end. Although it would be tempting to judge such strategies as an outright violation of disclosure rules, it should also be borne in mind that the legal rules that aim to protect informational transparency in this area could only catch behaviour that is blatantly illegal since its infancy. In other words, forward-looking information cannot be verified *ex ante* and it is preferable to treat it with caution as a hypothetical scenario that denotes only intention, not results, at the issuer level. Of course, this does not mean that issuers are not obliged to rectify the information when prevailing circumstances have changed, so as to inform the public of any further developments.

4.5 THE COMMUNICATION SCOPE OF PROSPECTUS DISCLOSURE OBLIGATIONS

4.5.1 The Vehicles of Disclosure

The PR provides a flexible framework by which issuers can choose between two prospectus presentation methods: they can either establish a prospectus via a unique document or via different documents (registration document, securities note and summary).[53] The registration document constitutes the main source of information related to the issuer. The information contained in this document relates to the periodic informational spectrum that will be examined in further detail in Chapter 5. For the purposes of this chapter, it is useful to note that issuers must be closely involved in drafting such documents since they contain a series of important information touching upon, *inter alia*, their profile, board of directors, shareholding structure and so forth. Aiming to facilitate the applicable framework for frequent issuers, the PR introduced a new and optional 'universal registration document' that allows for fast-track NCA approval when the prospectus will be required at a later stage.[54] Issuers can also

---

[52] See, for example, the empirical study by L. Bottazzi and M. Da Rin, 'Voluntary Information Disclosure at IPO' (2016), at https://ssrn.com/abstract=2810847.

[53] Article 6(3), PR.

[54] Article 9, PR.

satisfy periodic disclosure obligations – and more specifically the publication of annual and half-yearly reports – simply by having approved and published the universal registration document within four months after the end of the financial year for the annual reports and within three months after the end of the first six months of the financial year for the half- yearly reports.[55] This option considerably simplifies the overall disclosure-related requirements and reduces costs and resources for issuers.

The securities note must provide a description of the securities offered, their terms and conditions.

Lastly, the summary must include key information for the securities offered, in a language and a style that facilitate the understanding of the information; more specifically, the language needs to be clear, non-technical, concise and comprehensible for investors so that they can make an informed decision.[56] Summaries must be drawn up using a common format so that investors can compare them without any major difficulty, and they must also provide a warning that they should only be read as an introduction to the prospectus, whereas investment decisions should be based upon consideration of the whole prospectus, thus encouraging investors to examine all available documents and not to over rely on the summary.[57]

In the past, market actors have questioned the overall efficiency and usefulness of summaries, stating that they find it difficult to decipher the information disclosed. This is due to long-standing practices of drafting summaries with information copied from other documents and using very complex terms.[58] Issuers thus need to make more efforts, similar to the Delegated Regulation (EU) No 486/2012, in order to make disclosed information more accessible and summaries more useful to potential investors. The PR aims to further enhance the summary's accessibility and legibility by requiring a document[59] similar to the ones under the Regulation on key information documents for packaged retail and insurance-based investment products (PRIIPs).[60] Such required information might include the use of warnings, key information on the issuer/offeror/person asking for admission, the securities and the offer or admission, or a series of simplified subsections aimed at making the summary even more user-friendly.[61] Most importantly, what is particularly decisive is convergence among NCAs as to their expectations in prospectus applications

---

[55] For further detailed conditions, see Article 9(12), ibid.

[56] Article 7(2)(b), ibid.

[57] Article 7(5), PR.

[58] European Securities Markets Expert Group (ESME), 'Report on Directive 2003/71/ EC of the European Parliament and of the Council on the Prospectus to be Published when Securities are Offered to the Public or Admitted to Trading' (2007), 10, at http://ec.europa. eu/finance/securities/docs/esme/05092007_report_en.pdf.

[59] Article 7, PR.

[60] Regulation (EU) No 1286/2014 of the European Parliament and of the Council of 26 November 2014 on key information documents for packaged retail and insurance-based investment products (PRIIPs) [2014] OJ L 352/1.

[61] Article 7, PR.

for overall better investor protection at the EU level. ESMA has a very active role to play in that regard, with ongoing coordination initiatives and dialogue with and among NCAs.

4.5.2 Publication Methods

Another important factor for ensuring transparency in prospectus disclosure obligations is the use of consistent publication methods across the EU. Market actors need a clear view of the timing of the prospectus publication and the available sources so that they can find the necessary information and make informed investment decisions. Therefore, this type of information needs to be made available using the same publication methods and following the same time frame.

Regarding the applicable time frame, the PR provides that the prospectus must be filed with the NCA and made available to the public as soon as practicable and at a reasonable time in advance of the offer to the public or the admission to trading. Additionally, in the case of an IPO of shares not previously admitted to trading, the prospectus must be available at least six working days before the end of the offer.[62]

Regarding publication methods, the PD provided the following options: insertion in one or more newspapers circulating in the Member State where the listing is taking place or the offer to the public is made; availability in printed copies at the offices of the regulated market or the issuer and financial intermediaries (i.e. the banks or brokers placing or selling the securities); electronic publication on the issuer's or financial intermediaries' (placing or selling the securities) website;[63] electronic publication on the regulated market's website; or, lastly, electronic publication on the NCA's website. The new framework introduced by the PR opts for exclusive use of electronic publication[64] by removing the two above-mentioned print options (newspapers and printed copies);[65] the electronic publication must take place on any of the following websites:

- the website of the issuer, the offeror or the person asking for admission to trading on a regulated market

---

[62] Article 21, ibid.

[63] Electronic publication must be free of charge, registration and acceptance of liability disclaimer. Moreover, in order to facilitate access to the published information, the prospectus must be easily accessible when entering the website, in searchable and non-modifiable electronic format, and free from hyperlinks with the exception of links to the electronic addresses where information incorporated by reference is available: Commission Delegated Regulation (EU) 2016/301 of 30 November 2015 supplementing Directive 2003/71/EC of the European Parliament and of the Council with regard to regulatory technical standards for approval and publication of the prospectus and dissemination of advertisements and amending Commission Regulation (EC) No 809/2004 [2016] OJ L 58/13, Article 6.

[64] Article 21(2), PR.

[65] Copies on a durable medium may still be available upon request: Article 21(11), ibid.

- the website of the financial intermediaries placing or selling the securities
- the website of the regulated market where the admission to trading is sought.[66]

The NCA of the home Member State is also expected to publish on its website the prospectuses approved or at least the list of prospectuses approved with hyperlinks to the dedicated websites.[67] NCAs must also notify ESMA of the approval of a prospectus and provide the latter with an electronic copy of the prospectus as well as with the necessary data for its classification by ESMA in its own storage mechanism.[68] Indeed, another matter of crucial importance for investors and regulators is the creation of an online storage mechanism with a search tool facility that can be used for free.[69] ESMA is in charge of upgrading its pan-EU prospectus registry and creating this mechanism so that, on the one hand, investors can find, compare and analyse the disclosed information that will frequently be posted on this platform, and on the other hand, ESMA itself can have complete statistics on prospectuses at the EU level.

These measures enhance the availability of information given the considerable advantages of electronic publications in terms of cost, time and ease of access.

4.5.3 Prospectus Language

The language in which a prospectus is written is a very important issue for making sure that the disclosed information is accessible and understandable. The applicable language prospectus regime was undoubtedly one of the most highly debated issues in capital markets law before the FSAP. According to the pre-2003 PD regime, a Member State's NCA could demand that a prospectus be translated in its entirety into the local language of the market in which the issuer was seeking to raise capital.[70] This situation was extremely costly and cumbersome for issuers and offerors, to such an extent that their need to reduce these costs when attempting to raise capital was the driving force behind the PD reforms in 2003 that aimed to facilitate such operations.

The PD thus introduced an 'issuer-choice' model, whereby issuers can opt for a language customary in the sphere of international finance. In other words, English rapidly became the preferred language for capital-raising operations, an example that many Member States followed in order to attract more capital from issuers around the globe, with some notable exceptions.[71]

---

[66] Article 21(2), ibid.

[67] Article 21(5), ibid.

[68] Article 21(5), ibid.

[69] Article 21(7), ibid. See also Recital 63, ibid.

[70] P. Mattil and F. Möslein, 'The Language of the Prospectus: Europeanisation of Prospectus Law and Consumer Protection' (2008) 1 *Journal of International Banking & Financial Law* 27.

[71] Germany and France were the most notable exceptions in that regard, especially during and shortly after the enactment of the PD.

Nevertheless, the facilitation of such operations for the reduction of costs may appear slightly contradictory to the recurrent EU rhetoric for retail investor protection. Indeed, it is surprising to note that the proclaimed 'necessity' to inform investors efficiently does not go hand in hand with language accessibility, since they do not have a complete view of the prospectus in their native language. Although the prevalent issue is the facilitation of cross-listings, the persistent difficulties that investors may face in understanding and deciphering the information presented in another language is something that needs to be taken into account in the overall debate. Retail investors' predominant reliance on underwriters, analysts and other informed actors in the primary markets could resolve this conundrum by simply implying that such concerns are unfounded since individual retail investors would not in any case read prospectuses. Nevertheless, the scope of our analysis is to highlight the inconsistency of policymaking agendas that continue to claim such necessity for retail investor protection while creating an informational framework that still disconnects those investors from prospectuses.

The PR provides three different scenarios for determining the prospectus language, with the same degree of flexibility for issuers or offerors. First, when the offer is made or the listing is sought only in the home Member State, the language must be the one accepted by the NCA of that State.[72] Secondly, when the offer or the listing involve a State other than the home State, the language will be either the one accepted by that State or a language customary in the sphere of international finance; the final choice belonging to the issuer, offeror or person asking for admission.[73] The only prospectus item that a host Member State NCA may require to be translated into its official language is the prospectus summary.[74]

Thirdly, where the offer or listing is sought in more than one Member States, including the home Member State, the language will be either the one accepted by the home Member State and will also be made available either in one of the languages accepted by a host Member State or in the language customary in the sphere of international finance. Once again, the issuer or offeror decides which the language is used in the prospectus, and the NCA of each host Member State may only require that the prospectus summary be translated into its official language.[75]

This solution is a satisfactory one, at least for minimum information purposes, for investors to grasp a broad idea of an investment prospect. Nevertheless, it is easy to understand that this solution is not one that would efficiently protect retail investors in other Member States. Although retail investors' reliance on underwriters and analysts is still in evidence across the EU,[76] the

---

[72] Article 27(1), PR.
[73] Article 27(2), ibid.
[74] Article 27(2), ibid.
[75] Article 27(3), ibid.
[76] J. Armour, D. Awrey, P. Davies, L. Enriques, J. Gordon, C. Mayer and J. Payne, *Principles of Financial Regulation* (Oxford University Press, 2016), 162.

policymaking agenda of making financial products accessible to EU households does not meet the expectations of ordinary retail investors in this case, as rare as their presence may currently be. This goes hand in hand with financial literacy priorities that need to be taken into consideration very carefully in any future reforms so that retail investors can participate more actively in investing in capital markets.

4.5.4 The Exhaustiveness of the Rhythm of Disclosure

The PR has implemented a sophisticated time frame regarding the disclosure of prospectus information. Via the prospectus supplement, it aims to establish a 'perpetual transparency dialogue' with market actors in the presence of new facts of a certain importance that may arise after the prospectus is approved but before actual trading on the regulated market (or the closing of the offer to the public) takes place. The occurrence of such events, during a period that is particularly critical for the success of a capital-raising operation, may have a considerable impact on market actors' investment decisions. In such circumstances, the PR requires issuers to disclose these events in a prospectus supplement and to submit this supplement for approval.[77]

The disclosure obligation includes every significant new factor, material mistake or inaccuracy relating to the information included in the prospectus. The margin of appreciation left to national laws for implementing such a rule (as well as for sanctioning potential violations) in an appropriate way has been further clarified by a Delegated Regulation that provides regulatory standards specifying minimum situations that trigger the supplement's mandatory publication.[78] The term 'factor' should be welcomed since it can include a vast spectrum of situations arising during that period. This term should be preferred over the term 'change', which has created a series of interpretational difficulties in other jurisdictions due to its narrower conceptual spectrum and the potential it gives issuers to circumvent the rule by avoiding the disclosure of negative information during that critical period.[79]

The supplement to the prospectus obligation thus shows diligence in the search for transparency by an issuer during a critical phase in a capital-raising operation, who could otherwise have been tempted to maintain 'informational

---

[77] Article 23(1), ibid.

[78] Delegated Regulation (EU) No 382/2014 of 7 March 2014 supplementing Directive 2003/71/EC of the European Parliament and of the Council with regard to regulatory technical standards for publication of supplements to the prospectus [2014] OJ L 111/36.

[79] See, for example, the highly debated Canadian case *Kerr* v. *Danier Leather Inc.* 2007 CSC 44 around the interpretation of the term 'material change' by the courts and its implication for disclosure obligations in this framework: A. Anand and M. Condon, 'Weather, Leather, and the Obligation to Disclose: Kerr v. Danier Leather Inc.(c)' (2006) 44 *Osgoode Hall Law Journal* 727.

discretion' so as not to compromise its potential and attractiveness.[80] The supplement will be approved in the same way within seven working days maximum and will be published in accordance with the original publication arrangements of the prospectus. The summary of the prospectus must also be supplemented to reflect any new information that has arisen in the meantime.

4.6 THE SUPERVISORY FRAMEWORK OF PROSPECTUS DISCLOSURE OBLIGATIONS

4.6.1 The Auditors' Role

Accountants and auditors play a vital role in the area of prospectus disclosure obligations. Their gatekeeping function in securing informational transparency is needed not only in relation to the required reports that they must prepare to accompany the prospectus, but also in relation to information that is disclosed by issuers on a purely voluntary basis. The Regulation (EC) No 809/2004[81] contributed decisively to strengthening the gatekeeping function that auditors or accountants can play in this field. Nevertheless, concerns were raised regarding the administrative costs that issuers had to face in capital-raising operations. As a result, a new amending Regulation (EU) No 862/2012[82] aimed to soften some of the requirements for such reports.

The Regulation (EC) No 809/2004 provides the obligation for such reports to contain a series of information, such as profit forecasts or estimates,[83] pro forma financial information[84] and historical financial information.[85] Issuers obviously face the temptation to present an optimistic view of forward-looking information given the desire to make the prospectus attractive and to increase the likelihood of success of the capital-raising operation. The presence of accountants or auditors during this process is therefore vital so as to efficiently protect investors.

Beginning with the profit forecasts or estimates, the report that needs to be prepared by independent accountants or auditors must state that in their opinion 'the forecast or estimate has been properly compiled on the basis stated, and that the basis of accounting used for the profit forecast or estimate is consistent with the accounting policies of the issuer'.[86]

---

[80] It also needs to be borne in mind that such an eventual strategy is reasonable, especially given the fact that the PR allows investors to withdraw their acceptances within two working days following the publication of the prospectus supplement: Article 23(2), PR.

[81] Above n. 45.

[82] Delegated Regulation (EU) No 862/2012 of 4 June 2012 amending Regulation (EC) No 809/2004 as regards information on the consent to use of the prospectus, information on underlying indexes and the requirement for a report prepared by independent accountants or auditors [2012] OJ L 256/4.

[83] Annex I, 13.2, Regulation (EC) No 809/2004.

[84] Annex II, 7, ibid.

[85] Annex I, 20.1, ibid.

[86] This obligation is recurrent in the Regulation (EC) No 809/2004 for different schemes aiming to frame various types of financial instruments; see, for example, Annex I, 13.2, ibid.

Continuing with pro forma financial information, the report must state that in the independent accountant's or auditor's opinion, the information has been properly compiled on the basis stated and that that basis is consistent with the accounting policies of the issuer.[87]

The Regulation (EU) No 862/2012 aimed to facilitate this process by exempting issuers from accompanying their prospectus with an accountant's or auditor's report in the case where financial information relates to the previous financial year and contains non-misleading figures that are consistent with the final figures in the next annual audited financial statements for that previous year. The exemption can be triggered under the condition that the prospectus includes the following statements:

- that the person responsible for this financial information (if different from the one which is responsible from the prospectus) approves that information,
- that the accountants or auditors have agreed that this information is substantially consistent with the final figures to be published in the next annual audited financial statements, and
- that the financial information has not been audited.[88]

These cases are admittedly delicate since the accountants or auditors are not in a position to sign the audit report as the complete set of documents that form part of the annual financial statements are not available at that point in time. It therefore makes sense to exempt issuers from such reports, while simultaneously requiring the statements mentioned above. This is to ensure adequate informational investor protection.

Going beyond the formal requirements for these reports, it is also important to ensure a convergence in the interpretation of such requirements across the EU. The main problem in this area is that the term 'opinion' is not understood in the same way in various jurisdictions and, in the absence of a definition in the Regulation, NCAs have not explained its meaning either.[89] The interpretational difficulties continue with the absence of a definition regarding the expected degree of assurance from accountants or auditors, and the procedures that need to be taken in order to provide such assurance to prospectus users. Most importantly, the Regulation does not provide guidance with regard to the interpretation of the term 'properly compiled' (in reference to profit forecasts or estimates) that is therefore still subject to various interpretations

---

[87] Annex II, 7, ibid.
[88] See, for example, Annex I, 13.2, ibid.
[89] See, for example, IAASB CAG Paper, IAASB CAG Agenda Item D.1, 'Project Proposal, Assurance Reports on Prospectus Information' (2008), at http://www.ifac.org/system/files/meetings/files/3739.pdf; IAASB Prospectuses Working Group, 'Project Proposal, Assurance Reports on Prospectus Information' (2008), at https://www.ifac.org/system/files/meetings/files/3740.pdf.

across the EU.[90] Hence it is evident that the informational transparency and accessibility of such information cannot be guaranteed at the current stage as it is subject to various standards employed in various jurisdictions. Nevertheless, convergence efforts should be strengthened in this area so as to ensure similarity not only in terms of requirements (which has been achieved by the EU rules), but also in terms of their actual implementation across the EU. It is under this perspective that the gatekeeping function, which accountants or auditors are expected to exercise, will be fulfilled and prospectus users will be adequately informed on a cross-border basis.

Lastly, historical financial information must be audited, and the audit report must be presented together with the annual financial statements. This issue belongs to the periodic information spectrum but it is of critical importance to prospectuses[91] since auditors play a very important role at this stage of a capital-raising operation. Indeed, they can formulate reservations, including them in their report and thus inciting the issuer to rethink the content of periodic information and possibly to rectify some parts in order to make the disclosed information more transparent and the prospectus more attractive.

Auditors can also assume a complementary role regarding information that has been disclosed on an auxiliary basis. Regarding the registration document, issuers must indicate the other types of information that are included in the document and have been verified by auditors. For types of information that have not been subject to an audit process, issuers must specify their source and indicate that they have not been verified.[92] Concerning the securities note, auditors can verify or examine other types of information and establish a report.[93] Issuers must publish the content of such examination by reproducing the audit report or providing a summary. These optional measures contribute to the gatekeeping function that auditors are asked to play, but since they are not binding, investor protection depends upon the efficiency of audit checks on an ad hoc basis.

More generally, auditors can also contribute indirectly to the control of prospectus-related information. The PR provides that NCAs that have received an application for approving a prospectus have the power to require auditors of the issuer to provide information.[94]

---

[90] There are three main interpretations of 'properly compiled': the first one refers exclusively to the requirement for a mathematical exactitude of the estimates. The second one refers to the complete and reasonable character of estimates. Lastly, the third one refers to a more general interpretation of the term 'properly' going beyond the two above-mentioned criteria: Federation of European Accountants, 'Analysis of Responses to FEE Discussion Paper on the Auditor's Involvement with the New EU Prospectus Directive' (2005), 62, at https://www.accountancyeurope.eu/wp-content/uploads/Analysis_of_Responses_DP_Auditor_s_Involvement_with_the_New_Prospectus_Directive_051021102005321453.pdf.

[91] Chapter 5.

[92] Annex I, 20.4.3; Annex IX, 11.3.2; Annex X, 20.3.1; Annex XI, 11.3.2, Regulation (EC) No 809/2004.

[93] Annexe III, 10.2; Annexe V, 7.2, ibid.

[94] Article 32(c), PR.

4.6.2. The Role of NCAs

4.6.2.1 Pre-approval Prospectus Control

Before being published, prospectuses must first be approved by the NCA of the home Member State.[95] Approval by an NCA should not be perceived as an examination or an appreciation of the opportunity that a particular prospectus may represent for the investor community. Indeed, an NCA's sole role is to ensure that the required informational quality and compliance with applicable rules are satisfied. The PR further specifies that 'approval' means 'positive act at the outcome of the scrutiny by the home Member State's competent authority of the completeness, the consistency and the comprehensibility of the information given in the prospectus'.[96] Therefore, the formal examination of a draft prospectus cannot convey any positive or negative judgement of the quality of the prospectus itself, nor can it give reassurance to potential investors on its merits.[97] The regulatory neutrality and objectivity are the two main pillars of an efficient approval process.

The NCA has ten working days after the submission of the draft prospectus to inform the issuer, the offeror or the person asking for admission to trading on a regulated market of its decision regarding the approval of the prospectus.[98] This deadline is extended to 20 working days if the public offer involves securities issued by an issuer that does not have any securities admitted to trading on a regulated market and who has not previously offered securities to the public.[99] In the presence of incomplete documents, the NCA will notify the issuer accordingly.

The NCA of the home Member State may also transfer the approval of a prospectus to the NCA of another Member State, subject to the agreement of that authority. Such a transfer must be notified to the persons concerned in the submission of the draft prospectus.[100]

This initial approval phase marks the beginning of the *ex ante* control exercised by the NCA. The NCA will need to examine all the information provided in the submission of the draft prospectus and require the issuer, offeror or person asking for admission to trading on a regulated market to include supplementary information in the prospectus and to provide additional information and documents. The authority can also require auditors, managers and financial intermediaries related to the above-mentioned persons to provide information. It can also suspend a public offer or admission to trading for a maximum of ten consecutive working days, prohibit or suspend the advertisements for the

---

[95] Article 20(1), ibid.

[96] Article 2(r), ibid.

[97] The main risk being that some less experienced market actors may assume the contrary: see, more generally, P. Schammo, 'The Prospectus Approval System' (2006) 7 *European Business Law Review* 501.

[98] Article 20(2), PR.

[99] Article 20(3), ibid.

[100] Article 20(8), ibid.

same period of time, suspend or ask the relevant regulated markets to suspend trading for the same period of time and, more generally, prohibit a public offer, in the presence of suspicion of infringement of the provisions of the PR.

4.6.2.2 Post-approval Prospectus Control

Additional NCA supervision powers must be activated after the admission to trading on a regulated market. NCAs have the power to require issuers to disclose all material information that is likely to impact the assessment of the securities, to suspend or ask the relevant regulated market to suspend the securities from trading in the presence of a situation related to the issuer that raises concerns with regard to investors' interests, as well as to carry out on-site inspections in order to verify compliance with the provisions of the PR and delegated acts.[101]

Cooperation between NCAs is also crucial so as to enable them to carry out their duties efficiently and make optimal use of their powers. A typical example would be the presence of an issuer that has more than one home NCA, because of various classes of securities or where the approval of the prospectus has been transferred to the NCA of another Member State.[102] NCAs are expected to provide assistance to their homologues, as well as to exchange information and cooperate.[103] Cooperation between authorities becomes extremely useful in the presence of cross-listings, as various regulated markets will need to be constantly updated concerning the same issuer, especially in the presence of a suspension or prohibition of trading request for the optimal protection of market actors.

The overall efficiency of a supervisory system in the area of prospectuses, both on an *ex ante* and *ex post* basis, triggers further reflections about the current institutional arrangements anchored at the national level for prospectus approval and ongoing control.

Would ESMA be more suitable to be in charge of the above-mentioned procedures so as to ensure uniformity and high-level expertise across the EU?[104] The idea could be – to some extent – tempting since, in that scenario, convergence issues would not be a concern and investors could be protected better overall. Nevertheless, more realistic arguments regarding the magnitude of the supervisory task and the number of approval requests, as well as financial and staffing implications could dent this initial enthusiasm and reinforce the idea that what the current institutional structure needs are more sophisticated NCAs that are open to efficient cooperation. Indeed, it is more workable to

---

[101] Article 32, ibid.

[102] See above n. 100.

[103] Article 33, ibid.

[104] On this emerging issue in academic literature, as well as on the potential role of ESMA in becoming the Single Listing Authority in the EU, see E. Avgouleas and G. Ferrarini, 'The Future of ESMA and a Single Listing Authority and Securities Regulator for the CMU' in E. Avgouleas, D. Busch and G. Ferrarini (eds), *European Capital Markets Union* (Oxford University Press, 2018).

supervise a series of prospectus-related actions at national level and to continue to establish a viable dialogue with the concerned persons, instead of delegating these functions to a centralized EU agency and thus running the risk of regulators becoming disconnected from the market at large.[105]

4.7 THE ENFORCEMENT SPECTRUM OF PROSPECTUS DISCLOSURE OBLIGATIONS

The sanctions that can be imposed for prospectus disclosure obligation breaches are civil liability as well as criminal and administrative sanctions. Under a very general provision and '[w]ithout prejudice to the right [...] to impose criminal sanctions and [...] to their civil liability regime, Member States shall ensure, in conformity with their national law, that the appropriate administrative measures can be taken or administrative sanctions be imposed against the persons responsible, where the provisions adopted in the implementation of this Directive have not been complied with. Member States shall ensure that these measures are effective, proportionate and dissuasive.'[106]

The Prospectus Directive, cautious of the very sensitive and traditionally different civil and criminal liability regimes across the EU, thus endeavoured to accentuate the importance of administrative measures and sanctions as a more feasible way to combat prospectus disclosure obligation breaches. By doing so, it requires the satisfaction of effectiveness, proportionality and dissuasion, three notions that can be subject to various interpretations depending on the idiosyncrasies of national frameworks, as well as the size of the various capital markets that issuers have decided to access. In the following section, we will look briefly at the problems arising from the lack of sanction harmonization.

4.7.1 Civil Liability

Beginning with civil liability, Article 11 of the PR provides for a minimum harmonization framework limited to identifying the persons responsible for the information contained in a prospectus. Member States are required to ensure that this responsibility covers, at least, 'the issuer, or its administrative, management or supervisory bodies, the offeror, the person asking for the admission to trading on a regulated market or the guarantor, as the case may be'.[107] The above-mentioned persons must clearly be identified in the prospectus and must also declare that, to the best of their knowledge, the information included

---

[105] The examples of a centralized approval and supervision system, as in the case of credit rating agencies, is different in terms of its size and the supervisory capacity required for the accomplishment of such tasks.

[106] Article 38, PR.

[107] Article 11(1), ibid. The minimum harmonization on this issue can create further discrepancies among national laws due to the series of actors participating in the preparation of prospectuses and who may be exempted from liability in some jurisdictions but potentially liable in others.

therein is in accordance with the facts insofar as no omission has taken place which may affect its meaning.

Article 11(2) further specifies that the prospectus summary itself should not trigger any civil liability unless it is of a misleading, inaccurate or inconsistent character, or it does not provide key information to assist investors in their decision, when read together with the other components of a prospectus. The summary must also include a clear warning with regard to this matter,[108] as well as a warning that it should only be read as an introduction to the prospectus and that any investment decision should be based on the prospectus as a whole,[109] aiming to avoid any over-reliance by investors as well as an efficient defence mechanism for issuers against litigation claims. In the same line, the summary needs to include a warning that, where a claim relating to the information contained in a prospectus is brought before a court, the claimant may have to bear the translation costs of the prospectus before the initiation of legal proceedings.[110]

Indeed, it would appear rather difficult for an investor to file suit against an issuer using a summary containing general, fairly vague, information; the issuer could defend its disclosure strategy by invoking the introductory character of the summary. Academic commentators have already criticized this vague area, which can serve for various interpretative methods, by insisting on the fact that investors will not always be in a position to demonstrate negligence by the issuer, especially when the main prospectus is written in another language, taking into consideration that they are expected according to Article 7(5) to read the prospectus in its entirety. Issuers would thus be protected against litigation in an operating framework with long prospectuses drafted in another language, including various financial terms and complicated concepts that might also be interpreted in various ways by investors in different countries.[111]

It would therefore come as no surprise if national courts applied this framework in different ways, depending on their legal traditions, and resulting in different levels of investor protection across the EU. The persistent uncertainty around this issue and, more generally, around the fact that civil liability regimes are quite different in various jurisdictions clearly does not favour the creation of a rigorous accountability framework for issuers, as the risks of liability arbitrage among different jurisdictions will certainly continue to play a major role for issuers when choosing capital markets for seeking financing in the EU. In addition to these concerns, the uncertainty over the governing law

---

[108] Article 11(2), ibid.

[109] Article 7(5), ibid.

[110] Article 7(5), ibid.

[111] B. Breslin and D. Rabinowitz, 'The Prospectus Directive' (2004) 9 *Journal of Financial Services Marketing* 1. Nevertheless, see other academic views mentioning the considerable risks arising from issuer exposure to different liability regimes across the EU due to the lack of a passport system in the area of civil liability: Ferran, above n. 31, 470; Enriques and Gatti, above n. 19, 56.

for civil liability and the consequent liability exposure-related risks must not be neglected either.[112]

To highlight the deficiencies of the current EU civil liability framework, we can divide Member States into two broad categories, with the first developing national frameworks aimed at facilitating investor claims, and the second adopting a much more conservative approach, making successful claims in this area very difficult. Although the various components of national legal provisions on civil liability are not the subject of this chapter, various comparative analyses have continuously illustrated the considerable divergence among national frameworks and the subsequent risks to accountability in prospectus obligations.[113]

4.7.2 Administrative and Criminal Sanctions

Administrative sanctions seem to be at the centre of the PR since they are required from Article 38, as analysed above, in order to satisfy the criteria of efficiency, proportionality and dissuasion. Unfortunately, while these sanctions are required to satisfy the criteria, the divergence in their severity is striking. Some Member States – such as France[114] and the UK[115] – have opted for highly dissuasive penalties. Other Member States have less rigorous frameworks, with maximum penalties going up to €10,000 for natural persons or €100,000 for legal persons in Finland,[116] or up to €500,000 in Italy.[117]

Regardless of the variety of maximum penalties in different jurisdictions, the even more problematic issue related to administrative sanctions is the rarity of proceedings with the exception of some NCAs, such as France's Autorité des Marchés Financiers which has imposed dissuasive penalties in this area on several occasions.[118] What we can deduce with certainty given the divergence of penalties and the infrequent proceedings in different jurisdictions is the need for further harmonization as well as further convergence efforts among Member States and their authorities with regard to the conception and implementation of the criteria of effectiveness, proportionality and dissuasion.

Aiming to align the Prospectus regime with the Transparency and Market Abuse ones, the PR made a rather modest step towards the harmonization of administrative sanctions by recognizing a series of sanctions that NCAs may

---

[112] Ferran, above n. 33, 22.

[113] See, for example, the analysis in R. Veil (ed.), *European Capital Markets Law* (2nd edn, Hart Publishing, 2017), 301.

[114] Article L. 621-15 II and III *Code monétaire et financier* provides for a maximum of €100 million or double the amount of profits eventually made.

[115] Section 91(1A) FSMA does not provide for a maximum fine, thus making it highly dissuasive, at least in theory, for issuers.

[116] ESMA Annex III, 72.

[117] 148, ibid.

[118] For some interesting examples, see K. Sergakis, *La Transparence des Sociétés Cotées en Droit Européen* (IRJS Éditions, 2013), 138.

impose. These sanctions include administrative sanctions and measures, as well as minimum pecuniary sanctions frameworks. NCAs have the power to issue a public statement indicating the nature of the infringement and the identity of the person concerned, to publish an order requiring the concerned persons to cease the conduct constituting an infringement, and to impose maximum administrative pecuniary sanctions of at least twice the amount of the profits gained or losses avoided through the infringement. More specifically for pecuniary sanctions, they can impose maximum sanctions of at least €5 million for legal persons (or at least 3% of the total annual turnover of that legal person) and €700,000 for natural persons.[119] Member States may provide for additional sanctions or measures, or for higher levels of administrative fines.[120]

Therefore, in accordance with the Transparency and Market Abuse frameworks, this rather modest initiative constitutes a preliminary attempt to show a tendency of what sanctioning frameworks could look like at the national level, without resolving the key issue of efficient EU-level sanctions of violations in the prospectus area while achieving consistency among regulators. The consistency and convergence objectives are dealt with – to a certain extent – by the PR. This Regulation requires NCAs to take into account certain circumstances when determining the type and level of administrative sanctions and measures. These circumstances refer to the gravity and the duration of infringement, the degree of responsibility and the financial strength of the person subject to the sanction or measure, the impact of the infringement on retail investors' interests, the magnitude of the profits gained or losses avoided, the degree of cooperation of the concerned person with the NCA, previous infringements by that person, and the measures taken after the infringement by the person to prevent recurrence of such infringement.[121] This requirement is undoubtedly a useful driver for an indirect harmonization trend that may occur through gradual convergence among NCAs in this area, functioning with the same rationales, notwithstanding the persistent minimum and maximum levels of pecuniary sanctions as previously mentioned.

All decisions imposing sanctions or measures shall be published by NCAs by disclosing the type and nature of infringement, as well as the identity of the responsible persons.[122] This disclosure strategy for the publication of sanctions acts as a 'name and shame' exercise that may prove to be particularly dissuasive in the area of prospectus-related infringements in order to readjust the attractiveness of an investment opportunity and inform the public of a violation.

Nevertheless, the Prospectus Regulation also provides exemptions from such publication in cases that may justify a delay in the publication, an anonymous publication or even a complete absence of publication so as to protect the stability of financial markets (which could be at risk from such a publication)

---

[119] Article 38(2)(d)(e), Prospectus Regulation.
[120] Article 38(3), ibid.
[121] Article 39, ibid.
[122] Article 42(1), ibid.

or to maintain the proportionality of the publication of the measures taken for minor violations.[123]

As mentioned above,[124] criminal sanctions have not been harmonized in this area and have been left to Member States. This lack of harmonization has resulted in criminal provisions of varying rigour across the EU; this is admittedly a regrettable situation given the potential usefulness of criminal sanctions in the area of prospectus disclosure obligations that constitute the entry stage to the capital markets and necessitate the presence of sufficiently rigorous and deterrent mechanisms.

Going beyond the mere existence of sufficiently dissuading provisions, the common problem with criminal sanctions lies with the high level of proof required, which makes them quite rare and virtually confers criminal liability immunity to those involved in prospectus disclosure obligation breaches. The most characteristic examples are those of English,[125] German[126] and French[127] law. Regardless of variations in the duration of imprisonment or the amount of potential fines, the above-mentioned rigour in some jurisdictions is thus observed only 'in the books' and not 'in action', which raises questions on the marginalization of symbolically potent sanctions in this area.

4.8 CONCLUSION

EU law has contributed considerably to the creation and ongoing improvement of disclosure obligations in the area of prospectuses, as well as the harmonization of national disclosure frameworks across the EU. Numerous Directives, Regulations and convergence initiatives constantly aim to reinvigorate EU capital markets by attracting issuers and facilitating capital-raising operations. At a parallel level, EU law has the very difficult task of giving retail investors incentives to invest more in capital markets and aims to render the whole informational spectrum accessible and understandable to prospectus users. Notwithstanding the highly promising nature of EU initiatives, it is sensible to assess the overall efforts analysed in this chapter as an ongoing and rather conservative experimental approach.

Indeed, EU policymakers continue to attempt to facilitate issuers by showing a great degree of flexibility, while at the same time sustaining a rhetoric on the necessity to protect retail investors which is not always convincing.

---

[123] Article 42(2), ibid.

[124] See Section 4.7.

[125] Sections 89 and 92 of the Financial Services Act 2012, providing for a maximum of seven years of imprisonment, a fine, or both.

[126] Various general provisions can potentially be used with regard to incorrect information, incorrect description or embezzlement, but the three years' imprisonment in the case of fraud, provided in § 263 of the *Strafgesetzbuch*, are most characteristic.

[127] Article L. 465-1 and Article L. 465-3-1 alinéa 1 *Code monétaire et financier* provide for five years' imprisonment and €100 million. The fine can be increased to a maximum of twice the amount of profits eventually made, if they are higher than this maximum.

This is particularly true as prospectuses are more likely to be read, analysed and deciphered by a series of market actors that are not individual retail investors. The EU rules could therefore be seen as an aspiring framework for the development of a new generation of retail investors that nevertheless has not yet seen the light to date. This is due to the over-reliance on financial intermediaries and the ever-growing presence of institutional investors in capital markets.

This rather contradictory coexistence of the two imperatives can hardly be seen as the result of a meticulously structured approach since the facilitation of offers or admissions of securities does not go hand in hand with the efficient protection of prospectus users – as we have seen in this chapter. A notable example is the area of sanctions which still requires considerable improvement in order to secure investor expectations from prospectuses and to hold issuers accountable for deficient information. The example of civil liability regimes across the EU is striking in that respect. The latest initiatives developed by the PR in the area of administrative sanctions show a rather timid approach in this area which serves the sole purpose of transmitting a message of progress, without nevertheless reaching any substantial changes in the enforcement framework.

CHAPTER 5

Periodic Disclosure Obligations

5.1 INTRODUCTION

Periodic disclosure obligations give particular importance to the notion of informational transparency, whereby listed companies are subject to market evaluation on an ongoing basis, based on various reports that must be published at specific times. EU law has undoubtedly taken careful consideration of the market's need to receive information about issuers on an ongoing basis following the prospectus disclosure obligations (analysed in Chapter 4), which constitute the first heavily regulated informational release to the general public in a listed company's life. EU rules have therefore focused on introducing informational requirements that should coexist harmoniously with companies' business size, pace of operations and decision-making processes, while ensuring a fair, accurate and comparable context to the benefit of regulators and market actors interested in periodic information.

Information disclosed at predetermined points in time takes on special importance for various actors, and pressure for more frequent information disclosure is a significant issue for the shaping of the applicable legal rules. In order to address the ever-growing problem of short-termism, there have been some laudable recent efforts to channel investor expectations towards a longer-term perspective with a reduction of the frequency of disclosure of periodic reports. The most notable example was the lifting of the requirement for issuers to publish quarterly reports. Indeed, the connection between increasingly frequent disclosures and short-termism prompted the EU legislator to allow companies to win back some 'breathing space' by abandoning quarterly reports, while maintaining annual and half-yearly reports.

EU law therefore constantly tests its own suitability to business needs for flexibility on disclosure obligations during the financial year, on the one hand, and to market pressures for a steady stream of information, favouring ever-more frequent reports, on the other. A very delicate balance must be struck, and the overall efficiency and attractiveness of EU rules must be assessed also in comparison with other markets, such as the USA, which has made issuers more attractive to some types of short-term investors by requiring more frequent disclosure. While the prospects for international harmonization are far from clear and realistic, the choice for the degree of pressure placed on issuers is ultimately a matter of political decision-making since investor groups, depending on their nature and agenda, will have an increased or reduced appetite for short-term oriented and disclosed information. EU law has opted to enable both issuers and investors to adopt longer-term perspectives compared to US law. Nevertheless, the question remains as to the overall efficiency and quality of the disclosed information at the EU and international levels; discrepancies continue to exist. This is particularly true for the EU dimension, since the efforts to harmonize periodic disclosure obligations have stayed at a minimum level, allowing some Member States to impose additional requirements. The same observation holds true with regard to the storage mechanisms for such information. Such mechanisms continue to present challenges for information accessibility across the EU, notwithstanding some very positive recent initiatives regarding the interconnection of national storage mechanisms.

NCAs have been given a series of supervisory and sanctioning powers to ensure compliance with such disclosure obligations, and the need to ensure convergence of supervisory methods in practice remains at the top of the regulatory agenda. At the same time, EU law has endeavoured to remain attractive not only for foreign investor groups but also for third country issuers by facilitating their continuous existence in EU capital markets and by providing the means for regulators from both sides to supervise their activities accordingly.

Enforcement mechanisms have also been subject to recent harmonization initiatives and despite their merits in shaping the path for gradual convergence among national practices, the overall framework is perfectible and further initiatives are needed for a more meaningful harmonization to tackle illegal periodic disclosure practices efficiently.

5.2 THE EU REGULATORY SCOPE OF PERIODIC DISCLOSURE OBLIGATIONS

5.2.1 EU and Third Country Issuers

Periodic disclosure obligations at the EU level are provided by the Transparency Directive (TD)[1] and cover annual and half-yearly reports.[2] The TD has been considerably refined since 1979, when the first attempt to shape periodic disclosure obligations was made at the EU level.[3] The decisive step was, as in

---

[1] Directive 2013/50/EU of the European Parliament and of the Council of 22 October 2013 amending Directive 2004/109/EC of the European Parliament and of the Council on the harmonization of transparency requirements in relation to information about issuers whose securities are admitted to trading on a regulated market, Directive 2003/71/EC of the European Parliament and of the Council on the prospectus to be published when securities are offered to the public or admitted to trading, and Commission Directive 2007/14/EC laying down detailed rules for the implementation of certain provisions of Directive 2004/109/EC [2013] OJ L 294/13; N. Moloney, *EU Securities and Financial Markets Regulation* (3rd edn, Oxford University Press, 2014), 133.
[2] Articles 4 and 5, ibid.
[3] Directive 79/279/EEC co-ordinating the conditions for the admission of securities to official stock exchange listing [1979] OJ L 66/21.

previously examined areas of law, the FSAP. This plan proposed an impressive revamp of the ongoing transparency obligations by modernizing the provisions and framing them based on the 'Lamfalussy process'.[4] Focusing on the currently applicable framework, as revised in 2013, and apart from certain justifiable exceptions with regard to periodic disclosure obligations,[5] all issuers whose securities have been admitted to trading on a regulated market are expected to comply with the provisions that have been transposed into national law. EU law insisted on the necessity of equally accessible periodic information, adopting a rather prudent and reticent stance as to compromising various national political agendas on this issue.

The TD was marked, among other things, by the introduction of the concept of 'regulated information' that depicts this kind of compromise. This type of information is defined as all information that must be disclosed[6] under the TD, Article 17 of the Market Abuse Regulation,[7] or under the laws, regulations or administrative provisions of a Member State, if the latter has decided to provide for more stringent periodic disclosure obligations.[8] In other words, the introduction of this concept at the EU level constitutes a first step to understanding the extent of periodic information, as Member States can adopt the same broad framework that is harmonized at a minimum level even if the latter continues to vary to a considerable degree, depending on their discretionary powers (1) to subject an issuer to a more stringent disclosure framework than that adopted by the TD, while using the concept of 'regulated information',[9] or (2) not to adopt the notion of 'regulated information' at all in their national framework, by providing similar rules.

The situation is inevitably different for issuers whose registered office is outside the EEA and who wish to admit their securities to trading on a regulated market. The PR[10] provides that the NCA of the home Member State of these issuers may approve a prospectus that has been drawn up in accordance

---

[4] Commission, 'Communication from the Commission – Implementing the Framework for Financial Market: Action Plan', (1999) COM/99/0232 final, at http://eur-lex.europa.eu/legal-content/PL/TXT/?uri=celex:51999DC0232.

[5] Namely exemptions provided for States, regional or local authorities, public international bodies of which at least one Member State is a member, the European Central Bank (ECB), the European Financial Stability Facility (EFSF) established by the EFSF Framework Agreement and any other mechanism with the same 'financial stability'. The same exemptions also apply to issuers exclusively of debt securities admitted to trading on a regulated market, the denomination per unit of which is at least €100,000: Article 8(1)(b), ibid.

[6] Either by the issuer or by any person who has applied for the securities' admission to trading without the issuer's consent.

[7] Namely the episodic (ad hoc) disclosure obligations arising for issuers and analysed further in Chapter 6.

[8] Article 2(k), Directive 2013/50/EU.

[9] See, for example, the French regime: Article 221 – 1, *Règlement général de l'AMF*.

[10] Article 29, Regulation (EU) 2017/1129 of the European Parliament and of the Council of 14 June 2017 on the prospectus to be published when securities are offered to the public or admitted to trading on a regulated market, and repealing Directive 2003/71/EC [2017] OJ L 168/12 (hereinafter PR).

with the legislation of a third country, under the condition that (1) the NCA of the home Member State has concluded cooperation arrangements with the relevant supervisory authorities of the third country, and (2) the information requirements are equivalent to those provided in the PR. The equivalence framework that relates to prospectus disclosure obligations is followed, in a similar fashion, within the ambit of periodic disclosure obligations. The TD exempts issuers incorporated in third countries from periodic obligations applicable to EU issuers,[11] under the condition that the law of the third country provides for equivalent requirements or the issuer satisfies requirements of the law of the third country that are considered as equivalent by the NCA of the home Member State.[12] The latter also expects issuers to disclose all equivalent information every time they publish regulated information, and ensures that information that does not fall under the category of regulated information but may be important for the EU public is also published.

There is no doubt that EU law has shown a wise openness towards third countries by considerably reinforcing the EU internal market via the attractiveness of issuers incorporated in those countries, while guaranteeing the quality of periodic information within the ambit of the equivalence mechanism. The equivalence system has proven to be successful, facilitating the expansion of regulated markets and investor needs for a larger variety of investment perspectives. Going beyond market liability and prosperity imperatives, the equivalence mechanism may also trigger indirect convergence trends in the presentation and disclosure of periodic information among EU and third country issuers. In the future, this additional benefit may act as an underlying accommodating framework for further convergence of disclosure obligations at the international level. For the time being, such a scenario still seems to be unrealistic, given the fact that the TD has opted for minimum harmonization in periodic disclosure obligations, by allowing Member States to provide for more stringent requirements in this area.

5.2.2 The Degree of Harmonization

Contrary to the maximum harmonization level provided in the PR,[13] the TD provides that the home Member State may make issuers subject to more stringent requirements than those provided by the TD[14] with the exception of the requirement to publish periodic information on a more frequent basis than the

---

[11] Articles 4 to 7, Article 12(6) and Articles 14 to 18, ibid.
[12] Article 23, ibid.
[13] See Chapter 4.
[14] Article 3, ibid. For an overview, see Commission, 'Commission Staff Working Document – Report on More Stringent National Measures Concerning Directive 2004/109/EC on the Harmonization of Transparency Requirements in Relation to Information about Issuers whose Securities are Admitted to Trading on a Regulated Market', (2008) SEC(2008)3033, at http://ec.europa.eu/finance/securities/docs/transparency/report_measures_122008_en.pdf.

annual and half-yearly reports,[15] as well as the requirements provided in Article 17 of the Market Abuse Regulation.[16] The PR encapsulates informational requirements for companies' entry to capital markets. At that stage, the imperative is to reduce the informational asymmetry between investors and issuers whose profiles may not be well known. This is of paramount importance to attract capital and maintain investor confidence in the markets. Periodic information intervenes at a later stage when investors have gained a certain degree of familiarity with an issuer and, as previously mentioned, the main rationale for disclosure is no longer associated with the reduction of informational asymmetry, but with price efficiency that needs to be preserved at all times during an issuer's life in the capital markets.

It therefore becomes plausible to argue that minimum harmonization, notwithstanding its perfectible character and its ramifications for a series of concerned parties, may be justified in order to balance various prerogatives enjoyed by Member States, given that the priority is no longer to ensure a rigorous entry level of all issuers in the EU capital markets and to maintain investor confidence, but instead to enable market access to continue evaluating issuers at predetermined periods of time and for markets to be efficient. Variations arising from additional informational requirements in the periodic framework could therefore be more acceptable compared to the need for maximum harmonization in the prospectus framework.

Elevating the debate to the high-level political decision-making dimension on the desired degree of harmonization, it has become evident since the initial phase of the TD's negotiation that Member States with a traditionally more stringent approach to disclosure and with well-known and highly reputable capital markets wanted to maintain at all costs their additional requirements.[17] Would a maximum harmonization TD be in a position to frame periodic disclosure better? Even though the answer is not straightforward, we must observe that variable regimes in this area have not driven less rigorous frameworks towards more stringent approaches with an eventual convergence at the EU level. The only politically viable solution was therefore a minimum harmonization spectrum that allows the maintenance of national idiosyncrasies. This of course does not mean that the current situation is perfectly satisfactory for all concerned parties since, as the European Commission has noted, '[m]ore stringent national requirements […] are perceived as problematic by stakeholders. This results in real and costly implementation problems. This raises the question as to whether the current regime, namely minimum harmonization, is appropriate to achieve an effective level of harmonization of transparency requirements in the EU.'[18]

---

[15] For a detailed discussion of these reports and the abolition of quarterly reports, see 5.2.3.1.

[16] Article 3(2), Directive 2013/50/EU.

[17] The UK, France and Germany are the most notable examples.

[18] Commission, 'Operation of Directive 2004/109/EC on the Harmonization of Transparency Requirements in Relation to Information about Issuers whose Securities are Admitted to Trading on a Regulated Market' (2010) COM (2010) 243 final, SEC (2010) 611, 5, at http://ec.europa.eu/internal_market/securities/docs/transparency/directive/com-2010-243_en.pdf.

On the other hand, increased costs may arise for issuers when faced with additional requirements, as mentioned above, and accessibility difficulties for shareholders who may not be able compare periodic information efficiently. Within this multi-layered and complex issue, arguments for and against regulatory competition inevitably emerge and opinions vary as to the desired level of harmonization. If the current framework has not given rise to a 'race to the top' trend, it could be argued that the maintenance of the current system is unlikely to trigger that effect in the future. Nevertheless, regulatory competition may be desirable under the condition that more efficient cooperation between NCAs will take place and also ESMA's role in coordinating and enriching such cooperation will be strengthened. Indeed, a maximum harmonization framework, adopted in a straightforward manner, would most probably lead to disempowerment of rigorous frameworks and loss of an opportunity to improve the overall transparency of periodic information in the long term, by convincing gradually less stringent frameworks to follow more rigorous models.

5.2.3 The Periodic Disclosure Spectrum

5.2.3.1 Informational Spectrum

Periodic disclosure obligations aim to form a harmonious and complete informational spectrum as to issuers' various ongoing aspects. The TD provides a framework based exclusively on annual and half-yearly reports, having abolished the additional requirements for quarterly reports with the 2013 TD amendments, which still remain optional. Traditionally, the focus has been placed on financial accounting information that provides a coherent and widely understandable framework for all market actors, notwithstanding some interpretational issues of accounting standards that persist across the EU. The distinction adopted in EU law regards consolidated and individual accounts. On the one hand, for issuers who are required to prepare consolidated accounts,[19] these need to be drawn up in accordance with the International Financial Reporting Standards (IFRS)[20] standards,[21] together with the parent company's annual

---

[19] According to the (repealed) Seventh Company Law Directive, now consolidated within the Directive 2013/34/EU of the European Parliament and of the Council of 26 June 2013 on the annual financial statements, consolidated financial statements and related reports of certain types of undertakings, amending Directive 2006/43/EC of the European Parliament and of the Council and repealing Council Directives 78/660/EEC and 83/349/EEC [2013] OJ L 82/19.

[20] IFRS are issued by the International Accounting Standards Board (IASB) and the political controversy regarding the dubious merits of some accounting methods became particularly notable especially after the global financial crisis: see C. Laux and C. Leuz, 'The Crisis of Fair Value Accounting: Making Sense of the Recent Debate' (2009) 34(6–7) *Accounting, Organizations and Society* 826.

[21] Applicable to issuers whose securities are admitted to trading on a regulated market and adopted in EU law since 2002 with the Regulation (EC) No 1606/2002 of the European Parliament and of the Council of 19 July 2002 on the application of international accounting standards [2002] OJ L 243/1.

accounts, which are drawn up according to the national law of the Member State where the parent company is incorporated.[22]

On the other hand, if issuers are not required to prepare consolidated accounts, audited financial statements will simply include accounts that are drawn up according to the national law of the Member State where the parent company is incorporated.[23] This dual regulatory scheme has achieved a certain amount of convergence in the area of consolidated accounts,[24] but individual accounts inevitably present a degree of divergence, especially when national laws have not accepted the use of IFRS standards for both consolidated and individual accounts. More generally, the use of financial accounting information on an ongoing basis has so far offered the opportunity to the EU legislator to create a unifying framework for the widest possible use and with the potential to cover different informational needs from different interested parties, such as investor groups, regulators and others.[25]

Adding to this financial accounting framework, EU legislature moved towards a broader information framework to the benefit of stakeholders for work equally interested in periodic disclosure. Under its current form, periodic reporting now also includes environmental, social and governance (ESG) factors.[26] The new EU rules in this area inevitably make periodic reporting a matter of pivotal importance not only for shareholders but also for stakeholders who may be affected by companies' activities. Periodic disclosure policy thus encompasses a broader exposure and accountability focus for listed companies, and not the pure market efficiency focus traditionally prioritized by the various EU Directives.

Annual reports must include the audited financial statements,[27] the management report, and statements by those responsible within the issuer that the financial

---

[22] Article 4(3), Directive 2013/50/EU.

[23] Ibid.

[24] Even if interpretation issues regarding IFRS standards arise at the national level. Nonetheless, ESMA has developed an active role in the coordination of enforcement with regard to IFRS disclosures by organizing the European Enforcers Coordination Sessions (EECS), where enforcers participate in a forum that aims to provide a framework for sharing and comparing various practical experiences in this area: http://www.esma.europa.eu/page/ IFRS-Enforcement-0. This is undoubtedly useful for the gradual preparation of regulatory convergence in this area and testifies to a cultural change with regard to the use of indirect harmonization measures that may prove useful in the presence of persistent national divergent frameworks.

[25] For an interesting study on market reaction to the IFRS adoption at the EU level and various national laws, see C. Armstrong, M.E. Barth, A.D. Jagolinzer and E.J. Riedl, 'Market Reaction to the Adoption of IFRS in Europe' (2009), at http://ssrn.com/abstract=903429.

[26] Directive 2014/95/EU of the European Parliament and of the Council of 22 October 2014 amending Directive 2013/34/EU as regards disclosure of non-financial and diversity information by certain large undertakings and groups [2014] OJ L 330/1: Article 19(a); on this Directive, see D. Ahern, 'Turning Up the Heat? EU Sustainability Goals and the Role of Reporting under the Non-Financial Reporting Directive' (2016) 13(4) *European Company and Financial Law Review* 599.

[27] Financial statements need to be audited and the audit reports need to be disclosed in full together with the annual financial report to the public: article 4(4), Directive 2013/50/EU.

statements give a true and fair view of the issuer's overall position[28] and that the management report includes a fair view of the business' development and performance and the issuer's position along with a description of the principal risks and uncertainties.[29] Aiming to further enhance comparability of and accessibility to financial information and cost-efficient reporting methods, the 2013 amended TD provides for a single electronic reporting format at the EU level that will need to be assessed by ESMA with the perspective of being introduced on 1 January 2020. Annual reports must be published at the latest within four months after the end of each financial year and must remain available for ten years.[30]

Half-yearly reports must include the condensed set of financial statements, the interim management report and statements referring (in a similar fashion as to the one adopted in annual reports) to the condensed set of financial statements giving a 'true and fair view' of the issuer's overall position and to the interim management report including a fair review of all its required components.[31] They must include an audit report if they have been audited, or a statement that they have not been audited or reviewed by auditors.[32] They must also be published as soon as possible after the end of the six months of the financial year in question and, in any case, at the latest within three months after the end of that period, and they must remain available for ten years.[33]

As for the abolition of the quarterly reports requirement, this step was justified at the EU level in the light of the need to dissociate capital markets from short-term investment goals and to allow issuers to regain vital 'breathing space' when faced with continuous investor demands for fresh news. Indeed, corporate managers operate under constant pressure to generate positive news to continue to boost a company's share price. Companies are thus compelled to keep on showing a positive profile for current and prospective investors. The overall 'dependence of markets on constant company-relevant data streams as a basis for stock allocation decisions and associated professional communications' has been described as an 'informational centricity' phenomenon that creates a 'compelling pressure on corporate managers to generate fresh "news" indicative of perceived business "progress", in an effort to influence future share price movements'.[34]

---

[28] Namely of the issuer's assets, liabilities, financial position and profit or loss and the undertakings included in the consolidation taken as a whole.

[29] Article 4(2), ibid.

[30] Article 4(1), ibid. Some Member States require shorter periods of time than the one provided in the TD; this may be an additional attractive point for market actors.

[31] The interim management report needs to include at least indication of important events that took place during the first six months of the financial year as well as their impact on the condensed set of financial statements. Moreover, it needs to describe their impact on the condensed set of financial statements along with a description of the principal risks and uncertainties for the forthcoming six months of the financial year. They must also include major related parties' transactions: article 4(4), ibid.

[32] Article 4(5), ibid.

[33] Article 4(1), ibid.

[34] M.T. Moore and E. Walker-Arnott, 'A Fresh Look at Stock Market Short-Termism' (2014) 41(3) *Journal of Law and Society* 416, 418.

The abolition of quarterly reports does not necessarily mean that issuers will not continue using them if market demands persist. Nevertheless, it is encouraging to observe that listed companies have followed a longer-term disclosure trend by moving away from quarterly reporting in some Member States.[35] Conversely, Member States may still have the discretion to impose further requirements to publish additional information on a more frequent basis under the condition that the latter does not constitute a disproportionate financial burden in that Member State, especially for SMEs, and that its required content is proportionate to investment decision-making factors in that Member State.[36]

Attempting to emphasize the need for alleviating pressure on issuers, the TD also provides that Member States will need to assess, prior to making a decision on imposing additional periodic information requirements, whether such requirements may trigger an excessive focus related to the issuers' short-term results and performance, and whether SMEs may be negatively affected as to their access to the regulated markets.[37] The TD's amendment in 2013 therefore shows significant emphasis on investors' long-term goals, and makes potential additional requests subject to an *ex ante* evaluation in order to preserve the long-term investor decision-making and vital breathing space for corporate decisions that would otherwise be compromised with the ad hoc imposition of more frequent disclosure. Although the advantages of such provisions cannot be predicted with accuracy, given the fact that its beneficial character will depend upon Member States' prudence and sophistication, it could be argued that it is certainly a very positive first step towards the creation of a convergent mentality with regard to the merits and shortfalls of more frequent disclosure in capital markets.

Another less obvious advantage of the abolition of quarterly reporting may be the shifting of focus from the current 'curiosity' component of periodic information towards a more 'transparency' element for market actors. In other words, educating investors not to satisfy their mere (at times) short-sighted curiosity by accelerating the rhythm of disclosure may once again make periodic information a reliable vector of transparency, one that enables investors to obtain a holistic view of the issuer's situation, at fixed moments in time, rather than continuously informing them about some predominantly short-term agendas.

---

[35] Such as in the UK. This effort is *inter alia* related to the Stewardship Code that seeks, albeit with the adoption of methods of questionable efficiency, to enhance the quality of engagement between institutional investors and investee companies. More generally on the Stewardship Code, see B.R. Cheffins, 'The Stewardship Code's Achilles' Heel' (2011) University of Cambridge Faculty of Law Research Paper No 28/2011, at http://ssrn.com/abstract=1837344; A. Reisberg, 'The UK Stewardship Code: on the Road to Nowhere?' (2015) 15(2) *Journal of Corporate Law Studies* 217.

[36] Article 3(1)(a), Directive 2013/50/EU.

[37] Ibid.

Indeed, we must bear in mind that an accelerated disclosure rhythm may prove useless, especially in periods of volatility, since it accentuates the uncertainty and insecurity among investors who are faced with myriad information susceptible to change within a very short period of time. What is more preoccupying is that these alterations in business projects, reflected upon frequently disclosed information, have fewer chances of becoming decisive or representative of the issuer's real long-term prospects. It is thus crucial not to keep on nurturing a frenetic disclosure rhythm and investor mentality, but to ensure market confidence in capital markets via high-quality periodic information that reflects issuers' prospects in a concrete and efficient way, focusing on the informational content and not on disclosure frequency.

The articulation and coexistence of the above-mentioned documents presents a series of difficulties for both issuers and the public because all participants in the preparation of these issuer-related documents must have a clear and precise operational framework. Such a framework is needed in order to ensure overall compliance with the vast range of periodic disclosure obligations, on the one hand, and an optimal use of all the information disclosed for the investors through facilitated access corresponding to their need to be informed without having to dedicate disproportionate resources to reconstruct an 'informational puzzle', on the other hand.

5.2.3.2 Dissemination and Storage Mechanisms

The periodic (and episodic)[38] informational framework must be constantly updated with technological developments and offer modern and prompt disclosure means across the EU so as to enable investors to have concomitant access to a series of periodic information almost instantaneously. At the same time, all regulated information must be stored in a way that provides security and reliability of the information for the benefit of all its current and potential users.

The TD emphasizes the importance for such dissemination to take place free of charge, to ensure users' fast and non-discriminatory access to regulated information.[39] Issuers need to ensure such disclosure through the media, by communicating all regulated information in unedited full text or by communicating an announcement of the disclosure of regulated information by indicating their website where such information is available.[40] The home Member State is in charge of requiring issuers to use disclosure means that can be reasonably expected to ensure the effective dissemination of periodic information to the public across the EU.[41] The concept of effectiveness in this framework

---

[38] For a detailed analysis of episodic disclosure, see Chapter 6.

[39] Article 21(1), ibid.

[40] Commission Directive 2007/14/EC of 8 March 2007 laying down detailed rules for the implementation of certain provisions of Directive 2004/109/EC on the harmonization of transparency requirements in relation to information about issuers whose securities are admitted to trading on a regulated market [2007] OJ L 69/27: Article 12(3).

[41] Ibid.

corresponds to the need to ensure a pan-European and prompt disclosure to all investors within a very short period of time and independently from the information's source.[42] It is also important to note that effective dissemination does not equate to the mere availability of information since the latter needs to be 'pushed towards investors'.[43]

The above-mentioned 'free of charge' component of disseminated information is crucial to ensure the democratization of information itself for the benefit of all market actors. To that end, the use of electronic means, namely the Internet, is vital for effectively achieving the dissemination objective. Nevertheless, obvious risks emerge as to the security of the transmission process, the identification of the source of information[44] and the data accuracy. All these elements surround periodic information and may ultimately compromise its reliability. The need to have in place officially appointed mechanisms (OAMs) for the central storage of regulated information becomes evident, and the TD expects these mechanisms to satisfy the above reliability criteria for the stored information. The Commission is in charge of deciding on further initiatives related to minimum standards for the dissemination of regulated information, as well as for the central storage mechanisms for the benefit of both issuers and the public.

Accentuating therefore the importance of electronic access and further harmonization in this area, the TD 2013 provided for a web portal that will serve as a European electronic access point (EEAP), developed and operated by ESMA. To that effect, Commission Delegated Regulation (EU) 2016/1437 was adopted in 2016.[45] This portal's main function will be to interconnect the OAMs that will enable further access to information stored at the national level. It is therefore expected that the EEAP will reduce information access costs and search times, as well as enhance cross-border access to regulated information. Users of the EEAP will be able to access regulated information by using only the issuer's identity as a reference.[46] To guarantee the optimal cross-border use of the EEAP, it is also important to ensure harmonization of the presentation of regulated information across the EU and the 2016 Regulation

---

[42] According to Recital 25 of the TD, '[i]ssuers should benefit from free competition when choosing the media or operators for disseminating information under this Directive' and, according to Article 21(1), the home Member State cannot oblige issuers to use exclusively media whose operators are based on its territory.

[43] CESR, 'CESR's Final Technical Advice on Possible Implementing Measures of the Transparency Directive', CESR/05-407, June 2005, 11, at http://www.cmvm.pt/pt/Cooperacao/esma/DocumentosESMACESR/Documents/05_407.pdf.

[44] That could be compromised in the event of data corruption or non-authorized access by a third party.

[45] Commission Delegated Regulation (EU) 2016/1437 of 19 May 2016 supplementing Directive 2004/109/EC of the European Parliament and of the Council with regard to regulatory technical standards on access to regulated information at Union level [2016] OJ L 234/1.

[46] Namely, OAMs will use the legal entity identifiers as the unique identifiers: Article 7 of the 2016 Regulation.

includes a common list of types of regulated information that need to serve as classification criteria by the OAMs.[47]

The EEAP is undoubtedly an additional step towards the creation of a more accessible informational spectrum across the EU, but some delicate issues that have been observed in the past will need to be treated with the appropriate attention at the national level to enable this EU portal to fulfil its functions. Indeed, a study conducted for the assessment of a pan-European storage system[48] has already emphasized the need to overcome national idiosyncrasies that have, in the past, formed obstacles to a fully harmonized framework.[49] A more drastic alternative to the EEAP initiative would have been the introduction of an EU storage mechanism that would group all information submitted to NCAs from issuers, leading to the abolition of OAMs. According to the same study, this solution would be most adaptable to the objectives of transnational accessibility of information at the service of all users.[50] Nevertheless, the costs associated with such an initiative, together with the time needed for OAMs to converge their methods in order to accept the transfer of their functions to an EU mechanism, are non-negligible, making such a scenario very difficult to implement for the time being.

A matter of equal importance that will contribute greatly to the accessibility of information is the use of a common reporting language at the EU level that still needs to be adopted in a structured and decisive way. Indeed, although several Member States have started using the eXtensible Business Reporting Language (XBRL) format,[51] the users of information may encounter difficulties in comparing various reports in countries where such adoption has not taken place.[52] The distinctive advantage of the XBRL format is that it provides interactive data and facilitates ongoing and real-time disclosure of financial information. Investors will therefore be in a position to retrieve only the information that matters to them, instantaneously and via a simple keyword search among all the documents disclosed by issuers. It would therefore be beneficial for accessibility, comparability and cost-efficiency purposes for such a format to

---

[47] Article 9, ibid.

[48] K. Thomas and S. Gilbert, 'Feasibility Study for a Pan-European Storage System for Information Disclosed by Issuers of Securities – Final Report', 18 October 2011, ACTICA/ PB318D004 1.3, at, http://ec.europa.eu/finance/securities/docs/transparency/ markt-2010-17-f/final-report_en.pdf.

[49] For example, it is expected that the classification of different types of regulated information will resolve issues related to the variety of information available at OAMs that have depicted different informational spectrums, following the minimum harmonization as to the definition of 'regulated information', as analysed above, with the result of forming an 'informational puzzle' for investors in a cross-border dimension. Other OAMs have traditionally included information that does not belong to the 'regulated information' category: 20-21, ibid.

[50] 33, ibid.

[51] N. Enachi and I.I. Andone, 'The Progress of XBRL in Europe – Projects, Users and Prospects' (2015) 20 *Procedia Economics and Finance* 185, 186.

[52] And where other, more traditional, formats are used, such as PDF, HTML or Microsoft Word.

be officially endorsed by the European Commission in the future, even if the decisive factor, namely the political willingness to promote such an initiative, seems to be lacking at present.

Be that as it may, the utmost importance must be given to the sophisticated use of all available information. Facilitating access to that type of information may also encounter risks as to the shaping of investor behaviour, especially if users overestimate their analytical skills based on such facilitated access. Being able to retrieve important information without encountering the above-mentioned obstacles should not equate to being able to critically assess, with the same speed, its relevance for future investment decisions. Adopting reporting systems that individualize informational items with ease is a positive initiative, but it must be linked with a meticulous effort to evaluate issuers holistically.

5.3 CONTROL AND ONGOING SUPERVISION

5.3.1 Audit Control

Within the ambit of periodic disclosure obligations, auditors can play a major role by controlling *ex ante* annual and half-yearly reports. As previously seen, the TD mentions that audit reports must be disclosed in full to the public together with the annual financial report. This piece of information is therefore almost of equal importance to the annual report in terms of its benefit to investors and price efficiency.[53] Nevertheless, auditors cannot certify the veracity of information in the annual report since their role, in this specific framework, is limited (among other things) to protecting investors from information that has been generated through non-compliant methods. In other words, auditors are only in a position to certify the regularity and sincerity of the information disclosed, and the fact that the latter gives a true and fair view of the issuer's overall position. By including the audit report in the annual report, or even the auditors' refusal to audit the annual report, issuers convey to the market important information that potentially impacts investor decision-making.[54]

Moving on to half-yearly reports, the audit report (or audit review) remains optional for issuers.[55] If such an audit or review has taken place, the TD requires its full reproduction; if not, a mention that the half-yearly report has not been subject to either an audit report or a review is required so as to enable market actors to be fully informed. The half-yearly reports' audit control remains optional in most Member States,[56] and there is no common rule at the EU level with regard to the content and the spectrum of such control. The

---

[53] Article 4(4), Directive 2013/50/EU.

[54] Some issuers have also attempted to considerably delay such refusal to avoid a negative market reaction: see, for example, AMF, 8 December 2005, *Orco Property Group*, Revue AMF, April 2006, No 24, 55.

[55] See 5.2.3.1 and Article 5(5), Directive 2013/50/EU.

[56] Only two Member States require such control for half-yearly reports.

European Commission has suggested that the audit review should require at least limited control, which provides a moderate level of assurance, namely less than a full scope audit.[57] This type of review should therefore not be compared to the annual report's audit, since most Member States provide for a 'negative assurance' control, namely a control that concentrates on the observation that there are no significant anomalies or important modifications of the assessed information.[58]

Nevertheless, critiques have been formulated in the past regarding the optional character of the auditors' intervention in half-yearly reports, focusing upon the question of inequality and the eventual gaps in the quality control of periodic information across the EU.[59] Even if auditors in most Member States use the accounting standard ISRE 2400 'Engagements to review financial statements',[60] a mandatory audit in half-yearly reports could have accentuated the control of the information or quality of these reports. The European Commission, reflecting issuer concerns over considerable additional costs that such a control could generate, abandoned this proposal at an early stage.

Auditors' intervention in periodic disclosure obligations can also be expressed via the cooperation with the NCA when they deem necessary to inform the latter of any irregularity in this area to allow its prompt intervention.[61] NCAs also have the right to require auditors to provide information and documents.[62] It is important to mention that the TD aims to protect auditors in such NCA-triggered cases by providing that any disclosure by auditors following NCA requests will not constitute a breach of any disclosure restriction[63]

---

[57] Commission, 'DG Internal Market Services Commission Working Document on procedural arrangements for the choice of the home Member State, the content of the half-yearly financial report, the procedures for the notification and disclosure of acquisition or disposals of major holdings of voting rights, the dissemination of regulated information and the equivalence of third country issuers, under Directive 2004/109/EC on the harmonization of transparency requirements in relation to information about issuers whose securities are admitted to trading on a regulated market', Working Document ESC/34/2005 Rev. 2 (2005), 6, at http://ec.europa.eu/internal_market/securities/docs/prospectus/workingdoc-transparency-dir_en.pdf.

[58] CESR, above n. 43, 78.

[59] ECB, 'Opinion of the European Central Bank of 30 September 2003 at the request of the Council of the European Union on a proposal for a directive of the European Parliament and of the Council on the harmonization of transparency requirements with regard to information about issuers whose securities are admitted to trading on a regulated market and amending Directive 2001/34/EC', COM(2003) 138 final, CON/2003/21 [2003] OJ C242/6, 8.

[60] Issued by the International Federation of Accountants (IFAC) but not officially adopted at the EU level.

[61] See, for example, the *Generix* case in France where auditors contacted the NCA, mentioning a problem related to the accounting treatment of a contract since the issuer's CEO had not informed them about a contractual clause that was affecting considerably the disclosed turnover: *Décision AMF*, 6 January 2005, *Becquart et Generix*, Revue AMF, No 12, March 2005, 63.

[62] Article 24(4), Directive 2013/50/EU.

[63] Imposed by contract, law, regulation or administrative provision.

and will not trigger any auditor liability.[64] These provisions show a clear willingness to create an 'operational safety valve' for auditors to enable them to act as efficient gatekeepers in securing the quality of periodic information. A reinforced and efficient cooperation between auditors and NCAs may therefore be a more pragmatic solution in combating illegal practices within the periodic disclosure framework, given the unlikelihood of moving to a mandatory audit in half-yearly reports.

5.3.2 NCA Supervisory Framework

Following on from the NCA supervision model in prospectus disclosure obligations, the TD ensures consistency with the PR and maintains the ongoing supervision of periodic information with the NCA of the Member State in which the issuer has its registered office.[65] This centralized framework presents the advantage of reducing competition among NCAs, since issuers do not have the option of choosing another NCA,[66] but also has certain limits with regard to issuers incorporated in third countries. For the latter issuers, the TD refers to the importance of flexibility to be able to choose the Member State when they first decide to enter the EU capital market. Adding this flexibility to the TD's minimum harmonization, it is plausible to argue that regulatory arbitrage will persist for those issuers that will seek to choose a Member State according to their preferences.

Issuers are expected to disclose simultaneously to the public as well as to the NCA all regulated information, with the NCA in turn publishing that information on its website. The TD underlines the importance of a reinforced NCA status via a series of powers aiming to supervise issuers and to ensure compliance with the applicable legal framework. These powers, analogous to those provided by the PR, relate notably to the right to suspend or prohibit trading, to request from issuers and auditors (as well as other persons related to the issuer)[67] and persons that are in a control relationship with any of the above persons to provide information and documents and to carry out on-site inspections. Other powers are of particular interest and relate to the request for issuers to disclose periodic information to the public and to the publication of the fact that issuers do not comply with their obligations. These last powers aim to enhance transparency via the triggering of social sanctions, namely 'name and shame' mechanisms, expecting the markets to react to the NCAs' decisions.

---

[64] Article 24(6), ibid.

[65] Article 24(1), ibid.

[66] Member States may also designate another NCA (other than the central NCA) to be in charge of the examination of the periodic information and the taking of appropriate measures in case of infringements: Article 24(1). They also may allow their central NCA to delegate tasks: Article 24(2), ibid.

[67] Such as shareholders, holders of financial instruments, persons involved in the acquisition, disposal or exercise of major proportions of voting rights and persons that hold financial instruments with rights to acquire shares with voting rights.

The TD has striven to enhance NCAs' powers over the years but, as we will see later on, the efficient exercise of a series of prerogatives awarded to NCAs ultimately depends on adequate sophistication and resource levels that enable the regulator to perform its functions in a prompt and targeted way.

At the EU level, NCAs are expected to cooperate efficiently in the presence of cases that require a coordinated action.[68] The levels of sophistication regarding the combat of highly complex illegal practices in information disclosed periodically, as well as the resources dedicated to NCAs, still vary to a certain extent across the EU. Additionally, there may be cases where requests for cooperation may be rejected or not followed up promptly. ESMA's role then becomes crucial in settling any disagreements between different NCAs to ensure effective supervision across the EU. NCAs are also expected to cooperate with ESMA and to provide any information without delay so as to enable it to fulfil its functions. While respecting the obligation of professional secrecy,[69] NCAs can also exchange confidential information with or transmit such information to other NCAs, as well as ESMA and the European Systemic Risk Board (ESRB), in cases where their input is relevant and necessary.

The ongoing supervision of periodic disclosure obligations may be a more arduous task regarding third country NCAs or bodies, and cooperation agreements related to the exchange of information are needed as to facilitate the communication between different authorities. ESMA must be notified once such agreements are concluded.[70]

Assessing the overall efficiency of TD provisions in the area of NCA supervision, major attention needs to be paid to ESMA's coordinating role, in driving NCAs to a gradual convergence as to the methods employed for the ongoing supervision of periodic disclosure obligations and for the prompt responsiveness to a series of irregularities. The *ex ante* supervision framework is also closely connected with broader *ex post* enforcement mechanisms to which our attention will now turn.

5.4 THE ENFORCEMENT SPECTRUM

Violations of periodic disclosure obligations need to be adequately sanctioned for the protection of affected parties, market efficiency and investor confidence. The sanctions applicable are of a civil, criminal and administrative nature. Until the TD amendment in 2013, the sanctions framework was not sufficiently developed despite the willingness to foster investor confidence via such reforms even during earlier legislative steps.[71]

---

[68] Article 25(2), ibid.

[69] Article 25(1), ibid.

[70] Article 25(4), ibid.

[71] Indeed, the enhancement of sanctions in the Transparency Directive in 2004 was associated with the need 'to increase confidence in the accounts and annual reports on which investors base their decisions in the light of revelations of board misbehaviour in … corporate scandals': C. Villiers, *Corporate Reporting and Company Law* (Cambridge University Press, 2005), 72.

As previously mentioned, the TD attempted to enhance the accountability of a series of market actors operating within issuers by stipulating that they must include statements in annual[72] and half-yearly reports[73] by clearly indicating their names and functions and by stating that the information contained in these reports gives a true and fair view of the issuer's position and other components of its business. The clear identification of responsible persons for periodic information conveys, in theory, the message of forcing potentially liable persons to adopt more prudent strategies as their exposure is higher. Nevertheless, the TD does not provide any details as to the identity of the responsible persons within the issuer, and thus the choice of these people as well as their inclusion in the statements will ultimately depend on listed companies. Adding this flexibility to the persistent national divergences, it can be argued that the aim of enhancing the notion of accountability in this area will not be easily achieved, as listed companies and national legal frameworks will continue to maintain their idiosyncrasies and preferences.

5.4.1 Civil Liability

More generally, with regard to civil liability arising in this context, the TD provides, under Article 7, that Member States should ensure that responsibility for information prepared and disclosed according to Articles 4, 5, 6 and 16 should lie at least with the issuer or its own administrative, management or supervisory bodies, while the relevant liability provisions are applicable to the issuers, the above-mentioned bodies and the persons responsible within the issuers. Therefore, there is a key requirement about specific liability for the breach of periodic disclosure obligations. Nevertheless, the use of the conjunction 'or' in this framework has resulted in various national frameworks being able to continue to impose liability only on issuers and to exclude natural persons completely.[74] Although several national laws have introduced directors' liability in this framework,[75] others have considerably complicated its implementation.[76] Even more flexible,

---

[72] Article 4(2)(c), Directive 2013/50/EU.

[73] Article 5(2)(c), ibid.

[74] See, for example, the highly informative correspondence between Alexander Schaub (European Commission) and Lord Woolf (UK Financial Markets Law Committee) in 2006, at http://www.fmlc.org/uploads/2/6/5/8/26584807/issue_76_letter_to_schaub_european_commission.pdf, which emphasizes the freedom that Member States enjoy with regard to the level and the spectrum of liability in this area. See also recital 17 of the TD.

[75] Spanish law accepts issuer and members of the administrative board liability: Article 35 LMV, Article 10, 17 RD 1362/2007.

[76] See, for example, in French law, Article L. 225-251, alinéa 1er, *Code de commerce*, which requires the commission of a separable fault (*faute détachable*) to retain the directors' civil liability.

some national laws continue to exclude such liability for directors.[77] This is particularly problematic because entity responsibility shifts attention away from the moral agent behind the reprimanded behaviour. A combination of issuer and directors' liability should therefore be adopted as

> [t]he capacity to take action simultaneously against the entity and the individual provides further capacity for the threat of regulatory action to promote compliance since neither the firm nor the individual can be sure of transferring responsibility to the other: in that situation, some degree of 'constructive ambiguity' as to who will be held responsible may act as a useful deterrent even if action is only rarely pursued against individuals.[78]

Going beyond establishing specific liability for issuers or directors and examining more generally the openness of civil liability regimes to investor claims, similarly to prospectus disclosure obligations, the difference between national legal provisions is striking. Some Member States have traditionally been more receptive to the implementation of civil liability in this area,[79] contrary to others that continue to have highly complex or less protective civil liability provisions.[80]

5.4.2 Criminal and Administrative Sanctions

Criminal sanctions in the area of periodic reporting are even rarer. Some national legislation provides for very dissuasive criminal sanctions, with two, three or even seven years' imprisonment being the most notable examples

---

[77] UK law made an attempt, following the transposition of the TD, towards a better liability regime by introducing a provision which is, nevertheless, applicable to issuers and not to directors: Section 90A Financial Services and Markets Act 2000 (liability restricted only to intent or recklessness, excluding thus issuer liability in the case of ordinary negligence). Directors can thus be sued only under general liability provisions. For a critical analysis of the UK civil liability framework, see E. Ferran, 'Are US-style Investor Suits Coming to the UK?' (2009) 9 *Journal of Corporate Law Studies* 315, 342. See also J. Armour, B.S. Black, B.R. Cheffins and R. Nolan, 'Private Enforcement of Corporate Law: An Empirical Comparison of the UK and US' (2009) 6 *Journal of Empirical Legal Studies* 687, 712. Moreover, Germany abandoned the proposal for the introduction of a civil liability regime specifically for directors in this framework (*Kapitalmarktinformationshaftungsgesetz*). Of course, issuer liability may indirectly affect and deter directors who will be faced with the arduous task of managing sizeable losses associated with investor compensation: P. Davies, 'Liability for Misstatements to the Market: Some Reflections' (2009) 9 *Journal of Corporate Law Studies* 295, 301.
[78] I. MacNeil, 'Enforcement and Sanctioning' in N. Moloney, E. Ferran and J. Payne (eds), *The Oxford Handbook on Financial Regulation* (Oxford University Press, 2015), 280, 295.
[79] French law has shown a gradual receptiveness to investor claims for incorrect periodic reporting and has repeatedly sanctioned issuers (and less frequently directors due to the *faute détachable* obstacle as explained above): for some interesting examples, see K. Sergakis, *La Transparence des Sociétés Cotées en Droit Européen* (IRJS Éditions, 2013), 138, 171.
[80] Germany and Sweden being notable in this area.

under French,[81] German[82] and UK law,[83] respectively. However, courts have traditionally been very reluctant to impose criminal sanctions due to the requirement of intent.[84] This raises questions as to the current usefulness and dissuasive force of criminal provisions that seem to be largely marginalized and designed such that they are very difficult if not impossible to apply.[85]

The area of administrative sanctions appears to show more optimistic signs for convergence, especially after the amendment of the TD in 2013, which triggered a considerable wave of reforms in this area. The amended Article 28 requires administrative measures and sanctions for breaches of national provisions dealing with periodic obligations. Such sanctions must satisfy the criteria of effectiveness, proportionality and dissuasion. Member States are also required to ensure that the members of the administrative, management or supervisory bodies of the issuer, as well as other persons held responsible for breaches, can be potentially subject to sanctions, under the condition that this is provided for at the national level.[86] This provision aims to retain liability both for issuers and for natural persons in cases of periodic obligation breaches, while respecting national preferences with regard to the delineation of the liability spectrum, as previously analysed.

The most important element of the 2013 amendment of the TD is undoubtedly the increased harmonization in the area of administrative sanctions. New minimum sanctioning powers[87] have been conferred to NCAs with regard to,

---

[81] Article L. 465-1 and Article L. 465-3-1 alinéa 1 *Code monétaire et financier* provide for five years of imprisonment and €100 million fine. The fine can be increased to a maximum of twice the amount of profits eventually made, if they are higher than this maximum.

[82] Various general provisions can potentially be used with regard to incorrect information, incorrect description or embezzlement, but the three years' imprisonment in the case of fraud, provided in § 263 of the *Strafgesetzbuch*, are most characteristic.

[83] Sections 89 and 92 of the Financial Services Act 2012, providing for a maximum of seven years' imprisonment or a fine, or both.

[84] See, for example, in Germany, the Düsseldorf regional court in the *Mannesmann* case, retained only criminal liability for embezzlement, failing to establish the intentional element: LG Düsseldorf, *NJW* 3275, 2004. Moreover, in the highly publicized case of *EM.TV*, the court only fined the directors in an exemplary way (€1.2 million for Thomas Haffa and €240,000 for Florian Haffa) without imposing any imprisonment: 'Staatsanwalt Fordert für die Haffas eine Bewährungsstraffe,' *Frankfurter Allgemeine Zeitung*, 8 April 2003, No 83, 20; 'EM.TV's high-speed crash', *The Economist*, 7 December 2000.

[85] Alternatively, the criminal framework has been used in some countries for purely compensatory purposes. For example, under French law, compensation can be awarded to an investor in a criminal proceeding, joining the proceeding as *partie civile* and under the conditions that she will be able to show a personal and direct damage: Éric Dezeuze, 'La réparation du préjudice devant la juridiction pénale' (2003) 2 *Revue des sociétés* 261. This has been criticized as an indirect attempt to receive compensation by using the criminal framework in order to avoid the general civil liability provisions. Moreover, notwithstanding the legitimacy of the claim and the desire to be awarded damages, this indirect means of litigation risks transforming criminal sanctions into an easier compensatory tool and disempower their symbolic connotation and identity as a public enforcement dissuasive means.

[86] Article 28(1)(2), Directive 2013/50/EU.

[87] Public statement, order to cease the conduct that triggered the breach, and to avoid repetition of similar activities as well as administrative pecuniary sanctions.

at least, the breaches contained in Article 28(a) and related to the failure to make periodic information public within the set deadlines as well as to notify the acquisition or disposal of a major holding. The phrase 'at least' leaves room to NCAs to adopt the same measures on a wider scale and can serve as a first model for further harmonization in this area.

The administrative pecuniary sanctions provided under Article 28(b) are up to €10 million or 5% of the total annual turnover for legal persons and up to €2 million for natural persons. In both cases, sanctions can be up to twice the amount of the profits resulting from the breach, if such profits can be determined. Paragraph 3 of the same Article mentions that Member States can provide for higher levels of pecuniary sanctions, along with additional sanctions or measures. Therefore, it will be very interesting to see whether national laws will adhere to these new series of administrative sanctions, apart from the two types of breaches mentioned under Article 28(a) for which the sanctions are compulsory, and gradually converge with regard to the severity, frequency and intensity of sanctions imposed. Under the current framework, administrative sanctions continue to vary significantly, a fact that strengthens the argument for further harmonization.

In order to coordinate the exercise of sanctioning powers among NCAs, Article 28(c) provides a very useful guide that can be taken into account in determining the type and level of administrative sanctions or measures.[88] Indeed, the 2013 amendment accentuates the need for indirect harmonization in this area by focusing on the conceptual elements of sanctions and measures and by attempting to converge their perception, interpretation and implementation across NCAs. This indirect harmonization effort is, in our opinion, a positive step towards gradual uniformity in the interpretation of the three sanctions criteria required in various EU capital markets texts: efficiency, proportionality and dissuasion.

Lastly, Article 29 aims to accentuate the severity and deterrent effect of sanctions via compulsory disclosure requirements for NCAs, which are required to publish every decision on sanctions and measures, while providing information on the type and nature of the breach as well as the identity of the natural or legal persons affected by the decision. Aware of the risks involved in increased transparency in this area, the Directive also allows NCAs to delay such publication or to publish decisions anonymously if they believe that such an action would be disproportionate, would seriously jeopardize the stability of the financial system or an ongoing investigation, or would cause disproportionate and significant damage to related institutions or natural persons.

Mandatory disclosure of sanctions is undoubtedly a highly effective means of deterrence, as well as a strong trigger for market reaction. 'Naming and

---

[88] The gravity of the duration of the breach; the degree of responsibility and the financial strength of the natural or legal person; the magnitude of profits as well as the losses suffered by third parties due to the breach; the level of cooperation with the NCA and any possible prior breaches.

shaming' has traditionally been regarded as a social sanction that can theoretically become more serious than the sanction itself or even last longer, depending on the unpredictable cascading effects on investors, third parties and stakeholders at large.[89] Some Member States, such as the UK, France and Spain, have already adopted this practice with positive results. Nevertheless, other countries continue not to disclose the identity of concerned persons, citing concerns about disproportionality and unpredictable market reactions. It will therefore be challenging to see how these Member States will handle all the practices in the future, especially after the increasing demand for such disclosure from the EU.

5.5 CONCLUSION

Periodic disclosure obligations have been subject to continuous effort for improvement, alignment with issuer and investor needs, and gradual convergence across the EU. Contrary to the prospectus framework, the TD provides a minimum harmonization framework, given the fact that the primary concern in periodic disclosure is not to ensure the rigorous entry to capital markets, but rather to maintain price efficiency and ongoing investor confidence. Allowing for more national idiosyncrasies to be included in the content of periodic information and for regulatory arbitrage to play a non-negligible role is now seen as a reasonable political compromise. This has become evident as it may be the only realistic option for a long and gradual 'race to the top' trend regarding disclosure requirements across the EU under the condition that more efficient cooperation between NCAs will take place and also ESMA's role in coordinating and enriching such cooperation will be strengthened. This scenario would have been less likely in a maximum harmonization framework, whereas more rigorous frameworks would have lowered their standards while more flexible frameworks would have been faced with immediate issuer and regulatory costs.

Issuers are now faced with a straightforward framework, composed of annual and half-yearly reports, that allows them to avoid quarterly reports so as to be able to adopt more long-term strategies and to avoid investor pressure for more frequent disclosure. Investors are thus expected to lower their expectations regarding disclosure frequency and to understand the benefits of long-term investment projects. It is expected that issuers will follow this example,

---

[89] Although some empirical studies, focusing on the French authority *Autorité des Marchés Financiers*, have suggested that a negative market reaction is triggered from the stage of the investigation announcement and that the formal sanction announcement does not seem to adversely affect the share price in the same way: C. Djama, 'Fraudes à l'Information Comptable et Financière et Contrôle de l'AMF – Une Étude des Réactions du Marché Financier Français' (2013) 2(231) *Revue Française de Gestion* 133. For a more general analysis of reputational sanctions, see J. Karpoff and J. Lott, Jr., 'The Reputational Penalty Firms Face from Committing Criminal Fraud' (1993) 36 *Journal of Law and Economics* 757. See also C.R. Alexander, 'On the Nature of the Reputational Penalty for Corporate Crime: Evidence' (1999) 42 *Journal of Law & Economics* 489.

as has already started happening in some Member States, and will benefit from this abolition.

The access to periodic information across the EU is expected to be facilitated via the EEAP, which will interconnect OAMs. However, much more is needed for meaningful comparability of periodic information given the different types of reporting language used. If the EU law agenda is to channel investor expectations towards a longer-term perspective, it would be plausible to argue that further harmonization of reporting systems and accessibility to the remaining disclosed periodic information (annual and half-yearly reports) is even more vital to ensure the reliability and usefulness of that restrained disclosure framework. With persistent difficulties in accessing, comparing and ultimately evaluating disclosed information, it is highly unlikely that investors will change their stance towards issuer disclosure strategies.

As was also observed in this chapter, another area that needs more meaningful harmonization is the field of enforcement mechanisms. The recent efforts to harmonize administrative sanctions, at a minimum level, are a positive move towards gradual convergence among NCAs but a more binding framework is needed to bring more concrete results in the near future. Civil liability regimes and criminal sanctions also necessitate political willingness for a more visible level playing field among jurisdictions.

CHAPTER 6

Episodic Disclosure Obligations

6.1 Introduction

We have examined how issuers must disclose information to the market on specific occasions, such as prospectus (Chapter 4) and periodic obligations (Chapter 5). However, the demand for informational symmetry and transparency is incumbent on issuers at all times, and not just at the predetermined time frames applicable to prospectuses and periodic publications. Episodic disclosure obligations fill in this gap by requiring issuers to disclose to the public 'as soon as possible' any 'inside information' that directly concerns them.[1] Episodic obligations are needed since market actors should not wait for the predetermined times when information must be disclosed, such as prospectus and periodic transparency obligations. The reinforcement and harmonization of those obligations in EU law has undoubtedly affected episodic disclosure obligations that aim to maintain an informational equilibrium outside any predictable time frame. The instantaneity of the disclosure obligation, as well as the need to maintain constant informational symmetry between issuers and the rest of the market, makes these EU legal rules crucial for achieving price efficiency and protecting investors.

On the one hand, it is expected that through permanent informational exposure, issuers can respond to the continuous market demand for fresh news; on the other hand, it is also necessary to preserve a vital space for competition and confidentiality by allowing issuers to delay the disclosure of inside information. The harmonization efforts on this particular topic may nevertheless be compromised due to the varying perception of some elements of inside information, as well as the variable interpretations that may be given by different NCAs when delayed disclosure can be exceptionally allowed. The difficulty in defining the informational scope of inside information and the delay in its disclosure has always sparked a vivid debate around the need to find the optimal regulatory means to make listed companies truly transparent but within an *a priori* unpredictable informational landscape. The sophistication of NCAs is,

---

[1] Article 17, Regulation (EU) No 596/2014 of the European Parliament and of the Council of 16 April 2014 on market abuse (market abuse regulation) and repealing Directive 2003/6/EC of the European Parliament and of the Council and Commission Directives 2003/124/EC, 2003/125/EC and 2004/72/EC OJ L 173/1 (hereinafter 2014 MAR).

103

once again, crucial to ensure effective supervision of the permanent disclosure obligations in cooperation with other NCAs and ESMA. Such cooperation is needed for a truly integrated EU supervisory framework. Enforcement strategies are also crucial in this area since episodic disclosure of information may arise at any moment in time and the temptation to misuse the applicable legal framework, in order to influence the share price in an immediate way, is considerable and therefore requires an appropriate sanctioning response. Harmonization efforts towards that effect have recently been accentuated at a minimum level and much more is needed for meaningful convergence to take place.

6.2 THE EU INFORMATIONAL SCOPE

6.2.1 The Harmonization of Episodic Disclosure Obligations

The need to ensure a harmonized disclosure framework in episodic information has created a series of obstacles related to the exact content of the disclosure obligation and its contours that seem to be interpreted in various ways across the EU. The 2003 Market Abuse Directive (2003 MAD),[2] together with other EU texts, launched the first coordinated wave of harmonization and was subsequently replaced by the 2014 Market Abuse Regulation (2014 MAR), which followed on from the previous regime, and the new Market Abuse Directive (2014 MAD),[3] the latter dealing with criminal sanctions for certain market abuse offences. The attempt to discern the contours of the episodic disclosure obligations is a particularly arduous task given the very general character that the potentially disclosed information may have. The only reliable criterion used by the 2014 MAR, following on from the 2003 MAD framework, is to focus on the existence of inside information that directly concerns the issuer who needs to comply with the main disclosure obligation provided in Article 17, by informing the public of its existence as soon as possible.

A series of difficulties have arisen in the past as to shaping a coherent regulatory framework when it comes down to requiring the disclosure of inside information from issuers, as the concept of 'inside information' itself has been given a dual function, serving both the combat against insider dealing and the need for constant informational transparency. Even if both prerogatives serve the overarching market efficiency objective, it is dangerous to assume that the insider dealing threat in the market should force issuers to adopt an excessive pace of ad hoc disclosure just for the sake of combating insider dealing and thus preserving market stability. This is particularly true for cases in which inside information can remain private[4] in order not to compromise business

---

[2] Directive 2003/6/EC of the European Parliament and of the Council of 28 January 2003 on insider dealing and market manipulation [2003] OJ L 96/16 (hereinafter 2003 MAD).
[3] Directive 2014/57/EU of the European Parliament and of the Council of April 16, 2014 on criminal sanctions for insider dealing and market manipulation [2014] OJ L 173/179 (hereinafter 2014 MAD).
[4] Obviously under the condition that the information itself is not used to the detriment of other market actors.

opportunities for issuers.[5] Episodic disclosure obligations have therefore been mixed with insider dealing regulatory agendas and are continuously subject to pressure for more exposure to the market, by creating considerable difficulties to issuers, especially when other equally important interests need to be safeguarded for the companies' viability. The European Court of Justice has unfortunately failed to clarify the various facets of inside information either, simply focusing on examining more narrowly construed issues.[6] Most importantly, the degree of confusion regarding the breadth and applicability of legal rules in this area is considerable and has clear ramifications for the attractiveness of capital markets at large. In the end, the 2014 MAR opted for a unique function of 'inside information' and provided further clarification as to its applicability criteria.[7] The harmonization carried out at the EU level is thus inevitably restricted to a minimum level, reflecting the considerable difficulty in reaching a common understanding of the intellectual contours of 'inside information' to which our attention will now turn.

6.2.2 *The Criterion of Inside Information*

Attempting to define and interpret the notion of inside information proves to be, in turn, an equally complex task.[8] The 2014 MAR provides that inside information is any information which is precise, has not been made public, and relates, directly or indirectly, to one or more issuers (or to one or more financial instruments) and whose publication would be likely to have a significant effect on the price of the related financial instruments.[9] EU law has traditionally aimed to clarify each and every element of this definition to avoid divergent interpretations of the notion of inside information.

---

[5] For a critical approach of the 'dual function' as well as for the dangers of aiming towards a market efficiency through excessive ad hoc disclosure that triggers, in its turn, short-termism, see J. Lau Hansen, 'The Hammer and the Saw – A Short Critique of the Recent Compromise Proposal for a Market Abuse Regulation' (2012) Nordic and European Company Law Working Paper No 10-35, at http://ssrn.com/abstract=2193871.

[6] See, for example, Case C-19/11 *Markus Gelt* v. *Daimler AG*, 28 June 2012 (not reported). See also Section 6.2.2. For an interesting analysis, see J. Lau Hansen, ibid.

[7] See Section 6.2.2. For an overall analysis, see di C. Di Noia and M. Gargantini, 'Issuers at Midstream: Disclosure of Multistage Events in the Current and in the Proposed EU Market Abuse Regime' (2012) 9(4) *European Company and Financial Law Review* 484.

[8] Chapter 6 will mainly deal with the 'episodic disclosure obligations' facet of inside information, namely the need for continuous informational transparency so as to enable market actors to make informed investment decisions. For a detailed analysis of the 'inside information' concept from the 'insider dealing' aspect, namely the need to prohibit market abuse and cases where 'inside information' is used to the detriment of other market actors and markets' reliability at large, see Chapter 8.

[9] Article 7(1)(a), MAR 2014. On a more general note, the same article contains similar definitions for commodity derivatives [(1)(b), ibid.], emission allowances or auctioned products [(1)(c), ibid.] and execution of orders concerning financial instruments [(1)(d), ibid.] in an attempt to enlarge the applicability of episodic disclosure obligations in products or activities associated with various markets.

To begin with the inside information's precise nature, this concept has been subject to an ongoing debate since there are inevitably various steps during the formation of a situation which may give rise to precise information. The applicable rules must therefore frame the evolution of various situations that may give birth to such information and decide about the starting point that may trigger the respective disclosure obligations. In that respect, the 2014 MAR underlines that information of a precise nature is any information that indicates a set of circumstances or any event that may have taken place or is reasonably expected to take place, and that is specific enough that allow a conclusion to be formulated with regard to its possible effect on the prices of the related financial instrument.[10] This definition is opportune for the broadness of its scope, aiming to capture various interconnected circumstances that may relate to precise information. It is also important to note that this definition moves away from certainty and favours likelihood in the chain of different events that may lead to a more concrete informational outcome.

ESMA's predecessor Committee of European Securities Regulators (CESR) clarified that the decisive criterion confirms the existence of circumstances or the occurrence of an event would be 'firm and objective evidence for this as opposed to rumours or speculation'.[11] With regard to the more delicate issue of likelihood, CESR focused on 'whether it is reasonable to draw this conclusion based on the *ex ante* information available at the time'.[12] The issuer's position is, of course, delicate since some provisional data might not come to fruition, thus making the projected scenario untrue. It is therefore preferable to focus not on the inevitable element of unpredictability but on the eventual misleading character of any information resulting from its omission for a certain period.[13]

Notwithstanding its broad formulation, defining 'precise information' may be a relatively straightforward task in the case of events taking place in a relatively short period of time, especially compared with situations involving multiple and long-lasting events, whose contribution to the information itself may be particularly difficult to discern. The 2014 MAR specifies that a long-lasting process that has an intention to trigger, or actually triggers, particular circumstances or events may be considered precise information, together with all the intermediate steps of that process, as well as with those future circumstances or

---

[10] Article 7(2), ibid.

[11] CESR, 'Market Abuse Directive Level 3: Second Set of CESR Guidance and Information on the Common Operation of the Directive to the Market', CESR/06-562b, July 2007, 4, at www.fsc.bg/d.php?id=2011.

[12] Ibid.

[13] Issuers will therefore have to focus on a careful and reasonable calculation of risks and eventually formulate reservations with regard to some events that are already known and likely to affect those risks. Of course, the gap between forecasts and reservations cannot be wide since issuers will need to mention the uncertainty of the situation, all possible scenarios that may occur, the alterations that may be made to these projections and the different assumptions taken into account: *Eurodirect*, Cass.com., 22 November 2005, 03-20.600, unpublished.

event.[14] Intermediate steps can also be seen as inside information if they satisfy the above-mentioned criteria.[15]

Continuing with the significant effect of information on the prices of financial instruments if it were made public, this is seen in EU law from the reasonable investor's perspective and, more specifically, whether a reasonable investor would be likely to use this information as part of the basis for any investment decision.[16] This investor-oriented criterion exerts pressure on issuers who will have to carry out a very delicate assessment regarding the possible effect of the information on the investment decision process. It is obvious that the main focus of the episodic obligations falls on the need to preserve investor confidence by attributing to investors the decisive criterion for determining what type of information must be disclosed by issuers. Be this as it may, it is also important to underline the fact that issuers may not always be prepared to discern *a priori* the eventual effect of all types of information on the prices of financial instruments since the mere publication of some of them may give them much greater importance in the eyes of the public due to the sole fact and that they have become public. In other words, information may exert a discrete – but non-negligible – influence on the price, corresponding merely to the public appetite for fresh news, even if its initial potential to do so, based on its content, would be lower.

The European Court of Justice has endeavoured to provide legal certainty on these issues by mentioning that 'reasonable expectation' cannot mean a requirement of proof of a 'high probability' of realization of circumstances or events. Most importantly, precise information cannot include cases of 'implausible' occurrence. The focus therefore lies with the 'realistic prospect' of occurrence, and the probability of occurrence should not depend on the events' effect on the price, since the elements of 'precision' and 'likelihood of significant effect on prices' are not 'co-dependent'.[17]

EU law aims to frame informational equality by also ensuring the concomitant disclosure of information to all market actors. The concept of equality becomes crucial within the ambit of disclosure of inside information to third parties in the course of the exercise of an employment, profession or duties, such as press conferences organized by the issuer with a limited audience which cannot amount to the general notion of the 'public'.[18] The 2014 MAR therefore provides that in similar events, complete and effective public disclosure

---

[14] Ibid.

[15] Article 7(3), ibid. This follows on from the ECJ's ruling in case C-19/11 *Markus Gelt* v. *Daimler AG*, 28 June 2012 (not reported). For an interesting analysis, see J. Lau Hansen, above n. 5.

[16] Article 7(4), ibid.

[17] Case C-19/11 *Markus Gelt* v. *Daimler AG*, 28 June 2012 (not reported) paras 45–52.

[18] For an interesting example, see the administrative sanctions imposed on two issuers in France due to the announcement of the creation of a subsidiary during a press conference which was not accompanied with simultaneous disclosure to the public: Décision COB, *Ubi Soft*, 12 February 2002, Bull. COB, May 2002, No 368, 69.

of that information must take place in a simultaneous way if the disclosure is intentional and in a prompt way if the disclosure is non-intentional.[19] On a more general note, selective disclosure has not always been seen as destructive for market viability as the opinions on the topic vary.[20] Notwithstanding the arguments on both sides,[21] it is now accepted that selective disclosure would lead to a sort of informational discrimination that would harm investor confidence and cannot therefore be allowed, due to the increased importance paid to market confidence at the EU and international levels.

6.2.3 Ensuring Flexibility for Issuers

The desirable ongoing transparency must take into account legitimate reasons for which issuers may require flexibility to delay the disclosure of inside information without disorientating or misleading the public. The 2014 MAR, following the 2003 MAD framework, allows issuers this flexibility on the following conditions: immediate disclosure is likely to cause prejudice to their legitimate interests; the delay is unlikely to mislead the public; and issuers are able to ensure the confidentiality of that information.[22] In the potential case of a lengthy process with intermediate stages and with the intention or actual result of leading to a particular circumstance or event, issuers may delay disclosure of inside information following these same criteria. NCAs' contribution to this framework is fundamental, as issuers are required to inform them of this delay, as well as to provide a written explanation of how the above-mentioned criteria have been met, right *after* the disclosure of the inside information. Alternatively, NCAs may request a record of such explanations.[23]

Taking a closer look at this flexibility framework, there is a series of aspects that must be critically challenged. First of all, issuers may invoke the notion of legitimate interests in a distorted way in order to avoid disclosure. The 2014 MAR, following on from the repealed Directive 2003/124/EC, specifies that legitimate interest may, in particular, refer to ongoing negotiations whose normal pattern or outcome would be likely to be affected by the disclosure. A more tangible example is given in this respect, namely situations in which

---

[19] Article 17(8), ibid.

[20] E. Avgouleas, *The Mechanics and Regulation of Market Abuse* (Oxford University Press, 2005), 266.

[21] For a critical approach of the prohibition of selective disclosure, see D.C. Langevoort, 'Taming the Animal Spirits of the Stock Markets: A Behavioral Approach to Securities Regulation' (2002) 97 *Northwestern University Law Review* 135.

[22] Article 17(4), 2014 MAR. Of course, in the potential case where confidentiality of the inside information can no longer be ensured, issuers are required to disclose it to the public as soon as possible: Article 17(7), ibid. An important addition to the EU legal framework is the broadening of the flexibility with regard to the delay of disclosure of inside information regarding issuers that are credit institutions or financial institutions: Article 17(5), ibid. This flexibility is allowed in order to preserve the stability of the financial system. Examples given by the 2014 MAR relate to temporary liquidity problems that these types of issuers may face.

[23] Article 17(4), ibid.

the issuer's financial condition is in grave and imminent danger (nevertheless not within the ambit of insolvency law) and there is a need to preserve shareholder interests by finalizing negotiations aiming towards the issuer's long-term recovery and that would otherwise be undermined via the disclosure of related information.[24] This of course does not mean that if the negotiations fall through, or – being in a very difficult and irreversible situation – the issuer decides to inform the market too late, it is exempt from allegations of breach of the episodic disclosure obligations because the overall flexibility to delay disclosure of inside information is granted under the issuer's own responsibility.[25] It will thus ultimately depend on whether the arguments provided can justify *a posteriori* the delay of disclosure since, even in the presence of very critical and confidential situations, the issuer may still be found in breach of disclosure obligations. The category of legitimate interests also includes decisions taken or contracts made by the management body needing the approval of another body of the issuer, whose disclosure – before the approval and with the announcement that the latter is pending – would compromise the public's correct evaluation of the situation.[26]

On a general note, also taking into consideration that the list of legitimate interests is not exhaustive, the overall conclusion must be in favour of the acceptance of a flexible framework with regard to the delay of disclosure in the light of positive initiatives that may be carried out during a critical period for the issuer.[27] Nevertheless, it is also challenging to assume that this delay would not, by any means, affect investor decision-making since every information has its own potential in affecting investors. The discretionary space given to issuers is therefore considerable, and it will ultimately be up to NCAs to monitor any critical situations on an ongoing basis in order to decipher any possible disclosure breaches.

Another issue that may attract critical comments relates to another criterion for which delay of disclosure may be accepted, namely when this delay is unlikely to mislead the public.[28] While this formulation seems justified and reasonable, to a certain extent, the core essence of inside information means that its disclosure *would* be likely to affect the reasonable investors' decision-making process. It may therefore be challenging to accept a situation where the delayed disclosure of inside information will not be likely to mislead the public, notwithstanding the fact that inside information itself is likely to affect reasonable investors. The flexibility

---

[24] Recital 50, ibid. For an interesting example of such incidents that were accepted by the French regulator, see Décision AMF, 23 February 2006 à l'égard de M. Denis Walter, Revue AMF, July–August 2006, No 27, 109. See also the *Cyrano* case in France, where the issuer had delayed the disclosure of a deficit which was four times higher than the market's estimate, information that would have been likely to have a significant effect on the share price if it had been disclosed: Décision COB, 13 February 2003, *Bull. COB*, October 2003, No 383, 7.

[25] Article 17(4), ibid.

[26] Ibid. This incident would occur in companies with separation between those bodies.

[27] See also J. Lau Hansen, above n. 5.

[28] Article 17(4)(b), MAR 2014.

in delaying disclosure therefore risks misleading the public since a component of the 'informational puzzle' is missing. The optimal way to tackle this conundrum would be a thorough examination by NCAs, on a case-by-case basis, of the market's expectations from a particular issuer, as well as of issuer's prospects. It is also true that the variable degrees of attention that a financial instrument may attract within a regulated market, the potential gap between the issuer's real situation and the rate of investors' responsiveness may become substantial pressure factors that could force an issuer to disclose inside information promptly.[29]

ESMA's contribution in coordinating further effort for convergence in this area will undoubtedly be beneficial across the EU. First of all, draft implementing technical standards related to the technical means for the disclosure of inside information, as well as for the delay of such information, will inevitably enhance convergence. Moreover, guidelines with regard to the establishment of non-exhaustive lists of information that would be expected or required to be disclosed according to a wide range of sources, such as EU and national law, market rules and so forth, are welcomed although transparency in this area will ultimately depend on an effective NCA supervision framework that will aim to monitor episodic disclosure on an ongoing basis with an optimal degree of sophistication and responsiveness.

6.2.4 Voluntary Episodic Disclosure

Following on from the general rule of Article 17 related to the disclosure of inside information as soon as possible, justified in terms of investor confidence and price efficiency, it could also be argued that episodic disclosure obligations give a unique chance to issuers to engage with investors between the predetermined periods of time where information must to be disclosed, namely prospectus and periodic transparency obligations.[30] Notwithstanding the ongoing market pressure for fresh news, which may ultimately compromise sound decision-making processes, the main challenge for each issuer is to preserve a viable communication channel with the investor community without compromising the reliability and quality of information to obtain short-term gains.

Indeed, the episodic disclosure framework may become subject to strategies aimed at choosing the right moment to trigger the desired reaction from the investor community. If companies know in advance that the news is accurate and very positive, they will seek to disclose it when it best serves the purpose of attracting as much more capital as possible.[31] Nevertheless, if they know

---

[29] These situations may serve as reliable indicators *a posteriori* to justify the levying of sanctions if, for example, the issuer had been the subject of continuous research from investors during the critical period, a situation that may justify the immediate disclosure of inside information and could thus weaken the argument that its delay was not likely to mislead the public.

[30] See Chapters 4 and 5.

[31] See the concept of 'informational centricity', as analysed in Chapter 5: M.T. Moore and E. Walker-Arnott, 'A Fresh Look at Stock Market Short-Termism' (2014) 41(3) *Journal of Law and Society* 416.

that the news is negative and they attempt to disclose wrongful information in order to make it appear positive, their strategy will be aimed at obtaining the best benefit from the market's reaction based on the short-term criterion of the effect of the disclosure itself. Moreover, we must bear in mind that breaches of episodic disclosure obligations can generate profits in a very short-term framework – virtually instantaneously – and the motives for such a breach must be countered with sufficiently strong dissuasive measures.[32]

Issuers in some cases have already used episodic disclosure to sustain prices artificially, give a very optimistic image about their financial condition and eventually delay an inevitable price fall following the publication of negative performance or news. A recurrent strategy is the disclosure of ad hoc earnings or other forecasts to create a euphoric investment trend and boost the share price by creating a speculative, short-term atmosphere in the market. The fact that disclosure of any kind of information that does not respect the require-ments of Article 17 is purely voluntary and not required at predetermined periods of time cannot of course be used as an argument to exempt issuers from any liability, as any disclosed information will fall within the general rule of disclosure that must enable a complete and correct assessment of the issu-er-related information by the public and the regulator.

6.2.5 The Vehicles of Episodic Disclosure

Safeguarding prompt access to the disclosed information, as well as its com-plete, correct and timely assessment by market actors across the EU, is another major concern for EU law. This task has proven to be very difficult due to the national idiosyncrasies in terms of both legal requirements and market prac-tices. The 2014 MAR relies on issuers to guarantee the above-mentioned access and assessment criteria by also referring to the use of an officially appointed mechanism, where applicable, for access to regulated information as provided in the TD.[33] The officially appointed mechanisms aim to become a safe com-munication channel that ensures the coherent disclosure of inside information. Indeed, disclosure of information in a dispersed way will inevitably create con-fusion and will not guarantee a level playing field among investors. Taking into account cross-listings and the EU dimension of the investment landscape, issuers need to ensure instantaneous access to inside information for all market actors in all Member States, materializing the informational equality princi-ple across the EU.[34] It is therefore up to Member States to define the optimal

---

[32] Profits in this scenario would be channelled to the potential buyers or sellers engaged in market activities during the period in which disclosure failures have taken place. More generally, companies would benefit less directly in this scenario, merely by triggering an increase in the share price but not by gaining in a straightforward way (as would have been the case had they issued new shares privately at a higher price than could have been achieved with full episodic disclosure).

[33] See Chapter 5 for a detailed analysis.

[34] Article 21(1), Directive 2013/50/EU.

vehicles of episodic information within their jurisdiction. The traditional position favours disclosure by the press, although electronic means continue to gain considerable ground among issuers for the cost efficiency and adaptability to technological evolutions in international capital markets.

Issuers are also required to post and maintain on their website all types of inside information that has been publicly disclosed for a period of at least five years,[35] so that market actors have continuous access to that information from a single source and over a long period of time. The risk of combining inside information with other types of information and creating a confusing message for investors was also tackled in the 2014 MAR, which prohibits the combination of inside information with the marketing of issuer's activities.[36]

Timely disclosure is also a key issue in the area of episodic information, in both a national and an EU context.[37] Issuers are required to disclose the information 'as soon as possible', but Article 17 does not further specify the time limits that are acceptable in this framework. While UK cases have shown that even a delay of one day may suffice for the breach of this obligation,[38] the situation is different in France, where eight days may be considered a very long period but no indication is given as to the absolute minimum allowed, or even in the USA, where a delay of four business days can be accepted.[39] While it is reasonable to expect divergence in this area due to the different sizes and circumstances of capital markets across the EU and internationally, it is worrisome to maintain this kind of flexibility and rely solely on NCAs to decipher, on a case-by-case basis, the acceptable time limits for such disclosure. Further cooperation between NCAs under the aegis of ESMA is therefore required to explore convergence opportunities in the supervision of episodic information.

The comprehensiveness of disclosed information is also a key issue that must be safeguarded across the EU. Issuers may be tempted to disclose different components of the information via different means[40] or to omit some parts of information by revealing only the positive ones. The tendency to misuse the episodic disclosure framework is also greater than in the periodic framework since ad hoc information can relate to any aspect of the company, going beyond

---

[35] Article 17(1), 2014 MAR.

[36] Ibid.

[37] For some interesting comparative examples on this issue, see T.M. J. Möllers, 'The "Immediateness" of ad hoc Disclosure Statements in the Context of National and European Legal Doctrine' (2007) 18 *International Company and Commercial Law Review* 369.

[38] *Marconi plc*, Public statement, 11 April 2003, FSA/PN/047/2003.

[39] Form 8-K Current Report, Pursuant to Section 13 or 15 8d) of the Securities Exchange Act of 1934.

[40] Issuers have tried to integrate episodic information into periodic disclosure obligations, whose deadline may be very close to the moment where inside information needs to be disclosed 'as soon as possible', by claiming that this is acceptable. This line of arguments cannot of course be accepted since the two frameworks are completely separate and with different purposes: *Société Parrot*, Décision AMF, 1ère section, 9 June 2009. Using different disclosure mechanisms can also happen in order to make the evaluation of the inside information more complex and possibly hide some negative information from investors.

information related to accounting and other issues. Taking into account all the possible communication channels as well as the variety of information potentially disclosed, it is essential to ensure a coherent disclosure strategy that does not make the inside information a complex puzzle that investors have to solve.

6.3 THE ONGOING SUPERVISION FRAMEWORK

The EU supervision framework of episodic disclosure obligations relies heavily on NCAs. This is due to the permanent and unpredictable nature of disclosure in this area, which necessitates a prompt and effective response by the legal framework when it does– or does not – occur. NCAs are the most suitable points of reference given their ongoing contact with issuers and their regulatory 'know-how'. Effective monitoring of compliance with episodic disclosure rules is admittedly an arduous task because it is hard to unveil suspicious practices when the company remains silent with regard to inside information.

The 2014 MAR provides for a supervision system articulated around NCAs and ESMA, including a series of powers, cooperation arrangements with ESMA and cooperation with the NCAs of Member States and third countries. The wide range of powers enables NCAs to monitor ongoing disclosure obligations. These powers refer, *inter alia*, to the right to have access to any document and data, to demand information, and to carry out on-site inspections and investigations.[41] NCAs are expected to cooperate with each other[42] and with ESMA in all areas deemed necessary for the purposes of the market abuse regime, and they shall exchange information without undue delay, as well as cooperate in investigation, supervision and enforcement activities.[43] Cooperation with third countries is also a valuable part of the supervisory chain, and the conclusion of cooperation arrangements is vital for the exchange of information between supervisory authorities, especially since their arrangements are also facilitated by guidance provided by ESMA.[44] As mentioned previously, the main challenge for an effective monitoring framework will be the gradual convergence of regulatory best practices in order to eliminate (to a certain extent) the current divergent interpretations of the broadly formulated EU rules.[45]

---

[41] Article 23, 2014 MAR.

[42] Article 25, ibid.

[43] Article 24, ibid. NCAs may refuse to cooperate for investigation purposes or act on an information-related request by invoking national security, adverse effects on their own investigations, ongoing judicial proceedings for the same case or final judgements regarding the same case: Article 24(2), ibid.

[44] Article 26, ibid.

[45] For example, on the interpretational difficulties among market actors and NCAs surrounding the notion of 'inside information', see J. Lau Hansen and D. Moalem, 'The MAD Disclosure Regime and the Twofold Notion of Inside Information: The Available Solution' 4(3) *Capital Markets Law Journal* 323 (2009). See also Di Noia and Gargantini, above n. 7, 510.

ESMA will undoubtedly contribute to these efforts by coordinating related activities not only via its guidelines and technical standards but, most importantly, by providing guidance to national NCAs as and when requested.

6.4 THE ENFORCEMENT FRAMEWORK

6.4.1 Criminal Sanctions

Criminal sanctions are typically rare and marginalized in this framework. Few Member States have provided for criminal sanctions for breaches of episodic disclosure obligations, a fact that denotes the rather auxiliary role that episodic disclosure obligations are supposed to play in this area.[46] Adding to this reality, it should also be borne in mind that criminal liability could be particularly difficult to establish in episodic disclosure strategies, as proving the intentional element can be arduous. This is true due to the instantaneous character of the disclosure itself, which may not always be helpful in establishing intent since the defendants could argue that they were not aware of the defective character of the information disclosed and that they did not have such intent when carrying out the disclosure. Moreover, the marginalization of criminal sanctions in this area may also be attributed to the fact that criminal liability can be established only with regard to the disclosure of defective information and not by the omission of disclosure of correct information – a situation that can be common in this framework.

The signs of EU-level harmonization on criminal sanctions for episodic disclosure obligations are not particularly encouraging. The 2014 MAD[47] implemented minimum harmonization in the area of criminal sanctions only with regard to serious and intentional infringements of some market abuse practices, such as insider dealing, unlawful disclosure of inside information and market manipulation.[48] Therefore, the provisions of the 2014 MAD do not cover breaches of episodic disclosure obligations, which continue to be determined solely by national laws. This is particularly unfortunate as further harmonization in this area would be particularly welcome and would discourage inappropriate ad hoc disclosure practices that can harm investor confidence, destabilize capital markets and have serious effects on the investor community. The 2014 MAD itself acknowledges the beneficial aspects of criminal sanctions for market abuse practices as a 'stronger form of social disapproval compared

---

[46] CESR, 'Executive Summary to the Report on Administrative Measures and Sanctions as well as the Criminal Sanctions Available in Member States under the Market Abuse Directive', CESR/08-099, 2008, 34, at http://www.esma.europa.eu/system/files/08_099.pdf.
[47] Directive 2014/57/EU of the European Parliament and of the Council of April 16, 2014 on criminal sanctions for insider dealing and market manipulation [2014] OJ L173/179.
[48] Articles 3 to 5, ibid.

to administrative penalties'.[49] Nevertheless, the level of harmonization introduced was minimal and with uncertain outcomes at the national level due to the remaining interpretation obstacles.[50]

6.4.2 Administrative Sanctions and Measures

Lastly, breaches of episodic disclosure obligations can trigger a series of administrative sanctions and measures. The most notable characteristic of the 2014 MAR was the introduction of new thresholds with regard to pecuniary sanctions. First of all, for breaches of Article 17, NCAs can impose maximum administrative pecuniary sanctions of at least three times the amount of the profits related to the infringement, when the amount of such profits can be determined.[51] Moreover, natural and legal persons can be subject to maximum pecuniary sanctions of at least €1 million[52] and €2.5 million[53] (or 2% of total annual turnover), respectively. It is also worth noting that Member States retain the possibility of providing for higher levels of sanctions.[54] The 2014 MAR thus aims to raise the minimum levels of maximum pecuniary sanctions, while leaving national legislators the discretion to increase the severity of sanctions.

Similarly to Article 28(c) of the TD, as analysed in Chapter 5, Article 31 of the 2014 MAR provides a useful guide to the elements that must be taken into account by NCAs when determining the type and level of administrative sanctions.[55] It is clear that this alignment with the TD aims to enhance indirectly a harmonization trend among NCAs that are now required to start designing, interpreting and implementing sanctions with regard to a fixed minimum of circumstances applicable at the EU level. As in the case of periodic disclosure obligations, this is definitely an encouraging step towards gradual convergence of the *modus operandi* of NCAs. It may prove even more useful than formal harmonization measures that deal with minimal penalties, insofar as it could accustom authorities to a new way of thinking and calculating the severity of

---

[49] Recital 6, ibid.

[50] Indeed, it will be particularly interesting to see how Member States will implement these provisions with regard to the 'seriousness' of a case that should trigger the harmonized sanction levels. Recitals 11 and 12 of the Directive provide some useful guidance in that respect, but room for divergence is still inevitably present.

[51] Article 30(2)(h), ibid.

[52] Article 30(2)(i) and (ii), ibid.

[53] Article 30(2)(j) and (ii), ibid.

[54] Article 30(3), ibid.

[55] The gravity of the duration of the breach, the degree of responsibility and the financial strength of the natural or legal person, the magnitude of profits and of the losses suffered by third parties due to the breach, the level of cooperation with the NCA, any eventual former breaches and any measures taken for the prevention of repetition of the breach.

sanctions, prompting them to adopt a much more holistic approach that may not necessarily coincide with traditional approaches.[56]

The alignment with the TD is also evident from Article 34 of the 2014 MAR, which deals with the requirement for NCAs to publish immediately on their website any decision imposing an administrative sanction or measure. The publication must include information with regard to the time and the nature of the breach, as well as the identity of the person concerned.[57]Also, in the presence of disproportionality with regard to the person concerned or of risks of this mobilizing the financial markets for compromising an ongoing investigation, NCAs may defer the publication, publish the decision anonymously or even opt not to publish.[58]

In acknowledging the EU framework's responsiveness to deficient disclosure strategies, another potential argument relates to the accentuation of sanctions in the case of information-based market manipulation. Indeed, Article 12 of the 2014 MAR considers market manipulation to be the dissemination of information, through the media or by any other means, that gives or is likely to give false or misleading signals regarding, *inter alia*, a financial instrument. According to Article 30(2)(j)(i) and (ii), the administrative sanctions applicable to Article 15 which prohibits market manipulation can be much higher for both natural and legal persons, who can be subject to maximum pecuniary sanctions of at least €5 million and €15 million (or 15% of total annual turnover), respectively. In this case, the 2014 MAD would also be applicable because, in characterizing this behaviour as market manipulation in its Article 5(2)(c), it provides for a criminal offence in its Article 6, as well as a maximum term of imprisonment of at least four years in its Article 7 for natural persons, as well as other types of sanctions for legal persons in its Article 9. More generally, an information-based market manipulation could also be related to similar violations of prospectus or periodic disclosure obligations.

---

[56] See, for example, the relatively modest rates of administrative sanctions by the FSA (predecessor of the FCA): P. Davies, 'Davies Review of Issuer Liability: A Discussion Paper' (2007) 29. Nevertheless, the FSA had imposed a £17 million penalty on Shell in 2004 for breach of disclosure obligations, at http://www.fca.org.uk/your-fca/documents/final-notices/2004/fsa-final-notice-2004-the-shell-transport-and-trading-company. On a much more frequent basis, the FCA has recently been levying highly dissuasive penalties: see for example the penalty of £539,800 imposed on Reckitt Benckiser Group Plc in 2015, at http://www.fca.org.uk/static/documents/final-notices/reckitt-benckiser-group-plc.pdf, and the £2.4 million penalty imposed on Lamprell Plc in 2013, at http://www.fsa.gov.uk/static/pubs/final/lamprell.pdf. Such a trend testifies to a more general shift towards a more active public enforcement agenda, inevitably triggered by the more general ramifications of the financial crisis: P. Schammo, *EU Prospectus Law: New Perspectives on Regulatory Competition in Securities Markets* (Cambridge University Press, 2011), 56. More generally on different economic, legal and institutional infrastructures as well as complementary mechanisms that influence this framework in the UK, see K. Cearns and E. Ferran, 'Non-Enforcement Led Public Oversight of Financial and Corporate Governance Disclosures and of Auditors' (2008) 8 *Journal of Corporate Law Studies* 191, 209–210, 223.

[57] Article 34(1), MAR 2014.

[58] Article 34(1)(a)(b)(c), ibid.

Could it therefore be reasonably argued that the applicability of market manipulation rules would solve the lack of harmonization or sufficient rigour of sanctions at the EU level? Enhancing the severity of sanctions in the presence of market manipulation can only be a positive sign, but the general framework in which courts and NCAs will be asked to exercise their functions deprives the legal system of a possibility to develop and apply more targeted enforcement tools against equally sophisticated corporate disclosure strategies. Moreover, the harmonization gap would persist due to the same pattern followed across the applicable EU Directives and Regulations.

It should also be borne in mind that market manipulation rules are only a subsect of the entirety of defective disclosure strategies. The key characteristic of market manipulation strategies in this area can be identified as their potential to interfere with the market price-efficiency principle by giving misleading signals regarding the financial instrument. It can therefore be plausibly argued that these strategies only touch on some of the defective disclosure strategies adopted by companies and, as such, cannot qualify for a blanket prohibition for all cases.

6.4.3 Civil Liability

Civil liability (as well as criminal and administrative sanctions) can result from breaches of episodic disclosure requirements. The 2014 MAR simply provides, under Article 30, that Member States, without prejudice to any criminal sanctions, must empower NCAs to impose administrative sanctions and measures with regard to a series of infringements specified under the same article.[59]

Civil claims face several potential obstacles in the area of episodic disclosure obligations, due not only to the considerable divergence of national legal provisions but also to the inherent difficulty of proving the causal link between the defective information and the decision to invest. Indeed, in this specific framework, information is disclosed instantaneously and its influence on investors, who carry the burden of proof of such link,[60] may not be straightforward, especially in the presence of other concomitant factors that may be equally important to an investment decision. Moreover, it is common for national frameworks to provide only for issuer liability, thus excluding the responsible persons behind defective ad hoc disclosure practices in which they are usually more involved at a personal level, such as in the case of an interview with the financial press.

National laws have treated this topic in different ways; most of them having maintained their general civil liability provisions,[61] and others have chosen to

---

[59] Article 30(1), ibid.

[60] With the exception of Austrian law, where it is sufficient for investors to show that the defective information was known to the market at the time of the investment or that the omitted information was subject to a disclosure obligation.

[61] French law deals with these breaches under Article 1383 of the *Code Civil*.

introduce specific provisions for this type of breach.[62] Although some highly publicized cases have been subject to severe sanctions in certain jurisdictions,[63] it would be fair to say that national courts are still reluctant to facilitate civil claims, maintaining a rather conservative view of the impact of ad hoc disclosed information on investment decisions.[64]

6.5 CONCLUSION

Gaining particular importance within the more general disclosure framework, episodic obligations complete the transparency spectrum with continuously applicable informational exposure to the market. The 2014 MAR, following on from the 2003 MAD, has attempted to clarify the notion of 'inside information' that must be disclosed 'as soon as possible' by issuers. Fine-tuning is still needed as confusion regarding the context of 'inside information' and the various interpretations at the national level will continue to create uncertainties for both issuers and NCAs. The concomitant functions of 'inside information' as to the need to inform the public on an ongoing basis and to combat insider dealing, arising from the use of inside information to the detriment of other market actors, will inevitably continue to drive a vivid debate as to their importance and coexistence in the EU regulatory agenda.

The arduous task of fine-tuning the contours of episodic disclosure obligations and safeguarding all affected parties and the market at large inevitably falls to NCAs. Under ESMA's indispensable guidance on operational methods and convergence benefits in supervision and enforcement of disclosure breaches, NCAs will be in a position to gradually contribute to an indirectly harmonized institutional framework. The current harmonization efforts by 2014 MAR in the area of enforcement certainly help accentuate this convergence trend, albeit with some timid steps that will have to be further developed during a future MAR review.

---

[62] German law has introduced paragraphs 37b (omission to disclose inside information) and 37c (disclosure of incorrect information) in the *WpHG* dealing with episodic disclosure obligations. UK law has introduced Section 90A Financial Services and Markets Act 2000, which establishes issuer liability together with Schedule 10A.

[63] Such as *Informatec* (*OLG* Munich, 23 *ZIP* 1989 [2002]), *EM.TV* (*BGH, NZG* 672 [2005]) or *Comroad* (*BGH, NZG* 386 [2008]) in Germany and *Flammarion* (CA Paris, 26 September 2003, *Soulier et autres c/Flammarion et autres*) or *Eurodirect* (Cass. com., 22 November 2005, *Eurodirect Marketing c/M. X*) in France: for an extensive analysis, see K. Sergakis, *La Transparence des Sociétés Cotées en Droit Européen* (IRJS Éditions 2013) 211–214.

[64] For example, under German tort law, paragraph 823(1) BGB deals with infringements of a protective law but German courts have traditionally, with some exceptions, conceived of disclosure obligations as aiming to protect the market at large and not investors in particular. It therefore cannot be used in a civil claim unless an investor can show that she belongs to a protected category. Paragraph 826 BGB, dealing with intentional damage of public policy, seems to be more appropriate for a civil claim in this area but requires a full level of proof, thus making successful claims very difficult.

Transparency of Ownership Structures

7.1 INTRODUCTION

An efficient legal framework for capital markets must address issuers' capital structure in order to secure an adequate level of transparency not only on an issuer's internal aspects (such as financial information),[1] but also on the issuer's relationship with its shareholders and with other companies in cases of takeovers. EU and international capital markets are constantly evolving with numerous ongoing 'buy/sell' transactions. These transactions inevitably affect the composition of issuers' capital structures, as well as their control by shareholders, by allowing new investors to participate and existing shareholders to divest. All capital movements must be constantly visible to existing and potential shareholders as well as regulators. As we have already seen, becoming a publicly traded company entails constant informational exposure to the public at large: changes in the capital structure may become valuable informational signals as to a share's value, the attractiveness of a particular issuer, the general developments in a particular sector and the potential shifts in the issuers' control.

This chapter will focus on disclosure obligations that pertain to holding structures of listed companies. It is divided into two sections: first, it will deal with disclosure obligations of major holdings and financial instruments, and secondly, it will examine the same type of obligations which are triggered during takeovers. It is important to cover these two topics in tandem since they deal, directly and indirectly, with holding movements and the market for corporate control.

Capital structures have been a major focus of EU capital markets for a long time[2] and legal provisions have endeavoured to gradually enlarge all elements that are important so as to decipher any potential activity that may exert an influence on ownership structures in publicly traded companies. Any relevant transaction must be targeted rapidly and efficiently, and must be supervised by the relevant NCA. It is crucial for legal provisions that not

---

[1] See Chapters 4, 5 and 6.

[2] Council Directive 79/279/EEC of 5 March 1979 coordinating the conditions for the admission of securities to official stock exchange listing [1979] OJ L 66/21; Council Directive 88/627/EEC of 12 December 1988 on the information to be published when a major holding in a listed company is acquired or disposed of [1988] OJ L 348/62.

only permit these movements within the capital structure over time to be traced, but also force shareholders who might be tempted to adopt opaque operational methods in order to increase their participation in a company, to disclose relevant information and without delay. The rationales for such disclosure obligations relate to the need to secure market efficiency as well as allow issuers and shareholders to be aware of who exerts influence (or is about to exert even greater influence) over issuers.[3] It is also important for national laws to provide efficient sanctions, arising both from the company and from regulators and the courts, to deter violations of these disclosure obligations.

Sizeable movements within the capital structure may also result in takeovers that trigger a change of control of the issuer, with a series of consequences both for shareholders and for stakeholders such as employees.[4] EU law faced several difficulties before reaching a rather modest agreement between Member States on the Takeover Directive.[5] The main difficulties involved the board neutrality and 'breakthrough' rules, which constitute important features of national laws' approach to the level of openness of issuers to takeovers, with divergent practices and traditions being maintained. Our study focuses solely on disclosure obligations during this type of operation so as to examine the efficiency of the EU legal framework that aims to protect all concerned parties during takeovers. This protection is anchored in the information that all concerned parties should receive relating to their future investment decisions. Although disclosure rules were the least controversial aspect of negotiations for the Takeover Directive, their harmonization at a minimum level denotes persisting differences between national laws and prevents market actors from taking advantage of investment opportunities in the EU. An even greater source of concern lies with the sanctions imposed for violations of disclosure obligations in this area; these sanctions show a wide level of divergence from one country to the next, failing to create an efficient framework for market actors who may be affected by such violations.

---

[3] N. Jul Clausen and K. Engsig Sørensen, 'Disclosure of Major Shareholdings: A Comparative Analysis of Regulation in Europe' (2002) 4 *International and Comparative Corporate Law Journal* 202; M.C. Shouten, 'The Case for Mandatory Ownership Disclosure' (2009) 14 *Stanford Journal of Law, Business and Finance* 127; M.C. Schouten and M. Siems, 'The Evolution of Ownership Disclosure Rules Across Countries' (2010) 10(2) *Journal of Corporate Law Studies* 451.

[4] On this topic, see B. Clarke, 'The Role of Employees in the Takeover Bids Directive' in J. Cremers and S. Vitols (eds), *Takeovers With or Without Worker Voice: Worker Rights under the EU Directive on Takeover Bids* (ETUI, 2016), 33; B. Clarke, 'The Takeovers' Directive – A Meaningful Contribution to Stakeholders Rights in Europe' (2013) 10(1) *International and Comparative Corporate Law Journal* 80.

[5] Directive 2004/25/EC of the European Parliament and of the Council of 21 April 2004 on takeover bids [2004] OJ L 142/12. For an overview, see P-H. Conac, 'Le droit européen et les OPA' (2014) 6 *Cahiers de droit de l'entreprise* 44.

7.2 The EU Notification of Major Holdings Regime

7.2.1 Applicable Disclosure Rules

7.2.1.1 Applicable Thresholds

Investors who change their holdings in companies with securities admitted to trading on regulated markets, by investing or divesting, are expected to inform the concerned issuer, the regulator and the public at large. EU law has strictly defined the regulatory perimeter applicable in this framework and has also gradually strengthened the disclosure obligation, thus reflecting a constant need to prioritize and secure the transparency of capital structures. The TD provides a mixture of minimum and maximum harmonization measures, depending on facets of major holdings.[6] Indeed, Member States are not allowed to adopt more stringent rules in relation to the calculation of notification thresholds, the aggregation of the voting rights held, or the exceptions to the notification requirements. Conversely, Member States are still permitted to provide lower or higher notification thresholds and to require equivalent notifications in relation to thresholds based on capital holdings. They can also continue to provide stricter rules related to the informational content, the process and the timing for ratification, as well as requiring additional information on major holdings which is not provided by the TD.[7] The legal framework is complemented by Directive 2007/14/EC[8] and Regulation 2015/761.[9]

Starting with the holding notification thresholds, there are several thresholds (5%, 10%, 15%, 20%, 25%, 30%, 50% and 75%)[10] that trigger a disclosure obligation for shareholders who acquire or dispose of shares of an issuer and to which voting rights are attached. The eventual suspension of voting rights does not influence the calculation of these thresholds. The gradual escalation of thresholds functions as an 'alarm system' for issuers and existing or potential

---

[6] Directive 2013/50/EU of the European Parliament and of the Council of 22 October 2013 amending Directive 2004/109/EC of the European Parliament and of the Council on the harmonization of transparency requirements in relation to information about issuers whose securities are admitted to trading on a regulated market, Directive 2003/71/EC of the European Parliament and of the Council on the prospectus to be published when securities are offered to the public or admitted to trading, and Commission Directive 2007/14/EC laying down detailed rules for the implementation of certain provisions of Directive 2004/109/ EC [2013] OJ L 294/13; R. Veil (ed.), *European Capital Markets Law* (2nd edn, Hart Publishing, 2017) 399.

[7] Recital 12, ibid.

[8] Commission Directive 2007/14/EC of 8 March 2007 laying down detailed rules for the implementation of certain provisions of Directive 2004/109/EC on the harmonization of transparency requirements in relation to information about issuers whose securities are admitted to trading on a regulated market [2007] OJ L 69/27. On this Directive, see P-H. Conac, 'L'incidence de la directive du 8 mars 2007 sur les franchissements de seuils' (2007) 3 *Revue Trimestrielle de Droit Financier* 7.

[9] Commission Delegated Regulation (EU) 2015/761 of 17 December 2014 supplementing Directive 2004/109/EC of the European Parliament and of the Council with regard to certain regulatory technical standards on major holdings [2015] OJ L 120/2.

[10] Article 9, ibid.

shareholders who may be concerned about sizeable holdings and eventual changes in the control of a company in a takeover scenario. Member States are free to impose additional thresholds so as to provide for a more stringent disclosure framework for a series of market actors.[11] Indicative examples are UK law, which provides for additional thresholds (for UK issuers) of 3%, 4%, 6%, 7%, 8%, 9% and additional 1% thresholds up to 100%,[12] or Italian law, which provides for thresholds of 3% (applicable only to Italian large caps), 66.6% and 90% of actual holdings.[13]

7.2.1.2 Triggering Conditions for Disclosure Obligations

Disclosure obligations are triggered both actively and passively, namely in the presence[14] or in the absence[15] of a voluntary act on behalf of the concerned person, since the TD provides that such an obligation includes situations where thresholds are triggered 'as a result of events changing the breakdown of voting rights'[16] and based on the information disclosed by the issuer who is under an obligation to disclose to the public the total number of voting rights and capital at the end of each calendar month during which any increase or decrease of these numbers has taken place.[17] Shareholders must therefore notify the issuer promptly, and in any case within four trading days after they are informed about such events affecting voting rights.[18]

Member States have transposed this provision into national legislation in different ways. For example, some of them only mention the alteration of holdings as the triggering factor,[19] raising doubts as to the extent to which such an obligation is incumbent on shareholders when they are unaware of information in the issuer's possession. While it could be reasonable to assume that the absence of knowledge should not risk triggering an eventual liability for violation of disclosure obligations, general national provisions of this type should be seen as a strengthened version of the TD, given the minimum harmonization framework that allows Member States to adopt more stringent requirements.[20]

The TD also triggers a notification obligation to the issuer when the shareholder learns of the acquisition or disposal of voting rights or, having

---

[11] Article 3, ibid.

[12] Disclosure Rules and Transparency Rules (DTR) 5.1.2. Non-UK issuers are subject to thresholds similar to those provided in Article 9 of the TD, ibid.

[13] *Decreto Legislativo 15 febbraio 2016*, No 25, *Gazzetta Ufficiale Serie Generale* No 52, 3 March 2016.

[14] For example, the purchase of shares.

[15] For example, the disposal of shares, accompanied by double voting rights, that modifies consequently the denominator to a greater extent.

[16] Article 9(2), ibid.

[17] Article 15, ibid.

[18] Article 12(2)(b), ibid.

[19] See, for example, Article L. 233-7, *Code de commerce*.

[20] P-H. Conac, 'Franchissement de seuils' (2007) 26 *Répertoire Société Dalloz* 8.

regard to the circumstances, should have learned of it.[21] Although the latter provision does not refer to disclosure arising from the issuer in order for shareholders to gain knowledge of alteration in voting rights, it is reasonable to assume that this line of interpretation is also accepted by the TD. Transparency considerations for the benefit of other shareholders in the market at large should, in our opinion, justify a more stringent standard and a higher expectation from the existing shareholders potentially subject to such disclosure even in the absence of knowledge. Indeed, shareholders should be incited to update the available information on a regular basis. Shareholders' level of sophistication, as well as their degree of participation in listed companies, are undoubtedly useful in litigation as evidence that may or may not justify the lack of knowledge should liability arise for an alleged violation of the disclosure obligation triggered by passive alterations of voting rights.

7.2.1.3 The Types of Financial Instruments and Their Calculation
In addition to notification with regard to shares, as mentioned above, the same obligation applies to situations that have similar effects as to the acquisition or disposal of major proportions of voting rights. This assimilation aims to subject market actors to an increased level of transparency for the benefit of the market and the issuer concerned. These situations relate, *inter alia*, to voting rights held by a third party and connected via an agreement with the concerned shareholder that obliges the latter to adopt, by concerted exercise of voting rights,[22] a lasting common policy regarding the management of the issuer, to voting rights attached to shares in which the concerned person has the life interest, to voting rights attached to shares deposited with the concerned person that it can exercise at its discretion, and to voting rights held by a third party in its own name on behalf of that person.[23] Actions in concert in the TD are examined under the 'corporate influence' notion, which may not necessarily lead to corporate control, as is the case in the area of takeovers. Indeed, the only requirement for the existence of action in concert is the establishment of a common policy that requires a certain level of commitment but not actual action. The role also relates to already acquired shares and not to any potential future acquisition. The nature of this rule can be explained in the light of the fact that notification of major holdings acts as a preventive measure, alerting issuers of possible future actions that could arise from such common policies.

Similar treatment in terms of disclosure obligations has been provided for direct or indirect holdings of financial instruments[24] that, upon maturity, give

---

[21] Article 12(2)(a), TD. Shareholders are deemed to have knowledge no later than two trading days following the transaction, according to Article 9 of the Commission Directive 2007/14/EC, above n. 6.

[22] Concerted actions in takeovers are defined and further explained at Section 7.3.1.3.

[23] Article 10, ibid.

[24] Transferable securities, options, futures, swaps, forward rate agreements, contracts for difference and any other contracts or agreements with similar economic effects: Article

the holder either the right or the discretion to acquire shares with attached voting rights and of financial instruments that are referenced to shares and with a similar economic effect.[25] All these methods for the exercise of voting rights should therefore be subject to the same disclosure framework. The 2013 TD reforms in this area should be welcomed, especially given various discrepancies among national laws with regard to the range of financial instruments covered by such disclosure obligations in the past.[26] Most importantly, the rapid expansion of sophisticated and innovatory financial instruments have prompted various market actors to adopt opaque holding practices, creating further market abuse and concerns regarding deficient disclosure.[27] The UK approach has undoubtedly been instrumental to such reforms, as it has traditionally focused on rules that are formulated in a principles-based way so as to capture all financial products with similar economic effect.[28]

The notification obligation must be accompanied with a set of information so that the issuer has a holistic view of the disclosed situation. Indeed, informational elements such as the resulting situation in terms of voting rights, the chain of controlled undertakings through which these rights are held, the date on which the threshold was reached or crossed, and the identity of the concerned shareholder must be included in the notification.[29] As previously mentioned, the maximum period allowed for such notification to take place is four trading days after the date on which the shareholder became aware or should have become aware of any of the above-mentioned situations.[30] Consequently, issuers are expected, within three trading days after receiving the notification, to make public all the information contained in the notification so as to inform other market actors of these changes in their ownership structure.[31] Issuers may be exempt from such obligation if the information contained in the notification is made public by the NCA, upon receipt of the notification, but no later than three training days thereafter.[32]

The calculation of voting rights notified under Articles 9, 10 and 13, as mentioned above, must take place in an aggregated spectrum with the number of the voting rights related to financial instruments held directly

---

13(1)(b), ibid. See also, ESMA Indicative list of financial instruments that are subject to notification requirements according to Article 13(1)(b) of the revised Transparency Directive, 22 October 2015, ESMA/2015/1598. For information that needs to be provided according to Article 13, see Article 11(3) of the Directive 2007/14/EC, above n. 6.

[25] Article 13, TD.

[26] P.-H. Conac, 'Cash-Settled Derivatives as a Takeover Instrument and the Reform of the EU Transparency Directive', in H. Søndergaard Birkmose, M. Neville and K. Engsig Sørensen, *The European Financial Market in Transition* (Kluwer Law International, 2012), 49.

[27] Recital 9, TD.

[28] FSA, 'Disclosure of Contracts for Difference – Questions & Answers: Version 2', 11 June 2009.

[29] Article 12(1), TD.

[30] Article 12(2), ibid.

[31] Article 12(6), ibid.

[32] Article 12(7), ibid.

and indirectly. Notifications will also include a breakdown of the number of voting rights attached to shares held in accordance with Articles 9 and 10, and voting rights related to financial instruments covered by Article 13. In the presence of a previous notification, additional notification must be given when the concerned person has actually acquired the underlying shares and such acquisition triggers the applicable notification thresholds by its total number of voting rights attached to these shares.[33] This aspect is particularly important because just as the range of financial instruments varied across the EU, so were aggregation methods also different at the national level, creating an unequal transparency framework for market actors. These provisions aim definitively to address the aggregation methods for all Member States.

7.2.1.4 Notification Exemptions

The TD exempts market actors from notification requirements in a set of circumstances that do not raise issuer transparency concerns, unlike the ones analysed above. Exemptions apply to shares acquired for the sole purpose of clearing and settling within the usual short settlement cycle, or to custodians holding shares in their custodian capacity provided that they can only exercise the voting rights attached to such shares under instructions given in writing or by electronic means.[34] An additional exemption applies to the acquisition or disposal of a major holding triggering the 5% threshold by market makers when they act in their capacity as a market maker. This exemption applies under the condition that such activity is authorized by the home Member State and when market makers simply ensure market liquidity without being involved in the management of the issuer or exerting any influence on the issuer to buy such shares or to support the share price.[35] A further exemption is provided in relation to voting rights that are held in the trading book of a credit institution or investment firm. This exemption applies when the voting rights do not exceed 5% and the shares to which they are attached are held in a trading book, are not exercised or otherwise used to intervene in the management of the issuer.[36] The same exemption applies to voting rights attached to shares acquired for stabilization purposes related to exemptions for buyback programmes and stabilization of financial instruments, under the condition that the voting rights attached to those shares are not exercised or otherwise used to intervene in the management of the issuer.[37]

Aiming to resolve interpretational difficulties around the calculation of the thresholds for market making and trading book exemptions, Delegated Regulation (EU) 2015/761 provides that the calculation of the 5% threshold shall

---

[33] Article 13(2), ibid.
[34] Article 9(4), ibid.
[35] Article 9(5), ibid. As a general observation, this exemption relates to notification to issuers, which leaves market actors under the general obligation of informing the NCA of their actions.
[36] Article 9(6), ibid.
[37] Article 9(6)(a), ibid.

be aggregated[38] and that, in the case of a group of companies, all holdings shall be aggregated at the group level.[39] The aggregate population ensures a better result in terms of detecting the level of participation in an issuer's capital structure, in the presence of these exemptions that may blur the overall picture as to the holdings that must be notified to the issuer and others that are exempt from such notification.

7.2.1.5 Notification of Intent

Bearing in mind the minimum harmonization level of the TD with regard to the informational content, and in the absence of an EU rule, some national laws have made the applicable disclosure framework even more stringent by requiring that shareholders declare their intent for the six forthcoming months at the time of notification and disclosure of major holdings. For example, French law requires such declarations of intent when the thresholds of 10%, 15%, 20% and 25% have been triggered.[40] Shareholders must notify not only the issuer, but also the NCA, of such intent; they must also proceed to a new declaration on the same matter should their intent change within the six-month period. The new declaration is not dependent on any particular circumstances, a situation that may offer shareholders the chance to create 'market noise' at their discretion and risk influencing issuers and other market actors in a potentially misleading way. The same Article aims to control such risks by requiring an exhaustive list of information in the notification of intent.[41] German law provides a similar requirement for shareholders that reach the 10%, 15%, 20%, 25%, 30%, 50% and 75% thresholds of voting rights.[42] The disclosure obligation relates to any strategic objectives, plans for the acquisition of additional voting rights, the change of the issuer's capital structure and of the composition of the supervisory board. Regrettably enough, there are no enforcement provisions for such notifications. As it has been opined, there is difficulty in enforcing such statements, since it is an arduous task to differentiate between plans that have not come to fruition due to uncertainty and plans that are not realized due to a lack of willingness.[43]

It becomes evident that information in the area of major holdings is of crucial importance to a series of market actors and national laws, like France and Germany, who are in search of variable solutions so as to decipher shareholders'

---

[38] Article 2, Regulation (EU) 2015/761.
[39] Article 3, ibid.
[40] Article L. 233-7(VII), *Code de commerce*.
[41] The information touches upon the financing methods for the acquisition; the eventual existence of concerted action; the likelihood of pursuing further acquisitions and of updating the control of the issuer; the strategy that the concerned person intends to employ as to the issuer; and the implementing operations as well as the agreements of temporary disposal of shares and voting rights: ibid.
[42] § 27(a) *Wertpapierhandelsgesetz (WpHG)*.
[43] K. Engsig Sørensen, 'Shareholders' Duty to Disclose' in H. Søndergaard Birkmose (ed.), *Shareholders Duties* (Kluwer Law International, 2017), 319.

future movements, especially in the light of eventual takeover bids. More stringent provisions may also provide for an additional level of information protection to market actors and to concerned issuers. EU law has not provided any rules on this matter, allowing national systems to decipher shareholders' intent. This situation is regrettable and warrants closer regulatory attention in the future. A notification of intent rule is nevertheless unlikely to be adopted at the EU level since it may convey the message of takeover deterrence, by not allowing flexibility to market actors when they reach certain thresholds and with an eventual takeover bid in mind.

7.2.2 Enforcement of Notification Rules

7.2.2.1 Enforcement at the Issuer Level
Given the minimum harmonization level of the TD in the area of enforcement, national laws provide that issuers have the possibility of securing transparency in the area of notifications of major holdings via the introduction of additional thresholds in their articles of association, ranging from 0.5% to 5%, as is the case under French law.[44] It becomes a matter of internal policy how to manage alterations of ownership structures and impose notification to existing shareholders, by also taking into account the time-consuming aspect of a multiplication of thresholds which may prove counterproductive, especially for listed companies with low levels of liquidity.

In addition to statutory thresholds, national laws must also provide that the violation of notification rules may result in disenfranchisement for the voting rights attached to shares.[45] Member States can provide that such sanctions apply only to the most serious breaches.[46] Disenfranchisement can last for six months under German law[47] or even for two years under French law, starting from the date of regularization of the notification.[48] The TD does not provide any procedural rules, and it therefore remains unclear who is supposed to apply such a sanction. The most plausible explanation would be that NCAs – or in some national laws the courts, following an NCA application – should in principle be empowered to impose such sanctions.

According to French law, it is also possible for issuers to trigger disenfranchisement only upon request by one or more shareholders holding shares equal to the smallest fraction of capital whose acquisition has not been notified. Nevertheless, the fraction cannot be higher than 5% of the issuer's capital. This deviation from the general rule must already be included in the articles of association. It will therefore be a matter for the general assembly to decide on the implementation of such a sanction. If there is no such provision in the articles

---

[44] See, for example, Article L. 233-7(III), *Code de commerce.*
[45] Article 28(b)(2), TD.
[46] Ibid.
[47] § 28 *WpHG.*
[48] Article L. 233-14, *Code de commerce.*

of association, it could be opined that automatic disenfranchisement should be maintained, not only for the sake of legal certainty but also for a more efficient enforcement framework in the presence of notification violations.

Nevertheless, by awarding a quasi total disenfranchisement right to the general assembly, national laws may also risk creating disputable cases in the presence of borderline incidents. These instances may not constitute a flagrant violation of notification obligations but may show some premature signs of concerted action or other strategies that may alert issuers who, in turn, may want to put obstacles in front of some shareholders by disenfranchising them, with the excuse that these shareholders had failed to file the appropriate notifications. French doctrinal views on this issue are divided, with some authors arguing that this is a legitimate role for the general assembly – even in borderline cases – and others acknowledging such power only to the judiciary. In the *Eiffage* case, French case law clarified that the general assembly does not have this right in the presence of contested concerted actions.[49] There is no doubt that acknowledging such a power to the general assembly would attest to the need to ensure an immediate enforcement mechanism within the issuer so as to protect companies and their shareholders from violations. Indeed, the courts could be rather slow in resolving such cases. Nevertheless, in the presence of borderline cases, the courts will have to decide about disenfranchisement so as to overcome controversial situations in which both the general assembly and allegedly non-compliant shareholders may wish to pursue dubious strategies. That said, it is also true that courts may never be in a position to decipher uncertain situations *ex post* in the absence of flagrant elements of notification violations.

7.2.2.2 Enforcement at the Public Level

The potential problems arising at the issuer level for the enforcement of sanctions for violations of notification obligations give the courts an important role in triggering disenfranchisement. Some national laws provide for total or partial judicial suspension of voting rights for a period which, in France, may not exceed five years and it is applicable not only to violations of notification obligations, but also to situations where the initial content of the declaration of intent was not respected by the shareholders concerned.[50] The judicial intervention, while much stricter than the powers accorded to the general meeting, has not been used extensively even though it can be potentially triggered by various actors, such as the shareholders, the board chairman or the NCA.

The TD includes a general provision with regard to criminal sanctions, allowing Member States to provide for such framework.[51] General criminal sanctions are provided in French law for misleading statements,[52] and they should also be applicable in the area of violations of notifications since the latter are equivalent

---

[49] *Cour de cassation, Chambre commerciale,* 15 May 2012, *pourvoi* n° 10-23389.
[50] Article L. 233-14, *Code de commerce.*
[51] Article 28, TD.
[52] Article L. 465-2, *Code monétaire et financier.*

to such statements, under the condition that the disclosed information would be likely to have an impact upon the share price once disclosed. It could be opined that this condition is met since notification of major holdings is an informational item of great relevance for the formation of share prices. Specific criminal sanctions are also provided in French law for violations of notifications for a series of persons occupying a position within the issuer or, more generally, for shareholders.[53] The penalty provided is €18,000, which seems particularly modest, failing to reach the desired levels of deterrence, especially taking into account the potential gains resulting from such violations.

The area of administrative sanctions appears to show more optimistic signs for convergence, especially after the 2013 TD amendment, which triggered a considerable wave of reforms in this area. The amended Article 28 requires administrative measures and sanctions for breaches of national provisions having transposed the TD dealing, *inter alia*, with notifications of major holdings. Such sanctions must satisfy the criteria of effectiveness, proportionality and dissuasion. Member States are also required to ensure that the members of the administrative, management or supervisory bodies of the issuer, as well as other persons held responsible for breaches, can be potentially subject to sanctions, on the condition that this is provided for at the national level.[54] This provision aims to retain liability for both issuers and natural persons in cases of periodic obligation breaches, while respecting national preferences with regard to the delineation of the liability spectrum, as previously analysed.

The most important element of the 2013 amendment of the TD is undoubtedly the increased harmonization in the area of administrative sanctions. New minimum sanctioning powers[55] have been conferred to NCAs with regard to, at least, the breaches contained in Article 28(a) and related to the failure to notify the acquisition or disposal of a major holding. The phrase 'at least' leaves NCAs leeway to adopt the same measures on a wider scale and can serve as a first model for further harmonization in this area.

The administrative pecuniary sanctions provided under Article 28(b) are up to €10 million or 5% of the total annual turnover for legal persons and up to €2 million for natural persons. In both cases, sanctions can be up to twice the amount of the profits resulting from the breach, if such profits can be determined. Paragraph 3 of the same Article mentions that Member States can provide for higher levels of pecuniary sanctions, along with additional sanctions or measures. Therefore, it will be very interesting to see whether national laws will adhere to these new series of administrative sanctions, apart from the two types of breaches mentioned under Article 28(a) for which the sanctions are compulsory, and gradually converge with regard to the severity, frequency and intensity of sanctions imposed.

---

[53] Article L. 247-2-I, *Code de commerce*.

[54] Article 28(1)(2), TD.

[55] Public statement, order to cease the conduct that triggered the breach, and to avoid repetition of similar activities, as well as administrative pecuniary sanctions.

National laws must also provide that the violation of notification rules may result in disenfranchisement of voting rights attached to shares.[56] Member States can provide that such sanctions apply only to the most serious breaches.[57] Disenfranchisement is currently treated very differently by various national laws, some of them opting for NCA intervention and others for a judicial imposition of such sanctions, as mentioned above. It seems that the TD opts for the former, since the obligation to provide for such sanctions is included under the NCA sanctioning powers in Article 28. The diverging solutions for imposing such sanctions, the applicability criteria and their uncertain effect raise serious doubts about whether the TD's provisions are effective.[58]

In order to coordinate the exercise of sanctioning powers among NCAs, Article 28(c) provides a very useful guide that can be taken into account to determine the type and level of administrative sanctions or measures.[59] Indeed, the 2013 amendment accentuates the need for indirect harmonization by focusing on the conceptual elements of sanctions and measures and by attempting to converge their perception, interpretation and implementation across NCAs. This indirect harmonization effort is, in our opinion, a positive step towards gradual uniformity in the interpretation of the three sanctions criteria required in various EU capital markets texts: efficiency, proportionality and dissuasion.

Lastly, Article 29 aims to accentuate the severity and deterrent effect of sanctions through compulsory disclosure requirements for NCAs, which are required to publish every decision on sanctions and measures, while providing information on the type and nature of the breach, as well as the identity of the natural or legal persons affected by the decision. Aware of the risks involved in increased transparency in this area, the Directive also allows NCAs to delay such publication or to publish decisions anonymously if they believe that full publication would be disproportionate, would seriously jeopardize the stability of the financial system or an ongoing investigation, or would cause disproportionate and significant damage to related institutions or natural persons.

Chapter 7 has so far been dedicated to the notification of acquisition or disposal of major holdings and aimed to highlight transparency concerns among market actors and their treatment by EU and national rules. One of the main assessments relates to the gradual enlargement of the persons that bear notification obligations as well as on the financial instruments that are subject to

---

[56] Article 28(b)(2), TD.

[57] Ibid.

[58] For a detailed analysis of various national laws in the area of suspension of voting rights, see M. Neville and K. Engsig Sørensen, 'Suspension of the Exercise of Voting Rights – A Step Towards Deterrent and Consistent Sanctioning of EU Transparency Requirements?' (2017) Nordic & European Company Law Working Paper No 16-25, at https://ssrn.com/abstract=2958677.

[59] The gravity of the duration of the breach, the degree of responsibility and the financial strength of the natural or legal person, the importance of profits as well as the losses suffered by third parties due to the breach, the level of cooperation with the NCA and any eventual former breaches.

notification, a regulatory evolution that should be welcomed. Information about major holdings relates to 'exogenous transparency' and relying therefore on actors other than the issuer to provide information regarding their participation in the issuer's ownership structure. Nevertheless, transparency concerns could not be limited to simple alterations of holdings since, upon numerous occasions, such strategies aim for obtaining control of the issuer[60] and potentially changing its profile, thus affecting a series of shareholders and stakeholders. In the second part of this chapter, we will turn to these control-related strategies.

7.3 THE EU TAKEOVER DISCLOSURE REGIME

7.3.1 The EU Takeover Disclosure Perimeter

Apart from the highly controversial provisions on board neutrality and breakthrough rules in takeovers (two topics not covered in this chapter),[61] EU law has endeavoured to introduce an adequate level of transparency into national laws, by maintaining a minimum harmonization spectrum and allowing Member States to maintain some of their distinctive cultural or economic features.[62] The efficiency of disclosure rules in takeovers is of vital importance not only to target companies but also to their shareholders, who need to receive adequate information so as to make an informed decision as to whether to sell their shares to the bidder. The Takeover Directive emphasizes the disclosure rationale via the concepts of market transparency and integrity for the securities of all the companies involved in or affected by a bid so as to prevent the publication or dissemination of false or misleading information.[63]

Disclosure rules are also aligned with the more general and permanent disclosure obligations applicable to listed companies during their lifetime (as analysed in Chapter 6), which continue to apply before, during and after takeover operations. The specific takeover disclosure framework must be ensured by Member States so as to allow shareholders access to readily and promptly available information and documents, at least in the regulated markets on which the target company's securities are admitted to trading, and to employee representatives of the target and the bidder.[64] Prioritizing the creation of accessible and quasi-instantaneous transparency in takeovers falls within the broader objective

---

[60] The Takeover Directive provides that where a person holds, directly or indirectly, voting rights that give her control of the company, she will be required to make a bid so where is to protect the minority shareholders of that company: Article 5.

[61] L. Enriques, 'The Mandatory Bid Rule in the Takeover Directive: Harmonization Without Foundation?' (2004) *European Company and Financial Law Review* 440; T. Papadopoulos, 'The Mandatory Provisions of the EU Takeover Bid Directive and Their Deficiencies' (2007) 1(6) *Law and Financial Markets Review* 525.

[62] More generally, on this regulatory approach, see B. Clarke, 'The Takeovers Directive – Is a Little Regulation Better Than No Regulation?' (2009) 15(2) *European Law Journal* 174.

[63] Article 8(1), Takeover Directive.

[64] Article 8(2), ibid.

of EU law to inspire and maintain investor confidence in capital markets. Nevertheless, we must bear in mind that EU law has not attempted to define or to harmonize the procedural framework of takeovers, acknowledging persisting national differences.[65] The remainder of this chapter will seek to analyse the EU rules for minimum harmonization, together with some national examples that highlight the differences between jurisdictions and the importance of further reforms.

7.3.1.1 Disclosure during the Pre-offer Announcement

The informational transparency imperative prior to the announcement of a bid is mainly concentrated between the offeror company and the NCA. The offeror company is subject to a detailed procedure, with fixed and short deadlines that enable a prompt compliance-check procedure. This is important not only to ensure transparency so as to decipher the intentions of a potential offeror promptly, but also to safeguard the reliability of information that is subject to NCA control. During this preliminary phase, the applicable rules do not involve the target company, except for some issues; this regulatory stance reflects the reticence to oblige the target company to expose itself prematurely, given the lack of an advanced and approved bid during this stage.

One of the most important issues during the pre-bid period is the management of rumours related to an eventual bid that raises potentially contradictory concerns. On the one hand, rules need to respect the necessary confidentiality of eventual and ongoing operations leading towards the bid so as to enable its success. On the other hand, rules need to promote transparency of every intention or project to take control of the offeree company, since opaque situations during this phase may have a severe impact on the offeree company's image and operations, as well as on market efficiency more broadly. The Takeover Directive does not attempt to address this issue. Instead, in a very general fashion, it provides that Member States must ensure that a bid decision is made public without delay and that the NCA is informed of the bid. Member States may also require that the NCA be informed before the publication of such a decision.[66] The EU framework therefore abstains from inciting – or even forcing – national laws to establish disclosure obligations during the pre-bid period. Indeed, several Member States[67] do not dispose of a specific disclosure framework for this matter and rely on general episodic disclosure obligations, as analysed in Chapter 6.

The UK model has undoubtedly been instrumental in this area by influencing other national laws and by offering a sophisticated and modern framework. Rule 2.2 of the City Code on Takeovers and Mergers (hereinafter 'Takeover

---

[65] See, for example, Article 7 of the Takeover Directive that set the limits of the acceptance period, with some exceptions, as well as Article 13 that leaves to Member States the freedom to provide for national rules as to other aspects related to the conduct of bids.

[66] Article 6(1), ibid.

[67] For example, Spain, Greece, Italy and Sweden.

Code') requires a bid announcement when, following an approach to the board of the target company by or on behalf of a potential offeror, the target company becomes the subject of rumour and speculation or there is an 'untoward movement' in its share price.[68] This rule goes even further and requires a bid announcement even in the absence of a prior approach by or on behalf of a potential offeror. In this case, a potential offeror must simply have actively considered an offer, while the target company is the subject of rumour and speculation, or there is an untoward movement in its share price and there are reasonable grounds for associating these incidents with the potential offeror's actions (or inactions with regard to security or otherwise).[69] The notion of 'untoward movement' is related to general market sector movements, publicly available information, trading activity in the target company's shares and the time period. Nevertheless, the Takeover Panel[70] will take all relevant facts into account, not just the percentage of the share price movements. Especially for Rule 2.2(c), the accompanying notes mention that the Panel should be consulted at the latest in situations of a price movement of 10% or more above the lowest share price since the time of the approach by the offeror company. Moreover, an abrupt price rise of a smaller percentage could also fall within the definition of 'untoward movement'.

Even more critically, the UK Takeover Code has been an inspirational point also in relation to the 'put up or shut up' rule,[71] which gives a potential offeror 28 days, following the date of the announcement in which it is identified, either to announce a firm intention to make an offer or to announce that it does not intend to make an offer. In the latter case, a period of six months is provided, during which another offer announcement (or acquisition of interest in shares of the target company that would trigger a mandatory offer obligation) cannot take place.[72] The impression gathered from the UK framework is that the rules aim to force offerors to assume responsibility, even at a preliminary stage, with or without prior contact with the offeree company, of their actions or inactions. The motives for this regulatory stance towards offeror companies are various: firstly, these rules may be seen as a rebalancing mechanism of the takeover power, by making the whole process more cumbersome to potential bidders. Secondly, they may testify to the Panel's willingness to counterbalance the Code's 'strong bias towards the "facilitation" of takeovers'.[73]

During this pre-bid phase, the offeree company may also be subject to an announcement. This will take place if its board has been approached.[74]

---

[68] Rule 2.2(c), The Panel on Takeovers and Mergers, *The City Code on Takeovers and Mergers* (2016), at http://www.thetakeoverpanel.org.uk/wp-content/uploads/2008/11/code.pdf?v=12Sep2016.

[69] Rule 2.2(d), ibid.

[70] The UK's supervisory authority in the area of takeovers.

[71] Rule 2.6, ibid.

[72] Rule 2.8, ibid.

[73] D. Kershaw, *Principles of Takeover Regulation* (Oxford University Press, 2016), 179.

[74] Rule 2.3(c), ibid.

Moreover, potential offerors are not supposed to attempt to prevent the board from making an announcement as to a possible offer or the offeror's identity, at any time the latter considers appropriate.[75] The second category is when a purchaser is being sought for an interest in shares representing 30% or more of the target company's voting rights, or when its board is seeking one or more potential offerors and the company becomes the subject of rumour and speculation or there is untoward movement in its share price.[76] The sophistication of the UK framework can be seen from rules that subject the offeree company to disclosure for simply receiving approaches from potential offerors or looking for purchasers, so as to protect – even at a preliminary stage – its shareholders and price efficiency at large.

Other national frameworks have been strongly inspired by UK law in terms of intervening during the pre-bid period and imposing disclosure obligations, but they have maintained their own distinctive features. In France, a person may be required to declare its intentions to the *Autorité des Marchés Financiers* (hereinafter AMF) in the presence of reasonable motives regarding its takeover projects, especially if there is a significant movement in the target company's share price.[77] French rules do not specify the spectrum covered by the notion of 'reasonable motives' or what a 'significant movement' should actually represent so as to trigger the AMF's intervention, by offering the latter considerable discretionary power to force market actors to declare their intentions, including cases that simply involve rumours.[78] The General Regulation of the AMF, which determines the whole procedure, refers generally to 'large price swings or unusual trading volumes' that may trigger regulatory intervention. It also provides indicative examples of what could represent a reasonable motive regarding takeover projects, such as the holding of discussions between the issuers concerned or the appointment of advisors in view of preparing a bid.[79] The deadline for the publication of the declaration of intent will be fixed by the NCA and a news release will first have to be submitted to the NCA for approval and then disclosed publicly.[80] French law offers a more generic operational framework than the UK one, upon which the AMF can intervene and force market actors to disclose their intentions.

By orientating the debate towards the UK and the French approaches during the delicate period leading up to a potential bid announcement, it is striking to see how different NCAs are in their powers and co-operation mentality with various market actors. For example, the Takeover Panel must be consulted in advance by market actors, on numerous occasions, and engage in a fruitful and pedagogic dialogue with them, so as to filter the information that is subsequently disclosed to the public. Within this dialogue framework, if

---

[75] Rule 2.3(d), ibid.
[76] Rule 2.2(f), ibid.
[77] Article L. 433-1(V), *Code monétaire et financier.*
[78] Article 223-32, *Règlement général de l'AMF.*
[79] Ibid.
[80] Ibid.

a concerned person is not in a position to confirm its intention to launch a bid unequivocally, the Takeover Panel will not force it to disclose further its intention. This situation may take place with a company that may not be entirely prepared to launch a bid or its intentions may still be at an embryonic stage. Nevertheless, the AMF has the power to force the concerned persons to answer its questions and proceed to an eventual announcement by requesting such a response via an injunction,[81] or even through the courts.[82] French law adopts a much more interventionist approach during the pre-bid period, relying exclusively upon public powers, whereas the UK approach introduces a constant dialogue between the Takeover Panel and concerned persons.

These differences at the national level should lead the EU framework to harmonize disclosure obligations during this delicate phase by introducing an 'anti-rumour' policy and subsequently adequate disclosure obligations so that market actors can, in due time, understand takeovers that are about to take place.

7.3.1.2 Disclosure during and after the Offer Announcement

After communicating the offer document to the NCA and receiving approval, the offeror company is required to make this document public in good time. The boards of both the offeror and the offeree company will then communicate the document to their respective employees. The offer document shall be recognized in any other Member State on the market of which the offeree company's securities are listed without prior approval of the NCA of that Member State.[83] EU takeover rules pay attention to the informational exhaustiveness of the offer document that is addressed to all market actors, obliging the offeror company to disclose various types of information about the takeover project. The document must include at least the following items: the terms of the bid; the offeror's identity – and the identity of any other person(s) acting in concert with the offeror; the securities or the class or classes of securities for which the bid is made; the consideration offered; the compensation offered for the removed rights as a consequence of the breakthrough rule;[84] the maximum and minimum percentages or quantities of securities that the offeror aims to acquire; the existing holdings of the offeror – and of any other person(s) acting in concert – in the offeree company; the bid's conditions; the time for acceptance of the bid; the financing methods for the bid; and, lastly, the governing national law of contracts that will follow the bid between the offeror and the offeree company's shareholders.[85]

---

[81] Article L. 621-14, *Code monétaire et financier*.

[82] Article L. 621-15, ibid.

[83] Article 6(1) and (2), Takeover Directive. The NCA of that other Member State may also require additional information in the offer document so as to comply with information that is specific to that national framework, to formalities for the acceptance of the bid or to the tax arrangements relevant to the consideration offered to the target company's shareholders.

[84] Article 11(4), ibid.

[85] Article 6(3), ibid.

The offer document enables the concerned persons to be able to react in due time by eventually triggering the NCA's intervention instead of risking discovering some aspects and initiating litigation at a later stage. This document is particularly useful for forward-looking information included in the disclosure spectrum. Indeed, the offeror must disclose her intentions with regard to the future business of the offeree company and its own business, up to the extent that it is affected by bid, and with regard to the jobs and management of both companies. The document must also include any material change in employment conditions and, more specifically, the strategic plans for the two companies and the likely consequences of employment and the locations of both companies' places of business.[86] As a general assessment of the efficiency of such a rule, an external study has shown that employee representatives are not satisfied with this disclosure requirement since there are delays and deficiencies in disclosing such information. Most importantly, they have opined that there is no follow-up procedure to verify the reliability of disclosed information compared to the actions that the offeror will actually undertake in employment issues.[87]

Notwithstanding the undeniable importance of forward-looking information in this framework, the majority of offeror companies abstain from describing this type of information in great depth so as to avoid taking a firm position that will bind them in future business initiatives.[88] While such reticence for additional informational exposure may seem legitimate, since a very detailed strategy may become counterproductive in the presence of new circumstances, it is also true that transparency in this delicate period for the offeror is sacrificed due to a realistic – and not easily verifiable – level of uncertainty.

The offeror company is not the only one exposed at the informational level since the offeree company is also bound to provide information on a series of matters. Under a general obligation applicable to all publicly traded companies, it must publish detailed information in its annual report regarding a series of issues:

- structure of capital and different classes of shares;
- eventual restrictions on transferable securities;
- significant direct and indirect holdings;
- shareholders with special control rights and a description of those rights;
- all systems of any employee share schemes where the control rights are not exercised directly by the employees;
- voting rights restrictions and deadlines for exercising such rights;

---

[86] Article 6(3)(i), ibid.

[87] Sørensen, above n. 43, 329; Commission, Report from the Commission to the European Parliament, the Council, the European Economic and Social Committee and Committee of the Regions: Application of Directive 2004/25/EC on takeover bids, Brussels, 28 June 2012, COM(2012) 347 final, 9.

[88] For an overall analysis and some very interesting examples, see Kershaw, above n. 73, 278.

- shareholder agreements that are known to the company and may result in restrictions on the transfer of securities and/or voting rights;[89]
- rules relating to the appointment and replacement of board members and the amendment of the articles of association;
- board members' powers, and in particular powers related to share buybacks;
- eventual significant agreements that bind the company and may be triggered, altered or terminated in the presence of a change of control of the company as well as their effects; and, lastly
- eventual compensation agreements between the company and its board members or employees in the case of resignation or redundancy without a valid reason or termination of employment due to a takeover bid.[90]

All this information should be seen as intrinsically associated with the 'public company' status within EU capital markets. Disclosure is used to facilitate the visibility of issuers to market actors and to contribute to the multiplication of ownership-related operations among issuers, by inciting them to search for and target ownership structures that are sufficiently receptive to takeover projects. Although this disclosure obligation is expected to be applied in the same way across the EU, we must bear in mind that certain national laws have transposed the article by introducing a subjective element that depends on a company's discretion, at the expense of transparency.

For example, French law provides that this obligation is applicable to publicly traded companies who are expected to expose and, if applicable, explain the above-mentioned informational items, but on the condition that they are susceptible to have an effect (*incidence*) in a takeover scenario.[91] First of all, companies have the discretion to evaluate the rationale for disclosure in this area. Secondly, the concept of 'effect' is not explained further so as to constrain companies to disclose this type of information. Thirdly, it is difficult to decipher the exact content of an eventual explanation of these informational items by companies since most of them will prefer a simple description of the items that must be disclosed, whereas others may opt for a truly pedagogic explanation for the benefit of market actors. The need to increase the harmonization level for this type of disclosure is therefore clear in order to eliminate persisting discrepancies among national laws for the benefit of transparency and market actors interested in corporate control operations.

---

[89] Notwithstanding the informational usefulness of such a requirement, it is also true that it will not always be feasible for the company to determine such agreements in advance as the annual report will be published before the time of their bid. Clarke has opined that this requirement could be extended to expect disclosure by shareholders to the company and to the public of such arrangements upon their occurrence; nevertheless, this would constitute a considerable disclosure obligation and should be treated with caution: B. Clarke, 'Reinforcing the Market for Corporate Control' (2011) 22 *European Business Law Review* 517.

[90] Article 10, ibid.

[91] Article L. 225-100-3, *Code de commerce*.

The offeree company is also obliged to express its opinion on the bid once an announcement has been made about an offer. Indeed, its board must prepare and publish a document including its opinion and the reasons on which this opinion is based. It is also expected to express its views on the effects of the implementation of the bid on all the company's interests and, more specifically, employment issues, as well as on the offeror's strategic plans, as explained in the forward-looking information, mentioned above and contained in the offeror's bid announcement. The board of the offeree company is also supposed to communicate its opinion to the employee representatives and may also append the latter's' opinion on the effects of the bid on employment.[92] The emergence of conflicts of interest may be inevitable in this framework, due to a possible replacement of the members of the board of the offeree company and the willingness to frustrate the bid, and this may be reflected upon the information contained in the board's document containing its opinion of the bid.

National laws have endeavoured to enhance the informational quality of this document, in the presence of eventual conflicts of interest, by requiring or encouraging companies to solicit independent experts before they publish their opinion. For example, French law requires the appointment of an independent appraiser if the transaction is likely to cause conflicts of interest within the board of directors, supervisory board or governing body, risking to impair the objectivity of their opinion or to jeopardize the fair treatment of shareholders of the offeree company.[93] The independent appraiser will prepare a report on the financial terms of the offer or transaction including a statement of independence,[94] and the offeree company will then have to distribute the report at least ten trading days before the general meeting convened for the authorization of the transaction.[95] French law moved to compulsory appointment of an independent appraiser when transposing the Takeover Directive, since before that period, such an appointment was optional and rare. Nevertheless, the overall efficiency of this requirement may be overestimated, since the offeree company's board may assume responsibility for not disclosing certain information in the independent appraiser's report in order to protect its legitimate interests and on the condition that such an omission of disclosure is unlikely to mislead the public.[96] The definition of 'legitimate interests', as well as the likelihood of not misleading the public by not disclosing information, contains a certain degree of vagueness and may also be used by offeree companies to present a more subjective overall image about certain aspects of the bid.

UK law provides a simpler, but much more sophisticated requirement, for obtaining competent independent advice. The board of the offeree company must obtain such advice with regard to the fairness and reasonableness of the

---

[92] Article 9(5), Takeover Directive.
[93] Article 261-1, *Règlement général de l'AMF.* The same Article also contains a non-exhaustive list of situations that may constitute potential conflicts of interest.
[94] Article 262-1, ibid.
[95] Article 262-2, ibid.
[96] Article 231-19, ibid.

financial terms of an offer, and must also communicate the substance of such advice to the offeree company's shareholders.[97] The UK requirement is broadly applicable and not dependent on the eventuality of conflicts of interest, whereas the French requirement only triggers this obligation for the board if there is a likelihood of such conflicts. The UK rule also provides that the appointment of an independent advisor may take place at a much earlier stage, compared to the French requirement, namely as soon as the offeree company becomes aware of the possibility of an offer. The transposition of the Takeover Directive and additional independence requirements therefore continue to vary among Member States, by offering a variable degree of information quality after an offer announcement has taken place.

7.3.1.3 Acting in Concert

Acting in concert has traditionally been conceived as a facilitating and successful method for obtaining consolidated control of a target company or frustrating an offer through collective and organized shareholder action. This action may take the form of an express or tacit, oral or written agreement between natural or legal persons.[98] The Takeover Directive has opted for a broadly formulated definition that includes as many coordinated actions as possible in this framework to ensure a higher level of transparency applicable to a wider spectrum of market actors. National laws continue to interpret the features and treatment of such actions by takeover rules in a diversified way, depicting – without any doubt – different political agendas about the merits and shortfalls of facilitating or obstructing takeover operations.[99]

Concerted parties may be on both sides, namely on the offeror or offeree company's side, depending on their respective objectives. Legal provisions must increase the visibility of both scenarios, so as to treat equally both offerors and offerees given the ramifications that takeovers may trigger on both sides. The importance of actions in concert in the area of notification of major holdings and, most importantly, of takeovers is evident since acting in concert can trigger mandatory bids at a quicker pace through the calculation of the total sum of voting rights not only by one person concerned but also by all persons acting in concert.[100]

When parties are deemed to be acting in concert, their disclosure obligations change. The criteria for deciding whether various parties are included (or not included) in such concerted action need to be harmonized at the EU level in order to provide equal treatment to the concerned persons in similar

---

[97] Rule 3.1, Takeover Code.

[98] Article 2(1)(d), Takeover Directive.

[99] For an overall analysis on the ongoing legal conundrums in this area, see R. Ghetti, 'Acting in Concert in EU Company Law: How Safe Harbours Can Reduce Interference with the Exercise of Shareholder Rights' (2014) 11(4) *European Company and Financial Law Review* 594.

[100] Article 5(1), ibid. The applicable thresholds in mandatory bids vary across the EU. The most common threshold is 30% (applicable in France, Germany and the UK among many other Member States).

circumstances. National laws continue to deal with actions in a contestable way, and this situation suggests a rather pessimistic view of the realistic prospects for convergence. A restrictive definition of acting in concert may actually facilitate takeovers by allowing investors to build up a significant position that may not be detected in due time by NCAs or, on the contrary, by blocking takeovers by allowing shareholders of the offeree company to successfully develop an opaque strategy so as to thwart a bid.

On the contrary, an overly broad definition of acting in concert may have harmful consequences since it may trigger several mandatory bids as well as disclosure obligations to shareholders who simply wish to exercise their voting rights up to a certain limit. This could, in turn, harm shareholder activism at large, since the adoption of apathetic behaviour would be less costly in terms of disclosure obligations or eventual mandatory bids. Therefore, the balance that needs to be maintained in the area of concerted actions in takeover bids is a very delicate one. The optimal balance between ensuring transparency to a wide extent and not interfering with constructive engagement with issuers may not be easily achieved. Some examples from national laws are highly indicative of the ongoing conundrum surrounding the practicalities and instrumentalization of actions in concert.

French law has traditionally adopted a substantially broad interpretation of actions in concert so as to increase transparency in capital movements and to alert issuers in relation to unexpected takeover bids. All potentially concerned shareholders must be extremely vigilant, even in the absence of personal participation in a supposedly concerted action, since they can be classified as a party acting in concert on a simple decision by the NCA – resulting in possible sanctions that they may face together with other shareholders.[101] In the highly publicized *Eiffage* (target company) case, the AMF determined the existence of action in concert between *Sacyr* and other shareholders[102] – and the ensuing obligation to make a mandatory bid – based on a series of facts that could not be seen as a fortuitous conjunction of individual and autonomous operations and could only be explained within the ambit of a strategy aiming to gain control of *Eiffage*. Indeed, it was impossible to prove an agreement among the shareholders to form part of an action in concert, but the AMF – and the *Cour d'Appel de Paris*[103] – interpreted a series of facts in

---

[101] See, for example, the *De Dietrich* case where the *Commission des opérations de Bourse* (*COB*) – *AMF*'s predecessor – sanctioned two shareholders (*Wyser-Pratte* and *Verneuil Finance*) who were supposedly acting in concert for not notifying the acquisition of shares which had nevertheless taken place only in the case of one of them (*Wyser-Pratte*): COB, 15 June 1999, *Rapport annuel COB 1999*, 110. *Verneuil Finance* (the other shareholder) claimed that there was no personal participation in the supposed violation but the Court of Appeal judged that personal participation was irrelevant and that the sole element of party in concert would suffice for the imposition of the sanctioned by COB: *Cour d'Appel de Paris*, 1ère *chambre*, section H, 1 February 2000.

[102] Décision de l'AMF n° 207C1202 sur la conformité du projet d'offre publique d'échange visant les actions de la société Eiffage, 26 June 2007.

[103] *Cour d'Appel de Paris*, 1ère *chambre*, section H, 2 April 2008.

a very extensive and vague way so as to decide that such action existed and was expressed at *Eiffage*'s general meeting when *Sacyr* aimed to merge the two companies.

The same *lato sensu* interpretation was observed in the *Gecina* case. Three parties had signed a separation agreement aiming to reshape *Gecina*'s shareholding structure for the benefit of two of these parties. The AMF[104] – and subsequently the *Cour d'Appel de Paris*[105] and the *Cour de cassation*[106] – concluded that an action in concert existed between two of these three shareholders, compelling them to launch a mandatory bid. The line of reasoning seems contestable since a separation agreement, denoting a separation trend and not a concerted one among shareholders, is nevertheless considered able to trigger a common, solid and binding behaviour for the acquisition and exercise the voting rights in this case. The regulator and the courts proceed to an analysis that extracts fragmented features of a separation agreement, which may show some elements of concerted action, and generalizes their importance by concluding that action in concert actually does exist.

What becomes clear from the *Eiffage* and *Gecina* cases is that the focus of regulators and the courts is not on the existence of a common objective regarding a target company – which should be the only reliable criterion to decide whether action in concert exists – but regarding shareholders themselves. The extensive interpretation of the pursuit of a common objective, so as to qualify an action in concert, is therefore related to all types of common objectives that may be of interest to shareholders. Regrettably, under this interpretation spectrum, numerous instances will be seen as action in concert, triggering obligations to make mandatory bids, whereas these actions should be seen simply as various facets of shareholder activism and engagement within the company.[107]

It is also notable that in French law there is a series of mechanisms to increase transparency of actions in concert. For example, the AMF may force concerned persons to disclose their supposedly common objective, within the ambit of an action in concert, through injunctions[108] or it may even trigger the intervention of the President of the *Tribunal de grande instance de Paris* so as to seek to put an end to any irregularities.[109] Moreover, supposedly involved parties in an action in concert may be forced to declare such action by any other interested party that considers that her interests are threatened by the opacity of

---

[104] Décision de l'AMF n° 207C2792 sur la conformité du projet d'offre publique de rachat initiée par la société sur ses propres actions, *Société Gecina*, 13 December 2007.

[105] *Cour d'Appel de Paris*, 1ère *chambre*, section H, 24 June 2008.

[106] *Cass. com.*, 27 October 2009, *pourvois* n° 08-17782, n° 08-18779 et n° 08-18819.

[107] P-H. Leroy, 'Démocratie actionnariale et action de concert' (2007) 3 *Revue Trimestrielle de Droit Financier* 38.

[108] Article L. 621-14, *Code monétaire et financier*.

[109] See, for example, *Tribunal de grande instance de Paris*, ord. prés., 13 July 2005, unpublished; confirmed by the *Cour d'appel de Paris*, 14ème *chambre*, section A, 19 October 2005.

such strategies, such as minority shareholders, and seeks such declarations so as to oblige these parties to assume their responsibility and proceed with a mandatory bid.[110]

German law had traditionally followed a stricter interpretation of actions in concert, by allowing actions to be classified as such only in instances where they were taking place at the general meeting of the target company.[111] Although an optimistic assessment could be made of this approach, which seems more rational than the French one, when supposed actions in concert are deciphered, the German legislative framework[112] defines action in concert as any type of behaviour among shareholders, including coordination actions before the general meeting of the target company or even independently from the acquisition of voting rights. This extensive interpretation includes any instances beyond formal agreements that may risk creating an even more hazardous interpretational framework in German takeover law. Such a broadly formulated provision could also be seen as testimony of a political will to counterbalance the strict judicial interpretation of supposed actions in concert.[113]

UK law seems to strike a more sophisticated balance between the need to force shareholders to make a mandatory bid, while leaving them the necessary discretionary space to engage with each other and with the company without risking being viewed as participating in a concerted action. Indeed, Rule 9.1 of the Takeover Code only requires an agreement or understanding between shareholders in respect to a board control-seeking proposal whose result would be that future acquisitions of interests in shares could give rise to an offer obligation. It should also be noted that unlike other national frameworks, the Takeover Panel does not normally consider shareholders voting together on a resolution to be indicative of an action in concert.

This overview of French, German and UK rules aims to highlight not only the current differences among these national laws but, most importantly, the various political agendas that over the years have shaped the degree of restriction (or flexibility) of shareholder movements within publicly traded companies by an extensive (or strict) interpretation of actions in concert. The need to secure issuers from concerted shareholder action seems to prevail across the EU, driving us to the conclusion that a common legislative approach at the EU level seems unrealistic.[114]

---

[110] See, for example, *Cour d'appel de Paris*, 1ère chambre, section H, 20 February 1998.

[111] *Bundesgerichtshof*, 18 September 2006, BGHZ 169, 98.

[112] § 30(2), *Wertpapiererwerbs – und Übernahmegesetz*, *(WpÜG)*, 20 December 2001, BGBl. I, 3822.

[113] H. Baum, 'The Adverse Effects of Politically Induced Capital Markets Legislation on Corporate Governance: The German Takeover Act of 2001 and the "Risk Limitation Act" of 2008' (2009) 1 *Revue Trimestrielle de Droit Financier* 152.

[114] The European Securities Markets Expert Group (ESME) emphasized the need for a harmonized approach in this area by mentioning that '*[d]e facto* the directive should be considered by member states and NCAs, with respect to the acting in concert notion, as a maximum harmonization one': ESME, 'Preliminary views on the definition of "acting in concert" between the Transparency Directive and the Takeover Bids Directive',

More recently, ESMA issued a public statement on information in the area of acting in concert, aiming to assist institutional investors in their activities in relation to their eventual classification as acting in concert.[115] A 'White List' of activities was drawn up, encouraging shareholders to consult NCAs for guidance as early as possible regarding these matters. These activities relate to cooperation among shareholders that will not, 'in and of itself', lead to a conclusion that there is a concerted action. Examples are entering into discussions about possible matters to be raised with the company's board, making presentations to the company's board about company policies, practices or actions, exercising shareholder rights or agreeing to vote the same way on a particular resolution (other than in relation to the appointment of board members).[116] The ESMA statement also mentions that NCAs will take into consideration all relevant factors when deciding on the eventual existence of an action in concert, with each case being determined based on its own particular facts.

Although the objectives of convergence and enhancement of shareholder activism are laudable and aim for the creation of a balanced legislative framework, we must bear in mind that the ESMA statement is not legally binding. Moreover, it acknowledges the inherent limitations arising from the various national rules and their implementation methods by NCAs. Notwithstanding the above-mentioned divergent political agendas, which still seem to be insurmountable, national laws will need to adopt a common binding approach in the future on how to classify actions in concert. This will allow shareholders to fully explore and make use of their rights without the risk of triggering obligations to make mandatory offers.

7.3.2 The Enforcement of Takeover Disclosure Rules

7.3.2.1 The Neutralizing Sanctions of Opaque Practices

Enforcement in the area of takeover rules is left up to Member States. The Takeover Directive requires effective, proportionate and dissuasive sanctions regardless of their type.[117] Nevertheless, going beyond the classic categorization of administrative, civil and criminal sanctions,[118] a different type of sanction has emerged in the area of takeovers, aiming to neutralize the effects of opaque practices in order to protect concerned parties from the lack of transparency. For example, French law provides that agreement clauses that allow preferential terms and conditions to be applied to the sale and purchase of shares, amounting to at least 0.5% of the capital of voting rights of a listed company, must be submitted to the company and the AMF within five trading

---

17 November 2008, at http://ec.europa.eu/internal_market/securities/docs/esme/acting_in_concert_20081117_en.pdf.

[115] ESMA, 'Information on shareholder cooperation and acting in concert under the Takeover Bids Directive', 20 June 2014, ESMA/2014/677.

[116] Ibid., 5.

[117] Article 17, Takeover Directive.

[118] See Section 7.3.3.2.

days following the agreement. If such disclosure does not take place, the effects of these clauses are suspended and the concerned parties are not bound by their undertakings.[119]

Moreover, once a draft offer has been filed with the AMF, restrictive clauses with a potential impact upon the assessment of the offer or its outcome must be disclosed to the parties concerned by the offer, the AMF and the public; non-declaration faces the same sanctions in this case.[120] It is also plausible to question whether actions in concert could potentially be neutralized if they are not declared, since they present an affinity with agreement clauses allowing for preferential terms and conditions applicable to the sale and purchase of shares. The final decision must be made by the AMF, which has the power to classify any sort of agreement as an action in concert and can suspend its effects. Regrettably enough, the AMF has only infrequently exercised this power.[121] Disclosure therefore becomes a validity criterion for these types of activities, and suspending their effects is a means to stabilize the market from undesirable effects of non-declared strategies.

7.3.2.2 Repressive Sanctions
Apart from the possibility of using civil liability and criminal sanctions in the area of takeovers in order to achieve high levels of dissuasion and deterrence, it is striking that both types of sanctions occupy a marginal place in national laws. EU law has underlined the importance of interconnecting opaque takeover practices with market abuse, by indicating indirectly to Member States the possibility of using the concepts covered in the MAR[122] to protect investors from illegal practices in takeovers. Under a different perspective, it can also be opined that criminal sanctions may not be the most appropriate enforcement scheme in takeovers, as these may require a different sanctioning approach due to their complex structures and – at times – to the impossibility of tracing and sanctioning all aspects of illegal practices. For example, criminal sanctions could be applicable for lack of disclosure in takeover strategies under the general framework of ad hoc disclosure obligations that prohibit the disclosure of false or misleading information to the market.[123]

The difficulty in sanctioning all information contained in takeover practices is that some types of information may not be covered by the broad ad hoc disclosure obligations. For example, although the description of intentions by the offeror company and its evaluation of the offeree company are included in this disclosure framework, other types of information (such as certain features of an eventual offer) cannot be included since they do not relate to the offeror company's prospects or situation. Moreover, the information needs to relate

---

[119] Article L. 233–11, *Code de commerce.*
[120] Article 231-5, *Règlement général de l'AMF.*
[121] See, for example, the *Audika* case, *décision AMF,* 23 March 2004.
[122] Recital 27, MAR. See also Chapter 6.
[123] See Chapter 6.

to shares admitted to trading on a regulated market for the ongoing disclosure obligations and related criminal sanctions to apply.[124]

Civil liability could also be relevant in takeovers in cases of losses suffered due to a lack of informational equilibrium that could have allowed in investors to make informed decisions. Civil liability regimes vary considerably at the national level, with some of them maintaining a general framework applicable to any type of deficient information[125] and others opting for specific and more protective provisions in this area.[126] Investor protection through civil liability is still at an embryonic stage in the area of takeovers even though this type of liability can prove to be very efficient, since it is perfectly aligned with the offeror company's incentives to influence the outcome of a takeover via an alteration of its image and intentions with regard to the offeree company. The well-known difficulties related to the proof of a causal link between the loss suffered and the deficient information, as described in previous chapters, are equally applicable to takeovers. The additional obstacle that claimants must overcome is that takeovers inevitably constitute complex strategies at both the operational and informational levels. Moreover, the multitude of factors that can influence investment decisions as well as the outcome of a control operation is considerable, and a clear link between the loss and the deficient information may not always be proven.

A potential reform at the national level would be the adoption of the German provisions in this area, by allowing investors to bring a civil claim without the burden of proof of the causal link between the offer document and the investor's decision to accept the offer.[127] In this way, investor protection would be an additional confidence factor for shareholders for expecting reliable information in offer documents. It would also correspond to the real impact that offer documents have on a series of market actors concerned by takeovers, since, even if a direct association between the content of an offer document and the loss suffered may not always be straightforward, the potential motivation triggered within the investor community from offer documents can be assimilated to the one created by prospectuses, analysed in Chapter 4. The reason for this assimilation lies with the assumption that both operations invite potential investors to rely on an unknown scenario that will prove to be conformant (or less conformant) to the initial predictions made by another company seeking to either raise capital (prospectus) or convince shareholders to sell their shares (offer document).

---

[124] É. Dezeuze et D. Rebut, 'Offres publiques d'acquisition et droit pénal' in Guy Canivet, N. Molfessis and Didier Martin, *Offres publiques d'acquisition* (édition *Litec*, 2009) n° 428.

[125] See, for example, Article 1382, *Code civil français*.

[126] See, for example, § 12(3)(1), *Wertpapiererwerbs-und Übernahmegesetz* that provides for reversal of the burden of proof of such causal link between the offer document and the investor's decision to accept the offer, by allowing investors to bring a civil claim in a much more facilitated way.

[127] Ibid.

The dynamics of these two operations have in common the creation of an investment trend and the need to protect investors more efficiently given the lack of proximity and familiarity with the initiating of the respective operations. Accepting, therefore, a reversal of the burden of proof in the area of takeovers would not be a controversial development in the area of civil liability, since it would align with what already exists in prospectus civil liability, where the 'fraud of the market' theory prevails and exempts harmed investors from having to prove that they relied on a specific document to make an informed decision.

An additional difficulty in civil liability claims would be determining the loss suffered by claimants, which would typically be categorized as the opportunity loss compared to investing in an informed way. Nevertheless, demonstrating a difference between the offer price and the price that the claimant could have benefited from during the sale of his/her shares, had the information contained in the offer document been accurate and not produced distorted effects on the share price, may not be a straightforward task. This is due to the numerous factors that could have influenced the formation of the share price during that period, and that could be dissociated from the takeover itself.

Acknowledging the limitations of criminal and civil sanctions in the area of takeovers, the regulatory focus is inevitably focused on the sanctions that NCAs can impose in a much more facilitated way due to their constant contact with involved parties during the takeover period. Beginning from the initial contact made between the NCA and the offeror company, the NCA has the power to refuse approval of the offer document and thereby to protect any parties concerned by such an operation due to non-compliance with the applicable takeover rules. Injunctions may also be used by NCAs in this framework, as we have seen in the case of the AMF, in order to force the offeror company to adopt a higher degree of transparency.

Administrative sanctions can also be levied after the offer document has been approved in the presence of deficient information and by applying the episodic disclosure obligations regime, provided in the MAR, which relates to the constant need to ensure accurate and reliable information.[128] All sanctions imposed in this framework relate to deficient information contained in the offer document which aims to influence in an undue way the shareholders of the offeree company.[129]

7.4 CONCLUSION

This chapter focused on the EU transparency provisions relating to any movement in an issuer's capital structure, both via the notification of major holdings and via takeover operations.

---

[128] See Chapter 6.

[129] See, for example, *Décision COB, Ciments français, Bull. COB*, 2 September 1993, n° 271, 93; *Décision AMF, M. Rombi et Stés Les laboratoires Arkopharma et Imarko*, 17 December 2009.

From a major holdings perspective, the applicable disclosure obligations are the principal motive for a constant enlargement of transparency across various actors and financial instruments that are related to issuers. This exogenous transparency shows to what extent it is important to strengthen the informational rigour towards market actors that may exert an influence on the informational equilibrium and the general operation of issuers through their decisions and capital participation projects. Issuers may dispose of internal mechanisms to protect themselves from shareholders with distorted incentives and undue influence that do not comply with the applicable disclosure rules. Moreover, courts and NCAs are also potentially involved in sanctioning the lack of compliance in this area so as to secure an appropriate degree of capital transparency. The main obstacle for further harmonization across the EU is the persisting national differences in approaching and sanctioning disclosure violations. These differences do not allow us to be particularly optimistic on the future of capital-related transparency. Further convergence among NCAs, especially in the light of minimum harmonization of administrative sanctions, should constitute one of the main items on ESMA's agenda in the near future in order to secure disclosure of major holdings more efficiently.

From a takeover perspective, disclosure serves the need to guarantee the reliability of takeover offers as well as promising perspectives for the market for corporate control. All market actors involved must unequivocally be subject to disclosure obligations before and during offers. This type of disclosure, of a much broader nature than the one imposed in the notification of major holdings, requires a much more prominent NCA presence during all operational phases that are susceptible to interest the market, ranging from the pre-offer rumour and speculation management, to the safeguarding of the entire takeover process until its completion. The different layers of contact between the offeror and offeree companies determine the degree of transparency and the rhythm of escalation of disclosure obligations applicable to all parties engaging in control operations. Nevertheless, as mentioned on several occasions, national divergences after the transposition of the Takeover Directive continue to compromise harmonization and transparency at the EU level. New forms of public interventionism in this area are therefore needed so that legal provisions can re-establish their influential role on market forces and secure optimal transparency in takeover operations. The reinforcement of civil liability and the constant presence of NCAs during these operations constitute two realistic ways forward for potential reforms.

PART III

Inappropriate Market Practices and Market Integrity

CHAPTER 8

Insider Dealing

8.1 INTRODUCTION

Insider dealing is one of the most emblematic and controversial issues in the market abuse regulatory agenda. Numerous theoretical and empirical rationales have been put forward for the legitimization or the prohibition of insider dealing. Nowadays, it is commonly accepted that insider dealing is a harmful activity in capital markets that should be prohibited because it destabilizes market integrity and hampers investor confidence. Nevertheless, the legal response to insider dealing has not always been sophisticated enough to tackle its complexity and technicalities. After several decades of a rather timid legal approach, EU law has attempted to introduce a minimum common framework to combat insider dealing and, with more recent reforms, it has now introduced a uniformly adopted, sophisticated and widely applicable framework that can be viewed as a positive step forward.[1]

Notwithstanding the regulatory advances in this area, interpretational issues around core components of the EU legal framework – such as the concept of 'inside information' – may still hinder its potential success and may require further fine-tuning. Moreover, the supervision of insider dealing remains a quintessentially national matter, as NCAs are expected to perform this role on an ongoing basis. This situation raises concerns for efficient supervision and convergence of monitoring practices across the EU to ensure a safeguarded functioning of capital markets from insider dealing practices. Cooperation among NCAs in supervising such practices, coordinated under ESMA's aegis, is crucial for the future regulatory stance across the EU.

Enforcement mechanisms have traditionally been left to Member States, and this decision has resulted in national idiosyncrasies, cultural perceptions of insider dealing and regulatory approaches to combating such practices through different types of sanctions. A recent wave of harmonization has been aimed at driving convergence, and it remains to be seen whether national laws will strive for more severity in adopting stricter provisions and in implementing them in a meaningful and more frequent way. Administrative sanctions have been the main focus of these reforms, aiming to foster convergence among NCAs.

---

[1] H. McVea, 'Supporting Market Integrity' in N. Moloney, E. Ferran and J. Payne (eds), *The Oxford Handbook of Financial Regulation* (Oxford University Press, 2015), 650.

Criminal sanctions have been gathering pace in the last decade, but only in some Member States and with mixed results. Civil liability still faces various obstacles at the national level and is largely marginalized. The variable degree of enforcement is a concern not only across the EU but also around the globe, since insider dealing is potentially harmful to all capital markets, given their interconnectivity as well as the ramifications of price fluctuations in the context of international cross-listings. Be that as it may, the legal response from various jurisdictions is not always similar, and further research is needed to foster convergence not only at the EU but also at the international level.[2]

8.2 UNDERPINNINGS OF INSIDER DEALING LAWS

8.2.1 Arguments for the Acceptance of Insider Dealing

As mentioned above, insider dealing has not always been viewed as a destabilizing, illegitimate and harmful market practice. Indeed, US literature has put forth a series of arguments to counterbalance an interventionist legal approach for these practices. First of all, various academics have opined that insider dealing laws are the result of a misconception since insider dealing relates to the existence of inside information that belongs to the company and therefore should be used at the company's discretion.[3] The existence of such property right should also allow companies to compensate managers adequately for their work since they will be incentivized to acquire and develop inside information that they can exploit by trading on it.[4]

This exploitation may also resolve incentivization, renegotiation of managerial contracts and other agency problems within the company by allowing insider trading and transforming it into a 'reward of success' mechanism.[5] Under this view, the legalization of insider dealing would also enable managers to become much more entrepreneurial in their approach and less risk-averse, since inside information would be more likely to be produced based on the existence of business risks that managers would be ready to take, knowing that they would then benefit from its use.

Legalizing insider dealing would also ensure an optimal disclosure mechanism for companies since they would be able to channel information at their discretion, without incurring the burdens of exhaustive and complete disclosure to the public.[6] In turn, this selective disclosure could also aid price

---

[2] For an interesting empirical study of different types of enforcement in Australia, Canada (Ontario), Hong Kong, Singapore, the UK and the USA, see L. Bromberg, G. Gilligan and I. Ramsay, 'The Extent and Intensity of Insider Trading Enforcement – An International Comparison' (2017) 17(1) *Journal of Corporate Law Studies* 73.

[3] See, for example, J.R. Macey, *Insider Trading: Economic, Politics, and Policy* (1991) American Enterprise Institute for Public Policy Research.

[4] D.W. Carlton and D.R. Fischel, 'The Regulation of Insider Trading' (1982–1983) 35 *Stanford Law Review* 857, 866.

[5] 871, ibid; H.G. Manne, *Insider Trading and the Stock Market* (The Free Press, 1966), 138.

[6] 866, ibid.

efficiency – by signalling to investors new information in a less costly way – as well as an efficient allocation of resources. An additional line of reasoning related to investors is that insider dealing is a faceless or victimless crime since, in a trading transaction, buyers and sellers do not know each other and transactions would occur in any case, regardless of insider dealing practices. Investors could also benefit from insider dealing since the share price could increase thanks to additional demand.

8.2.2 Arguments for the Prohibition of Insider Dealing

While arguments for insider dealing may appear controversial, it is important to look at these arguments seriously in order to reinforce *a contrario* the arguments against insider dealing that have served as a 'normative safety valve' for the creation and furtherance of a strict regulatory stance around the globe. Beginning with the view that inside information is a property right belonging to companies and should be used as they see fit, it is nowadays widely accepted that information is a public good that needs to be shared with the market so that various actors can make informed investment decisions. Contemporary disclosure theories also refute the argument about the merits of issuer selective disclosure. Indeed, notwithstanding the burden of continuous exposure to the market, compulsory and complete disclosure enhances price efficiency and secures informational transparency by avoiding destabilizing trends that may arise from opaque practices.[7]

The argument about incentivizing managers and resolving agency, renegotiation and compensation issues should also be rejected since there are many other corporate law mechanisms that can be – and have been – implemented to address these issues. Allowing managers to privately benefit from inside information cannot ensure resolution of the above concerns and can endanger the creation of distorted incentives, as well as moral hazard risks.[8] This can also amplify a culture of excessive risk-taking combined with an 'entitlement' to benefit privately from inside information at the expense of other (uninformed) market actors. More general arguments about the dubious moral aspects of insider dealing,[9] as well as its negative impact on business ethics, have been

---

[7] From a vast literature, see F.H. Easterbrook and D.R. Fischel, 'Mandatory Disclosure and the Protection of Investors' (1984) 70 *Virginia Law Review* 669; J.C. Coffee Jr., 'Market Failure and the Economic Case for a Mandatory Disclosure System' (1984) 70 *Virginia Law Review* 717.

[8] For example, if managers profit from negative information via the use of put options, they will pursue a counterproductive strategy at the expense of the company's value. At the same time, managers would be interested in exploiting positive inside information about the company. The potential exploitation of all different types of information by managers would then make them indifferent to the continuous success of the company and would shift their interest only to ad hoc occasions during which they could benefit from inside information (regardless of the positive or negative outcome for the company itself).

[9] K. Lane Schepple, '"It's Just Not Right": The Ethics of Insider Trading' (1993) 56 *Law and Contemporary Problems* 123.

advanced, aiming to highlight the overall ramifications of allowing such practices and, most importantly, the exploitation of information only to a certain
category of actors who have a competitive advantage compared to other
investors.

Other similar arguments have been put forward in the academic literature.
These arguments relate to the harmful consequences of insider dealing on the
allocation of resources and the cost of capital,[10] investor confidence that is
inevitably harmed by the perception of an unfair trading mentality being legit-
imized, and more generally, the creation of a volatile and disorderly market,
driven by distorted ad hoc strategies aimed at exploiting privately available
information. Although it is true that insider dealing is a victimless crime, we
must bear in mind that the loss of confidence in the functioning of the markets
destroys investment incentives, essentially 'victimizing' the market as a whole.

The above-mentioned debate around the legalization or prohibition of
insider dealing has paved the way for a new series of arguments based on
empirical analysis. These empirically driven arguments aim to decipher whether
legal rules have a rational existence in the area of insider dealing by employing
market efficiency criteria and by testing the effect of insider dealing laws upon
various elements, such as the volatility of stock markets, ownership structures,
price accuracy and market liquidity.[11] Notwithstanding the undoubted usefulness of empirical analyses in this area, the use of non-market values should be
preferred so as to decide whether insider dealing should be regulated or not.
This is because empirical studies are themselves based on market theories that
cannot be tested empirically.[12]

Regulating insider dealing therefore becomes a legal imperative, aiming
to ensure the proper functioning of markets, their safeguarding from illegal
practices, and the maintenance of investor confidence in the premise that the
markets offer a fair trading environment in a context of informational equality
and transparency.

8.3 LEGISLATIVE FRAMEWORK

8.3.1 Legal Sources and Harmonization Objectives

EU law moved to the first experimental approach in prohibiting insider dealing
practices in 1989,[13] following variable reactions at the national level, with some
Member States opting for hard law prohibitions and others for soft law recommendations. The next decisive step for a more sophisticated legal framework

---

[10] U. Bhattacharya and H. Daouk, 'The World Price of Insider Trading' (2002) 57(1) *Journal of Finance* 75.

[11] McVea, above n. 1, 641.

[12] 642, ibid.

[13] Council Directive 89/592/EEC of 13 November 1989 coordinating regulations on insider dealing [1989] OJ L 334/30.

was the 2003 Market Abuse Directive.[14] Together with other EU texts, this directive launched the first coordinated wave of harmonization.[15] Subsequent to the growing regulatory agenda that was driven by the global financial crisis and the *de Larosière* Report,[16] the 2003 MAD – which was considered a success but was somewhat lacking in ensuring supervision and enforcement convergence[17] – was subsequently replaced by the 2014 MAR.[18] This new Regulation followed – in most parts – the previous regime by extending market abuse prohibitions,[19] and was accompanied by the new Market Abuse Directive[20] that deals with criminal sanctions for certain market abuse offences, as we will see below.

The 2014 MAR also has the advantage of being the first single rulebook of market abuse, concentrating in a single source, by ensuring direct applicability, legal certainty and less complexity for market actors. This new piece of EU legislation emphasizes a series of prerogatives that justify a more concentrated and harmonized approach to market abuse and, more specifically for the purposes of this chapter, insider dealing. The notion of market integrity is pivotal and is based on full and proper informational transparency, market efficiency and integration. Another focal point that justifies the current insider dealing prohibitions is, according to the 2014 MAR, the unfair advantage obtained from inside information at the expense of third parties and the ensuing undermining of investor confidence.[21]

It becomes evident that the EU legal framework is based on market-oriented justifications, aiming to safeguard the proper and smooth functioning of the markets, to eradicate unfair practices and informational asymmetry, so as to

---

[14] Directive 2003/6/EC of the European Parliament and of the Council of 28 January 2003 on insider dealing and market manipulation [2003] OJ L 96/16 (hereinafter 2003 MAD).

[15] On the benefits of harmonization, see G. Ferrarini, 'The European Market Abuse Directive' (2004) 41(3) *Common Market Law Review* 711, 717.

[16] The High-Level Group on Financial Supervision in the EU Report, Brussels, 25 February 2009, at http://ec.europa.eu/internal_market/finances/docs/de_larosiere_report_en.pdf: the Report highlighted deficiencies in the enforcement framework across the EU and the need for greater harmonization.

[17] See, for example, ESME, 'ESME Report – Market Abuse EU Legal Framework and its Implementation by Member States: A First Evaluation', 6 July 2007, Brussels, at http://ec.europa.eu/internal_market/securities/docs/esme/mad_070706_en.pdf.

[18] Regulation (EU) No 596/2014 of the European Parliament and of the Council of 16 April 2014 on market abuse (market abuse regulation) and repealing Directive 2003/6/EC of the European Parliament and of the Council and Commission Directives 2003/124/EC, 2003/125/EC and 2004/72/EC OJ L 173/1 (hereinafter 2014 MAR).

[19] In order to encapsulate as many illegal practices as possible, the 2014 MAR extended market abuse rules to all types of trading venues, as well as to all types of conduct or action related to financial instruments, regardless of whether they did or did not take place on the trading venue.

[20] Directive 2014/57/EU of the European Parliament and of the Council of April 16, 2014 on criminal sanctions for insider dealing and market manipulation [2014] OJ L 173/179 (hereinafter 2014 MAD).

[21] Recital 23, 2014 MAR.

foster confidence in investing, and to control the existence and potential exploitation of inside information. This regulatory approach is in sharp contrast with the US approach that is concerned with the fiduciary relationship between directors and issuers. Via a complex *convivium* of case law,[22] legislation[23] and administrative regulations, US law rejects the EU regulatory imperatives of informational equality and market egalitarianism as the main rationales for the prohibition of insider dealing. Instead, under US law, insider dealing is prohibited insofar as it constitutes a breach of fiduciary duty.

This breach can emerge in different scenarios: first of all, if the person trading owes a fiduciary duty to the company[24] and trades in its securities, then this person is seen as breaching the fiduciary duty to the company's shareholders (who are the parties participating in the trading transaction with this person). Secondly, if the concerned person does not owe a fiduciary duty to the company, liability will arise from a breach of duty of confidence and trust to the source of information under the 'misappropriation theory'. Lastly, 'tippees'[25] may also be found liable for trading on inside information, but under the condition that that tipper has violated a duty (either a fiduciary one or a confidence and trust one, as mentioned above) in disclosing the information to the tippee and that the latter is aware of such a violation, as well as of the tipper's expectation to obtain a personal gain.[26]

Although the US enforcement system is much more stringent and more frequently applicable, we must bear in mind that this mixture of various legal sources for the regulation of insider dealing has created a series of interpretational difficulties for legislators and courts that could easily be swept away if the US framework opted for a clearer and more straightforward prohibition of insider dealing. An obvious example would be the EU approach, which is not based on the relationship that may emerge between the trading person, the concerned issuer and third parties (as shown in the three categories above) but adopts a market-based approach that determines liability based on the mere possession of inside information and the potential impact that such possession may have upon the market. Shifting the attention from a purely company law perspective, as is still the case in the USA, towards a capital markets perspective[27] would not only offer the US system

---

[22] See, for example, *Chiarella* v. *US* 445 U.S. 222 (1980); *Dirks* v. *SEC* 463 U.S. 646 (1983).

[23] Section 10(b) of the Securities and Exchange Act 1934 and Rule 10b-5 (a general anti-fraud provision).

[24] For example, company directors and officers (primary insiders), but also lawyers and accountants working for the company (temporary or constructive insiders).

[25] See Section 8.3.3.

[26] For an overview of the US framework, see M. Ventoruzzo, 'Comparing Insider Trading in the United States and in the European Union: History and Recent Developments' (2014) 4 *European Company and Financial Law Review* 554.

[27] For an overview of these two regulatory approaches, see P. Davies, 'The European Community's Directive on Insider Dealing: From Company Law to Securities Market Regulation' (1991) *Oxford Journal of Legal Studies* 92.

a more workable legal framework, but would also ensure a harmonized legal response against insider dealing at the international level.

8.3.2 Criterion of Inside Information

Attempting to define and interpret the notion of inside information proves in its turn to be an equally complex task.[28] Following the definition provided by the 2003 MAD, the 2014 MAR stipulates that inside information is any information which is precise, has not been made public and relates (directly or indirectly) to one or more issuers (or to one or more financial instruments), and whose public disclosure would be likely to have a significant effect on the price of the related financial instruments.[29]

Before embarking on an explanation of these three different criteria of inside information, we must remember that an additional layer of interpretational difficulty and confusion arises from the fact that 'inside information' is a concept used both for episodic disclosure obligations, applicable to issuers, and as a pillar of the combat against insider dealing. For the former category, issuers must disclose inside information that is related directly to them.[30] For the latter category, inside information can be information that is related to the issuer directly or indirectly.[31]

This slightly differentiated approach – among other elements – may create confusion for issuers who are expected to disclose as soon as possible inside information and at the same time safeguard the markets from inappropriate exploitation of such information by certain market actors.[32] Focusing on the notion of 'inside information', EU law has traditionally aimed to clarify each and every element of this definition to avoid divergent interpretations of the notion of inside information.

8.3.2.1 Precise Information
The precision of inside information has been subject to ongoing debate since it may be subject to various interpretations. For example, as a situation takes shape which may give rise to precise information, various steps may inevitably occur leading

---

[28] Chapter 6 dealt with the 'episodic disclosure obligations' facet of inside information, namely the need for continuous informational transparency as to enable market actors to make informed investment decisions. This chapter deals with the 'inside information' concept from the 'insider dealing' aspect, namely the need to prohibit market abuse, and examines 'inside information' when it is used to the detriment of other market actors and markets' reliability at large.

[29] Article 7(1)(a), MAR 2014. On a more general note, the same Article contains similar definitions for commodity derivatives [(1)(b), ibid.], emission allowances or auctioned products [(1)(c), ibid.] and execution of orders concerning financial instruments [(1)(d), ibid.] in an attempt to enlarge the applicability of episodic disclosure obligations in products or activities associated with various markets.

[30] Article 17(1), ibid.

[31] Article 7(1)(a), ibid.

[32] For a critical and complete assessment of this situation, see J. Lau Hansen, 'Say When: When Must an Issuer Disclose Inside Information?' (2016) Nordic and European Company Law Working Paper No 16-03, at https://ssrn.com/abstract=2795993.

up to the final event. The applicable rules must therefore frame the evolution of various situations that may give birth to such information and decide about the starting point that may constitute 'precise information' in and of itself, and should therefore trigger the respective insider dealing prohibitions at an earlier stage.

The 2014 MAR underlines that information of a precise nature is any information that indicates a set of circumstances, or any event that may have taken place or is reasonably expected to take place, and that is specific enough to allow a conclusion to be formulated as to its possible effect on the prices of the related financial instrument.[33] This definition is appropriate for the broadness of its scope, aiming to capture various interconnected circumstances that may relate to precise information.[34] It is also important to note that this definition favours likelihood in the chain of different events that may lead to a more concrete informational outcome.

ESMA's predecessor (CESR) clarified that the decisive criterion confirms the existence of circumstances or the occurrence of an event would be 'firm and objective evidence for this as opposed to rumours or speculation'.[35] With regard to the more delicate issue of 'likelihood', CESR focused on 'whether it is reasonable to draw this conclusion based on the *ex ante* information available at the time'.[36] The issuer's position is of course delicate since some provisional data might not come to fruition. It is therefore preferable to focus not on the inevitable element of unpredictability, but on the eventual risks that may arise from the exploitation of any information during that period so as to serve the market egalitarianism and investor confidence, as defended by EU rules.

The European Court of Justice (ECJ)[37] has also rejected the 'probability/ magnitude formula' whereby the level of probability required may vary according to the effect that certain events may have on prices. In other words, if the potential for affecting the prices is high, it would be sufficient for the occurrence of any event to be simply possible, whereas if the potential for affecting the prices is low, the probability of occurrence would need to be higher. This formula is not adequate in this framework since it creates further uncertainty to concerned persons by insider dealing prohibitions as well as the market actors affected by inside information.

Regarding the duration of events, the definition of precise information may be fairly straightforward in the case of events taking place in a relatively short

---

[33] Article 7(2), ibid.

[34] This follows on from the ECJ's ruling in case C-19/11 *Markus Gelt* v. *Daimler AG* [2012] (not reported). On this case, see H. Krause and M. Brellochs, 'Insider Trading and the Disclosure of Inside Information after *Geltl v Daimler* – a Comparative Analysis of the ECJ Decision in the *Geltl v Daimler* Case with a View to the Future European Market Abuse Regulation' (2013) 8(3) *Capital Markets Law Journal* 283.

[35] CESR, 'Market Abuse Directive Level 3: Second Set of CESR Guidance and Information on the Common Operation of the Directive to the Market', CESR/06-562b, July 2007, 4, at, www.fsc.bg/d.php?id=2011.

[36] Ibid.

[37] Case C-19/11 *Markus Gelt* v. *Daimler AG* [2012] (not reported), para 50.

period of time. Nevertheless, problems inevitably arise with situations involving multiple or long-lasting events, whose contribution to the information itself may be particularly difficult to discern. The 2014 MAR specifies that a long-lasting process that has an intention to trigger, or actually triggers, particular circumstances or events may be considered precise information together with all the intermediate steps of that process, as well as with the future circumstances or event.[38] Intermediate steps can thus be seen as inside information if they satisfy the above-mentioned criteria.[39]

8.3.2.2 Non-public Information

Inside information must be non-public, namely any information that has not been shared with the public, as recommended to issuers in Article 17(1) of the 2014 MAR within the episodic disclosure framework.[40] Once the information has become public, there is no reason to maintain insider dealing prohibitions since market informational equality is guaranteed and it is up to investors to analyse and use the available information.

A reasonable argument could be formed as to the extent of disclosure of information as well as the spectrum of recipients (for example, financial analysts/institutional investors or the public at large) so as to satisfy the 'public' information status and not to raise any concerns about the prohibited exploitation of inside information. It would suffice to say that if selective disclosure to a restricted circle of persons would indicate that the information has become 'public', this would lead to a legitimate use of the information only by some people and would constitute informational discrimination that would harm investor confidence. Such interpretation therefore cannot be allowed, due to the increased importance paid to market confidence and integrity at the EU and international levels. Disclosure to the public at large is the decisive criterion that transforms private information into public information.

Even if this reasoning is perfectly in line with the wider EU market-oriented objectives, would it be unreasonable to argue that selective disclosure to a series of actors, who can trigger a market reaction with their investment positions and therefore integrate that inside information into the affected prices, could be tantamount to making the information public?[41] Adopting such criteria to assess the private character of inside information may be helpful in some

---

[38] Ibid.

[39] Article 7(3), ibid. See the ECJ's ruling in case C-19/11 *Markus Gelt* v. *Daimler AG* [2012] (not reported). For an interesting analysis, see J. Lau Hansen, 'The Hammer and the Saw – A Short Critique of the Recent Compromise Proposal for a Market Abuse Regulation' (2012) Nordic and European Company Law Working Paper No 10-35, at http://ssrn.com/abstract=2193871.

[40] See Chapter 6.

[41] S. Gilotta, 'The Regulation of Outsider Trading in EU and the US' (2016) 4 *European Company and Financial Law* 631, 656; P.K. Staikouras, 'Four Years of MADness? – The New Market Abuse Prohibition Revisited: Integrated Implementation Through the Lens of a Critical, Comparative Analysis' (2008) 19(4) *European Business Law Review* 775, 783.

cases, but it cannot constitute a reliable and widely applicable method. Insider dealing allegations need to be examined on a case-by-case basis and in accordance with other circumstances that inevitably vary.

8.3.2.3 Information with Significant Effect on Prices

The significant effect of information on the prices of financial instruments, if such information were to be made public, is the third criterion of inside information. In EU law, this criterion is assessed from the reasonable investor's perspective and, more specifically, whether the information in question would be likely to be used by a reasonable investor as part of the basis for any investment decision.[42] Recital 14 of the 2014 MAR also specifies that reasonable investors base their investment decisions upon *ex ante* available information, and it is that moment in time that is relevant for assessing the eventual price impact. Such an assessment will need to take into account the anticipated impact of the information, by factoring in the totality of the issuer's activity, the reliability of this source of information, and any other market variables potentially affecting the financial instruments.[43]

This investor-oriented criterion exerts pressure on issuers, which have to perform a very delicate assessment regarding the possible effect of the information on the investment decision process. It is also important to underline the fact that issuers may not always be prepared to discern *a priori* the eventual effect of all types of information on the prices of financial instruments since the mere publication of some of them may give them a much more important character to the eyes of the public due to the sole fact that they become public. In other words, disclosure may exert a discreet – but non-negligible – influence on the price, corresponding merely to the public appetite for fresh news, even if its initial potential to do so, based on its content, would be less likely.

It ultimately remains a matter for NCAs to decipher, on a case-by-case basis, whether the criterion of significant price impact is met or not so as to trigger the inside information characterization. Of course, this situation bears the risk of generating slightly diverging interpretations across the EU, especially in the absence of a common understanding or of more specific guidelines.

8.3.3 Concerned Persons

The persons concerned by the insider dealing prohibitions are those who possess inside information as a result of being a member of the administrative, management or supervisory bodies of the issuer, having a holding in the issuer's capital, having access to information through the exercise of employment, a profession or duties (primary insiders), or being involved in criminal activities. The same prohibitions also apply to persons who possess inside information in a way that differs from the abovementioned instances, where they know or

---

[42] Article 7(4), ibid.
[43] Recital 14, ibid.

ought to know that it is inside information (secondary insiders or 'tippees'). When a legal person is concerned, the prohibition also applies to the natural persons participating in the decision to carry out the acquisition, disposal, cancellation or amendment of an order for the legal person's account.[44]

While these categories are sufficiently inclusive and aim to extend prohibitions to a wide range of market participants, it is doubtful whether – in the absence of more specific criteria – their interpretation will be uniform across the EU. For example, should a particular threshold for holdings in a company be established, or should any person with a holding be included in this category of insiders? Another layer of concern arises in relation to persons who have access to inside information through the exercise of their employment, profession or duties. Article 8 does not specify either the degree of connection to the company or the financial instruments affected. Given the widely applicable objectives of EU rules related to market informational equality and investor confidence, a *lato sensu* interpretation should be preferred for all these cases and no further criteria should be envisaged in order for the abovementioned persons to be subject to insider dealing prohibitions.

8.3.4 Prohibited Insider Dealing Practices

Following the categorization of prohibited insider dealing practices, the 2014 MAR refers to three types of violations: engaging or attempting to engage in insider dealing, recommending that another person engages in insider dealing or inducement of another person to engage in insider dealing and, lastly, the unlawful disclosure of inside information.[45]

8.3.4.1 Acquisition or Disposal of Financial Instruments

Insider dealing relates to the possession and use of inside information leading to the acquisition or disposal of financial instruments related to that information. The acquisition or disposal may be done directly or indirectly and for the inside dealer's own account or for the account of a third party. As mentioned above, buy or sell transactions based on inside information cannot be seen as acceptable market practices since they harm market efficiency, informational equality and investor confidence in market transactions. Aiming to include as many destabilizing practices as possible, the 2014 MAR also considers insider dealing to encompass the cancellation or amendment of an order concerning a financial instrument to which the inside information relates where the order was placed before the inside dealer possessed the information.[46]

---

[44] Article 8(4)(5), 2014 MAR.

[45] Article 14, ibid.

[46] Article 8(1), ibid. The same article also provides that, in relation to auctions of emission allowances or other auctioned products, the use of inside information shall also comprise submitting, modifying or withdrawing a bid by a person for its own account or for the account of a third party.

A further clarification of the notions of 'possession' and 'use' of inside information is necessary so as to clarify situations in which it may be legitimately defended that there is no infringement of insider dealing prohibitions if the concerned person claims that it only possessed but never used such information. Recital 24 of the 2014 MAR specifies that the possession of inside information implies its use when insider dealing takes place, but such presumption is without prejudice to the right of the defence. Indeed, the defence needs to maintain the right to rebut presumption of insider dealing, and the crucial question is to examine the concerned behaviour in the light of the purpose of EU rules, aiming to protect market integrity and investor confidence.

Following the interpretational pattern developed in the *Spector* case,[47] the 2014 MAR provides a list of legitimate behaviours whereby the mere possession of inside information does not imply its use.

First of all, the list refers to legal persons in two separate circumstances that constitute legitimate behaviour:

- legal persons have established, implemented and maintained adequate and effective internal arrangements and procedures that ensure that natural persons – who either decided on its behalf to acquire or dispose of financial instruments or had an influence on that decision – were not in possession of the inside information
- legal persons have not encouraged, recommended, induced or influenced the person who acquired or disposed of financial instruments on their behalf.[48]

Secondly, the list includes legitimate behaviours for natural persons in two instances:

- where they are market makers or are authorized to act as counterparties, and the transaction is made legitimately in the normal course of the exercise of these roles
- where they are authorized to execute orders on behalf of third parties and the transaction is made to execute such an order legitimately in the normal course of the exercise of their employment, profession or duties.[49]

The same article also provides a legitimate behaviour category for transactions carried out in the discharge of an obligation that has become due in good faith and not to circumvent insider dealing prohibitions. That obligation must result from an order placed or agreement concluded before possession of inside

---

[47] Case C-45/08 *Spector Photo Group NV* v. *Commissie voor het Bank-, Financie- en Assurantiewezen* [2009] ECR I-12073; L. Klöhn, 'The European Insider Trading Regulation after Spector Photo Group' (2010) 2 *European Company and Financial Law Review* 347.
[48] Article 9(1), 2014 MAR.
[49] Article 9(2), ibid.

information, or the transaction must be carried out so as to satisfy a legal or regulatory obligation that came into existence before such possession.[50] The same article also provides for legitimate behaviour in the context of public take-overs or mergers when inside information is obtained in the conduct of such activities and used only for the purpose of proceeding with the merger or the public takeover. In order for such exemption from the presumption of use of inside information to apply, the inside information in question must have been made public or must have ceased to constitute inside information at the point of the approval of the merger or acceptance of the offer by the shareholders of the target company.[51]

The overall assessment of Article 9, which deals with legitimate behaviours and distinguishes 'possession' from 'use' of inside information, is a positive one since EU rules now contain some very instructive examples that allow rebuttal of the presumption of the use of inside information. Nevertheless, concerns could be raised in relation to the (apparently) exhaustive character of this list. Indeed, it is not clear whether this is only an indicative list that allows for other examples to be included in this 'legitimate behaviour' category. It would have been preferable for the EU framework to specify if the 'legitimate behaviour' list is a non-exhaustive one.

Moreover, Article 9 itself provides that, in respect of the abovementioned instances of legitimate behaviour, infringements may still be accepted if an NCA believes that there was an illegitimate reason for the orders, transactions or behaviours concerned.[52] It will be particularly interesting to see how NCAs will exercise this provision in practice since the interpretational difficulties will be numerous so as to override the abovementioned classification of a certain behaviour and to deduce a straightforward infringement of inside dealing provisions.

8.3.4.2 Recommendation or Inducement to Engage in Insider Dealing

Another form of insider dealing prohibition is the recommendation or inducement to engage in such action.[53] The recommendation/inducement of another person to acquire or to dispose of financial instruments[54] must be based on the possession of inside information that relates to these instruments.[55] In order for the use of such recommendations or inducements to amount to insider dealing, their recipient and user must know (or is supposed to know) that they are based on inside information.

Deciphering the term 'inducement' is also necessary in order to understand the scope of the prohibition. The disclosure to a third party of the specific content of the insider information is not necessary, as what ultimately counts is the influence exercised upon its investment actions.

---

[50] Article 9(3), ibid.
[51] Article 9(4), ibid.
[52] Article 9(6), ibid.
[53] Article 14(b), ibid.
[54] Or to cancel or amend an order concerning a financial instrument.
[55] Article 8(2), ibid.

8.3.4.3 *Unlawful Disclosure of Inside Information*

The unlawful disclosure of inside information is the third and last pillar of insider dealing prohibitions.[56] It relates to the possession of inside information and its disclosure to any other person outside the spectrum of the normal exercise of employment, a profession or duties. The prohibition applies equally to natural and legal persons, as well as to primary and secondary insiders.[57]

In the presence of onward disclosure of recommendations or inducements to engage in insider dealing, unlawful disclosure of inside information is deemed to have taken place when the person disclosing the recommendation or inducement knows or is supposed to know that it was based on inside information.[58]

The *Grøngaard/Bang* case is particularly enlightening with regard to the interpretation and scope of this prohibition.[59] According to the ECJ, the prohibition is not absolute since it does not apply to the disclosure of inside information by an insider in the normal course of her employment, profession or duties. The ECJ is also aware of the fact that the rule can potentially cover very different situations, hence the need for a strict interpretation.[60] In other words, this exception requires a close link between the disclosure and the exercise of the employment, profession or duties,[61] as well as that it is strictly necessary for with the exercise of such employment, profession or duties to disclose such information.[62] Also relevant in this interpretation spectrum is the sensitivity of the inside information. The ECJ provides as an example the inside information that relates to a merger between two listed companies.

Since the exemption relates to the exercise of employment, a profession or duties, it is inevitable that national labour law and company law will be used, in the absence of harmonization in this area.[63] It therefore becomes a matter for national courts to decide whether disclosure of inside information is justified in a particular case, taking into consideration the national applicable framework as well as the criteria provided by the ECJ.

A perfectly legitimate disclosure of inside information made in the normal exercise of a person's employment, profession or duties is disclosure via a market sounding. Market soundings are communication strategies that are purported to measure the interest of potential investors in a possible transaction, as well as the relevant conditions of this transaction (size, price, etc.). The communication of information may be done by the issuer, a secondary offeror of a financial instrument, an emissions allowance market participant, or a third party acting on their behalf or on their account.[64]

---

[56] Article 14(c), ibid.
[57] Article 10(1), ibid.
[58] Article 10(2), ibid.
[59] Case C 384/02 *Grøngaard/Bang* [2005] ECR I-9961.
[60] Ibid., para 27.
[61] Ibid., para 31.
[62] Ibid., para 34.
[63] Ibid., paras 39–40.
[64] Article 10(1), 2014 MAR.

In order to be considered a legitimate practice outside the scope of the unlawful disclosure of inside information, the person disclosing the information must, prior to making the disclosure, obtain the consent of the receiving person to receive the inside information, inform that person that she is prohibited from using it or attempt to use it, and that she is under an obligation to keep it confidential.[65]

8.4 THE ONGOING SUPERVISION FRAMEWORK

8.4.1 *Insider Lists*

Assembling various provisions that were found in various texts[66] and attempting to reduce administrative costs for SME issuers,[67] the 2014 MAR reshaped the insider list regime by establishing uniform data fields and by offering a more flexible framework for SME issuers.[68] Insider lists are drawn up by issuers or persons acting on their behalf or on their account, contain details about persons who have access to inside information while working for them under a contract of employment,[69] and must be communicated to NCAs immediately upon request.[70] Therefore, there is no obligation to provide the list to NCAs unless requested to do so.

Persons included on the insider list must acknowledge in writing the legal and regulatory implications, as well as to be aware of the applicable sanctions for the violation of insider dealing prohibitions.[71] Insider lists assist NCAs in their investigation tasks of possible market abuse practices and at the same time serve issuers in their need to control the flow of inside information and manage their confidentiality issues on an ongoing basis.

The details included in insider lists relate to the identity of persons having access to inside information, the reason for their inclusion, the date and time at which they gained access to inside information, and the date on which the list

---

[65] Article 10(5), ibid. For more detail, see Commission Delegated Regulation (EU) 2016/960 of 17 May 2016 supplementing Regulation (EU) No 596/2014 of the European Parliament and of the Council with regard to regulatory technical standards for the appropriate arrangements, systems and procedures for disclosing market participants conducting market soundings [2016] OJ L 160/29. See also, ESMA, 'MAR Guidelines – Persons receiving market soundings', 10 November 2016, ESMA/2016/1477, at https://www.esma.europa.eu/sites/default/files/library/2016-1477_mar_guidelines_-_market_soundings.pdf.

[66] For example, see Article 6(3), 2003 MAD and Article 5 of the Commission Directive 2004/72/EC of 29 April 2004 implementing Directive 2003/6/EC of the European Parliament and of the Council as regards accepted market practices, the definition of inside information in relation to derivatives on commodities, the drawing up of lists of insiders, the notification of managers' transactions and the notification of suspicious transactions [2004] OJ L 162/70.

[67] Recital 56, 2014 MAR.

[68] Article 18, ibid.

[69] Or otherwise performing tasks through which they have access to inside information, such as advisors, accountants or credit rating agencies.

[70] Article 18(1), ibid.

[71] Article 18(2), ibid.

was drawn up.[72] The list can also contain other types of information that must be updated promptly in the presence of a change in the reason for including a person on the list, when new persons have access to inside information and they therefore must be included, or when already included persons on the list stop having access to inside information.[73] Insider lists must be kept on record for a period of at least five years after their creation or last update.

In order to reduce administrative burdens for SME issuers, the 2014 MAR exempts them from drawing up a list if they take all reasonable steps to ensure that persons with access to inside information acknowledge the legal and regulatory implications and are aware of the applicable sanctions for the violation of insider dealing prohibitions, and if they are able to provide NCAs with an insider list upon request.[74]

8.4.2 NCAs

The EU supervision framework for insider dealing practices relies heavily on NCAs. This is due to the highly complex and sophisticated practices in the area of insider dealing that necessitate a prompt and effective response by the legal framework. NCAs are the most suitable points of reference given their ongoing contact with market actors and their regulatory 'know-how'.

The 2014 MAR provides for a supervision system articulated around NCAs and ESMA. This system includes a series of powers, cooperation arrangements with ESMA, and cooperation with Member States' as well as with third countries' NCAs. The wide range of powers enables NCAs to detect insider dealing activities and they refer to, *inter alia*, the right to have access to any document and data, to require information, and to carry out on-site inspections and investigations.[75] NCAs are expected to cooperate with one other[76] and with ESMA in all areas deemed necessary for the purposes of the market abuse regime, and they shall exchange information without undue delay as well as cooperate in investigation, supervision and enforcement activities.[77] Cooperation with third countries is also a valuable part of the supervisory chain, and the conclusion of cooperation arrangements is vital for the exchange of information between supervisory authorities, especially since their arrangements are also facilitated

---

[72] Article 18(3), ibid.

[73] Article 18(4), ibid.

[74] Article 18(6), ibid. See also the light regime prescribed by ESMA, 'Final Report – Draft Technical Standards on the Market Abuse Regulation', 28 September 2015, ESMA/2015/1455, 62, at https://www.esma.europa.eu/sites/default/files/library/2015/11/2015-esma-1455_-_final_report_mar_ts.pdf.

[75] Article 23, ibid.

[76] Article 25, ibid.

[77] Article 24, ibid. NCAs may refuse to cooperate for investigation purposes or act upon an information-related request by invoking national security, adverse effects upon its own investigations, initiated judicial proceedings for the same case or final judgments regarding the same case: Article 24(2), ibid.

by guidance provided by the ESMA.[78] As previously mentioned, the main challenge for an effective monitoring framework is the gradual convergence of regulatory best practices in order to eliminate, up to a certain extent, the current divergent interpretations of the broadly formulated EU rules.[79]

ESMA will undoubtedly contribute to these efforts by coordinating related activities not only via its guidelines and technical standards but, most importantly, by its ongoing guidance to national NCAs when requested.

8.5 THE ENFORCEMENT FRAMEWORK

8.5.1 Administrative Sanctions and Measures

The 2014 MAR makes administrative sanctions and measures for insider dealing infringements stricter by enriching them in great depth and detail.[80] This initiative is particularly welcome, especially compared to the previous 2003 MAD framework that only required effective, proportionate and dissuasive administrative sanctions and measures.[81] The 2014 MAD's most notable characteristic is the introduction of new thresholds for pecuniary sanctions. First of all, for breaches of Article 14, NCAs can impose maximum administrative pecuniary sanctions of at least three times the amount of the profits related to the infringement, when the amount of such profits can be determined.[82] Moreover, natural and legal persons can be subject to maximum pecuniary sanctions of at least €5 million[83] and €15 million[84] (or 2% of total annual turnover), respectively. It is also worth noting that Member States retain the possibility of providing for higher levels of sanctions.[85]

The 2014 MAR thus aims to raise the minimum levels of maximum pecuniary sanctions, while leaving national laws the discretion to increase the severity of sanctions if they wish. Notwithstanding the unquestioned merits of such minimum harmonization, the introduction of minimums in pecuniary sanctions would have been an even more beneficial step to increasing their dissuasiveness across the EU.

Similarly to Article 28(c) of the TD, as analysed in Chapter 5, Article 31 of the 2014 MAR provides a useful guide to the elements that must be taken

---

[78] Article 26, ibid.

[79] For example, on the interpretational difficulties among market actors and national regulators surrounding the notion of 'inside information', see J. Lau Hansen and D. Moalem, 'The MAD Disclosure Regime and the Twofold Notion of Inside Information: The Available Solution' (2009) 4(3) *Capital Markets Law Journal* 323. See also C. Di Noia and M. Gargantini, 'Issuers at Midstream: Disclosure of Multistage Events in the Current and in the Proposed EU Market Abuse Regime' (2012) 9(4) *European Company and Financial Law Review* 484, 510.

[80] Article 30, 2014 MAR. On this new framework, see P-H. Conac, 'Le nouveau cadre européen de la répression des abus de marché' (2016) *Bulletin Joly Bourse* 71.

[81] Article 14(1), 2003 MAD.

[82] Article 30(2h), 2014 MAR.

[83] Article 30(2)(i) and (i), ibid.

[84] Article 30(2)(j) ad (i), ibid.

[85] Article 30(3), ibid.

into account by NCAs when determining the type and level of administrative sanctions.[86] It is clear that this alignment with the Transparency Directive aims to enhance indirectly a harmonization trend among NCAs, which are now required to start designing, interpreting and implementing sanctions with regard to a fixed minimum of circumstances applicable at the EU level. This is undoubtedly an encouraging step towards gradual convergence of the *modus operandi* of NCAs. It may prove even more useful than formal harmonization measures, which deal with minimal penalties, insofar as it could accustom authorities to a new way of thinking and calculating the severity of sanctions, adopting a much more holistic approach that may not necessarily coincide with traditional approaches.

The alignment with the Transparency Directive is also evident from Article 34 of the 2014 MAR, which deals with the requirement for NCAs to publish immediately on their website any decision imposing an administrative sanction or measure. The publication must include information with regard to the time and the nature of the breach, as well as the identity of the person concerned.[87] Also, in the presence of disproportionality with regard to the person concerned or of risks of this mobilizing the financial markets for compromising an ongoing investigation, NCAs may defer the publication, publish the decision anonymously or even avoid the publication.[88]

8.5.2 Criminal Sanctions

The signs of harmonization of criminal sanctions at the EU level for insider dealing are to some extent – but not overwhelmingly – encouraging, especially considering that according to the previous 2003 MAD framework, criminal sanctions were purely optional since Member States only needed to provide for effective, proportionate and dissuasive administrative measures and sanctions.[89] The 2014 MAD made criminal sanctions compulsory and implemented a minimum harmonization.[90] This welcomed evolution nevertheless applies only with regard to serious and intentional insider dealing infringements, leaving discretionary space to national laws to shape their criminal frameworks accordingly.[91] Member States have already provided for criminal sanctions for insider dealing practices, but the implementation of criminal provisions remains

---

[86] The gravity of the duration of the breach, the degree of responsibility and the financial strength of the natural or legal person, the importance of profits as well as the losses suffered by third parties due to the breach, the level of cooperation with the NCA, any eventual former breaches and any measures taken for the prevention of repetition of the breach.

[87] Article 34(1), MAR 2014.

[88] Article 34(1)(a)(b)(c), ibid.

[89] Article 14(1), 2003 MAD.

[90] M.G. Faure and C. Leger, 'The Directive on Criminal Sanctions for Market Abuse: A Move Towards Harmonizing Insider Trading Criminal Law at EU Level?' (2014–2015) 9 *Brooklyn Journal of Corporate, Financial and Commercial Law* 387.

[91] Articles 3(1) and 4(1), 2014 MAD.

problematic.[92] Criminal liability could be particularly difficult to establish in insider dealing practices, as proving the intentional element can be arduous.

The Directive provides that insider dealing and unlawful disclosure of inside information should be deemed serious in cases where the impact on market integrity, the actual or potential profit derived or loss avoided, the level of damage caused to the market or the overall value of the financial instruments traded is of a high level. Offences that have been committed within the framework of a criminal organization or prior commission of the same offence are also indicators of seriousness, without of course precluding national laws from adopting additional criteria for criminal liability in this area.[93] The limitation of criminal liability to serious offences is particularly unfortunate as further harmonization in this area would be particularly welcome and would discourage inappropriate insider dealing practices that can harm investor confidence, destabilise capital markets and have serious effects on the investor community.

The Directive itself acknowledges the beneficial aspects of criminal sanctions for market abuse practices as a 'stronger form of social disapproval compared to administrative penalties'.[94] Nevertheless, the level of harmonization introduced was minimal and with uncertain outcomes at the national level due to the remaining interpretation obstacles.[95] The same Directive also provides that inciting, aiding and abetting these offences is also punishable as a criminal offence, as is the mere attempt to commit any of these offences.[96] These new provisions broaden the applicability of criminal provisions and increase the deterrence of enforcement. Natural persons may face criminal penalties that must satisfy the criteria of effectiveness, proportionality and dissuasiveness.[97] The Directive also operates a minimum harmonization of imprisonment by providing that insider dealing and recommendation or inducements to engage in insider dealing offences are punishable by a maximum term of imprisonment of at least four years.[98] The unlawful disclosure of inside information is punishable by a maximum term of imprisonment of at least two years.[99]

---

[92] For a general overview of the pre-MAD 2014 framework across the EU, see CESR, 'Executive Summary to the Report on Administrative Measures and Sanctions as well as the Criminal Sanctions Available in Member States under the Market Abuse Directive', CESR/08-099, 2008, 34, at http://www.esma.europa.eu/system/files/08_099.pdf.

[93] Recital 11, ibid.

[94] Recital 6, ibid. On the effectiveness of imprisonment for the implementation of insider dealing laws, see J. Öberg, 'Is it "Essential" to Imprison Insider Dealers to Enforce Insider Dealing Laws?' (2014) 14(1) *Journal of Corporate Law Studies* 111.

[95] Indeed, it will be particularly interesting to see how Member States will implement these provisions with regard to the 'seriousness' of a case that should trigger the harmonized sanction levels. Recitals 11 and 12 of the Directive provide some useful guidance in that respect but room for divergence is still inevitably present.

[96] Article 6(1) and (2), ibid.

[97] Article 7, ibid.

[98] Article 7(2), ibid.

[99] Article 7(3), ibid.

It remains to be seen if national laws will make full use of these new minimum maximums of imprisonment and will raise considerably their standards so as to increase the dissuasiveness of criminal enforcement. The same text also provides criminal liability for legal persons[100] and, in addition to criminal or non-criminal fines, an indicative list of other sanctions potentially included in national provisions, such as exclusion from entitlement to public benefits or aid, disqualification from the practice of commercial activities, placing under judicial supervision, or court-ordered winding-up and closure of establishments used for committing the offence.[101] Member States nevertheless remain free to only impose upon legal persons the administrative sanctions provided in the 2014 MAR since they are considered sufficient by the Directive.[102]

The 2014 MAD also provides details with the various types of conduct covered by insider dealing prohibitions, such as insider dealing,[103] recommending or inducing another person to engage in insider dealing,[104] and unlawful disclosure of inside information.[105]

8.5.3 Civil Liability

There is no specific mention of a civil liability regime in the 2014 MAR, and the eventual provisions in this framework could only emerge from national provisions. For multiple reasons, civil claims for insider dealing cannot be conceived in a straightforward way. First of all, as it was mentioned above, infringements of this type constitute a faceless crime as they destabilise market integrity and price efficiency, but without the courts being in a position to determine which particular investors (claimants) have suffered damages. NCAs can trigger the courts' intervention via a restitution order,[106] but the same identification problems inevitably arise. Moreover, the inherent difficulty of proving the causal link between the insider dealing infringement and the loss suffered by investors means that any potential claim is bound to fail.

National laws have treated this topic in different ways, most of them having maintained their general civil liability provisions[107] and others having chosen not to introduce any specific provisions for this type of breach. It would be fair to say that national courts are still reluctant to acknowledge civil claims in insider dealing infringements, maintaining a rather conservative position, in light of the abovementioned difficulties. For example, French courts have

---

[100] Article 8, ibid.
[101] Article 9, ibid.
[102] Recital 18, ibid.
[103] Articles 3(2), ibid.
[104] Articles 3(6), ibid.
[105] Article 4, ibid.
[106] See, for example, in UK law, Section 382 Financial Services and Markets Act 2000.
[107] French law deals with these breaches under Article 1383 of the *Code Civil*.

either indirectly[108] or directly[109] treated the eventuality of civil claims in insider dealing cases within the scope of criminal proceedings, but with no success so far. In the *Sidel* case, investors claimed compensation and, although this was in principle acceptable by the courts, the damage could not be proved since the insider dealing was related to a small fraction of the listed shares and its impact upon the share price was insignificant. This approach restricts the number of potential claimants to the ones that were counterparties to the trading of shares affected by insider dealing practices.[110] This restriction makes such claims virtually impracticable given the numerous and anonymous transactions that take place, making it impossible to identify counterparties so that they can claim compensation.

Another solution would be to follow the fraudulent misrepresentation claim under UK law[111] in order for the victim to claim compensation. Nevertheless, the same identification obstacles would arise since such claims would require proof that, due to a false statement or fact, the claimant was intentionally induced by the defendant to enter into an agreement by relying on such a statement or fact. Such a link between the defendant and the claimant cannot be established in the anonymous trading venues of capital markets.

8.6 CONCLUSION

Insider dealing harms market integrity and investor confidence with unpredictable results for the future of capital markets. A strict, widely applicable and efficient legal response is vital to preserving the markets from inappropriate use of inside information. EU rules adopt a market egalitarianism approach that aims to ensure informational equality among investors, as well as to enhance their confidence in the functioning of capital markets. This market-based approach is in sharp contrast with the US one, which adopts a fiduciary-based approach with a series of interpretational difficulties. The EU model has therefore provided a convincing and sophisticated case for the combat of insider dealing practices.

The 2014 MAR, following on from the 2003 MAD, attempted to clarify the notion of 'inside information' which is the pillar of insider dealing prohibitions. Nevertheless, as it has also been mentioned in Chapter 6, fine-tuning is still needed as confusion regarding the context of 'inside information' and the various interpretations at the national level will continue to create uncertainties for issuers, market actors and regulators. The concomitant functions of 'inside

---

[108] *Cour d'Appel de Paris*, 15 January 1992, *9ème chambre, Société Générale de Fonderie*: the Court of Appeal merely mentioned that the civil parties in criminal proceedings had not claimed any compensation in the light of insider dealing offences for which the concerned persons were prosecuted, allowing thus an *a contrario* interpretation that would be in favour of such claims.

[109] *Cour d'Appel de Paris*, 17 October 2008, *9ème chambre, Section B, n° 0609036 Sidel.*

[110] AMF, 'Rapport relatif à l'indemnisation des préjudices subis par les épargnants et les investisseurs', 25 January 2011, 30.

[111] Misrepresentation Act 1967.

information' as to the need to inform the public on an ongoing basis and to combat insider dealing, arising from the use of inside information to the detriment of other market actors, will inevitably continue to drive a vivid debate as to their importance and coexistence in the EU regulatory agenda.

The arduous task of supervising insider dealing practices and safeguarding all affected actors and the market at large inevitably falls upon NCAs. Under ESMA's vital guidance as to operational methods and convergence benefits in supervision and enforcement of insider dealing infringements, NCAs will be in a position to gradually contribute to an indirectly harmonized institutional framework. The 2014 MAD's current harmonization efforts in enforcement certainly accentuate this convergence trend, albeit with some timid steps that will need to be further developed in a future MAR review.

CHAPTER 9

Market Manipulation

9.1 Introduction

Market manipulation has a long series of consequences upon markets. It affects price formation mechanisms by subjecting them to illegal practices which aim to destabilize the market while generating profit from price fluctuations (of the manipulated financial product or other related products) and moving security prices in a certain direction. The interference with the formation of prices also damages market integrity with regard to volatility which, increased by such strategies, can reduce liquidity and make markets less trustworthy and subject to systemic crises. Undoubtedly, at the heart of all these consequences stands investor confidence, which is adversely affected by market manipulation, with possible long-lasting deleterious effects on market viability. It is necessary to ensure that investors remain confident in the price formation mechanism which, despite its imperfections and unpredictability, represents the conventional wisdom of investment risk, commonly understood as a 'supply and demand game'. Determining what constitutes manipulation may be a delicate task since many strategies can appear excessively risky but do not actually amount to market manipulation, merely representing ordinary trading practices.[1] As EU law currently stands, manipulative practices are based on three large categories: manipulative transactions, dissemination of false or misleading information, and benchmark manipulation.

Another important question relates to whether regulation of market manipulation is actually needed or whether manipulative practices should simply be left to market mechanisms to continuously adjust prices, namely before and after manipulative incidents. Indeed, it has been suggested that market manipulation may not necessarily lead to profits – due to price fluctuations that may be independent of manipulative trades – and hence the need for a regulatory framework may not be evident, except for purely fictitious trades.[2] Adding to these assumptions, important cultural factors with regard to the acceptance of certain practices across different jurisdictions have also played a role in shaping

---

[1] E. Avgouleas, *The Mechanics and Regulation of Market Abuse* (OUP 2005), 108; L. Gullifer and J. Payne, *Corporate Finance Law: Principles and Policy* (2nd edn, Hart Publishing, 2015), 584.

[2] D. Fischel and D. Ross, 'Should the Law Prohibit "Manipulation" in the Financial Markets?' (1991) 105 *Harvard Law Review* 503, 553.

and maintaining divergences in regulating market manipulation.[3] Is it the vagueness of the concept of manipulation itself or the mere existence of concomitant factors in the price formation mechanism that can justify the absence of any regulation in this framework? In fact, neither scenario can be accepted nowadays. Numerous empirical studies[4] have supported that market manipulation does matter as, even if manipulative trading cannot ensure profits per se, the dynamics that it creates for other market actors – if the latter assume that the manipulative traders dispose of private information with regard to the security's true value – are enough to trigger price changes and generate profits for the person engaged in manipulation.[5]

An additional concern is the plethora of advantages offered to traders via manipulative strategies. These advantages are not confined to fixing the price of a single security for their benefit. For example, interlinked financial products in different trading venues may be subject to market manipulation not for the sole purpose of increasing or decreasing the price in one market, but instead for the benefit of other similar strategies in other markets. It can first be seen that market manipulation does matter and should therefore be subject to a rigorous regulatory framework in terms of both banned activities and effective sanctions imposed for violations. Nevertheless, in order for the legal response to these strategies to become appropriate, the contours of such practices must be defined. This crucial task may not always be straightforward.

9.2 THE INHERENT DIFFICULTIES IN REGULATING MARKET MANIPULATION

9.2.1 Defining the Contours of Market Manipulation

Market manipulation has never been clearly defined in a legal text, given the considerable difficulty for the legislator to understand manipulative behaviours, to distinguish them from legitimate ones and to position manipulation within constantly evolving market practices. The lack of clarity and the broad wording of legal definitions around the globe have triggered – quite unsurprisingly – vivid

---

[3] A characteristic example can be seen between the USA and the UK laws on this matter in the nineteenth century: US law – prior to the major reforms that took place with the Securities and Exchange Act of 1934 – had traditionally been reluctant to impose any liability upon persons being engaged in transactions purported to unduly influence security prices. Liability was largely left to the realm of private regulation, namely under stock exchanges rules: A.A. Berle, 'Liability for Stock Market Manipulation' (1931) 31 *Columbia Law Review* 264, 272. The difference was striking with UK courts already in the nineteenth century considering as fraudulent schemes purported to issue buy orders to sustain market prices: *Scott* v. *Brown* [1892] 2 QB 724.

[4] For an interesting overview, see T.J. Putniņš, 'Market Manipulation: A Survey' (2012) 26(5) *Journal of Economic Surveys* 952.

[5] F. Allen and D. Gale, 'Stock Price Manipulation' (1992) 5(3) *The Review of Financial Studies* 503, 508. Allen and Gale generally categorize market manipulation in three broad categories: action-based manipulation, information-based manipulation and trade-based manipulation.

debates regarding the contours of market manipulation and the desired legal framework for effectively monitoring and sanctioning it.

The main difficulty with market manipulation lies in setting the limit between legitimate (even risky or overly optimistic/pessimistic) trading and manipulative trading. Inevitably, each and every trade affects the price of a particular security or even other securities, or may even have repercussions upon other trading venues with linked products. It is also true that trades convey a certain message to other market participants, depicting a preference or dislike for an investment opportunity. Strategy in trading also forms part of the conventional wisdom of a 'skilled or intelligent investor', but we must bear in mind that market liquidity is largely facilitated by these practices.[6] It is thus particularly arduous for regulators to distinguish between the two settings and to move to building an enforcement case with (most of the time) very few elements in hand that could show a manipulative incident.

Several doctrinal contributions have paved the way for considerable reflection on the optimal definition and framework within which market participants could be concerned about manipulation allegations. In a highly thought-provoking study,[7] Fischel and Ross argued in favour of 'bad intent' as the decisive criterion for trade-based market manipulation, by excluding cases where traders with good intent cause severe damages in the market with their transactions, and thus making the whole accountability framework extremely subjective. The objective harm doctrine, which moves away from intent and focuses exclusively on an incident's impact on the market,[8] is therefore the preferred one since it encapsulates a larger series of incidents without tackling the conundrum of attempting to decipher the person's state of mind. Notwithstanding the attractiveness of this latter doctrine, shared by many jurisdictions, clear limitations arise with regard to drawing the line between legitimate (and beneficial to the market) trading and market manipulation.[9] Different legal systems have followed both approaches in their own characteristic way and with some slight variations that create a rather blurred image across the globe.[10] EU law has traditionally adopted an 'effects-based' approach, focusing

---

[6] See more generally W.L. Silber, 'On the Nature of Trading: Do Speculators Leave Footprints?' (2003) 29 *The Journal of Portfolio Management* 64.

[7] D. Fischel and D. Ross, above n. 2, 503.

[8] S. Thel, '$850,000 in Six Minutes — The Mechanics of Securities Manipulation' (1994) 79 *Cornell Law Review* 219, 288.

[9] 298, ibid.

[10] US law focuses generally upon 'manipulative or deceptive devices or contrivance' (Section 10(b) of the Securities Exchange Act 1934) and acts operating 'as a fraud or deceit upon persons' (SEC Rule 10b-5, general anti-fraud rule) which may risk applying to informed traders engaging in large transactions (although US courts have insisted on the demonstration of intent to constitute manipulation): on the relationship between fraud and manipulation, see Avgouleas, above n. 1, 113. There is also a provision requiring explicitly intent in the case of a 'series of transactions in any security [...] with respect to such security creating actual or apparent active trading in such security, or raising or depressing the price of such security, for the purpose of inducing the purchase or sale of such security by others': Section 9(a)(2) of

primarily on the impact of the alleged incident on the market. Nelemans has developed a slightly different and very interesting approach, focusing on the concept of 'unsupported price pressure' that creates societal costs and cannot be justified by sufficient information.[11]

9.2.2 The EU Position

Turning our focus to EU law, following the major overhaul of the 2003 Market Abuse Directive[12] in 2014 with the Market Abuse Regulation[13] and the new Market Abuse Directive,[14] market manipulation became subject to a more extensive and up-to-date legal regime with regard to technological and market innovations in manipulative strategies. There is no doubt that market manipulation includes (and will continue to include) a vast series of highly complex and sophisticated tactics that aim to interfere with price formation and the market's overall functioning. Following the initial 2003 MAD framework,[15] the 2014 MAR shaped a sophisticated but perfectible regulatory spectrum around manipulative practices based on three large categories: manipulative transactions, dissemination of false or misleading information, and benchmark manipulation.

One of the most interesting 2014 MAR and 2014 MAD reforms was undoubtedly the inclusion of *attempted* manipulation in the market abuse prohibitions.[16] The attempt covers of course all types of market manipulation, as defined in the 2014 MAR and the 2014 MAD. This extension of the regulatory scope should be welcomed as a complementary initiative to facilitate

---

the Securities Exchange Act 1934. Nevertheless, it has not been used extensively due to the subjective test and the difficulty in reaching the high burden of proof. EU law underlines the importance of abnormal or artificial prices by adopting an objective approach, and Australian law restricts itself to artificial prices having removed references to intent (although the latter keeps on being used by courts as a determinant factor to establish manipulation). For an interesting analysis on all three jurisdictions, see M. Nelemans, 'Redefining Trade-Based Market Manipulation' (2008) 42 *Valparaiso University Law Review* 1169, 1171.

[11] 1183, ibid.

[12] Directive 2003/6/EC of the European Parliament and of the Council of 28 January 2003 on insider dealing and market manipulation (hereinafter 2003 MAD).

[13] Regulation (EU) No 596/2014 of the European Parliament and of the Council of 16 April 2014 on market abuse (market abuse regulation) and repealing Directive 2003/6/EC of the European Parliament and of the Council and Commission Directives 2003/124/EC, 2003/125/EC and 2004/72/EC OJ L 173/1 (hereinafter 2014 MAR).

[14] Directive 2014/57/EU of the European Parliament and of the Council of April 16, 2014 on criminal sanctions for insider dealing and market manipulation [2014] OJ L 173/179 (hereinafter 2014 MAD).

[15] For an excellent analysis accompanied with very interesting examples, see M. Siems, 'The EU Market Abuse Directive: A Case-Based Analysis' (2008) 2 *Law and Financial Markets Review* 39.

[16] Articles 12 and 15, 2014 MAR ('[a] person shall not [...] attempt to engage in market manipulation') and Articles 5 and 6, 2014 MAD ('the attempt to commit [market manipulation] is punishable as a criminal offence').

enforcement, especially in the light of difficulties that NCAs kept facing in collecting information and proof in the ambit of their supervisory tasks given the high complexity of manipulative strategies.[17] More generally, such an extension is also welcomed since market manipulation attempts may simply be the result of a failed trading strategy that was not completed for various reasons but nonetheless constitutes an (incomplete but equally harmful) manipulation.[18]

Nonetheless, on a more critical note, it would be very ambitious to expect a uniform application of this framework by NCAs and national courts, as the wording of both EU texts is quite vague.[19] Even if by lowering the burden of proof NCAs and national courts can legitimately overcome previous obstacles to proving manipulation, it is also crucial to provide a clearer definition of 'attempt' to enhance the legitimacy of their effort, as well as to provide legal certainty to all potentially affected persons.

The sophistication of NCAs and national courts will probably be the only safeguard for ensuring a balanced approach is maintained in this area, since it is very difficult to understand when an attempt should trigger administrative or criminal sanctions. But even in the presence of regulatory/judicial know-how, the overall image will not be reassuring across the EU since other countries will continue to fall behind in deciphering 'attempts' and whether sanctions should be triggered for some incidents. At some point in the near future, EU law will need to further specify the theoretical and practical framework for attempts, at least to an extent that enables Member States to go one step further and take advantage of a perfectible but opportune initiative to tackle market manipulation.

9.2.3 A Dearth of Conclusive Empirical Studies

Empirical studies have not been particularly enlightening as to the particular features of manipulative practices. This is due to the extremely vast and complex structure of market manipulation tactics, as well as their constantly evolving nature that can be grasped and deciphered only to a limited extent. Moreover, most empirical studies have based their conclusions on a limited range of data (especially when attempting to categorize and theorize unknown or even well-known manipulation cases) given the considerable difficulty in

---

[17] As it was mentioned by CESR in 2009, '[s]upervisors may face some difficulties in building up cases for market manipulation stemming from the need to obtain enough pieces of evidence to substantiate the case, which is not always easy due to the complex structures [...] it is difficult for regulators to prove perfected manipulation': CESR, 'CESR's response to the European Commission's call for evidence on the review of Directive 2003/6/EC (Market Abuse Directive)', 9 July 2009, CESR/09–635, 7, at https://www.esma.europa.eu/sites/default/files/library/2015/11/09_635.pdf. See also M. Siems and M. Nelemans, 'The Reform of the EU Market Abuse Law: Revolution or Evolution?' (2012) 19 *The Maastricht Journal of European and Comparative Law* 195.

[18] Recital 41, 2014 MAR.

[19] E. Herlin-Karnell, 'White-Collar Crime and European Financial Crisis: Getting Tough on EU Market Abuse' (2012) 37 *European Law Review* 481, 490.

gathering such data.[20] Another more compelling argument against the absolute reliability of empirical studies is the plethora of factors that may give rise to certain trading tactics that interfere with the market, cannot be explained solely under the manipulation spectrum, but may nevertheless affect share prices. It is therefore the very existence of alternative explanations of certain phenomena in the market that makes empirical studies in this area certainly enriching but also subject to further debate. This leads us to the conclusion that empirical studies cannot, at least for the time being, act as the only reliable 'safety valve' for further regulatory initiatives that could be based upon concrete and verifiable assumptions.

9.2.4 Limitations of Disclosure Obligations

Mainstream regulatory strategies whereby the legal framework expects to ensure investor confidence and market stability are not perfectly suitable to tackle the idiosyncrasies of market manipulation phenomena. For example, disclosure obligations that aim to make practices or intentions visible, as mentioned in previous chapters, cannot easily be considered to be an optimal regulatory strategy in market manipulation practices. This is particularly true in the light of the nature of market manipulation incidents, which are expressed via actions and not disclosure tactics to the market. Disclosure therefore becomes irrelevant in this context and can only intervene when certain practices are deemed to be legitimate by the legal framework and hence disclosure obligations need to complement some rules to ensure that these accepted practices are well understood by both the regulator and the market actors.[21]

Moreover, manipulation may be carried out by a series of actors who may or may not be connected to the issuer of securities. Disclosure obligations may therefore be unsuitable for detecting potentially manipulative tactics at an early (or even at a late) stage, since these obligations are mostly focused on a specific number of actors associated with companies, such as the companies themselves, their directors or major shareholders. It is therefore troublesome to use disclosure obligations in an area which can be more efficiently controlled with a series of simple prohibitions related to the activities that amount to market manipulation.

9.3 TYPES OF MARKET MANIPULATION

Manipulative practices fall into three large categories: manipulative transactions, dissemination of false or misleading information, and benchmark manipulation.

---

[20] Putniņš, above n. 4, 952.
[21] For example, this is the case with buyback programmes and stabilization measures that will be analysed at Section 9.4.2.

Starting with manipulative transactions, the 2014 MAR covers instances in which a person enters into a transaction, places a trading order, or engages in any behaviour which emits (or is likely to emit) false or misleading signals related to the supply, demand or price of a financial instrument (or a related spot commodity contract or an auctioned product based on emission allowances) or achieves (or is likely to achieve) an artificial or abnormal price for that instrument (or for a related spot commodity contract or an auctioned product based on emission allowances).[22] Moreover, the same prohibition applies for transactions, order placing, or any other behaviour employing fictitious devices or any kind of deception or contrivance that may have an actual or potential impact on the prices of the above-mentioned products.[23]

Moving to the dissemination of false or misleading information via the media (including the internet) or by any other means, the 2014 MAR includes these types of activities in the prohibited market abuse practices due to their actual or potential impact on the supply, demand or price of a financial instrument (or a related spot commodity contract or an auctioned product based on emission allowances), or on the formation of an artificial or abnormal price for that instrument (or for a related spot commodity contract or an auctioned product based on emission allowances). The distinctive feature of this manipulation category is that intention is required as the person involved in the dissemination must have known, or should have known, that the information was false or misleading.[24]

The above-mentioned framework also includes prohibitions for the transmission of false or misleading information or the provision of false or misleading inputs with regard to benchmarks, including any other behaviour associated with the manipulation of a benchmark calculation. An intention requirement also applies to this category.[25]

The 2014 MAR also specifies to great length, but – quite wisely so – on a non-exhaustive basis, the types of behaviour which may amount to market manipulation in the area of manipulative transactions, as analysed above. The list includes the following types of behaviour:[26] securing a dominant position on the 'supply and demand' spectrum of a financial instrument (or a related spot commodity contract or an auctioned product based on emission allowances) with the actual or likely effect of fixing, in a direct or indirect way, purchase or sale prices or of creating other unfair trading conditions;[27] buying or selling financial instruments, at the opening or closing of the market, with

---

[22] Article 12 (1)(a), 2014 MAR. These techniques are commonly known as 'painting the tape'. The provision should not be seen as requiring the maintenance of price at an abnormal or artificial level for more than a certain duration in order to apply: Case C-445/09 *IMC Securities BV v. the Netherlands Authority for the Financial Markets*, ECR 2011 I-05917, para 31.

[23] Article 12 (1)(b), ibid.

[24] Article 12(1)(c), ibid.

[25] Article 12 (1)(d), ibid.

[26] Article 12 (2), ibid.

[27] These are known as 'cornering the market' and 'squeezing the market' techniques.

an actual or a likely effect of misleading other market actors basing their decisions on the affected prices;[28] placing orders – via, most notably, algorithmic and high-frequency trading tactics – with 'dominant position' or 'open-close' manipulative tactics;[29] voicing an opinion in any type of media about a financial instrument (or a related spot commodity contract or an auctioned product based on emission allowances) while having taken a prior position on this product without disclosing the conflict of interest to the public;[30] and carrying out any purchase or sale transactions on the secondary market of emission allowances (or related derivatives) prior to an auction in order to fix the auction clearing price at an abnormal or artificial level or to mislead auction bidders.

The 2014 MAR further extends its provisions by providing an equally detailed – and non-exhaustive – list containing indicators related to fictitious devices, deception or contrivance, false or misleading signals, and price fixation.[31] The non-exhaustive indicators do not necessarily constitute market manipulation by themselves, but they must be taken into consideration when market actors or NCAs assess transactions or orders. This testifies to the need to preserve a certain amount of operational flexibility for market participants and not to trigger market manipulation allegations in a quasi-automatic way.

---

[28] Commonly known as 'marking the open' and 'marking the close' tactics. Their importance is non-negligible and has been highlighted by numerous empirical studies that have shown that a significant proportion of manipulation occurs on month- and quarter-end days: C. Comerton-Forde and T.J. Putniņš, 'Stock Price Manipulation: Prevalence and Determinants' (2014) 18 *Review of Finance* 23.

[29] By actually or potentially disrupting or delaying trading systems, by creating actual or potential obstacles to the identification of genuine orders on trading systems (usually called 'quote stuffing') or by emitting (or being likely to emit) false or misleading signals with regard to the 'supply and demand' spectrum of a financial instrument.

[30] Usually referred to as 'scalping'.

[31] Annex I, ibid. The non-exhaustive indicators of false or misleading signals and price fixation depend on the extent to which trading orders/transactions amount to a significant proportion of the daily volume of transactions in the relevant product; the extent to which trading orders/transactions effectuated by market factors with an important buying or selling position in a product lead to significant changes in its price; the fact that the transactions in question do not result in changing the level of beneficial ownership of a product (commonly known as 'wash sales'); the extent to which the trading orders/transactions include position reversals in a short period of time and constitute a significant proportion of the daily volume of transactions in the relevant product (commonly known as 'pump and dump' when the long position held after having created an artificial price is then sold out); the extent to which trading orders/transactions are included within a short time trading spectrum and result in a price change that is then reversed; the extent to which trading orders change the representation of the best bid/offer prices in a product or change the representation of the order book and are finally removed before their execution; and the extent to which trading orders/transactions take place at or around the calculation time of reference prices/settlement prices/valuations and lead to the change of prices with a subsequent influence upon such prices and valuations.

The non-exhaustive indicators of fictitious devices or any other form of deception or contrivance depend on whether trading orders/transactions are linked to *ex ante* or *ex post* dissemination of false or misleading information (this is another form of 'pump and dump' mentioned above) or to the production/dissemination of investment recommendations that are erroneous, biased or demonstrably affected by material interest.

Notwithstanding the details provided in the above-mentioned 2014 MAR framework, it is reasonable to assume that reaching a common conception and application of these rules and indicators may not be a straightforward task across the EU. On the one hand, market participants must be aware not only of the applicable rules, but also of the way that NCAs intend to use them in the presence of market abuse allegations. This should be a concern for market participants who are behaving appropriately but may be caught by some provisions within the 'effects-based' approach adopted by the 2014 MAR.[32] On the other hand, NCAs must be transparent as to their degree of familiarity, understanding and expectations of what amounts to market manipulation, at least to an approximate level, given the fact that such an estimate can never be perfected.[33] The balance between legal certainty and regulatory transparency is thus a very delicate one, especially considering that an 'effects-based' approach is more likely to encompass several incidents which may emerge in the future and for that reason remains the preferred option across the EU.

The decisive factor to enable all constituencies to coexist in this regulatory framework should therefore be an ongoing effort to accentuate supervisory convergence and transparency across NCAs. ESMA (and previously CESR)[34] aims with its various guidance and technical advice reports to enhance this kind of convergence and to gradually ensure that the market participants understand the applicable legal provisions in the same way.[35] Of course, respondents to the ESMA consultation on the 2014 MAR provisions have expressed a series of concerns with regard to their broad and subjective wording that may make it difficult to monitor market manipulation incidents effectively, while also citing the practical difficulties that market participants may face when integrating the non-exhaustive indicators into their automated surveillance systems (with the further risk of the generating 'false positive' alerts).[36] There also seems to be an ongoing confusion on the element of intent and its significance in triggering market manipulation.[37]

---

[32] The accepted market practices regime that has been introduced to tackle this delicate issue is functioning well but there is considerable space for improvement. See Section 9.4.1 below.

[33] For example, the criterion of 'significant proportion' of the daily volume of transactions, which serves as a market manipulation indicator, may be subject to different interpretations by NCAs given that national markets have different trading levels: I. H-Y. Chiu, *Regulatory Convergence in EU Securities Regulation* (Kluwer Law International, 2008), 115.

[34] For example, see CESR, 'Market Abuse Directive: Level Three – First Set of CESR Guidance and Information on the Common Operation of the Directive', May 2005, CESR/04-505b, at www.fsc.bg/d.php?id=2009.

[35] For recent technical advice with highly informative explanations with regard to types of market manipulation, see ESMA, 'Final Report: ESMA's Technical Advice on Possible Delegated Acts Concerning the Market Abuse Regulation', 3 February 2015, ESMA/2015/224, 14, at https://www.esma.europa.eu/sites/default/files/library/2015/11/2015-224.pdf.

[36] 76, ibid.

[37] See Section 9.6.1.

The overall conclusion from the feedback received on the 2014 MAR provisions may give a positive sign of the major regulatory overhaul undertaken, but it is also evident that much more needs to be done to strengthen the common understanding and use of rules by both market participants and NCAs. It remains to be seen whether further regulatory fine-tuning will take place or more resources will be invested in achieving market and supervisory convergence. In our view, the latter option is much more realistic and decisive for achieving truly integrated, manipulation-free markets.

9.4 Ensuring Flexibility for Firms

9.4.1 Accepted Market Practices

Accepted market practices (AMP) have traditionally been seen by national laws and regulators as a way to maintain a rational approach to operational flexibility for activities which, notwithstanding their interference with share price formation, can be justified in the light of legitimate purposes envisaged by market participants. The most notable examples include price stabilization mechanisms and share buybacks, which we will analyse below. Examining AMPs from an EU perspective, we immediately notice the divergence among Member States as to which practices can be included in the AMP category.

Persons involved in such activities must show that they have performed these activities for legitimate reasons and that they comply with the AMP status in their jurisdiction. For that purpose, NCAs are expected to introduce AMPs taking into consideration a series of criteria.[38] Of course, the discretion given to NCAs cannot have an EU-wide effect and will only be applicable to other markets in other countries upon acceptance of the practice by another NCA.[39]

The debate on whether harmonization is desirable and feasible has been vivid at the political level. The 2014 MAR has found a compromise between the willingness at the national level to retain freedom in choosing which activities can benefit from the AMP operational scope and the impetus of EU harmonization. An NCA that wishes to introduce an AMP must notify ESMA as well as the other NCAs of this initiative three months prior to its intended establishment. Following this notification, ESMA must publish an opinion within two months on its website. This opinion is nonbinding, and gives ESMA's view on the compatibility of the proposed AMP with the above-mentioned criteria and other regulatory standards,[40] as well as its potential impact on market

---

[38] Outlined in Article 13(2): the degree of transparency of the practice in the market, the practice's high level of operational 'safety valve' for market efficiency purposes, its impact on market liquidity, its harmonious existence with the trading mechanism of the relevant and related markets, any precedent by any NCA or authority which has investigated this practice in relation to market abuse or codes of conduct violations and, lastly, the characteristics of the relevant market potentially affected by this practice.

[39] Ibid.

[40] These standards touch on the criteria, the procedure and the requirements for establishing AMPs: ESMA, 'Final Report: Draft Technical Standards on the Market Abuse Regulation',

confidence at the EU level.[41] Even if ESMA's opinion is negative, the NCA remains free to adopt its proposed AMP, subject to publishing the reasons for its decision on its website within 24 hours after establishing the AMP.[42] The 2014 MAR also provides for an intermediary role played by ESMA in the interesting scenario where another NCA views the AMP in question as not compatible with the required criteria, as outlined in Article 13(2). In such a case, ESMA must accompany the NCAs in reaching an agreement. If no agreement can be found, then ESMA may decide on the issue itself.[43]

We believe that the overall design of this framework is positive in the sense that it allows for considerable flexibility and discretion at the national level but ultimately depends on ESMA's final decision in cases where another NCA seems to be concerned about the AMP's compatibility with the 2014 MAR criteria. It thus remains to be seen whether or not ESMA will be intervening in this field (and if so, to what extent), and with which kind of outcomes for ensuring market confidence at the EU level. The 2014 MAR also invites NCAs to constantly review AMPs, particularly in the presence of market changes.[44] ESMA is tasked with monitoring the application of AMPs, submitting a relevant annual report to the Commission, and publishing a list of AMPs on its website. These measures will undoubtedly contribute to market participants' familiarity with the overall picture at the level and potential convergence of established AMPs.

9.4.2 Buyback Programmes and Stabilization Measures

The exemption from market manipulation prohibitions with regard to buyback programmes and stabilization measures can be seen as a facilitating tool for listed companies to alleviate the pressure stemming from speculation in capital markets. These practices cannot realistically be seen as manipulative despite the fact that they do intervene in the price formation process. Nevertheless, potentially abusive practices behind these facilitating mechanisms cannot be ruled out and can prove to be quite harmful to the markets and to investor confidence. The informational and procedural safeguards that aim to legitimize these practices must therefore be rigorous and applied consistently at the EU level. Adding to initial regulatory dilemmas in this area, the EU spectrum was very diverse before the 2003 MAD, a situation that created legitimate reasons for intervention and harmonization rules. The 2003 MAD introduced a harmonized regime at the EU level, which was further complemented by a Buyback and Stabilization Regulation in 2003[45] which ensured – at least

---

28 September 2015, ESMA/2015/1455, at https://www.esma.europa.eu/sites/default/ files/library/2015/11/2015-esma-1455_-_final_report_mar_ts.pdf.
[41] Article 13(4), MAR 2014.
[42] Article 13(5), ibid.
[43] Article 13(6), ibid.
[44] Article 13(8), ibid.
[45] Commission Regulation (EC) No 2273/2003 of 22 December 2003 implementing Directive 2003/6/EC of the European Parliament and of the Council as regards exemptions

in theory[46] – straightforward and uniform application of the EU rules at the national level while providing a 'safe harbour' that protects firms from potential market abuse allegations.

Starting with buyback programmes, these activities[47] aim to reduce the company's capital for various purposes, from enhancing the value of the remaining shares in the market to increasing shareholder dividends.[48] It is nevertheless crucial to ensure the presence of legitimate motives behind such decisions in order to avoid abusive practices, such as an artificial increase in buy orders or 'last-minute' attempts to buy back shares before the disclosure of negative information. At the same time, legal rules should facilitate these transactions by encouraging firms to repurchase their own shares when this is deemed beneficial for their purposes. The 2014 MAR, following the 2003 MAD rules that largely satisfied this positive signalling effect to firms,[49] therefore requires a series of safeguards that rely heavily on disclosure obligations and on the satisfaction of certain operational characteristics to ensure that all market actors and regulators are well informed about the details of such operations. Disclosure obligations apply to the full details of the programme before the start of trading in own shares[50] and the reporting of these trades as part of buyback programmes to both the NCA and the public.[51] With regard to the operational characteristics, buyback programmes must have as their sole purpose a reduction in the issuers' capital, the compliance with obligations stemming from their financial instruments (exchangeable into equity instruments) or from share option programmes (or other allocations of shares).[52]

Continuing with stabilization mechanisms, these include operations after the offering which purport to sustain the price during its initial trading phase that can be subject to downturns in the presence of (potentially speculative) sell orders. Stabilizing the price aims to ensure price accuracy with regard to the security's value. Offering the opportunity for legitimate interference in the price formation mechanism to a series of market actors who are behind the offering, entails other types of risk, such as insider dealing and the creation of an artificial price by intervening for an extended period of time in the trading

---

for buyback programmes and stabilization of financial instruments OJ L 336/33 (hereinafter 2003 Commission Regulation).

[46] For some persisting discrepancies and interpretational differences among NCAs, see ESME, 'Market Abuse EU Legal Framework and its Implementation by Member States: A First Evaluation', Brussels, 6 July 2007, 15, at http://ec.europa.eu/finance/securities/docs/esme/mad_070706_en.pdf.

[47] Of a constantly growing importance in both the USA and the EU: M. Siems and A. De Cesari, 'The Law and Finance of Share Repurchases in Europe' (2012) 12 *Journal of Corporate Law Studies* 33, 37.

[48] For a detailed discussion, see J.M. Fried, 'Open Market Repurchases: Signalling or Managerial Opportunism?' (2001) 2 *Theoretical Inquiries in Law* 865.

[49] See the very interesting study by M. Siems and A. De Cesari, above n. 47.

[50] Article 5(1)(a), 2014 MAR.

[51] Article 5(1)(b), ibid. Disclosure elements to the NCA are further exemplified in Article 5(3), ibid.

[52] Article 5(2), ibid.

of shares[53] with the excuse of aiming to stabilize a price that is vulnerable to speculation. The regulatory balance that therefore must be struck between risks associated with speculation coming 'from the outside' and manipulation coming 'from the inside' is undoubtedly a very delicate one.

Following on the first harmonization wave initiated by the 2003 MAD and the 2003 Commission Regulation that aimed to eliminate discrepancies among national laws with regard to stabilization mechanisms, the 2014 MAR requires certain disclosure and organizational safeguards in order for the safe harbour framework to apply to these transactions.[54] Stabilization needs to be carried out for a limited period, and information on transactions in this framework must be disclosed to the NCA (within seven daily market sessions following the execution day of stabilization transactions) by issuers, offerors or other entities in charge of the stabilization.[55]

Most importantly and with regard to both buyback programmes and stabilization measures, trading must comply with regulatory technical standards developed by ESMA that will specify, in turn, the conditions for trading, time and volume restrictions, disclosure and reporting obligations and price conditions.[56]

9.5 Ensuring an Adequate Supervision Framework

9.5.1 ESMA and NCAs

As for insider dealing, the 2014 MAR provides for a supervision system articulated around NCAs and ESMA and including a series of powers,[57] cooperation arrangements with ESMA[58] and cooperation with Member States'[59] as well as third countries' NCAs.[60] As mentioned in Chapter 8, the success of this multi-layered supervision mechanism will largely depend on the NCAs' responsiveness towards the impetus of EU convergence in regulatory capacity. ESMA will undoubtedly have to accentuate its existing initiatives, especially in the area of market manipulation. This is particularly true in the light of the distinctive features of such incidents pertaining to the difficulty of detection, the complexity of adopted strategies and the constant evolution of technological means at their service, as explained above.

One other equally important feature that needs to be further explored in the area of market manipulation, in terms of both research and regulatory initiatives, relates to cross-market surveillance limitations and their impact upon a

---

[53] G. Ferrarini, 'The European Market Abuse Directive' (2004) 41(3) *Common Market Law Review* 711, 735.
[54] Article 5(4), ibid.
[55] Article 5(5), ibid.
[56] See ESMA, above n. 40, 13–20.
[57] Article 23.
[58] Article 24, ibid.
[59] Article 25, ibid.
[60] For a detailed analysis, see Chapter 8.

sound supervisory framework. Market manipulation practices can also be conducted across different markets with the purpose of trading in one market in order to influence the price in another market.[61] These practices are highly sophisticated and not easily detectable due to the inherent limitation in understanding whether orders and trading in one market have underlying links with a financial product in another market with the ultimate purpose of manipulating its price. The 2014 MAR has taken this element into account by insisting on the need to enable NCAs to have the necessary supervisory mechanisms for effective cross-market order book surveillance.[62] NCAs supervising different markets are therefore expected to cooperate efficiently to ensure exchange of information and prompt detection of these incidents.[63]

ESMA has been keen to encourage market participants to report suspicious behaviours to NCAs in order to detect this type of market manipulation.[64] ESMA also acknowledges that they may not always be in a position to decipher any potential cross-market manipulation elements in orders or transactions because they cannot have a holistic view of the market. It nevertheless insists on their obligation to go beyond their internally available information and to take into account public information as well when they assess such cases, a task that may not be always straightforward.[65] There is no doubt that cross-market manipulation is related to more general international surveillance issues since it cannot be solely seen as a European problem.[66] An additional problem arising is related to the collection of data in a standardized form which varies significantly at the international level, with Europe falling behind in this area compared to Canada and the USA.[67] An important initiative that may therefore bring concrete results at a quicker pace is the establishment of an EU cross-market order book surveillance framework. The Commission is expected to submit a report by 2019 assessing this possibility and formulating relevant recommendations. This will undoubtedly be an effective way to tackle cross-market surveillance limitations and to safeguard markets from manipulative practices.

---

[61] For example, in the case of manipulation of financial instruments being connected with commodity derivatives and vice versa: Recital 20, 2014 MAR.

[62] Recital 68, ibid.

[63] Directive 2014/65/EU of the European Parliament and of the Council of 15 May 2014 on markets in financial instruments and amending Directive 2002/92/EC and Directive 2011/61/EU.

[64] ESMA, 'Final Report: ESMA's Technical Advice on Possible Delegated Acts Concerning the Market Abuse Regulation', 3 February 2015, ESMA/2015/224, 11-12, at https://www.esma.europa.eu/sites/default/files/library/2015/11/2015-224.pdf.

[65] 12, ibid.

[66] Apart from the obvious assumption that it is acknowledged as a problem on other continents too, sophisticated manipulative strategies can be manifested not only with regard to different markets in one country but also across borders since cross-border elements can also be present.

[67] J. Austin, 'Unusual Trade or Market Manipulation? How Market Abuse is Detected by Securities Regulators, Trading Venues and Self-Regulatory Organizations' (2015) 1(2) *Journal of Financial Regulation* 263, 280.

Taking the debate to an international level, the International Organization of Securities Commissions (IOSCO) also needs to be given a much more active role in coordinating different national regulators by enhancing the exchange of information between these regulators.[68] IOSCO has already expressed its concerns about cross-market surveillance given the difficulties arising from technological evolution of manipulative practices and the above-mentioned difficulties in collecting and using data.[69] Costs associated with these initiatives and with more general organizational and 'know-how' convergence issues among regulators[70] may lead us to the conclusion that reforms in this area are not realistic in the very near future. Adding to these concerns, the reluctance of various markets to be subject to a more stringent and overarching supervisory mechanisms should also be taken into account and may prove to be particularly arduous to overcome, both in terms of cultural and regulatory transformation.

9.5.2 The Close Cooperation with Market Actors

Having previously analysed the importance of effective enforcement and the seemingly unsurmountable difficulty in identifying and sanctioning market manipulation incidents, regulatory attention is inevitably shifted towards the exploration of alternative methods that will help NCAs monitor this area more effectively. The most efficient way forward – both economically and strategically – is to have recourse to other market actors, such as stock exchanges,[71] market operators and investment firms to provide NCAs with information regarding potential violations. The 2014 MAR provides that the market operators and investment firms operating a trading venue are required to set up and maintain effective arrangements, systems and procedures for the prevention and detection of, *inter alia*, market manipulation and attempted market manipulation.[72] There is also a reporting obligation for orders (an addition of the 2014 MAR regime) and transactions that could constitute such behaviour to the NCA of the trading venue without delay.[73] These two requirements seem quite straightforward and can be smoothly satisfied by market actors.[74]

---

[68] 275, ibid.

[69] IOSCO, 'Technical Challenges to Effective Market Surveillance-Issues and Regulatory Tools: Final Report', April 2013, at http://www.iosco.org/library/pubdocs/pdf/IOSCOPD412.pdf.

[70] D. Cumming and S.A. Johan, 'Global Market Surveillance' (2008) 10 *American Law Economic Review* 454.

[71] For example, in Germany, Bafin is in charge of market surveillance at the federal level, and stock exchange supervisory authorities deal with market surveillance at the Länder level in collaboration with the respective offices of each stock exchange: IOSCO, above n. 69, 9.

[72] In accordance with Articles 31 and 54 of Directive 2014/65/EU: Article 16(1), 2014 MAR.

[73] (1), ibid.

[74] As has been shown in various countries, such as the UK and Germany, where a substantial amount of market manipulation cases are still being triggered from such reports, highlighting

However, this is not the case with another requirement regarding persons professionally arranging or executing transactions bearing the same obligation of setting up and maintaining effective arrangements, systems and procedures for the detection and reporting of suspicious orders and transactions.[75] The obstacle lies in the fact that the notification obligation for such persons to the NCA without delay is triggered when they have a reasonable suspicion that an order or transaction could constitute market manipulation or attempted market manipulation.[76] There is no doubt that the reasonableness of the underlying suspicion, as well as the likelihood of constituting market manipulation, are two criteria that are by far uncertain with regard to their understanding and use across different trading venues in the EU. It remains to be seen whether further convergence could be achieved gradually, especially taking into account the ESMA regulatory technical standards touching upon the appropriate arrangements, systems and procedures, as well as notification templates used by the concerned persons.[77]

On a parallel level, whistleblowing measures are also provided in the 2014 MAR to assist NCAs in their monitoring task. The EU provisions contain a non-exhaustive list of measures that must be ensured at the national level, such as procedures for the receipt of infringement reports, protection of personal data mechanisms for employees reporting or being involved in such incidents.[78] Financial incentives may also be provided by Member States to persons with no pre-existing legal or contractual duties to report relevant information on the condition that the information is new and that it results in the levying of sanctions or measures for a relevant violation.[79]

9.6 SANCTIONS

9.6.1 Introductory Comments

The issue of sanctions applicable to market manipulation is one of the most challenging matters that both Member States and the EU have been confronting for many years with mixed results.[80] At a parallel level, it is important to ensure that potentially concerned parties are able to understand

---

the usefulness of having recourse to market actors in this area to assist NCAs in detecting violations: Austin, above n. 67, 270, 272.

[75] Regardless of the training venue, by enlarging considerably the scope of application of this notification obligation.

[76] (2), ibid.

[77] Even in the presence of the ESMA standards, regarding more technical than substantial issues, it is likely that the more subjective evaluation of such incidents will keep on being subject to variable interpretations and may thus compromise the rationale of these provisions.

[78] Article 32, MAR 2014.

[79] (4), ibid.

[80] J. de Larosière et al., 'Report by The High-Level Group on Financial Supervision in the EU', 25 February 2009, at http://ec.europa.eu/internal_market/finances/docs/de_larosiere_report_en.pdf.

in advance the meaning of the applicable legal framework, its enforcement criteria, as well as its ongoing use by NCAs and national courts. Back in 2007, the Commission emphasized the importance of a transparency exercise with the basic aim to inform market participants of the national provisions in place to ensure the avoidance of interpretational conundrums across the EU in the gradual creation of a more consistent understanding and enforcement of legal provisions.[81]

The 'law on the books' rigour needs to be ensured first in order to provide a dissuasive legal framework against potential violations. Following on from a considerably variable sanction regime across the EU, the 2003 MAD adopted a rather modest and experimental step in harmonizing sanction provisions by requiring appropriate administrative measures and sanctions fulfilling the criteria of effectiveness, proportionality and dissuasiveness (without any further clarification). Civil liability and criminal sanctions were left untouched, shaping a very embryonic agenda.[82] The 2014 MAR thus had a broad scope of intervention that it managed to use in a perfectible way with regard to administrative measures and sanctions, as well as criminal sanctions and with considerable space for improvement. Would this mean that further harmonization of legal provisions would ensure the sanctions' framework efficiency? The answer lies more with the assumption that theoretical dissuasiveness is realistically less relevant to ensure enforcement efficiency.[83]

Indeed, the 'law in action' rigour is what ultimately counts since, even in the hypothetical absence of regulatory arbitrage, the implementation of provisions and their ongoing use by NCAs and national courts will ultimately provide a more accurate view of the quality of the sanctions regime and its success. The element of intent is one characteristic example in this sense. It seems that there are still confusing areas with regard to the legal framework's expectation from market participants. In a recent consultation process, a number of respondents asked ESMA to expressly detail the element of intent and requested that the examples, which are already provided in the 2014 MAR and in ESMA's Technical Advice, should include it as well.[84] ESMA has nevertheless made it clear that 'where an example seems to require that a conduct is characterized by a manipulative intent, this does not imply that, in the absence of the intent that conduct might not fall

---

[81] CESR, 'Report on Administrative Measures and Sanctions available in Member States under the MAD', 17 October 2007, CESR/07-693, 4, at https://www.esma.europa.eu/sites/default/files/library/2015/11/07_693_u_2_.pdf.

[82] L. Enriques and M. Gatti, 'Is There a Uniform EU Securities Law After the Financial Services Action Plan?' (2008) 14(1) *Stanford Journal of Law, Business, and Finance* 43, 61.

[83] See, for example, the very interesting empirical study on Libor manipulation showing that the mere presence of legal rules cannot suffice to tackle misconduct in the markets: P. Gandhi, B. Golez, J.C. Jackwerth and A. Plazzi, 'Financial Market Misconduct and Public Enforcement: The Case of Libor Manipulation' (2016), at http://ssrn.com/abstract=2342075.

[84] ESMA, above n. 35, 76.

within the scope of the definition of market manipulation'.[85] As seen above, some jurisdictions, like Australia, have removed requirements of intent in order to move towards an 'effect-based' approach (but intent remains relevant in court to constitute manipulation),[86] while others, like the USA, adopt a mostly 'intent-based' approach.[87] The 2014 MAD also notes that '[w]hereas offences should be punishable under this Directive when committed intentionally and at least in serious cases, sanctions for breaches of Regulation (EU) No 596/2014 do not require that intent is proven or that they are qualified as serious'.[88]

Even if harmonization across the EU – and around the globe – would not be feasible in this area, the general trend towards removal of references of intent for the establishment of market manipulation testifies to the willingness to facilitate enforcement as well as to the inherent difficulty in building up enforcement cases. Nevertheless, this does not mean that intent is likely to become irrelevant, as courts and regulators will continue to seek its establishment in the ambit of their tasks. It is our belief that the 'effect-based' approach is one of the main symptoms of a highly politicized agenda, especially after the ramifications of the global financial crisis, which satisfies the public demand for more enforcement and a very efficient communication tool towards market participants that the legal framework has enlarged its scope and more cases may be subject to its realm. Of course, a considerable amount of work still needs to be done in order to respond to market demands for more clarity in this area, and ESMA will inevitably be called on for the delicate task of engaging in a further ongoing dialogue with market actors.

Our focus will now turn to administrative measures and sanctions that highlight difficulties of enforcement in market manipulation cases, as well as the prospects for further harmonization across the EU. A crucial matter that needs to be further enhanced is the cooperation between NCAs and other market actors in identifying and reporting such incidents. Our analysis will also touch on criminal sanctions and the latest developments of the 2014 MAD, as well as their coexistence with administrative sanctions in the enforcement landscape. Particular attention will be paid to civil liability in this framework, a matter that continues to be treated in a largely variable way around the globe and needs a closer look with regard to its legitimacy.

---

[85] ESMA, 'Consultation Paper: ESMA's Draft Technical Advice on Possible Delegated Acts Concerning the Market Abuse Regulation', 11 July 2014, ESMA/2014/808, 8, at https://www.esma.europa.eu/sites/default/files/library/2015/11/esma_2014-808_consultation_paper_u_on_mar_draft_technical_advice_0.pdf.

[86] See above n. 10.

[87] Ibid. UK law distinguishes between criminal and regulatory offence as well as its precise nature in order to determine the mens rea element. For example, Sections 89–91 of the Financial Services Act 2012 (criminal offences) require the mens rea element, but Section 118(6) Financial Services and Markets Act 2000 (regulatory offences) does not and Section 118(7) opts for a negligence standard.

[88] Recital 23, 2014 MAD.

9.6.2 *Administrative Measures and Sanctions*

As discussed in Chapter 8, the 2014 MAR attempted to harmonize applicable sanctions for market abuse to a certain extent, following from a rather modest approach adopted in the 2003 MAD that provided at the time that Member States should implement appropriate administrative measures or sanctions, without any further specification as to their type. Focusing on market manipulation violations, the 2014 MAR provides for administrative measures, further specified in Article 30(2),[89] by further enhancing the harmonization spectrum in this area by making them compulsory. On an even more interesting note, Article 30(2)(j), (i) and (ii) provides for administrative pecuniary sanctions applicable to both natural and legal persons, who can be subject to maximum pecuniary sanctions of at least €5 million and €15 million (or 15% of total annual turnover), respectively, thus allowing national laws to provide for even higher maximums. These 'minimum maximums' are a first step towards further harmonization that needs to be at the centre of the EU agenda in the future since the 2014 reform allows considerable space for divergence at the national level.[90] Administrative sanctions can also be of at least three times the amount of the profit gained or losses avoided. NCAs are expected, as in the case of other market abuse cases, to take into consideration a series of factors when they decide on the type and level of administrative sanctions.[91] The provisions related to the publication of decisions levying administrative sanctions or measures, analysed in Chapter 8, apply equally to market manipulation infringements.[92]

Another delicate matter that inevitably influences the efficiency of the enforcement framework in Member States relates to the capacity of public prosecutors and NCAs. Indeed, the numbers may look modest and more resource investment should be channelled towards staffing.[93] Sophistication and regulatory 'know-how' are also very important issues in the detection and sanctioning of market manipulation cases, and much more needs to be done for meaningful convergence to take place among NCAs.[94]

---

[89] The list is non-exhaustive and relates to orders to cease the infringement, to the disgorgement of the profits gained or losses avoided, to public warnings, to the withdrawal or suspension of the authorization of an investment firm, to temporary or permanent bans from exercising management functions and investment firms, and to temporary bans from dealing.

[90] For some examples from a relatively recent report, see ESMA, 'Report: Actual Use of Sanctioning Powers under MAD', 26 April 2012, ESMA/2012/270, 12, at https://www.esma.europa.eu/sites/default/files/library/2015/11/2012-270.pdf. See also D. J. Cumming, A.P. Groh and S. Johan, 'Same Rules, Different Enforcement: Market Abuse in Europe' (2016) TILEC Discussion Paper No 2014-019, at http://ssrn.com/abstract=2399064.

[91] Article 31, 2014 MAR.

[92] Article 34, 2014 MAD.

[93] T. M.J. Möllers, 'Investor Protection in the System of Capital Markets Law: Legal Foundations and Outlook' (2010) 36(1) *North Carolina Journal of International Law* 57, 76. See also H.E. Jackson and M.J. Roe, 'Public and Private Enforcement of Securities Laws: Resource-Based Evidence' (2009) 93(2) *Journal of Financial Economics* 207.

[94] As Siems notes, 'for instance, the complex criteria for market manipulation may be no problem for authorities in London or Frankfurt but this may be different in Vilnius or Sofia': M. Siems, above n. 15, 46.

9.6.3 Criminal Sanctions

Criminal law in the area of market manipulation has a strong dissuasive connotation but, as seen in previous chapters, is lacking in extensive and frequent use of its provisions. In theory, it presents the advantage of being more convincing as a sanction, compared to administrative alternatives, but its practical contours also need to be clarified in order to ensure its effectiveness. This does not appear to be the case even after the 2014 EU reforms.

2014 MAD, an entirely new Directive aimed exclusively at criminal sanctions in the area of market abuse, attempted to convey a clear – more symbolic than realistic – message about the harmonization of criminal sanctions. As a preliminary comment, Recital 3 emphasizes that providing for a rigorous enforcement mechanism and at the same time being able to ensure its effective implementation across the EU is key to preserving market integrity and investor confidence. Even though the link between sanctions and investor confidence may be much more straightforward, the Directive does not define market integrity despite its explicit reference to this kind of prerogative for criminal sanctions.[95] Furthermore, a hypothesis that criminal sanctions can guarantee market integrity would be fallacious as the latter can depend on various factors. It therefore seems that the rhetoric adopted serves a mostly communicative and pedagogical purpose rather than a meticulously designed legal framework that could further enhance the legitimacy of the proposed measures in the 2014 MAD.

To start with the scope of market manipulation offences, the 2014 MAD mentions that market manipulation constitutes a criminal offence at least in serious cases and when committed intentionally.[96] The element of intent having been analysed previously, the second criterion seems quite vague as further specifications with regard to the notion of 'serious cases' do not seem to ensure sufficient clarity. Indeed, in its Recital 12, the 2014 MAD provides a non-exhaustive list of cases according to which market manipulation should be considered serious. These cases refer to the high level of impact on market integrity, of profit gained/loss avoided, of damage to the market, of alteration to financial products' value and of the funds originally used. There is an additional criterion related to the identity of the person involved in market manipulation, namely someone who works or is employed in the financial sector or in a supervisory or regulatory authority. Aside from the fact that these criteria are reasonable, it would be particularly optimistic to expect them to become indicators of convergence across the EU given their broad wording which leaves non-negligible scope for variable interpretations from national courts.

The definition of market manipulation is given in Article 5 and is generally similar to the one provided in the 2014 MAR with the difference that

---

[95] E. Herlin-Karnell, above n. 19, 485.
[96] Article 5, 2014 MAD.

the 'likely' effect of an action has been removed, as has any reference to the level of knowledge in order to delineate the intent requirement mentioned above. The 2014 MAD provides for criminal sanctions in cases of inciting, aiding and abetting market manipulation offences, but retaining a very broad and neutral provision regarding their type since it only mentions 'effective, proportionate and dissuasive criminal penalties'.[97] Therefore, these types of behaviour are not subject to any meaningful harmonization for the time being. With regard to market manipulation itself, a maximum term of imprisonment of at least four years is provided in Article 7 for natural persons, as well as other types of sanctions for legal persons in Article 9. As stated in Chapter 8, the 'minimum maximum' is a perfectible way forward for convergence in this area, acknowledging nonetheless the national reluctance to concede sovereignty in this area and accept a more significant compromise in the fixation of sanction levels.

As an overall conclusion of the new criminal legal framework, it seems that the main contribution of the 2014 MAD will be mostly symbolic and less pragmatic due to the broad wording of the contours of the criminal offences and, hence, the reluctance of criminal courts to impose criminal sanctions on a frequent basis.[98] Moreover, the high level of proof, the long duration of criminal proceedings and the concern that it is much more difficult to impose criminal sanctions due to these reasons may also deter NCAs from referring enforcement cases to criminal courts.[99]

It is also interesting to note that Member States have the discretion not to introduce rules for administrative sanctions when the concerned infringements are already subject to criminal sanctions. This is undoubtedly due to the complex relationship between these two types of sanctions, especially in the light of the case *Grande Stevens and others* v. *Italy*,[100] regarding a well-known market manipulation case, where the ECHR confirmed that administrative sanctions are in substance criminal sanctions. The European Convention of Human Rights is therefore applicable, rendering administrative proceedings subject to the conventions protective provisions for all affected parties. Moreover, national laws that allow the potential application of both types of sanctions may violate the principle *ne bis in idem* that forbids the imposition of sanctions twice for the same facts. This of course does not mean that administrative sanctions are not needed in the presence of criminal ones, the latter being marginalized due to the above-mentioned difficulties, but that their harmonious coexistence is needed and optimal cooperation between NCAs and criminal courts is also crucial for an effective enforcement landscape.

---

[97] Article 6, 2014 MAD.

[98] V. Tountopoulos, 'Market Abuse and Private Enforcement' (2014) 3 *European Company and Financial Law Review* 297, 326.

[99] 327, ibid.

[100] *Grande Stevens and others* v. *Italy* App nos 18640/10, 18647/10, 18663/10, 18668/10 and 18698/10 ECHR (4 March 2014).

9.6.4 Civil Remedies

As in the case of insider trading, private enforcement rules in the area of market manipulation may be very difficult to design and to introduce in national laws due to the fundamentally different perception of the decisive criteria that must be satisfied in the ambit of a civil claim. For example, according to some national laws, like the UK one, there must be a fraudulent misrepresentation with the intention of inducing the affected party to rely on the manipulative strategy,[101] which is almost impossible to prove within the anonymous trading spectrum. To continue with another obvious obstacle, market manipulation inevitably affects the market as a whole but it is a rarity to be able to identify each and every investor who may have suffered damage from these types of violations in trading venues where anonymity prevails. The 'victimless crime' characterization denotes the inherent difficulty in proving reliance on a manipulative strategy and excludes, in most cases, any further possibility in pursuing a civil claim. On a more general note, allowing private enforcement within a very generalized and anonymized context, which could potentially include all investors affected by manipulative strategy, could very well trigger litigation floodgates as well as the acknowledgement of a very broad and disproportionate liability. Adding to this concern, other investors buying or selling securities during the day when the manipulative strategy took place could also benefit from the awarding of damages, thus making private enforcement mechanisms even more controversial.

The above-mentioned arguments may explain why, with the exception of one Member State,[102] civil claims are not provided in this area across the EU. This is not of course the case with other continents, the most notable example being the USA, which facilitates civil claims with class actions and accepts the 'fraud on the market' theory for market manipulation. Reliance on manipulative strategies therefore becomes irrelevant since the only decisive criterion for the acceptance of civil claims (within the general securities fraud claims framework of the SEC Rule 10b-5) is the proof of transaction.[103] Adding to this facilitating tool, the efficient capital markets hypothesis (hereinafter ECMH)[104] becomes relevant by serving as a further argument to show that the market is constantly evaluating securities and that market prices themselves reflect all available information; therefore, investor reliance can easily be presumed in an indirect way as long as the 'efficient market' criterion – when the manipulated security was trading – can be shown in court.[105]

---

[101] *Smith* v. *Chadwick* (1884) 9 App Cas 187.

[102] Austrian law accepts private enforcement in this area under § 48(a) BörseG, which is considered to provide protection to the rights of investors.

[103] *Basic* v. *Levinson* 485 US 224 (1998).

[104] E.F. Fama, 'Efficient Capital Markets, A Review of Theory and Empirical Work' (1970) 25 *Journal of Finance* 383.

[105] Of course, this can be challenged by the defendant in the presence of factors serving against the plaintiff's claim.

Nevertheless, it is also important to note that, notwithstanding its merits in other market abuse areas, the ECMH may not be suitable for market manipulation incidents which, according to empirical studies, are more likely to occur in inefficient markets that are small and illiquid.[106] The market efficiency requirement may thus risk interrupting the chain of indirect causation instead of facilitating the presumption of reliance.[107] Should this argument lead us to the conclusion that the 'fraud on the market' theory together with the ECMH should be abandoned after all? Fischel has opined that maintaining the current framework simply as a procedural facilitating tool to prove a reliance – but not considering it as a general liability standard that may complicate things even further – would be the preferred way forward.[108] Under this perspective, investors who rely – or at least should rely – on market prices should be protected accordingly.[109] This kind of 'juristic grace'[110] is therefore justified within the market manipulation area because investors are in a way entitled to be protected by manipulators who do not merely aim to mislead them, but to profit from fluctuations in the market by harming the market price's integrity.

As can be observed, even the US rules that aim to facilitate civil claims in market manipulation cases have been subject to criticism and show certain elements of confusion and contradiction. The 'juristic grace' is certainly welcomed but lacks a stable foundation with regard to the specificities of market manipulation cases as mentioned above, and can be only accepted as an overarching regulatory prerogative aiming to protect the investor community. The above-mentioned analysis leads us to the conclusion that the US framework is perfectible. Lessons

---

[106] R.K. Aggarwal and G. Wu, 'Stock Market Manipulations' (2006) 79(4) *Journal of Business* 1915, 1917. More generally, on the relationship between market manipulation and illiquid markets, see V. Tountopoulos, 'Manipulation in Illiquid Markets – A Tale of Inefficiency?' (2017) 3 *European Company and Financial Law Review* 1.

[107] Furthermore, Korsmo argues that even the concept of reliance shows signs of incoherence in market manipulation cases. This is due to the fact that investors do not actually rely on anything, especially in the case of trade-based manipulation, since there is no statement or omission per se to rely upon. What is more, it is not possible to argue that investors trade in an efficient market during the manipulative strategy since, if they rely on a manipulated optimistic price signal – believing that it shows new information and that it is therefore likely to drive the price even higher – they testify to a rather inefficient market mentality. This is true because in an efficient market, investors would accept that the current market prices reflect all past prices of a security and that they are essentially 'an example of a martingale'. Nevertheless, if they believe that the current price will affect future price movements, they show their disbelief in an efficient market: C. Korsmo, 'Mismatch: The Misuse of Market Efficiency in Market Manipulation Class Actions' (2011) 52 *William and Mary Law Review* 1111, 1155. Of course, this is not the case with manipulative strategies associated with the dissemination of false or misleading information (if the market relies by reacting to the information and by influencing the price accordingly), but the argument remains relevant for trade-based manipulation incidents.

[108] D.R. Fischel, 'Use of Modern Finance Theory in Securities Fraud Cases Involving Actively Traded Securities' (1982) 38 *The Business Lawyer* 1, 9.

[109] Charles Korsmo, above n. 107, 1156.

[110] D.C. Langevoort, 'Basic at Twenty: Rethinking Fraud on the Market' (2009) 2 *Wisconsin Law Review* 151, 171.

from the US system need to be learned and taken into consideration when the debate focuses upon potential similar reforms in EU law.

More specifically, EU rules will need to design a broad civil liability regime to respect national idiosyncrasies in this area in a first experimental approach, but caution is needed to avoid a disproportionate and unfiltered regime. The academic debate in this area has highlighted the need to provide for an effective protection to harmed investors in the area of market abuse.[111] Tountopoulos opines that the arguments can be twofold: firstly, in their majority, market abuse offences have been completed when detected,[112] making requests from harmed parties to cease the violation and avoid repetition – for public interest purposes – less relevant[113] and by strengthening further the importance of the right to compensation.[114] Secondly, the new EU market abuse framework may give the message that, by choosing as a legislative tool a Regulation and not a Directive, it aims mainly to constrain traders to avoid practices that harm market integrity. If the primary purpose of the 2014 MAR is therefore to enhance investor confidence, it may be argued that harmed investors may not need to rely on NCAs to trigger the enforcement of relevant sanctions.[115] This analysis is certainly interesting but it remains to be seen whether the EU regulatory agenda will shift towards an 'enforcement outsourcing strategy' to civil claims in order to complement its enforcement agenda, currently dominated by criminal and administrative sanctions. Reforms are needed in this area, but the regulatory design of a civil liability regime needs to be equally meticulous. The current possibilities for compensation, involving NCAs having at their disposal the right to apply to court for restitution orders, are certainly meaningful but ultimately depend on the sophistication and resources of NCAs.[116]

9.7 Conclusion

Market manipulation offences are very complex, constantly evolving and have blurred contours. The tasks of defining, monitoring and sanctioning them with legal certainty and effectiveness is substantially arduous. EU law progressed into a much more mature regulatory framework with the adoption of the 2014

---

[111] For example, see the proposal for a private right of action formulated by Avgouleas, above n. 1, 486.

[112] And are not always ongoing, like in other areas of law such as competition law.

[113] Those claims belonging to the plaintiff's right to pursue the public interest following, for example, a competitor's violation of legal rules. See Case C-253/00 *Muñoz and Superior Fruiticola* v. *Frumar and Redbridge* [2002] ECR I-7289, para 31: '[t]he possibility of bringing such proceedings strengthens the practical working of the Community rules on quality standards [...] actions brought before the national courts by competing operators are particularly suited to contributing substantially to ensuring fair trading and transparency of markets in the Community.'

[114] V. Tountopoulos, above n. 98, 329.

[115] Ibid.

[116] For example, in UK law, see S. 383 FSMA for restitution orders triggered when the FCA believes that compensation is justified for certain parties affected by market abuse offences.

MAR and the 2014 MAD, by imposing broadly defined rules able to include a large series of manipulative strategies and, at the same time, by offering flexibility to security issuers to engage in legitimate activities that could otherwise be seen as interfering in the price formation mechanism. The overall assessment of these provisions is a positive one, but closer regulatory attention needs to be paid with regard to supervision and enforcement mechanisms. Notwithstanding the broad range of powers that NCAs have now been given, considerable space for improvement still exists with regard to convergence initiatives that need to be further enhanced under the aegis of ESMA to ensure that regulatory sophistication will be ensured across the EU.

Enforcement mechanisms will also need to be subject to further harmonization trends in the future. The 2014 MAD attempted a first but perfectible wave of harmonization that will need to be re-examined later on, and the 2014 MAR included positive reforms with regard to the type and the quanta of administrative measures and sanctions, but more is needed for meaningful harmonization to take place. Private enforcement has been left outside EU reforms, due to the seemingly insurmountable obstacles to allow for civil claims in market manipulation, but the arguments in favour of a civil liability regime are equally convincing and merit closer reflection.

CHAPTER 10

Short Selling

10.1 Introduction

One of the most criticized activities in capital and financial markets,[1] short selling has been subject to a stringent EU regulatory framework since 2012,[2] following the well-known and widely publicized incidents related to sovereign credit default swaps, combined with the collapse of major financial services firms.[3] Regulatory bodies intervened due to market stability concerns, reflecting the popular (mis)conception of short selling's detrimental effects on market functioning and stability. Inherently experimental, politically driven[4] and, according to empirical studies, counterproductive,[5] temporary bans nevertheless acted as a temporary antidote to further market volatility and fears of potentially destructive ramifications. As a result of this general mistrust of short selling activities combined with market destabilization risks, short selling practices became an ideal scapegoat,[6] justifying further intervention in response to constantly growing public outrage about greed in the capital and financial markets.

---

[1] 'The fact that short sellers profit by selling something which they do not own at the time is felt to be morally dubious, and runs counter to the general idea that parties in a market entering an economic exchange for profit must have property rights over the traded asset. The fact that the most common short sellers are hedge funds has added to the idea that short sellers are unscrupulous traders making a risk-free one-way bet that destabilizes the markets': J. Payne, 'The Regulation of Short Selling and Its Reform in Europe' (2012) 13 *European Business Organization Law Review* 413. See also, L. Gullifer and J. Payne, *Corporate Finance Law: Principles and Policy* (2nd edn, Hart Publishing, 2015), 616.
[2] Regulation (EU) 236/2012 of the European Parliament and of the Council of 14 March 2012 on short selling and certain aspects of credit default swaps [2012] OJ L 86/1 (hereinafter EU Regulation).
[3] On this topic, see B. Saporito, 'Are Short Sellers to Blame for the Financial Crisis?' (Time Business, 18 September 2008), at http://content.time.com/time/business/article/0,8599,1842499,00.html.
[4] L. Enriques, 'Regulators' Response to the Current Crisis and the Upcoming Reregulation of Financial Markets: One Reluctant Regulator's View' (2009) 30(4) *University of Pennsylvania Journal of International Law* 1147.
[5] M. Clifton and M. Snape, 'The Effect of Short Selling Restrictions on Liquidity: Evidence from the London Stock Exchange' (2008), at http://www.lseg.com/sites/default/files/content/documents/short selling-restriction-market-quality-december-2008.pdf.
[6] As has been wisely mentioned, '[r]ailing against short sellers seems to be shooting the messenger rather than listening to the message': R. Karmel, 'IOSCO's Response to the Financial Crisis' (2011–2012) 37 *Journal of Corporation Law* 849, 880.

As a side effect, short selling of listed companies' shares, the focus of this chapter, also became subject to a set of requirements, sparking considerable debate about their nature, scope and efficiency.[7] The EU Regulation introduced a series of disclosure duties for natural or legal persons. These disclosure duties are owed to the regulator and the public at large and are triggered when certain net short position thresholds[8] are reached by the concerned parties. The focus on short selling of listed companies is not simply a consequence of an EU political agenda because there are clear theoretical rationales for the introduction of some rules, as we shall see below, although there was no obvious empirical case for such a framework. So how can this vast regulatory action be justified? The interconnection of operations taking place in capital and financial markets was decisive in developing an overinclusive regulatory approach to the types and features of various short selling practices. The advantage of applying broad short sale restrictions and imposing a series of duties thus became a necessity to convey the message of 'regulator responsiveness' to market access and to the public on the widest possible scale.

In the case of listed companies, short sellers seek to make a profit out of a fall in share prices by borrowing shares at an initial price, selling them to a third party, and expecting a price decline during a certain period of time in order to repurchase the respective number of shares at a lower price for delivery back to the lender.[9] In the event that the share price increases, short sellers suffer loss because they must pay more to purchase the same number of shares for delivery. This kind of expectation with regard to the investee company's share price is rather unorthodox in that it breaks with the 'conventional wisdom' of higher profits expected for the company and, given a resulting rise in the share price, for its shareholders.

This misalignment of short sellers' incentives with those of the rest of the company's members can be problematic on two levels. Firstly, the misalignment of interests can affect a company's future prospects since its corporate governance system will be subject to divergent influences. Secondly, short selling practices may adversely affect share prices on a wider market level if their ramifications become amplified and expressed in various companies. It is therefore essential to assess critically the current regulatory framework for short selling practices.

Following the analysis of these regulatory concerns, touching upon market stability and corporate governance issues, this chapter will examine the efficiency

---

[7] The EU Regulation also imposes duties and restrictions on short selling activities related to sovereign debt (Articles 7 and 13) and in sovereign credit default swaps (Articles 8 and 14).

[8] A net short position is the position resulting after deducting the long position from the short position taken on the issued share capital: Article 3(4) of the EU Regulation.

[9] According to Article 2(1)(b) of the EU Regulation, '"short sale" in relation to a share or debt instrument means any sale of the share or debt instrument which the seller does not own at the time of entering into the agreement to sell including such a sale where at the time of entering into the agreement to sell the seller has borrowed or agreed to borrow the share or debt instrument for delivery at settlement ...'.

of some operational constraints on short selling activities, such as short selling bans and circuit breakers. It will then focus on the introduction of a series of disclosure duties, according to the EU Regulation, which aim to make these activities visible to the regulator and to the market at large. Special attention will be paid to the supervisory and investigating powers conferred on NCAs and ESMA, as well as potential sanctions that can be imposed for breaches of the EU Regulation. Lastly, the analysis will aim to question whether the current EU regulatory framework should be reinforced, and if so, in which direction? More generally, is there a clear rationale for placing more restrictions on short selling activities, or will a new reform wave mainly serve a political agenda?

10.2 SHORT SELLING REGULATORY CONCERNS

10.2.1 Market Stability Concerns

The EU Regulation aims to address market stability concerns given the impact that short selling activities may have on the markets at large. These concerns have been consistently used as a justification for regulation in this area by referring to a series of potential risks that can be grouped under the following broad categories. First of all, there is a risk of a trading trend with the expectation of price falls that can result in prices being driven further down due to a constant pressure in that direction.[10] Secondly, the risk of amplification of short selling practices and their impact upon share prices can be further exacerbated by the adoption of inappropriate practices, such as the spreading of false rumours (constituting market manipulation) or the exploitation of inside information (triggering insider dealing practices).[11] Thirdly, there is also a settlement risk in the case of uncovered (or 'naked') short selling,[12] as short sellers may wish to

---

[10] Despite this well-known (and highly publicized) concern, numerous studies have shown that short selling is not the source of drastic price declines and that the short selling bans did not curtail such declines despite the expectation that prices would increase in the absence of short selling activities: E. Boehmer, C.M. Jones and X. Zhang, 'Shackling Short Sellers: The 2008 Shorting Ban' (2013) 26 *Review of Financial Studies* 1363; R. Battalio, H. Mehran and P. Schultz, 'Market Declines: Is Banning Short Selling the Solution?' Federal Reserve Bank of New York Staff Report No 518 (2014), at http://www.newyorkfed.org/research/staff_reports/sr518.html.

[11] Nevertheless, empirical studies have shown that there is no relevant evidence and that short sellers are able to process available information and act accordingly in the market: B. Blau and J.M. Pinegar, 'Are Short Sellers Incrementally Informed Prior to Earnings Announcements?' (2013) 21 *Journal of Empirical Finance* 142; B. Blau and C. Wade, 'Informed or Speculative: Short Selling Analyst Recommendations' (2012) 36 *Journal of Banking and Finance* 14. But see *contra* N. Massoud, D. Nandy, A. Saunders and K. Song, 'Do Hedge Funds Trade on Private Information? Evidence from Syndicated Lending and Short Selling' (2011) 99 *Journal of Financial Economics* 477. Moreover, see other arguments related to the 'unconvincing' market abuse rationale in short selling advanced by E. Avgouleas, 'A New Framework for the Global Regulation of Short Sales: Why Prohibition is Inefficient and Disclosure Insufficient' (2010) 15 *Stanford Journal of Law Business and Finance* 376, 381.

[12] Uncovered short selling is now subject to a certain number of conditions provided in Article 12 of the EU Regulation.

engage in important sale transactions of securities, driving prices down further, without having made adequate arrangements for the borrowing of the same number of securities.[13]

Although the above-mentioned concerns are well justified in theory, it must be emphasized that, according to numerous empirical studies,[14] there appears to be no clear association between short selling activities and the above-mentioned market stability risks. Of course, nothing prevents short sellers from engaging in activities that can materialize these risks at the expense of other market actors and the market at large; this is why the current regulatory framework was needed. However, even if such a scenario proved to be real, it would have to have a substantial impact for the regulatory framework to be reinforced and for new duties to be imposed since a legal reform in the absence of major scandals or repeated inappropriate practices would risk becoming counterproductive and damping the short selling market.

The EU Regulation thus reflects these concerns, while also acknowledging that short selling has beneficial aspects for market actors and markets at large, opting for a balanced interventionist approach and avoiding overly restrictive prohibitions. Without constituting the main focus of our study, the beneficial aspects of short selling can be summarized as follows: short selling can contribute to price discovery and accuracy, increase market liquidity, and reduce market volatility.[15] Beginning with price discovery and accuracy, short sellers are seen as experienced traders able to decipher available information[16] and, acting upon these skills, reinforce informational quality by bridging the gap between an overvalued share price and its more fundamental value.[17] Price discovery also results from increased market liquidity since short selling reinforces the informational flow, helping market actors benefit from lower transaction costs while being able to operate in a liquid market.[18] Analysing liquidity as a separate beneficial aspect of short selling, it is well known that this kind of activity has traditionally provided facilitation in matching sell and buy orders

---

[13] See, more generally, the interesting analysis of these concerns by Payne, above n. 1, 418.

[14] See above n. 3 and n. 4. See also Avgouleas, above n. 11, 403.

[15] IOSCO Technical Committee, *IOSCO Regulation of Short Selling – Consultation Report* (2009) 22, at http://www.iosco.org/library/pubdocs/pdf/IOSCOPD289.pdf.

[16] T. Christensen, M. Drake and J. Thornock, 'Optimistic Reporting and Pessimistic Investing: Do Pro Forma Earnings Disclosure Attract Short Sellers?' (2014) 31 Contemporary Accounting Research 67.

[17] See, for example, A. Curtis and N. Fargher, 'Does Short Selling Amplify Price Declines or Align Stocks with Their Fundamental Values?' (2014) 60 *Management Science* 2324. See also Avgouleas, above n. 11, 395; see, more generally, E.M. Miller, 'Risk Uncertainty, and Divergence of Opinion' (1977) 32 *Journal of Finance* 1151, 1162. See also Payne, above n. 1, 419 that underlines that '[t]here is one, potential, caveat to this analysis. Short selling is a good tool for arbitrage in a normal market, but where the problem is not a price spike but a precipitous price fall, the arbitrage required is not sales but purchases. As a result, short selling is likely to be less beneficial to price discovery in a falling market than in a rising market.'

[18] E. Boehmer and J. Wu, 'Short Selling and the Price Discovery Process' (2013) 26 *Review of Financial Studies* 287.

and increased trading volume of less liquid stocks, as was also shown during a wide international trend of short selling bans and the ensuing decrease in market liquidity during the global financial crisis.[19] Lastly, market volatility is reduced in the presence of short selling since market actors benefit from short sellers' perception about shares' fundamental value, which helps reduce market uncertainty in general.[20]

As an overall assessment, the EU Regulation comprises a reasonable solution based on market stability risks, reflecting the politicized agenda that triggered the various reforms in this area. Other types of concerns, related to the impact of short selling activities on companies and their members, have therefore been left outside the scope of the Regulation. Despite this regulatory choice, it is important to examine these concerns in order to assess their relevance as a potential rationale for imposing duties on short sellers.[21]

10.2.2 Corporate Governance Concerns

Corporate governance concerns have arisen in literature following highly sophisticated risk reduction or elimination strategies, commonly known as 'negative decoupling',[22] employed by shareholders (typically hedge funds). Indeed, under a basic scenario, a shareholder with a long position could be interested in having an equivalent (or partial) short position to hedge the risk of an equity investment since, whichever outcome would occur in the event of an increase or decrease in the share price, the shareholder would avoid negative returns.[23] Shareholders obviously retain any voting rights attached to the long position and are therefore able to influence corporate decision-making, but with the difference that the ownership (e.g. voting) and the financial (economic exposure) interests become partially or entirely separate with the adoption of this risk hedging strategy.

More generally, any combination of long and short positions creates an underlying dissonance with other shareholders and the company since it is unpredictable how these misaligned incentives will be expressed not only in

---

[19] R. Battalio and P. Schultz, 'Regulatory Uncertainty and Market Liquidity: The 2008 Short Sale Ban's Impact on Equity Option Markets' (2011) 66 *Journal of Finance* 2013.

[20] M. Bohl, A. Klein and P. Siklos, 'Short selling Bans and Institutional Investors' Herding Behavior: Evidence from the Global Financial Crisis' (2014) 33 *International Review of Financial Analysis* 262.

[21] See 10.4.

[22] W-G. Ringe, 'Hedge Funds and Risk Decoupling: The Empty Voting Problem in the European Union' (2013) 36 *Seattle University Law Review* 1027, 1030. See also Luz María García Martínez, *Nuevas Formas de Ejercicio del Voto: La Escisión Entre la Propriedad de las Acciones y los Derechos de Voto* (Tesis doctoral, Universidad Computense Madrid, 2017).

[23] An increase in the long position's value would be offset by a decrease in the short position's value and vice versa. More complicated structures exist involving the use of other financial instruments (e.g. equity swaps, futures, forwards, puts or calls, etc.) but our study will exclusively focus on the combination of long and short positions, as highlighted above, to analyse these corporate governance concerns.

terms of voting strategies but, more generally, in terms of shareholder engagement throughout the company's life. The combination of long and short
positions has been identified as one of the many 'empty voting' techniques,[24]
with voting rights operating in a vacuum in the absence of related economic
rights (as in the case of a 'classic' shareholder whose economic exposure forms
an inherent part of the investment strategy) or, more generally, voting rights
being much greater than the economic ones. By reinventing the shareholder
status and transforming voting rights into a malleable instrument that market
actors may potentially abuse, risk decoupling strategies (i.e., for the purposes
of our study, any combination of long and short positions) can favour distorted
corporate decision-making and weaken shareholder democracy.

By allowing shareholders that have practically no economic responsibility
for their positions to influence a company's future, the exercise of voting rights
becomes even riskier as it is directly associated with a series of opaque factors
that are outside the corporate agenda and not visible to other shareholders.
This unorthodox shareholder profile can create even more serious concerns
when the short position outweighs the long one and the major interest is to
engage in value decreasing initiatives since the profit will mostly come from
the short position. But even in the scenario of long and short positions being
equal, risk-free shareholders will be in a position to influence the company with
their voting power and may drive the administration in an opposite direction to
that expected by other shareholders.

All the above-mentioned concerns reflect the canonical view of the typical
shareholder that should coexist harmoniously (up to a certain extent) with
the company's 'conventional wisdom' and other shareholders' similar agendas,
under the 'one share, one vote' principle. This principle is aimed at sustaining and promoting value-enhancing decisions for the benefit of the company[25]
and the shareholder body.[26] Notwithstanding the merits of this traditional
approach, there can be no certainty that the mere combination of long and
short positions will always trigger manipulative behaviour by risk-free shareholders (although this risk always remains possible). Furthermore, it can be

---

[24] Empty voting can also occur in a typical share lending scenario where shares are borrowed in
order to increase voting rights for a short period of time, to influence the company and deliver
them back to the lender (risk decoupling in a purely long position scenario). This is possible
since there is a transfer of ownership between the lender and the borrower and therefore of
the voting rights as well. These strategies have been criticized for allowing shareholders with
a purely temporary interest (and not the respective risk exposure) to exercise voting rights:
ICGN, *Securities Lending Code of Best Practice* (2007), at https://www.icgn.org/files/icgn_
main/pdfs/best_practice/sec_lending/2007_securities_lending_code_of_best_practice.pdf.
On various empty voting strategies more generally, see the seminal work of H. T.C. Hu and
B.S. Black, 'The New Vote Buying: Empty Voting and Hidden (Morphable) Ownership'
(2006) 79 *Southern California Law Review* 811.

[25] S.J. Grossman and O.D. Hart, 'One Share-One Vote and the Market for Corporate Control'
(1988) 20 *Journal of Financial Economics* 175.

[26] F.W. Easterbrook and D.R. Fischel, 'Voting in Corporate Law' (1983) 26 *Journal of Law
and Economics* 395.

argued that unorthodox shareholder profiles could, in some cases, be in a better position to take the lead in changing the company's mainstream approach due to their sophistication and analytical skills. More generally, 'negative decoupling' could also be seen as a way to facilitate shareholder engagement and the effective monitoring of the company's administration since more active monitoring could arise in the absence of risk exposure. Other shareholders would thus benefit from risk-free shareholders' actions and their overall strategy and objectives for the company's future development.

Contrary to the canonical view, under the market efficiency perspective that has shaped modern corporate and capital market law, it is perfectly legitimate to borrow, buy and sell shares; thus, the above-mentioned concerns would not justify the imposition of any further duties on shareholders (and short sellers). Moreover, share transfers are not exclusively purported to serve 'empty voting' strategies since they also entail the transfer of a bundle of rights (beyond voting rights), such as management and property rights. Under this approach, shareholders should be entirely free to combine long and short positions for whichever purpose they want to, and risk hedging strategies should not be primarily conceived as a manipulative strategy against the best interests of the company.

Corporate governance concerns regarding short selling could also be unanimously accepted as a reasonable basis for a more interventionist approach, as explained below, under the condition that short sellers[27] would be the only actors in a company (or at least the most tempted) to try to manipulate prices and the market at large with their misaligned incentives. This assumption can nevertheless not be accepted in the light of recent empirical evidence that shows no significant increase in manipulative practices in short sellers compared with long traders, with both categories being seen as equally manipulative (when these types of behaviour are observed).[28] In other words, the reduction or elimination of risk exposure is not the decisive trigger for corporate governance concerns[29] since even shareholders with exclusively long positions are able to manipulate the corporate structure in order to serve their own misaligned agendas.

Even if shareholders with exclusively long positions would not necessarily be willing to manipulate prices, they could still have their own misaligned incentives and try to advance their own agendas while disregarding other shareholders' desires and the mainstream or commonly shared position in the company. Acknowledging that initiatives with a 'value decreasing' objective are not necessarily a feature of short selling, the arguments for using corporate governance concerns as an additional basis for determining or reinforcing short

---

[27] And more generally actors acting after having eliminating their risk exposure towards an investment.

[28] J. Blocher, J. Engelberg and A. Reed, 'The Long and the Short of It: Evidence of Year-End Price Manipulation by Short Sellers' (2012) Working Paper, at http://papers.ssrn.com/sol3/papers.cfm?abstract_id=1364835.

[29] And therefore justify the imposition of more duties or the reinforcement of the existing ones, as it will be seen at Sections 10.4 and 10.6.1.

seller duties thus become weaker. It is important therefore to repeat that the only basis upon which these duties should, for the time being, be shaped and imposed is the market stability agenda, as used in shaping the EU Regulation. Having analysed both market stability and corporate governance concerns, our analysis will now turn to the efficiency of the operational constraints on short selling activities, as they have been envisaged at the EU level, following similar experiences in the USA.

10.3 OPERATIONAL CONSTRAINTS ON SHORT SELLING ACTIVITIES

10.3.1 Short Selling Bans

Temporary short selling bans became popular in various countries following the collapse of Lehman Brothers in the USA.[30] At that stage, such bans seemed to be the only viable solution to restrict the destructive ramifications of price volatility and precipitous falls in financial stocks' prices, 'however blunt and ineffective a tool [they] subsequently turned out to be'.[31] Different approaches with regard to the applicability spectrum of these bans (namely bans on short selling activities of all listed securities or only of financial stocks) created a rather inconsistent regulatory response at the international level,[32] making a harmonization process even more necessary. In addition to short selling bans at large, various jurisdictions further distinguished between covered and uncovered short sales, touching upon uncovered in the first instance but then backtracking and including covered as well.[33] The overall impression of the regulatory responses to short sales during the crisis is therefore not particularly encouraging for the harmonization prospects internationally, as various jurisdictions were caught up in their old standards and legal traditions, failing to participate in a more coordinated framework to tackle these issues.

Given the settlement risks associated with short sales, but also being aware of strong political concerns in this area related to sovereign CDS transactions, the EU Regulation drew a decisive line between covered and uncovered short sales, allowing only the covered ones in the following manner: with regard to the focus of our chapter, a short sale is allowed only when the shares have been borrowed (or alternative provisions have been made leading to the same result) or in the presence of either an agreement to borrow the shares (or of

---

[30] See Payne, above n. 1.

[31] N. Moloney, *EU Securities and Financial Markets Regulation* (3rd edn, Oxford University Press, 2014) 541. See also recent empirical data that argue that the bans did not result in a reduction in return volatility, price drops and probability of default: A. Beber, D. Fabbri and M. Pagano, 'Short Selling Bans and Bank Stability' (2016) CEPR Discussion Paper No DP11090, at http://ssrn.com/abstract=2733024.

[32] A. Beber and M. Pagano, 'Short Selling Bans around the World: Evidence from the 2007–2009 Crisis' (2013) 68 *Journal of Finance* 343.

[33] J.G. Hill, 'Why Did Australia Fare so Well in the Global Financial Crisis?' in E. Ferran, N. Moloney, J.G. Hill and J.C. Coffee Jr., *The Regulatory Aftermath of the Global Financial Crisis* (Oxford University Press, 2012), 257.

an absolutely enforceable claim regarding the transfer of ownership of a cor-responding number of securities and resulting in settlement when it is due) or, lastly, in the presence of an arrangement with a third party confirming that the share has been located and that arrangements have been made with third parties for the short seller to have a reasonable expectation that settlement will take place when due.[34]

Of particular importance is the last criterion, namely the 'locate rule', which is further detailed in the Implementing Regulation No 827/2012. Indeed, there is a general requirement, prior to the short sale, of a locate confirmation, that is, confirmation by the third party that it will be able to make available the number of shares required to enable settlement. In the presence of liquid shares or same day sales, the Regulation also requires a confirmation that the shares are easy to borrow or purchase. In the presence of illiquid shares, there is a requirement for a 'put on hold' confirmation, that is, a confirmation by the third party that it has put on hold the number of shares required to cover the forthcoming short sale.[35]

It is therefore rather straightforward to understand that the above-mentioned rules constitute quintessentially a ban on uncovered short sales with a broad range of applicability, since all types of shares are envisaged in these rules. The EU framework thus aims higher than the temporary bans put into effect during the global financial crisis in various countries and which focused on financial stocks.

10.3.2 Circuit Breakers

Circuit breakers aim to maintain control of precipitous price falls by imposing temporary restrictions on short selling activities. According to the EU Regu-lation, NCAs must consider whether they should impose such restrictions or prohibitions upon natural or legal persons in the presence of a fall in value of 10% or more for liquid shares[36] during the same trading day, the amount being calculated with regard to the previous day's closing price on the same venue.[37] The restrictions will be activated until the end of the next trading day and can be renewed for two additional trading days in the presence of a price fall

---

[34] Article 12(1), EU Regulation. Similar provisions (and restrictions) are provided in Articles 13 and 14 for short sales in sovereign debt and credit default swaps respectively.

[35] Article 6 of the Implementing Regulation (EU) 827/2012 of 29 June 2012 laying down implementing technical standards with regard to the means for public disclosure of net position in shares, the format of the information to be provided to the European Securities and Markets Authority in relation to net short positions, the types of agreements, arrangements and measures to adequately ensure that shares or sovereign debt instruments are available for settlement and the dates and period for the determination of the principal venue for a share according to Regulation (EU) No 236/2012 of the European Parliament and of the Council on short selling and certain aspects of credit default swaps [2012] OJ L 251/11.

[36] For illiquid shares and other types of financial instruments, see Commission Delegated Regulation (EU) no 918/2012.

[37] Article 23, EU Regulation.

(despite the initial circuit breaker).[38] ESMA also has the power to intervene in the presence of exceptional circumstances and to prohibit or impose conditions on short selling activities.[39] The EU framework therefore relies on national regulators, which are expected to assess the appropriateness of such prohibitions or restrictions and eventually impose them on market actors. The overall impression from these circuit breaker rules is that the EU has adopted a rather strict approach. Indeed, as Payne suggests, '[i]n most cases such a fall, especially of non-financial stocks, will reflect the macro or micro-economic fundamentals, and not short selling giving rise to systemic risks'.[40]

The USA has a very different historical background with regard to circuit breakers and uptick rules, the latter being triggered in the presence of an 'uptick' for the restriction of short sales to be waived.[41] After a series of criticisms with regard to the appropriateness of the uptick rule,[42] it eventually adopted a variation of the initial rule (the 'alternative uptick rule') integrating a circuit breaker into its function. According to this rule, restrictions on short sales are imposed in the presence of a price fall of more than 10% (in comparison with the previous day's closing price) but, unlike the EU rule, these restrictions can be waived if the price rises above the best bid at the national level. Regardless of the opportunity in amending the previous regime and aiming to improve the 'uptick rule', empirical studies[43] have raised concerns that remain valid with regard to the questionable efficiency of this rule in preventing prices from further declines and to its influence on the execution of short sales.

In addition to the above-mentioned operational constraints that may be adopted in specific circumstances with the aim to protect market stability from risky short selling activities, the EU Regulation focuses primarily on the introduction of disclosure duties to safeguard the operational framework of short selling.

10.4 INFORMATIONAL CONSTRAINTS ON SHORT SELLING ACTIVITIES

10.4.1 Disclosure Duties towards the Regulator

The EU Regulation provides that a natural or legal person with a net short position equivalent to 0.2% or higher of a listed company's issued share capital has the obligation to notify the national regulator of that position and of any further 0.1% increase in that position.[44] The notification to the

---

[38] Article 23(2), ibid.

[39] Article 28, ibid. For further discussion, see Section 10.5.1.2.

[40] Payne, above n. 1, 439.

[41] A further distinction with regard to 'uptick' types has to be made: 'plus tick' concerns a short sale which has to be at a higher price compared to the previous sale and 'zero plus tick' regards a short sale at an equal price (to the previous sale) but which was higher than the previous different price.

[42] G.J. Alexander and M.A. Peterson, 'Short Selling on the New York Stock Exchange and the Effects of the Uptick Rule' (1999) 8 *Journal of Financial Intermediation* 90.

[43] Ibid.

[44] Article 5(1) and (2), EU Regulation.

regulator serves the basic purpose of keeping the NCA informed so that it can efficiently supervise short selling activities on an ongoing basis. Moreover, the 0.2% threshold theoretically makes it easier for the authority to submit further enquiries to the market actors concerned with the aim to prevent aggressive short selling that may have detrimental effects on the investee company's operations and the market functioning.[45] The relatively low threshold applicable in this case is mainly justified by the need to supervise any potentially inappropriate and destabilising short selling practices in a timely manner, leaving the disclosure to the market to a later stage, as will be shown below.

Nevertheless, the initial 0.2% threshold has, unsurprisingly, been viewed by market actors (e.g. institutional investors) as very easy to reach in a relatively short time and therefore unduly burdensome given the exposure, costs and time concerns involved in disclosure obligations.[46] Moreover, the threshold has been criticized for potentially overloading regulators with notifications by short sellers, possibly reducing their capacity to make the best use of the available data. Other sources, such as the Committee on Legal Affairs of the European Parliament, have also noted the shortfalls of such a low threshold and have proposed a 1% threshold instead.[47]

Although it remains unclear whether the future regulatory position will raise this threshold, the EU Regulation has, for the time being, provided that ESMA may issue an opinion to the Commission in order to adjust the thresholds, taking into consideration developments on financial markets. We should therefore not rule out such an amendment in the future, especially if we view the 0.2% threshold as an initial 'safety valve' in the midst of a highly politicized agenda that could be relaxed if there are no major scandals involving short selling of listed companies' shares.

A second layer of concerns relates to the lack of harmonization of reporting rules, triggered according to the previously mentioned thresholds, among regulators at the EU level. This would ideally be resolved through the introduction of a centralized system.[48] The EU Regulation praises uniformity in the application of the reporting rules,[49] but this objective is left up to ESMA's

---

[45] FSA, 'Short Selling Discussion Paper 09/1' (February 2009) 29.

[46] Oliver Wyman Inc., 'The Effects of Short Selling Public Disclosure of Individual Positions on Equity Markets' (2010), 43, at http://www.managedfunds.org/wp-content/uploads/2011/06/plugin-Oliver_Wyman_Financial_Services_Report.pdf.

[47] European Parliament, 'Report on the Proposal for a Regulation of the European Parliament and of the Council on Short Selling and Certain Aspects of Credit Default Swaps' (A7-0055/2011) 48. For a similar position from the London Stock Exchange (in 2009) see Letter from Anita Collett, *Regulatory Strategy, London Stock Exchange to Carlo Comporti*, at http://www.londonstock exchange.com/about-the-exchange/regulatory/response-cers-call-evidence-short selling.pdf.

[48] See some very interesting examples from various jurisdictions described by E. Howell, 'Short Selling Reporting Rules: A Greenfield Area' (2015) 12(2) *European Company Law* 79, 82. For the same issue at a global level, see the analysis by E. Zlotnikova, 'The Global Dilemma in Short Selling Regulation: IOSCO's Information Disclosure Proposals and the Potential for Regulatory Arbitrage' (2010) 35 *Brooklyn Journal of International Law* 965, 977.

[49] Recital 3.

coordinating efforts that may not currently be sufficient due to different operational methods adopted at the national level. One possible way forward, which
is unfortunately unlikely to receive support at the current stage,[50] would be the
creation of an EU website grouping together all disclosed data or the creation
and circulation by ESMA of a reporting form that would need to be used by
all national regulators.[51] While the first option seems quite unpopular,[52] the
second could be much more realistic at the current stage and would most likely
ensure uniformity among regulators.

10.4.2 Disclosure Duties towards the Market

The EU Regulation introduced an obligation for natural or legal persons to
disclose to the public any net short position of 0.5%, with additional disclosure
obligations at every additional 0.1%. Extending beyond the above-mentioned
necessity for the regulator to monitor short selling activities at a relatively early
stage, the disclosure to the public occurs at a later stage, with 0.5% being
considered an important threshold that needs to be known to the rest of the
market. The justifications for such a disclosure obligation are, as in similar disclosure obligations in capital markets law and among many factors, the increase
in market transparency, the possibility for market actors to have greater insight
into the dynamics of long and short positions in an investee company, and the
constraint on inappropriate short selling practices.[53] It is hoped that sharing
this information with the rest of the market will make these activities subject to
market scrutiny and will enhance their legitimacy by enabling other actors to
trade upon a wider informational spectrum. It therefore becomes obvious that
the overall arguments for the imposition of a rather low threshold of 0.5% rely
upon market stability concerns with the aim to instrumentalize transparency in
this area to ensure an optimal trading framework.

Although the transparency arguments are worthy of attention and can clearly
legitimize disclosure obligations, it should be borne in mind that disclosure to
the public may also have undesirable effects. First of all, short sellers might

---

[50] Only a small minority of national regulators was in favour of a centralized system at the EU
level, the majority claiming that the current arrangements run smoothly, the costs would be
increased, they would not be in a position to monitor the data and potentially react in real time
and that, in the eventual transfer of the net short positions to an EU system, information would
be fragmented (with regard to other types of issuer-related information) disclosed by some
regulators: ESMA, 'Final Report: ESMA's Technical Advice on the Evaluation of the Regulation
(EU) 236/2012 of the European Parliament and of the Council on Short Selling and Certain
Aspects of Credit Default Swaps' (ESMA/2013/614), 19, at https://www.esma.europa.eu/
sites/default/files/library/2015/11/2013-614_final_report_on_ssr_evaluation.pdf.
[51] Howell, above n. 48, 83.
[52] Ibid.
[53] European Commission, 'Impact Assessment – Accompanying Document to the Proposal
for a Regulation of the European Parliament and of the Council on Short Selling and
Certain Aspects of Credit Default Swaps' (SEC(2010) 1055), 58, at http://ec.europa.eu/
smart-regulation/impact/ia_carried_out/docs/ia_2010/sec_2010_1055_en.pdf.

be unduly exposed to strategic market behaviour that may compromise the beneficial aspects of their practices.[54] Secondly, they may find themselves in a 'short squeeze' situation and incur significant losses due to increased transparency of their positions that could enable shareholders of the investee company to keep their shares and be reluctant to sell when the short sellers are interested in buying them back to fulfil their contractual duty towards the lender.[55] Thirdly, the above-mentioned undesirable effects may make short selling a much less attractive activity and dissuade market actors from selling short (or simply maintaining their positions right under disclosure thresholds).[56] As previously mentioned, this would inevitably lead to a decrease in market liquidity.[57] Adding to that scenario, market actors might find even more opaque areas of activities to conduct their business without being subject to these disclosure requirements. This will have the consequence not only of creating an even 'darker operational spectrum' but also of transforming the current rules into a 'dead letter' framework.

Lastly, the increase in transparency will inevitably trigger excessive or unnecessary herding behaviour.[58] This is due to the fact that, although herding is a common phenomenon in financial markets, it can prove to be disastrous in this area if market actors perceive net short positions as a constant precursor for abusive short selling and react accordingly, i.e. by deciding to dissociate themselves from the alleged negative effects of short positions by selling their shares, without realising that these short positions may simply be a mixture of legitimate hedging practices and not a sign of mistrust of the expected company's progress.[59]

Contrary to the herding issue, it could be plausibly argued that increased transparency could also generate a 'free rider' problem since other market actors will be tempted to mimic short selling positions, benefiting from increased disclosure in this area without having to bear the disclosure-related

---

[54] Payne, above n. 1, 437.

[55] O. Bernal, A. Herinckx and A. Szafarz, 'Which Short Selling Regulation is the Least Damaging to Market Efficiency? Evidence from Europe' (2014) 37 *International Review of Law and Economics* 244; A.J. Kammel, 'The Dilemma of Blind Spots in Capital Markets – How to Make Efficient Use of Regulatory Loopholes?' (2009) 10(5) *German Law Journal* 605.

[56] ESMA, above n. 50, 13. See also the interesting empirical study with regard to the reduction of trading volumes and the increase in volatility as a consequence of disclosure requirements: O. Bernal, A. Herinckx and A. Szafarz, ibid.

[57] Oliver Wyman Inc., above n. 46, 43.

[58] On the concept of herding, see D. Scharfstein and J. Stein, 'Herd Behavior and Investment' (1990) 80 *American Economic Review* 465.

[59] Bearing especially in mind that, apart from rational market actors acting upon information, there are also 'noise' traders acting upon imperfect information and who will be willing to imitate 'short selling related' actions without an *a priori* informational analysis: A. Shleifer and L.H. Summers, 'The Noise Trader Approach to Finance' (1990) 4 *Journal of Economic Perspectives* 19 analysed in Avgouleas, above n. 11, 395; see also, on this topic, Zlotnikova, above n. 48, 987.

costs.[60] This can also lead to a decrease in the incentives to look for information since empirical studies have shown that high-quality disclosure can discourage market actors from seeking new information, as they simply grow accustomed to depending on the enriched disclosed data.[61]

Disclosure of short selling positions has nevertheless received a considerable amount of support from some studies that show that, contrary to public perception, disclosure duties in this area can actually enhance market liquidity.[62] Short selling can therefore function as a highly informative signal for other market actors who will be able to decipher (or at least understand for their own decisions) short sellers' trading behaviour, namely trading upon the expectation of a price decline. These signals will provide market actors with a more holistic view of market activity and will make them more willing to participate in transactions.[63]

The quest for transparency is undoubtedly a legitimate one, but the thresholds that trigger such objectives may need to be fine-tuned in the future since it would appear that short sellers, as well as other sources,[64] find them unreasonably burdensome, both for short sellers and for regulators, and unnecessary. Most importantly, the evidence of the overall effect of disclosure remains inconclusive; although disclosure in this area may have some repercussions on short selling activities, it seems unlikely that it would reduce short selling to a level that would significantly affect market liquidity and the resulting informational quality.[65]

10.5 SUPERVISION AND SANCTIONS

10.5.1 Supervisory and Investigatory Powers

10.5.1.1 NCAs
The EU Regulation provides for a series of powers of intervention for NCAs in particular circumstances. These relate to the imposition of additional disclosure requirements, temporary bans or, more generally, conditions on short selling practices.[66]

Beginning with additional disclosure requirements, the association of notification obligations and the politicized agenda can be seen in the power that NCAs

---

[60] A.N. Licht, 'Regulatory Arbitrage for Real: International Securities Regulation in a World of Interacting Securities Markets' (1998) 38 *Vanderbilt Journal of International Law* 563, 567.

[61] S. Brown and S.A. Hillegeist, 'How Disclosure Quality Affects the Level of Information Asymmetry' (2007) 12 *Review of Accounting Studies* 443.

[62] A. Beber and M. Pagano, 'Short Selling Bans Around the World: Evidence from the 2007–09 Crisis' (2013) 68 *Journal of Finance* 343.

[63] G. Pownall and P.J. Simko, 'The Information Intermediary Role of Short Sellers' (2005) 80 *Accounting Review* 941; T. Arnold, A.W. Butler, T.F. Crack and Y. Zhang, 'The Information Content of Short Interest: A Natural Experiment' (2005) 78 *Journal of Business* 1307.

[64] See above n. 45 and n. 46.

[65] P.K. Staikouras, 'The EU Short Selling Regulation Revisited: New Evidence, Different Perspective?' (2015) 26(4) *European Business Law Review* 531.

[66] All these measures can be applicable for a three-month period and are potentially renewable for another three-month period: Article 24, EU Regulation.

have, according to Article 18 of the EU Regulation, to require notification of net short positions taken by natural or legal persons according to thresholds set by the regulators and in exceptional circumstances. These circumstances may refer to the presence of adverse events or developments that seriously threaten financial stability or market confidence. Moreover, notification can be required when considered appropriate to the threat in question and without triggering detrimental (and disproportionate) consequences for the efficiency of financial markets.

Even if this power does not relate to net short positions in a company's issued share capital, this is a particularly interesting area that may give highly informative examples of the ad hoc powers exercised at a national level and the way in which they are chosen by a regulator as an interventionist means whose benefits outweigh the costs arising from the additional notification obligation. Bearing this in mind, close attention must be paid to the pre-existing levels of sophistication of national regulators in order for these powers to be exercised efficiently, namely in a timely and well-adjusted manner with regard to each situation that may arise in this context.

Article 18 also provides the same intervention power with regard to the imposition of additional and exceptional cases that will trigger market disclosure of details of the net short position. Similar reserves need to be formulated regarding this power since it will need to be exercised in a well-balanced and timely way, also requiring an adequate preparation and supervisory capacity of the regulator, which will enable a prompt intervention. Moreover, the EU Regulation does not provide any indication with regard to potential incidents that may trigger such intervention and this is something that needs to be further clarified.

The exceptional circumstances, clarified in a non-exhaustive list,[67] can also justify restrictions on short selling and similar transactions,[68] as well as on a sovereign credit default swap transactions.[69]

A different measure can be imposed in the presence of a significant fall in price, without requiring the presence of exceptional circumstances. This measure relates to the imposition of a circuit breaker, as analysed above, in the presence of a fall of 10% for liquid shares.[70]

With regard to investigatory powers, NCAs dispose of an extensive range of means to conduct their supervision tasks, such as access to documents, information-related requests, on-site inspections, orders to cease inappropriate practices and others.[71] In line with other EU texts, the cooperation among NCAs,[72] with third countries[73] and with ESMA[74] will be of crucial importance

---

[67] Article 24, Commission Delegated Regulation (EU) no 918/2012.

[68] Article 20, EU Regulation.

[69] Article 21, ibid.

[70] For illiquid shares and other types of financial instruments, see Commission Delegated Regulation (EU) no 918/2012.

[71] Article 33(2), EU Regulation.

[72] Articles 35 and 37, ibid.

[73] Article 38, ibid.

[74] Article 36, ibid.

to the effective supervision of short selling practices, not only within the EU but also in the third countries concerned by the enforcement of obligations related to the EU regulation.

10.5.1.2 ESMA

ESMA has been given a predominantly supervisory role among national regulators aiming to ensure the facilitation and coordination of the exercise of their powers and, most importantly, the consistency in the way that all measures or restrictions are taken at the national level.[75] All the above potentially imposed measures and restrictions must be notified, prior to their entry into force,[76] to ESMA providing the necessary amount of details.[77] ESMA is also expected to issue an opinion[78] related to the appropriateness and proportionality of the proposed measure (and its duration) to address the exceptional circumstances.[79] National authorities remain free to take action that does not coincide with ESMA's opinion by publishing the reasons for such derogation within 24 hours.[80] This possibility does not of course mean that ESMA is completely unarmed in this kind of scenario since it can still make use of its intervention powers in exceptional circumstances under Article 28. More generally, this Article provides for intervention powers in the presence of a threat to the orderly functioning and integrity of the markets or to the financial system's stability with cross-border implications and in the absence of measures taken by national authorities (or if the measures already taken by these authorities are deemed to be insufficient to tackle the threat in question).[81]

It therefore becomes evident that ESMA has a significant role to play in the presence of exceptional circumstances given its quite broad scope for intervention. More specifically, ESMA can require natural or legal persons to make disclosures to the national authority or the public; it can also prohibit or impose conditions on short sales.[82] ESMA is expected to take into consideration a series of factors to ensure that the exercise of these powers constitutes an adequate means of dealing with the exceptional circumstances in question. The EU Regulation also provides for a continuous dialogue in these situations,

---

[75] Article 27, ibid.

[76] The notification must occur not less than 24 hours before the measures or restrictions take place, except for the presence of exceptional circumstances which justify a notification in less than 24 hours: Article 26(3), ibid.

[77] Article 26(2), ibid.

[78] The opinion must be issued within 24 hours, except in the case of a circuit breaker, given the imminent need to impose such a restriction, where no opinion is issued.

[79] Article 27(2), ibid. ESMA can also indicate whether similar measures can be taken by other national regulators to address the concerned situation.

[80] Article 27(3), ibid. In a circuit breaker scenario, ESMA will still have to be notified but there is no obligation for the national authority to justify its different position. ESMA is thus left with a general coordinating task to ensure the avoidance of ramifications in the presence of instruments traded in various markets.

[81] Article 28(2), ibid.

[82] Article 28(1), ibid.

with a series of notifications to the national authorities of ESMA's measures and publications of these measures or any renewal thereafter.[83] It should also be highlighted that ESMA's adopted measures prevail over any prior measures taken by national authorities.[84]

The EU Regulation thus aims to create an adequately coordinated operational framework within which national authorities retain a certain amount of freedom in exercising their intervention powers under ESMA's overarching coordinating responsibility. ESMA can considerably curb this freedom but only in exceptional circumstances, while maintaining the informational requirements for ESMA that aim to preserve communication with national authorities. This escalation of exercising power within this 'two-speed' decision-making framework represents, for the time being, an optimal solution given the recent character of reforms in this area and may leave space for further developments in the future, especially with regard to the reinforcement of ESMA's intervention role.

Nevertheless, it is also crucial to note that ESMA needs to be very cautious when it has the opportunity to exercise the above-mentioned powers on an ad hoc basis, especially as Member States have strongly questioned the legitimacy of these powers.[85]

10.5.2 Sanctions

With regard to sanctions applicable in the area of short selling practices, the EU regulation provides in Article 41 that it is the Member States' task to establish rules on penalties and administrative measures fulfilling the criteria of effectiveness, proportionality and dissuasiveness. Acknowledging the quite recent regulatory developments in this area, it would be particularly interesting to see any convergence trends among NCAs, in the absence of which any future amendment of the EU regulation should include commonly accepted factors to be taken into consideration by these authorities in the exercise of their powers. These factors could be similar to those mentioned in the Transparency Directive[86] and Market Abuse Regulation[87] and could lead to an indirect harmonization trend among regulators which will further enhance the existence of a level playing field in the area of enforcement. According to the same Article,

---

[83] Article 28(3–10), ibid.
[84] Article 28(11), ibid.
[85] See, for example, the UK's challenge to Article 28 of the EU Regulation, advancing the argument, among many others, that it is not in line with the delegation of powers framework, as it has been shaped by the *Meroni* and *Romano* doctrines. The UK's challenge was not successful since the European Court of Justice decided to uphold ESMA's powers: Case C-270/12 *United Kingdom v. Council of the European Union and European Parliament* (ECJ, 22 January 2014); C. Di Noia and M. Gargantini, 'Unleashing the European Securities and Markets Authority: Governance and Accountability after the ECJ Decision on the Short Selling Regulation (Case C-270/12)' (2014) 15 *European Business Organization Law Review* 1, 31.
[86] See Chapter 5.
[87] See Chapter 6.

ESMA can issue guidelines to that effect, and it receives annual and aggregate data on penalties and administrative measures from national regulators which will prove most probably very useful in the convergence task.

10.6 TOWARDS A REINFORCED BUT LESS RESTRICTIVE FRAMEWORK

10.6.1 Enhanced Disclosure Duties

One possible further regulatory intervention in the area of short selling would be to enhance disclosure duties, namely by introducing a disclosure obligation for any short position held with regard to the listed company's issued share capital.[88] As we have already seen, the current disclosure obligations in the area of short selling relate to net short positions. Moreover, Article 9 of the Transparency Directive[89] provides for shareholder disclosure obligations of long positions, associated with voting rights, which must be notified to the issuer.[90] In theory, it would therefore make sense to reinforce the current regulatory framework with disclosure of short positions in listed companies.

Would an enhancement of disclosure duties foster transparency in short selling activities, enable market actors to make more informed decisions, and ensure an optimal monitoring framework? To answer this question, we must first decipher the inherent justification for such an enhancement. If the rationale behind such an initiative is based on market stability concerns, which have triggered the above-mentioned EU reforms, it would be plausible to assert that a reinforcement in this direction would not serve any additional purpose. Indeed, the current measures with net short position thresholds of 0.2% (notification to the regulator) and of 0.5% (disclosure to the market) largely respond to these concerns, even in an overly cautious way, given the amount of criticism exercised by institutional investors as noted above. Market stability is not necessarily threatened by any short position but potentially when a net short position is of a certain size. Therefore, the duty to notify and disclose should arise as a preventive measure against abusive short selling.

Nevertheless, if the rationale behind such a reform is based on corporate governance concerns, namely the need for the company and other shareholders to be aware of any short position in order to be able to anticipate future potentially abusive practices, the answer might not be straightforward. On the one hand, the arguments for other shareholders and the company to be aware

---

[88] Ringe, above n. 22, 1120.

[89] Directive 2013/50/EU of the European Parliament and of the Council of 22 October 2013 amending Directive 2004/109/EC of the European Parliament and of the Council on the harmonization of transparency requirements in relation to information about issuers whose securities are admitted to trading on a regulated market, Directive 2003/71/EC of the European Parliament and of the Council on the prospectus to be published when securities are offered to the public or admitted to trading, and Commission Directive 2007/14/EC laying down detailed rules for the implementation of certain provisions of Directive 2004/109/EC [2013] OJ L 294/13.

[90] The thresholds are 5%, 10%, 15%, 20%, 25%, 30%, 50% and 75%: Article 9(1), ibid.

of any short position are reasonable in the sense that short selling activities, whether or not combined with long positions, may constitute important signals of a behaviour that does not necessarily coincide with the company's 'conventional wisdom' given the fact that profit is expected out of a fall in the share price. Under this perspective, the members of the company and the company itself would benefit from receiving information about a short position that would otherwise not be disclosed under the current framework.[91] This would enable them to be better prepared to react to an increased participation of a short seller in its long and short positions, or simply an increased percentage of a short position, both scenarios being potentially alarming as the short sellers' interests are not aligned with the company's.

On the other hand, close attention must be paid to the overall ramifications of disclosure of any short position both inside the company and in the market at large. First of all, shareholders could be alarmed by any short position disclosed, without necessarily being equipped to distinguish between more and less important cases. This could accidentally trigger investment or divestment decisions based upon less sophisticated factors and could potentially disrupt the regular investment flow in the company. Secondly, the company itself could be unnecessarily alarmed by the disclosure of all short positions and even invest resources and time to analyse all the information received without necessarily being in a position to prevent or control future movements in this area. Thirdly, regulators (in case such an obligation were extended to the regulator) would be overloaded by the increased volume of disclosure, facing the same problems with regard to resources and time invested in analysing all the data, as well as the fact that not all short positions would be alarming or relevant for monitoring purposes. Lastly, market actors would be much more inclined to herding behaviour since the multiplication of data would add substantial, constant 'noise', giving the impression that all short positions are able to transmit a significant signal and therefore influence other investors' decision-making.

---

[91] In that respect, Ringe, above n. 22, 1103–1104 provides some very interesting examples: A hedge fund with a 0% net short position (7% long and 7% short position), a hedge fund with a 0.5% net short position (1% long and 1.5% short position) and, lastly, a hedge fund with no net short position (10% long and 5% short position). In the first case, there is a disclosure duty for the long position but no disclosure duty for the net short position (according to the EU Regulation). From a corporate governance angle, it is crucial for the rest of the company as well as for investors to be aware of this 'risk elimination' strategy. In the second case, there is no disclosure duty for the long position but there is a duty of disclosure for the net short position notwithstanding the relatively insignificant position of the risk-free shareholder in this case. Nevertheless, the recipients of the information cannot decipher the size of influence of the shareholder and hence the 'net short position' information might not be the optimal regulatory choice as it can be subject to various interpretations (the same net short position would result from a 4.9% long and 5.4% short position but the shareholder's influence on the company is much greater hence the need for the simple short position to be disclosed separately). In the third and final case, although there is no net short position, a shareholder who has decided to reduce the risk exposure by half might be tempted to promote a misaligned agenda that needs to be known to the other shareholders and the company.

The last factor, namely the increase in herd behaviour, seems to be the main argument against the introduction of reinforced disclosure duties in this area. Although it is reasonably expected that the information produced would theoretically benefit the company and its shareholders, any proposal in that direction must be weighed against the inevitable increase in herd behaviour.[92] Such an increase could prove to be much more alarming or destabilising than the short selling activities themselves insofar as the undesired risks would outweigh the expected benefits of increased disclosure. It is therefore supported that, for the time being, and in the absence of major and repeated scandals in this area, the most efficient approach is to continue with the current framework, namely disclosure of net short positions.

An alternative and interesting proposal has been formulated by Emilios Avgouleas, focusing on the need for different thresholds based on stock liquidity levels.[93] For example, a 0.3% threshold is suggested for listed securities that are part of a market's main index, 0.6% for stocks traded outside the main market index (thus presenting lower liquidity levels), and 1% for stocks traded OTC. Further disclosure obligations would occur at additional increments of 0.25% (for all listed shares) and 0.5% (for OTC shares). Under this scheme, liquidity would go hand in hand with thresholds, taking into account different realities when disclosure occurs, and short sellers are protected from traders potentially aiming to adopt an opposite strategy, since they are allowed to have a narrower or larger trading margin without being obliged to disclose their positions.[94]

Whatever the future implications of the above-mentioned proposals, it seems rather unlikely that the current disclosure rules will change, as has been stated by ESMA[95] and the Commission.[96]

10.6.2 Shareholder Disenfranchisement

Another line of argumentation could focus on alternative ways that could effectively restrict the negative ramifications of short selling practices and, as a result, ensure that short sellers fulfil their ongoing duties without destabilising investee companies. For example, shareholder disenfranchisement in the case of risk elimination activities could prohibit short sellers from influencing corporate

---

[92] More generally on this concern, the FSA [now FCA] pointed out that '[I]f investors respond irrationally [...] the price decline may be excessive (price overshooting) and may be misleading about the value of the stock(s). Overshooting can become a self-fulfilling prophecy for firms in sectors experiencing stress, resulting in disorderly markets': FSA, above n. 45, 4.

[93] Avgouleas, above n. 11, 418.

[94] Ibid., 419.

[95] ESMA, above n. 50, 12.

[96] Commission, 'Report from the Commission to the European Parliament and the Council on the Evaluation of the Regulation (EU) No 236/2012 on Short Selling and Certain Aspects of Credit Default Swaps', Brussels, COM(2013) 885 final, 13 December 2013, at http://ec.europa.eu/transparency/regdoc/rep/1/2013/EN/1-2013-885-EN-F1-1.Pdf.

decision-making with the ultimate aim of driving the company's share price down or, more generally, of serving their own misaligned agenda. Of course, risk elimination activities are not solely confined to short selling practices, as seen above, and any reform in that respect must be applicable not only to these strategies but also to all strategies with risk elimination results. Such prohibition would be based on the fact that:

> [i]f the risk exposure is the real justification for shareholders entitled to vote at all, this justification disappears where the shareholder is able to eliminate that risk. A risk-free shareholder cannot fulfil the function of the vote—to express the best possible decision for the strategic direction of the company. A risk-free shareholder will always exercise his voting rights for purely selfish and potentially detrimental social considerations. The right to vote in this way loses its positive function, while a rational actor would exercise it in the spirit of the firm community. It potentially becomes an instrument prone to abuse, leading to self-benefit.[97]

Among the proposals made in that respect, there seems to be a broad consensus on the necessity to restrict shareholders' voting power in risk-decoupling cases.[98] Nevertheless, examining the concept of disenfranchisement for the purposes of our current study, it would be useful to question whether a general voting prohibition, applicable to shareholders with risk elimination strategies, could resolve all the problems arising from abusive short selling. This assumption could be true since voting power would be eliminated and the concerned shareholders would, in theory, be unable to impose their misaligned approach to the rest of the company. In practice, however, the same shareholders could have alternative means of influencing corporate boards, such as informal meetings, which could lead us to the conclusion that a general voting prohibition would not necessarily protect the company and its shareholders from all risks in this area. Moreover, such a prohibition could be seen as an overly cautious and unduly restrictive approach that could deter short selling at large in the first place and thus deprive both the company and the market of some beneficial aspects of this kind of activity.[99]

A less strict solution would thus need to be found which would enable an ad hoc intervention only in exceptional circumstances where voting prohibition would be justified. A very interesting proposal, with regard to risk-decoupling activities in general, has been advanced more recently,[100] advocating the

---

[97] Ringe, above n. 22, 1073–1074.
[98] See, for example, H. T.C. Hu and B. Black, 'Equity and Debt Decoupling and Empty Voting II: Importance and Extensions' (2008) 156 *University of Pennsylvania Law Review* 625, 701. For short selling in particular, see a similar proposal by S.P. Martin and F. Partnoy, 'Encumbered Shares' (2005) 3 *University of Illinois Law Review* 775, 793.
[99] For example, see the arguments under Sections 10.2.1 and 10.2.2 *supra* with regard to the facilitation of shareholder activism via short selling activities when the risk is reduced or eliminated as well as the overall benefits drawn from this sector for price efficiency and so on.
[100] Ringe, above n. 22, 1109–1112.

introduction of such an ad hoc power accorded to national regulators. The latter would be able to decide individually on each case taking into account a series of factors, such as 'the actual scope and extent of the risk-decoupling situation [...] the timing of the situation [...] [and] the potential harm of the risk-decoupled situation'.[101] Such a proposal would be welcome in short selling activities, as it would allow the regulator to decipher, insofar as this is possible, the distinctive features of each and every case and eventually impose voting restrictions in the presence of abusive or overly aggressive strategies.

A significant problem would nevertheless remain with regard to such an additional power accorded to national regulators (and combined with enhanced disclosure duties, namely disclosure of all short positions).[102] The multiplication of disclosed data, along with the expectation for a regulator to intervene on an ad hoc basis, would inevitably affect the latter's supervisory capacity and result in an overload that could lessen, in theory, its potential contribution to the timely confrontation of serious cases. It therefore remains to be seen whether policymakers would be willing to move in that direction in the future, acknowledging the limitations mentioned above (if national regulators were not equipped with the staff and expertise to face these challenges).

10.7 CONCLUSION

Short selling has undoubtedly created a considerable amount of controversy related to its impact on companies, shareholders and markets at large. Market stability and corporate governance concerns have been used in literature as justification for introducing or expanding short seller duties. As we have seen, only the former category (market stability) has been used by regulators, as corporate governance concerns are still marginalized as a rationale for the imposition of duties. The question of whether duties should be imposed on short sellers, and to what extent, was central to this chapter that aimed to portray not only the array of these duties, but also the wider implications of the current EU regulatory framework.

The disclosure duties, operational restrictions and various powers potentially exercised in particular circumstances were introduced by the EU Regulation as a result of the highly politicized agenda following the well-known incidents of sovereign credit default swaps and the collapse of financial services firms. It was therefore inevitable for the 'market stability' rhetoric to prevail in the regulatory agenda, but this should not lead future reforms to enhance duties without a clear raison d'être.[103] Regulators seem to be reluctant to impose further restrictions, not only due to the lack of empirical evidence supporting such a decision but also in the presence of inconclusive assumptions around the merits and

---

[101] Ibid.

[102] See Section 10.6.1.

[103] As has been wisely mentioned, 'any regulation of short selling should aim to tackle legal or economic concerns, rather than any moral issues raised by this issue': Payne, n. 1, 415.

flaws of short selling practices that are still subject to debate. It could therefore be plausibly argued that if regulators hesitate to go beyond legal certainty and the mainstream market concepts on which modern capitalism is based, the likelihood of becoming evidence of radical change and more intrusive legal intervention in the operation of short selling activities is minimal.

Moreover, since corporate governance concerns do not show any indisputable rationale for the extension of short sellers' duties and given the fact that there are no signs of a shift from a 'market stability' towards a 'corporate governance' agenda at the EU and the international regulatory levels, it would be preferable to maintain the status quo until conclusive empirical data can demonstrate an imminent risk in companies' life from risk-free shareholders employing short selling activities. This observation cannot obviously predict to what extent scandals may (or may not) occur in the future since manipulative behaviour with a 'risk-free' allure cannot be ruled out.

In the lack of substantial evidence with regard to the widespread character of manipulative transactions in the area of short selling, any further imposition of duties would be unduly burdensome and counterproductive. Thus, similarly to what has been suggested in previous chapters, the central focus needs to be the reinforcement of coordination of supervisory actions among NCAs and their efficient cooperation with ESMA. An optimally operational supervisory framework will probably suffice, at least at this stage, to implement the 'market stability' rationale that was crucial to the introduction of the EU short selling regulatory regime.

PART IV

Gatekeepers

CHAPTER 11

Investment Firms

11.1 INTRODUCTION

Investment firms can indirectly become important gatekeepers in capital markets since they offer, among many things, access to financial products (by trading on behalf of their clients) and advisory services to investors. They are therefore well placed to offer high-quality services to enable their clients to make informed decisions and to have access to various products. By performing their role efficiently, they can channel investment towards issuers by safeguarding the efficient allocation of resources and market liquidity. It is their unique position between investors and issuers that grants them a gatekeeping function and places them under a strict regulatory framework to protect investors from unqualified, inefficient or fraudulent investment firms. Not all investors have the same level of understanding, knowledge and capacity to buy or sell shares, and many will inevitably use investment firms' services. It is therefore crucial to guarantee a series of requirements that pertain to the optimal functioning of investment firms and the quality of their services.

EU law has endeavoured to introduce and subsequently refine applicable rules for the authorization, functioning and supervision of investment firms with a series of Directives and Regulations.[1] Legal provisions in the area of investment firms are constantly being challenged by technological and market developments, and need to be adaptable to revision so as to respond promptly to new and uncertain[2] challenges and to protect efficiently users of investment services from potential risks.[3] It is not easy to strike a balance between the regulatory need to maintain a legal framework that provides a sufficient level of sophistication, on a par with financial innovation, and the market's need to allow investment firms to perform their functions as financial intermediaries in the least cumbersome way possible. A heavily regulated operational framework could theoretically prevent excessive risk-taking or, more generally, a laissez-faire approach in the provision of investment services. However, it could also

---

[1] See Section 11.3.

[2] On the notion of uncertainty, see I. MacNeil, 'Uncertainty in Commercial Law' (2009) 1 *Edinburgh Law Review* 68.

[3] J. Black, 'The Rise, Fall and Fate of Principles Based Regulation' (2010) LSE Law, Society and Economy Working Papers 17/2010, at http://eprints.lse.ac.uk/32892/1/WPS2010-17_Black.pdf.

endanger the benefits of a vibrant and innovative financial intermediary industry. Principles-based regulation therefore emerges as a laudable and reasonable approach. Despite the fair amount of criticism it has come under as it has developed, this approach offers the necessary amount of flexibility to investment firms to comply with various requirements while maintaining their specificities.[4]

This chapter will give a comprehensive overview of the legal spectrum that aims to ensure the proper functioning of investment firms, as well as the rules by which they can offer services to their clients. Focusing solely on investment firms' gatekeeping function, it will deal only with areas closely related to the relationship between investment firms and their clients, along with the legal mechanisms that ensure the proper enforcement of such rules. Our analysis will attempt to determine whether the gatekeeping function is duly preserved from a series of obstacles (such as conflicts of interest) that may compromise it. In parallel, it will critically assess the powers given to NCAs and ESMA to safeguard investors and markets from potential violations of the applicable framework, in terms of both supervisory and enforcement capacity, as well as the feasibility of other enforcement regimes.

11.2 REGULATORY RATIONALES AND PRINCIPLES-BASED APPROACH

The rationales for introducing and maintaining a regulatory framework for investment firms are broadly focused on avoiding any type of distorted incentives that could place the firm's clients at risk, while also macro-managing systemic risks. These two rationales go hand in hand with the more general financial regulation objectives of preserving market confidence and economic prosperity at large.[5]

Similar to other areas of capital markets law, informational asymmetry is a common and recurrent challenge that also manifests itself between investment firms and their clients. The inherent capacity of clients to share – and understand – any type of information in the same way may give rise to agency costs since investment firms may have distorted incentives. The most notable example is the existence of conflicts of interest that may lead investment firms to act not in their clients' best interests but in their own interest. The well-known remuneration criteria and performance targets in financial intermediation[6] have repeatedly generated and exacerbated distorted incentives and strategies to further the firms' or their employees' own agendas at the expense of their clients,[7] via the increase of fees and other fraudulent practices.

A second regulatory rationale extends beyond the microcosm of the relationship between firms and their clients and touches upon more general regulatory concerns related to market stability that can be threatened by the spread

---

[4] On these benefits, see N. Moloney, *How to Protect Investors* (Cambridge University Press, 2010), 209; D. Awrey, W. Blair and D. Kershaw, 'Between Law and Markets: Is there a Role for Culture and Ethics in Financial Regulation?' (2013) 38 *Delaware Journal of Corporate Law* 191.
[5] E. Avgouleas, *Governance of Global Financial Markets: The Law, the Economics, the Politics* (Cambridge University Press, 2012), 217.
[6] Chapter 3.
[7] More generally, on the EU investor protection regime, see N. Moloney, 'The Investor Model Underlying the EU's Investor Protection Regime: Consumers or Investors? (2012) 13 *European Business Organization Law Review* 169.

of distorted incentives. Investment firms characterized by excessive risk-taking and distorted incentives may create a much bigger avalanche of destabilizing practices, with important systemic risks,[8] if generalized on a wider scale. Highly complex and poorly understood financial products, aggressive trading practices, and an excessive focus on generating commission fees, among other factors, have in the past created a dangerous mix of risk factors that can have a systemic impact around the globe. The concepts of size, substitutability and interconnectedness have been used as reliable criteria for the identification of the systemic importance of markets and institutions.[9] Their relevance in the area of financial intermediation is obvious, given the current financial landscape that relies primarily – together with issuers and investors – on intermediaries for most market activities.

The creation of a regulatory strategy that is able to understand, target and address the above-mentioned risks via the introduction and development of legal provisions is an undoubtedly delicate task. For a series of reasons, a principles-based approach has been favoured with regard to the regulation of financial intermediaries. First of all, the inherent regulatory inability to oversee business relationships between firms and their clients by simply imposing exogenous rules has made regulation 'from the inside'[10] a vital component of financial regulation. Indeed, involving investment firms in the regulatory landscape indirectly[11] by requiring them to adopt a series of 'conduct of business' rules at the internal level as well as other types of rules (such as corporate governance ones) succeeds in creating a multi-layered meta-regulatory mechanism, shifting from internal to external operational imperatives that form a common and acceptable framework for the conduct of investment firms.

The existence of the multi-layered and highly complex deficiencies creates a regulatory incentive to tackle current and future challenges by becoming more intrusive and more attentive to the endogenous problematic aspects of investment firms. Legal rules require investment firms to regulate themselves internally and to safeguard their own operational spectrum, prior to any activity or service, depending on their own specificities, size and structure. Aiming to trace and remedy deficiencies in investment firms requires such a regulatory approach since the mere expectation of outcomes via compliance to exogenous – to investment firm specificities – and strict 'one size fits all' rules would not resolve such deficiencies efficiently.

The principles-based approach has been viewed in a critical light due to the broadly formulated rules that do not prescribe a specific conduct spectrum but primarily rely on the broad implementation of 'safety valves' within investment

---

[8] M. Brunnermeier, A. Crockett, C. Goodhart, A.D. Persaud and H. Shin, *The Fundamental Principles of Financial Regulation* (2009) Centre for Economic Policy Research, Geneva Reports on the World Economy, 11.

[9] FSB, IMF and BIS, 'Report to G-20 Finance Ministers and Governors. Guidance to Assess the Systemic Importance of Financial Institutions, Markets and Instruments: Initial Considerations' (2009) 2, at http://www.bis.org/publ/othp07.pdf.

[10] I. H-Y. Chiu, *Regulating (from) the Inside: The Legal Framework for Internal Control in Banks and Financial Institutions* (Hart Publishing, 2015).

[11] J. Black, 'Regulatory Styles and Supervisory Strategies' in E. Ferran, N. Moloney and J. Payne (eds), *Oxford Handbook of Financial Regulation* (Oxford University Press, 2015), 217.

firms. There is a plausible risk of an inferior quality of overall compliance.[12] Given the need to address endogenous deficiencies in a highly complex and constantly evolving framework, this regulatory approach is considered to be the most workable way forward.[13] As we will see in this chapter, most requirements contain broadly formulated terms, such as 'appropriate', 'adequate', 'sound', 'proportionate' and 'effective'. The main purpose is therefore to invite investment firms to a subjective evaluation of their own operational systems and to ensure a broadly similar approach to these high-level regulatory objectives.

11.3 EU LEGAL SOURCES

EU law made a decisive step towards framing investment firms' activities with the Directive 2004/39/EC[14] that, following a series of weaknesses observed after the financial crisis, was replaced by Directive 2014/65/EU[15] and Regulation 600/2014/EU.[16] The new regulatory framework is applicable as of 3 January 2018 and will also be enriched by an administrative rulebook (Level 2 legislative acts). ESMA is also expected to produce regulatory technical standards and technical implementing standards for a series of issues.

Observing the evolution of EU norms in attempting to regulate investment firms, the gradual strengthening of requirements in various areas, as we will see in this chapter, goes hand in hand with the constant revelation of various deficiencies that takes place during major crises. Starting from a Code of Conduct in 1977[17] that provided broadly formulated high-level principles, and experiencing national divergences for many years in the way investment firms

---

[12] J. Black, 'Paradoxes and Failures: "'New Governance" Techniques and the Financial Crisis' (2012) 75 *Modern Law Review* 1037.

[13] D. Awrey, W. Blair and D. Kershaw, above n. 4.

[14] Directive 2004/39/EC of the European Parliament and of the Council of 21 April 2004 on markets in financial instruments amending Council Directives 85/611/EEC and 93/6/EEC and Directive 2000/12/EC of the European Parliament and of the Council and repealing Council Directive 93/22/EEC [2004] OJ L 145/1 (hereinafter MiFID I).

[15] Directive 2014/65/EU of the European Parliament and of the Council of 15 May 2014 on markets in financial instruments and amending Directive 2002/92/EC and Directive 2011/61/EU Text with EEA relevance [2014] OJ L 173/349 (hereinafter MiFID II). MiFID II deals primarily with requirements related to the authorization and operating conditions of investment firms; the provision of investment services by third country firms; the authorization and operation of regulated markets as well as of data reporting services; and, most importantly, the supervision and enforcement by NCAs as well as their relationship with ESMA. This chapter will focus on the authorization and operating conditions of investment firms, as well as the supervision and enforcement by NCAs under the overarching role of ESMA.

[16] Regulation 600/2014/EU of the European Parliament and of the Council of 15 May 2014 on markets in financial instruments and amending Regulation 648/2012/EU [2014] OJ L 173/84 (hereinafter MiFIR). MiFIR deals with the requirements related to the disclosure of trade data to the public, the reporting of transactions to the NCAs, the trading of derivatives on organized venues, the provision of investment services by third country firms, the non-discriminatory access to clearing and to trading in benchmarks and the product intervention powers of NCAs, ESMA and EBA. MiFIR rules will not be the focus of this chapter.

[17] Commission Recommendation of 25 July 1977 concerning a European code of conduct relating to transactions in transferable securities [1977] OJ L 212/37.

operated and should be regulated, EU law was faced with the dilemma between preserving a fragmented regulatory landscape that impeded the creation of an integrated EU market, and laying the foundations for a harmonized legal framework that would revive the investment firm sector. The answer to this dilemma was somewhat different in that it favoured, during that period, a mutual recognition system with considerable room for manoeuvre on a national level.[18] The following regulatory steps were marked by the Directive 89/646/EC,[19] which awarded a passport facility to credit institutions and harmonized certain rules to a minimum, as well as by Directive 93/22/EC,[20] which extended rules to non-bank investment firms and also provided a minimum framework for authorization and operating purposes. Following the massive influence that the Financial Services Action Plan had on EU capital markets law in 1999,[21] MiFID I was undoubtedly the critical step towards a more harmonized and sophisticated regulatory framework that could provide the appropriate legal rules for constant and challenging technological and operational developments in investment firms.[22]

The considerable deficiencies spotted during the global financial crisis inevitably led EU law to further reform and to enrich the applicable rules by introducing the new MiFID II/MiFIR regime.

11.4 FUNCTIONAL APPROACH AND APPLICABILITY OF RULES

MiFID II adopts a functional approach in the sense that it applies to the provision of investment services and activities and does not link the applicability of its framework with the provider's identity or status. The crucial element is the provision of such services and activities, regardless of its source. Thanks to this functional approach, more and more investment services are subject to the MiFID II spectrum, and investors can operate and interact with investment services and activities providers in a supervised and regulated framework under an overarching 'functional' framework.

---

[18] Commission, 'Completing the Internal Market: White Paper' (1985), COM(85) 310 final, Brussels.

[19] Second Council Directive 89/646/EEC of 15 December 1989 on the coordination of laws, regulations and administrative provisions relating to the taking up and pursuit of the business of credit institutions and amending Directive 77/780/EEC [1989] OJ L 386/1.

[20] Council Directive 93/22/EEC of 10 May 1993 on investment services in the securities field [1993] OJ L 141/27.

[21] See Chapter 1.

[22] It was further enriched by Commission Directive 2006/73/EC of 10 August 2006 implementing Directive 2004/39/EC of the European Parliament and of the Council as regards organizational requirements and operating conditions for investment firms and defined terms for the purposes of that Directive [2006] OJ L 241/26 and by Commission Regulation (EC) No 1287/2006 of 10 August 2006 implementing Directive 2004/39/EC of the European Parliament and of the Council as regards record-keeping obligations for investment firms, transaction reporting, market transparency, admission of financial instruments to trading, and defined terms for the purposes of that Directive [2006] OJ L 241/1.

MiFID II provides a series of principles that aim to ensure investor protection.[23] It applies to investment firms, which are defined as 'any legal person whose regular occupation or business is the provision of one or more investment services to third parties and/or the performance of one or more investment activities on a professional basis'.[24] Member States retain a right to extend this definition to include undertakings that are not legal persons, under the condition that their legal status ensures a level of protection for third parties' interests equivalent to that afforded by legal persons, and that they are subject to equivalent prudential supervision rules that are appropriate for their legal form. Natural persons providing services involving the holding of third-party funds or transferable securities may also be considered to be an investment firm under certain conditions.[25] The definition of investment services and activities is given by reference to Section A of Annex I.[26] Such services and activities must relate to any of the instruments listed in Section C of Annex I.[27] Ancillary services are defined by reference to section B of Annex I.[28]

---

[23] Article 24, ibid.

[24] Article 4(1)(1), MiFID II.

[25] For more details, see Article 4(1)(1), ibid.

[26] Reception and transmission of orders in relation to one or more financial instruments; execution of orders on behalf of clients; dealing on own account; portfolio management; investment advice; underwriting of financial instruments and/or placing of financial instruments on a firm commitment basis; placing of financial instruments without a firm commitment basis; operation of an MTF and operation of an OTF.

[27] Transferable securities; money-market instruments; units in collective investment undertakings; options, futures, swaps, forward rate agreements and any other derivative contracts relating to securities, currencies, interest rates or yields, emission allowances or other derivatives instruments, financial indices or financial measures which may be settled physically or in cash; options, futures, swaps, forwards and any other derivative contracts relating to commodities that must be settled in cash or may be settled in cash at the option of one of the parties other than by reason of default or other termination event; options, futures, swaps, and any other derivative contract relating to commodities that can be physically settled provided that they are traded on a regulated market, a multilateral trading facility (MTF), or an organized trading facility (OTF), except for wholesale energy products traded on an OTF that must be physically settled; options, futures, swaps, forwards and any other derivative contracts relating to commodities, that can be physically settled not otherwise mentioned in point 6 of this Section and not being for commercial purposes, which have the characteristics of other derivative financial instruments; derivative instruments for the transfer of credit risk; financial contracts for differences; options, futures, swaps, forward rate agreements and any other derivative contracts relating to climatic variables, freight rates or inflation rates or other official economic statistics that must be settled in cash or may be settled in cash at the option of one of the parties other than by reason of default or other termination event, as well as any other derivative contracts relating to assets, rights, obligations, indices and measures, which have the characteristics of other derivative financial instruments, having regard to whether, *inter alia*, they are traded on a regulated market, OTF, or an MTF; emission allowances consisting of any units recognized for compliance with the requirements of Directive 2003/87/EC (Emissions Trading Scheme).

[28] Safekeeping and administration of the financial instruments for the account of clients; granting credits or loans to an investor to allow him to carry out a transaction in one or more

11.5 CLIENT CLASSIFICATION

A key component of the efficient provision of investment services is the assessment of suitability and appropriateness of clients to such services (the 'know your client' principle), as well as their classification to different categories that determines their relationship with the investment firm and the level of information and protection provided. This type of classification aims to tailor the applicability of conduct of business rules to different investor profiles so as to offer a flexible and less burdensome operational space for investment firms, while protecting clients depending on their sophistication level. Indeed, more sophisticated and experienced clients may not need the same level of information protection when they receive services from investment firms. Allowing the latter to classify them accordingly determines the level of information that must be provided and enhances the overall efficiency in the way they operate.

MiFID II maintained the classification of clients, as initially designed by MiFID I, as follows:

- eligible counterparties
- professional clients
- retail clients.[29]

Retail clients enjoy the full range of information or protection by investment firms since their status does not justify any relaxation or disapplication of the applicable rules.

Eligible counterparties are defined as investment firms, credit institutions, insurance companies, UCITS and their management companies, pension funds and their management companies, other financial institutions authorized or regulated under EU or national laws, national governments and their corresponding offices, central banks and supranational organizations.[30] Member States may also recognize as eligible counterparties other undertakings that

---

financial instruments, where the firm granting the credit or loan is involved in the transaction; advice to undertakings on capital structure, industrial strategy and related matters and advice and services relating to mergers and the purchase of undertakings; foreign exchange services where these are connected to the provision of investment services; investment research and financial analysis or other forms of general recommendation relating to transactions in financial instruments; services related to underwriting; investment services and activities as well as ancillary services of the type included under Section A or B of Annex 1 related to the underlying of the derivatives included under points (5), (6), (7) and (10) of Section C where these are connected to the provision of investment or ancillary services.

[29] MiFID I was generally successful in introducing such a classification system, but the repercussions of the financial crisis raised a series of concerns and warnings with regard to the sophistication and risk tolerance capacity of certain clients that they were supposedly not in need of a full investor protection package (for example, municipalities and local public authorities). MiFID II has therefore made the classification system more sophisticated in that it allows a better fluctuation of investor protection provisions in the professional markets, as explained later on in this section.

[30] Article 30(2), ibid.

meet predetermined proportionate requirements, including quantitative thresholds.[31] They may recognize as eligible counterparties third country entities equivalent to the above-mentioned categories.[32]

Investment firms that are authorized to execute orders on behalf of clients and/or to deal on own account and/or to receive and transmit orders, are not obliged – when they bring about or enter into transactions with eligible counterparties – to comply with the general conduct principles (Article 24), the suitability assessment (Article 25), the best execution principle (Article 27) and the client order handling rules (Article 28).[33]

The classification of clients allows for some flexibility in triggering an additional level of investor protection. For example, eligible counterparties retain a right to request, either generally or on a trade-by-trade basis, to be treated as clients whose business is subject to the above-mentioned rules and therefore oblige investment firms to respect them fully, notwithstanding the fact that they are 'eligible counterparties'.[34]

MiFID II defines professional clients as those clients that possess the experience, knowledge and expertise to make their own investment decisions and properly assess the risks incurred.[35] They are also subject to an additional series of criteria so as to be further broken down into those who are considered to be professionals or those who may be treated as such upon request.

Clients classified as professionals are, according to MiFID II, those entities that are authorized or regulated to operate in the financial markets,[36] including large undertakings meeting two out of three size criteria on a company basis (total balance sheet of €20 million, net turnover of €40 million and own funds of €2 million). This category also encompasses national and regional governments (including public bodies that manage public debt at the national or regional level), central banks, international and supranational institutions (such as the World Bank, the IMF, the ECB and the EIB) and, lastly, other institutional investors whose main business is to invest in financial instruments.[37]

Notwithstanding their classification as professionals, these entities can benefit from additional investor protection by requesting non-professional treatment. Prior to providing any services, investment firms must inform these clients that they are considered to be professional clients and will be treated as such unless they agree otherwise. They must also inform them that they can

---

[31] Article 30(3), ibid.

[32] Article 30(4), ibid.

[33] Article 30(1), ibid. There are some rules that must be fully respected by investment firms: Article 24(4)(5) and Article 25(6).

[34] Article 30(2), ibid.

[35] Annex II, ibid.

[36] Annex II(I)(1), ibid. The same paragraph also provides a list of such entities that includes credit institutions, investment firms, other authorized or regulated financial institutions, insurance companies, collective investment schemes and management companies of such schemes, pension funds and management companies of such funds, commodity and commodity derivatives dealers, locals and other institutional investors.

[37] Annex II(I)(2)-(4), ibid.

request a variation of the terms of the agreement in order to ensure a higher level of protection. It falls within the client's responsibility to ask for such additional level of protection when it considers that it cannot properly assess or manage the risks involved.[38]

Clients who can be treated as professionals on request must fulfil additional criteria, and they should not be considered to possess market knowledge and experience comparable to that of the eligible counterparties that are considered to be professionals, as described above. This category includes public sector bodies, local public authorities, municipalities and private individual investors.[39] Conduct of business rules may therefore be waived for these clients, but on the condition that investment firms conduct an adequate assessment of the expertise, experience and knowledge of the client, obtaining a reasonable assurance that it is able to make investment decisions and understand the risks involved.

As part of this assessment of the client's profile, two of the following three criteria must be satisfied:

- the carrying out of transactions of significant size on the relevant market at an average frequency of ten per quarter over the previous four quarters;
- a financial instrument portfolio exceeding €500,000 in value; and
- at least one year of previous financial market experience in a profession that requires knowledge of the envisaged transactions or services.[40]

The assessment test must be accompanied by a specific procedure that follows these steps:

- the client must declare to the investment firm in writing that it wishes to be treated as a professional;
- the firm must give a clear written warning of the protections and investor compensation rights the client may lose; and
- the client must confirm in writing that it is aware of the consequences of losing such protections.[41]

Investment firms are expected to implement appropriate written internal policies and procedures with regard to client classification. Professional clients are responsible for updating the firm about any change that could potentially

---

[38] Annex II(I)(4), ibid.

[39] The reason for their inclusion in this category is that serious concerns have been raised in the past with regard to their classification, given the considerable losses incurred during the financial crisis and the reconsideration of their status, now in need of additional investor protection.

[40] Annex II(II)(1), ibid. In order to further the protection of municipalities and local public authorities when they request to be treated as professional clients, Member States may adopt alternative or additional specific criteria for the assessment of their expertise and knowledge.

[41] Annex II(II)(2), ibid.

affect their categorization, and the firms are also able to alter such classification if they become aware that the client no longer fulfils the initial conditions.[42] Quite wisely so, the client classification becomes a malleable instrument that adapts to various circumstances over time and allows both parties to trigger additional levels of investor protection. An initial classification of a client by an investment firm should not be considered the final one, especially taking into account the length and potential spectrum of their relationship, which may include various circumstances, services and financial products.

11.6 REGULATORY SAFEGUARDS

11.6.1 Authorization Requirements

The EU regulatory spectrum imposes authorization requirements so as to protect potentially affected parties and broader marketability from investment firms that do not satisfy the pre-set minimum criteria for the provision of investment services and/or the performance of investment activities. Authorization is granted by the home Member State's NCA and notified to ESMA, which is in charge of establishing and regularly updating a publicly available list of all investment firms in the EU.[43] The authorization must specify the investment services or activities which the investment firm is authorized to provide, and it may cover one or more of the ancillary services listed in MiFID II.[44] A passport mechanism is provided upon authorization; this allows investment firms to provide the services or perform the activities that have been authorized throughout the EU.[45]

For the purposes of receiving authorization, investment firms must provide all information, including a programme of operations that sets out, among other things, the types of business envisaged and the organizational structure. A decision regarding the granting of authorization must be made within six months of the submission of a complete application.[46] MiFID II also requires compliance with a series of criteria related to the composition and the role of the management body of the firm[47] and to the identities of shareholders and members with qualifying holdings.[48]

Regarding the management body of an investment firm,[49] NCAs granting the authorization must ensure that investment firms and management

---

[42] Annex II(II)(2), ibid.

[43] Article 5, ibid.

[44] Annex I(B), ibid. Investment firms may also submit a request for extension of their authorization if they wish to extend their business to additional investment services or activities or ancillary services after having been authorized.

[45] Article 6, ibid.

[46] Article 7, ibid.

[47] Article 9, ibid.

[48] Article 10, ibid.

[49] According to MiFID II, 'management body means the body or bodies of an investment firm, market operator or data reporting services provider, which are appointed in accordance

bodies comply with Articles 88 and 91 of Directive 2013/36/EU.[50] These two articles refer to governance requirements that focus, *inter alia*, upon the management body's role in defining, overseeing and being accountable for the implementation of governance arrangements within the firm, as well as upon the management body's composition.

Governance arrangements must also include the definition, approval and overseeing of:

- the organization of the firm for the provision of investment services and activities and ancillary services, the resources, the procedures and the arrangements for the provision of services and activities;
- a policy as to the services, activities, products and operations offered or provided in accordance with the firm's risk tolerance and the characteristics and needs of its clients; and
- a remuneration policy for persons involved in the provision of services to clients that aims to encourage responsible business conduct, further treatment of clients and the avoidance of conflicts of interest.[51]

The management body must monitor and periodically assess the adequacy and the implementation of the firm's strategic objectives related to the provision of investment services and activities and ancillary services, the effectiveness of the investment firm's governance arrangements and the adequacy of the policies related to the provision of services to clients. It must also take any appropriate steps to address any deficiencies.

An additional authorization requirement is the profile characteristics that each member of the management body must satisfy. These refer to a sufficiently good reputation, possession of sufficient knowledge, skills and experience, and commitment of sufficient time in the performance of her functions within the investment firm. NCAs are also required, for authorization purposes, to delve into the management body's role with regards to the effective, sound and prudent management of the firm and to the adequate consideration of client interests and market integrity as indicators of the body's suitability.

Regarding the identities of shareholders and members with qualifying holdings, NCAs must be informed, prior to authorization, of the identities of the

---

with national law, which are empowered to set the entity's strategy, objectives and overall direction, and which oversee and monitor management decision-making and include persons who effectively direct the business of the entity': Article 4(1)(36), ibid.

[50] Directive 2013/36/EU of the European Parliament and of the Council of 26 June 2013 on access to the activity of credit institutions and the prudential supervision of credit institutions and investment firms, amending Directive 2002/87/EC and repealing Directives 2006/48/EC and 2006/49/EC [2013] OJ L 176/338. This chapter does not deal in detail with the 2013 Capital Requirements Directive, being mainly concentrated upon the relationship between investment firms and their clients as well as the gatekeeping function that firms can exercise in capital markets.

[51] Article 9(3), MiFID II.

shareholders or members (direct or indirect, natural or legal persons) with such holdings, as well as their amounts. If the shareholders or members are not deemed to be suitable, authorization may be refused.[52]

All the above-mentioned governance requirements aim to safeguard a proper governance mindset for investment firms, bringing their activities and services into line with the interests of their clients. The formulation of these requirements is broad in nature, maintaining the necessary flexibility so as to ensure wide applicability of these general principles from investment firms who compose – in their totality – a very diverse and heterogeneous landscape in terms of size, range of activities and sophistication.[53] Under MiFID II, senior management is a focal point for attention by assuming an overarching and strengthened role over the firm.[54] These latest reforms depict a more general reform wave and a reconceptualization of senior management's contribution to the operating framework of banks, investment firms and other institutions.

11.6.2 Organizational Requirements

11.6.2.1 General Requirements
Investment firms are expected to comply with a series of organizational requirements to ensure their proper functioning and the provision of investment services without being unduly affected by factors that can compromise their reliability. MiFID II, replicating the MiFID I framework, lays out several requirements for investment firms, notably:

- the establishment of adequate policies and procedures that are sufficient to ensure compliance of the firm, its managers, employees and tied agents with the applicable legal framework;
- the maintenance and operation of effective organizational and administrative arrangements so as to take all reasonable steps for the prevention of conflicts of interest;[55]
- the undertaking of reasonable steps to ensure continuity and regularity in the performance of investment services and activities through the adoption of appropriate and proportionate systems, resources and procedures;
- the undertaking of reasonable steps to avoid undue additional operational risk arising from outsourcing functions to third parties;[56]

---

[52] Article 10, ibid.
[53] K.J. Hopt, 'Better Governance of Financial Institutions' in G. Ferrarini, K.J. Hopt and E. Wymeersch (eds.), *Financial Regulation and Supervision. A Post-Crisis Analysis* (Oxford University Press, 2012), 337.
[54] See, for a complete overview, I. H-Y. Chiu, 'Corporate Governance and Risk Management in Banks and Financial Institutions' in I. H-Y. Chiu (ed.), *The Law on Corporate Governance in Banks* (Edward Elgar, 2015), 169.
[55] See Section 11.5.2.
[56] More generally, such outsourcing may not take place if it impairs in a material way the quality of investment, firm's internal control and the supervisor's ability to monitor the firm's overall compliance.

- the maintenance of records (including recording of telephone conversations or electronic communications) of all services, activities and transactions so as to enable NCAs to perform their supervisory and enforcement tasks; and
- the safeguarding of clients' ownership (and other) when an investment firm holds financial instruments on their behalf.[57]

Investment firms that engage in algorithmic trading must also have in place effective systems and risk controls suitable to its business to safeguard the resilience, capacity and proper functioning of their trading systems. They must have effective business continuity arrangements – in case of failure of their trading systems – and must fully test and properly monitor such trading systems.[58]

These requirements are formulated in a very broad and generic way, without being able to convey a more precise image of the organizational spectrum that investment firms should follow. 'Adequate', 'reasonable', 'appropriate' and 'proportionate' are some indicative examples that can be subject to varying interpretations by investment firms. As previously mentioned, the broad formulation of applicable rules is essential to the optimal adaptation of investing firms to these principles given the considerable diversity among firms in their operational environment. More specific requirements are set out in the Delegated Regulation 2017/565.[59]

According to the general organizational requirements, investment firms are required to:

- establish, implement and maintain decision-making procedures and an organizational structure that specifies reporting lines and allocates functions and responsibilities;
- ensure proper awareness of all the procedures that need to be followed by all their relevant persons;
- establish, implement and maintain adequate internal control mechanisms so as to secure overall compliance with decisions and procedures;
- employ persons with the necessary skills, knowledge and expertise;
- establish, implement and maintain effective internal reporting and communication of information;
- maintain adequate and orderly records of their business and internal organization; and
- ensure that the performance of various functions by relevant persons does not have an impact on the sound, honest and professional discharge of any particular function.[60]

---

[57] Article 16, MiFID II.
[58] Article 17, ibid.
[59] Commission Delegated Regulation (EU) 2017/565 supplementing Directive 2014/65/EU of the European Parliament and of the Council as regards organizational requirements and operating conditions for investment firms and defined terms for the purposes of that Directive [2017] OJ L 87/1.
[60] Article 21, ibid.

Investment firms are also expected to establish, implement and maintain systems and procedures that are adequate to ensure the security, integrity and confidentiality of information,[61] as well as a business continuity policy.[62] Lastly, they must have in place accounting policies and procedures to send their financial reports to the NCA upon request.[63]

11.6.2.2 Compliance Requirements

The compliance[64] requirements are additional to the general ones mentioned above and are also provided by the Delegated Regulation 2017/565,[65] so as to ensure the establishment, implementation and maintenance of an overall compliance system within investment firms.[66] It is therefore an internal compliance exercise that is expected from firms. The sophistication and extent of this exercise inevitably varies, depending on the nature, size and complexity of each firm's business, not to mention the range of services and activities involved in that operational sphere.

The requirement to establish and maintain a permanent, effective compliance function has broad applicability. The compliance system must monitor and assess the adequate and effective character of the adopted measures and procedures – whose aim is to ensure overall compliance – and the actions taken to address any deficiencies in the firm's compliance. It must also advise and assist the relevant persons who carry out investment services and activities, in their overall compliance with the applicable legal framework.[67]

Investment firms must ensure an appropriate framework for the compliance function to perform its tasks properly and independently. More specifically, they must make sure that this function disposes of the necessary authority, resources, expertise and access to all relevant information. The appointment of a compliance officer is also an important component of such a framework. Moreover, the persons occupying this function cannot be simultaneously involved in the monitored services or activities themselves, and their remuneration must be set in a way that does not (or us unlikely to) compromise their objectivity.[68]

Going beyond the legal compliance, namely compliance with the applicable legal provisions, Implementing Directive 2006/73 also provides requirements with regard to risk management,[69] which constitutes a more broadly defined compliance with a particular mindset that aims to protect investment firms and

---

[61] Article 21(2), ibid.
[62] Article 21(3), ibid.
[63] Article 21(4), ibid.
[64] Chiu, above n. 10, 41.
[65] Above n. 59.
[66] Article 22, ibid.
[67] Article 22(2), ibid.
[68] Article 22(3), ibid.
[69] Chiu, above n. 10, 77; M. Crouhy, 'Risk Management Failures During the Financial Crisis' in R.W. Kolb (ed.), *Lessons from the Financial Crisis* (John Wiley & Sons, 2010), 283; M.T. Moore, 'The Evolving Contours of the Board's Risk Management Function in UK Corporate Governance' (2010) 10 *Journal of Corporate Law Studies* 279.

their clients from various risks. Risk management therefore has a more over-arching function that is not concerned with formalistic compliance with the legal rules, but ensures a wider operational risk-related mentality within invest-ment firms. Risk management covers all types of risks that are relevant to the firm. Nevertheless, it should be borne in mind that non-compliance with legal requirements undoubtedly constitutes a risk to any investment firm and as such, should fall within the 'risk management' ambit. At the same time, compliance has its own risk-based approach since it must ensure the firm's overall compli-ance with the legal provisions that are related, *inter alia*, to risk management.[70]

Investment firms are required to establish, implement and maintain ade-quate risk management policies and procedures that identify risks and set the risk tolerance level for the firm. They must also adopt effective arrangements, processes and mechanisms for the management of risks, in light of the risk tol-erance level. Lastly, they need to monitor the adequacy and the effectiveness of risk management policies and procedures, the level of compliance with risk man-agement arrangements, processes and mechanisms, as well as the adequacy and effectiveness of measures that aim to address deficiencies in this framework.[71]

Investment firms are also expected to establish and maintain an independent risk management function that implements the above-mentioned policy and pro-cedures, while providing written reports and advice to senior management within investment firms.[72] Risk management therefore occupies a powerful place within firms, not only by covering all types of risks but also by overseeing all procedures related to such risks on an ongoing basis. At the same time, as mentioned above, it becomes part of the overall compliance function, since it is formed by and subject to legal requirements that dictate how its functions must be performed.

This overlap between compliance and risk management inevitably leads investment firms to adopt an integrated approach and to merge the two areas to optimize their close connection and coexistence within the same operational framework.

11.6.3 Conflicts of Interest

Conflicts of interest are undoubtedly one of the most important challenges that investment firms constantly face, given the complexity and interconnectiv-ity of various market situations that may easily give rise to such conflicts.[73] The impact of such conflicts on investment firms' operations and reputation is con-siderable, and the need to put in place carefully designed rules is non-negligible.

---

[70] For the risk-based approach that compliance should adopt, see ESMA, 'Final Report: Guidelines on Certain Aspects of the MiFID Compliance Function Requirements' (2012), ESMA/2012/388, 24, at https://www.esma.europa.eu/sites/default/files/library/2015/11/2012-388.pdf.
[71] Article 23(1), Commission Delegated Regulation (EU) 2017/565.
[72] Article 23(2), ibid.
[73] M. Andenas and I. H-Y. Chiu, *The Foundations and Future of Financial Regulation: Governance for Responsibility* (Routledge, 2013), 286.

Investment firms are required to take all appropriate steps to identify, prevent or manage conflicts of interests. The 'appropriate' character of such steps is a welcome step forward from MiFID I, which provided for 'reasonable' steps on this matter, leaving more space to investing firms for divergence and subjectivity. Such conflicts may exist between the firms, their managers, employees and tied agents and any other person – who is directly or indirectly linked to them by control – and their clients or between clients. If the organizational or administrative arrangements made by the investment firm, so as to prevent conflicts of interest from affecting the interests of a client, are not sufficient to ensure the prevention of risks of damage to the client, the firm is required to clearly disclose the nature and/or the sources of conflicts of interest to the client,[74] along with indicating the steps that it has taken to mitigate those risks before undertaking business on the client's behalf.[75] Nevertheless, we note that the formulation with 'and/or' allows investment firms not to disclose the nature and the extent of the conflict itself, a situation that fails to offer meaningful protection to clients.

Disclosure must be made in a durable medium and include sufficient detail by also taking into consideration the nature of the client so that the latter can make an informed decision regarding the proposed service in light to this conflict.[76] Of course, a distinction should be drawn between a generic disclosure which may take place at the beginning of the relationship with a client, and the need to inform the latter of any conflict of interest during the contractual relationship. The wording seems so broad that it is difficult to conclude with certainty how often such disclosure should take place.[77] In any case, clients are not protected in an optimal and meaningful way under these rules, in our view.

Conflicts may arise during the provision of any investment and ancillary services, including services triggered by the receipt of inducements from third parties or by the firm's own remuneration and other incentive structures.[78] Delegated Regulation 2017/565[79] gives further examples of the situations that may give rise to conflicts of interest that are potentially detrimental to the investment firm's client and requires firms to take them into account.

These may include, at a minimum, circumstances whereby the firm or the concerned person:

- is likely to make a financial gain (or avoid a financial loss) at the expense of the client;

---

[74] For a critical approach in this sense, see L. Enriques, 'Conflicts of Interest in Investment Services: The Price and Uncertain Impact of MiFID's Regulatory Framework' in G. Ferrarini and E. Wymeersch (eds), *Investor Protection in Europe: Corporate Lawmaking, the MiFID and Beyond* (Oxford University Press, 2006), 321, 326.

[75] Article 23(2), MiFID II.

[76] Article 23(3), ibid.

[77] Enriques, above n. 74, 331.

[78] Article 23(1), MiFID II.

[79] Above n. 59.

- has an interest in the outcome of a service provided to the client, or of a transaction carried out on its behalf, which is distinct from the client's interest in that outcome;
- has a financial or other incentive to favour the interest of another client or a group of clients over the interests of the client;
- carries out the same business as the client; or
- receives or will receive from a person other than the client any inducement, related to the service provided to the client (this may take the form of monies, goods or services), other than the standard commission or fee for that service.[80]

Delegated Regulation 2017/565 requires investment firms to establish, implement and maintain an effective conflicts of interest policy. This policy must be in writing and appropriate to the size and organization of the firm and the nature, scale and complexity of its business.[81] It must identify the circumstances that constitute or may trigger conflicts of interest that would generate a risk of damage to clients, as well as the procedures and measures for the management of such conflicts.[82]

Such procedures need to secure a degree of independence in the way a firm operates. They may relate, *inter alia*, to:

- the prevention or control of the exchange of information between relevant persons engaged in activities involving a risk of a conflict of interest;
- the separate supervision of relevant persons whose principal functions include carrying out activities on behalf of clients whose interests may conflict, or persons representing different conflicting interests;
- the removal of any direct link between the remuneration of various persons engaged in potentially conflicting activities;
- measures aimed at preventing or limiting persons from exercising inappropriate influence on other persons who carry out investment or ancillary services or activities; or
- measures aiming to prevent or control the concomitant or subsequent involvement of persons in a separate investment or ancillary services or activities that may potentially represent an obstacle to the proper management of conflicts of interest.[83]

Investment firms are also required to maintain and frequently regularly a record of all investment or ancillary services or investment activities that have been (or may be) associated with a conflict of interest that involves a material risk of damage to client interests.[84]

---

[80] Article 33, ibid.
[81] Article 34, ibid.
[82] Article 34(2), ibid.
[83] Article 34(3), ibid.
[84] Article 35, ibid.

Aiming to assess the general efficiency of broadly formulated conflicts of interest rules, we must bear in mind that the broad formulation of such rules has the advantage of being flexible across all types of investment firms, but it does not set any meaningful convergence in the way firms and concerned persons interpret, apply and use them on an everyday basis. The lack of such uniformity not only manifests itself at the national level, but also across the EU. Even though NCAs and courts will be invited to assess the importance of infringements *ex post*, it is at least illusory to expect their reactions to be similar given the different cultural, political and legal traditions, as well as varying levels of sophistication that continue to be non-negligible. The goal of harmonization is therefore unlikely to be achieved under these circumstances.[85]

Another recurrent issue in the area of conflicts of interest is the focus on the identification and prevention or management of conflicts of interest. Although identification and prevention is laudable, the management of such conflicts is in itself an ongoing conundrum for both regulators and clients. Indeed, there can be no absolute guarantee as to the efficiency of a procedure that manages such conflicts because the dividing line between the minimization of negative consequences arising from such conflicts and the materialization of such risks at the expense of clients – and potentially the markets at large – is a very delicate one.

Regrettably, EU regulatory trends continue to favour exclusively the management of such conflicts, without providing investment firms with the option of abstention from action. Moreover, the (perfectible) disclosure of conflicts of interest to clients, before undertaking business on their behalf, indirectly legitimizes the very existence of such conflicts and shifts attention away from the firm's questionable position and onto the clients' evaluation of their eventual importance within their decision-making process. Such legitimization weakens the argument for stricter rules, making conflicts of interest a malleable concept that, if disclosed and managed, can be viewed as perfectly acceptable situations within the investment firm and with regard to the client.

11.6.4 Conduct Regulation

MiFID II has been keen on framing the relationship between investment firms and their clients on a proper assessment of the client's profile that should determine the level and the range of the conduct of their business.[86]

Investment firms must act honestly, fairly and professionally in accordance with the best interests of their clients and comply with all the following principles:

- manufacturing of financial instruments designed to meet the needs of an identified target market within a relevant category of clients, and assessing the compatibility of such instruments with the needs of the clients;[87]

---

[85] Enriques, above n. 74, 333.

[86] Article 24(2)–(10), MiFID II.

[87] Investment firms must also ensure that financial instruments are offered or proposed only when this is in the interest of the client. For more details and specific requirements regarding

- disclosing information to clients (including marketing communications) in a fair, clear and not misleading manner;
- providing appropriate information – in good time and in a comprehensible form – related, among other things, to the firm, its services, the financial instruments and the proposed investment strategies;[88]
- not being involved in any fees or commissions or any non-monetary benefits related to the provision of an investment or ancillary service; and
- not having any conflicts between its staff's remuneration or performance assessment methods and its duty to act in the best interest of its clients.[89]

Investment firms must also obtain information related to their client's (current and potential) profile, touching upon the following three elements: their knowledge and experience in the investment field (that are relevant to the specific type of product or service); their financial position (including their ability to bear losses); and, lastly, their investment objectives, including risk tolerance. These factors should allow investment firms to recommend investment services and instruments that are suitable to their clients and to their level of risk tolerance and ability to bear losses.[90]

When providing other types of investment services, investment firms must seek information from their clients regarding their knowledge and experience in the investment fields that are relevant to the specific types of product or service in order to be in a position to assess whether such products or services are appropriate for these clients. If the firm assesses that such products or services are not appropriate, it must warn the client (in a standardized format). In the absence of information requested by the firm (or in the presence of insufficient information) regarding the client's profile, the firm will issue a warning (in a standardized format) about its inability to determine the appropriateness of the service or product.[91] Investment firms may be exempted from obtaining such information from their clients if they provide investment services that consist solely of execution or reception and transmission of client orders related, *inter alia*, to shares admitted to trading on a regulated market.[92]

---

the manufacturing of financial instruments, see Article 9, Commission Delegated Directive (EU) 2017/593 of 7 April 2016 supplementing Directive 2014/65/EU of the European Parliament and of the Council with regard to safeguarding of financial instruments and funds belonging to clients, product governance obligations and the rules applicable to the provision or reception of fees, commissions or any monetary or non-monetary benefits [2017] OJ L 87/500.

[88] Furthermore, the provided information must touch on the level of independence of the provided advice, include appropriate guidance on and warnings of the risks associated with investments and information on all costs and associated charges. Regarding the independent character of the investment advice, investment firms are expected to assess a sufficient range of financial instruments so as to ensure that the client's objectives are met.

[89] Article 24(2)–(10), MiFID II.

[90] Article 25(2), ibid.

[91] Article 25(3), ibid.

[92] See Article 25(4), ibid for the other types of financial instruments that justify such an exemption.

Investment firms are also expected to establish a record including all the documentation agreed with their clients, and must provide the latter with adequate reports on the service provided. Such reports must include periodic communications taking into consideration the type and the complexity of the financial instruments involved, along with the nature of the service provided to the client. In an attempt to providing optimal protection to clients, investment firms must provide them with a statement on their suitability, specifying the advice given and how such advice meets the preferences, objectives and other characteristics of the retail client. Such statement needs to be given prior to the transaction, allowing for an extra level of protection for the client.[93]

Notwithstanding the laudable, high-level and flexible character of conduct rules, we must bear in mind that the above-mentioned provisions are quite complex in nature. Moreover, if placed in the context of compliance and risk management rules, the risk for firms of becoming counterproductive by creating a single-minded approach to compliance, failing to inculcate an overarching philosophy about business conduct within firms, is plausible.[94]

11.7 SUPERVISION

11.7.1 NCAs

Member States are required to designate the NCAs that are in charge of enforcing the MiFID II and MiFIR duties and rules.[95] If more than one NCA has been designated by Member States, their roles must be defined clearly and they must cooperate closely.[96] NCAs are given a wide range of supervisory powers, including investigatory powers and powers to impose remedies. The powers refer, *inter alia*, to:

- access to any document or any other data
- requests or demands for information from any person (including the auditors of authorized investment firms, regulated markets and data reporting services)
- carrying out on-site inspections or investigations
- requisitioning existing recordings of telephone conversations or electronic communications
- freezing or sequestering assets
- enforcing a temporary prohibition on professional activity
- referring matters for criminal prosecution
- permitting auditors or experts to carry out verifications or investigations

---

[93] Article 25(6), ibid.
[94] For a critical approach, see I. MacNeil, 'Rethinking Conduct Regulation' (2015) 30(7) *Butterworths Journal of International Banking and Financial Law* 413.
[95] Article 67, MiFID II.
[96] Article 68, ibid.

- requiring temporary or permanent cessation of any practice or conduct that the NCA considers to be contrary to the applicable rules
- adopting any type of measure to ensure the compliance with the applicable rules by investment firms, regulated markets or any other persons
- suspending trading in a financial instrument and removing such an instrument from trading
- issuing public notices
- suspending the marketing or sale of financial instruments
- removing a natural person from the management board of an investment firm or market operator.[97]

MiFID II also provides a series of rules regarding the cooperation between NCAs and with ESMA, aiming to create a more effective supervisory framework across the EU.[98] The most notable cooperation mechanisms relate to the exchange of information and the coordinated exercise of supervisory powers.

11.7.2 ESMA

ESMA is in charge of supporting NCAs indirectly by fostering convergence in the way they exercise their powers, along with coordinating the supervisory framework across the EU. With its various guidelines and other convergence tools, it can nurture a common understanding of the optimal supervisory model across the EU. Nevertheless, we must bear in mind that NCAs are subject to different political, financial and cultural factors that enable or impede their ongoing progress towards a sophisticated supervisory model.

First of all, ESMA may receive notification from NCAs that have good reason to suspect possible infringements of the applicable rules in another Member State. NCAs will also notify their national homologues, which will report back to the notifying NCA and ESMA with the outcome of the action.[99] Host NCAs may find themselves in the position where they have clear and demonstrable grounds to believe that an infringement is taking place either by an investment firm acting within their territory, or by an investment firm with a branch in their territory. They must therefore notify the home NCA and refer the matter to ESMA.[100] ESMA is also notified for a series of other issues by NCAs.[101]

Secondly, ESMA may participate in the activities of the colleges of supervisors, including on-site verifications or investigations, when these are carried out jointly by two or more NCAs.[102] Thirdly, it may also receive information related to situations where a request among NCAs to carry out a supervisory activity or to exchange information within a cooperative framework has been

---

[97] Article 69, ibid.
[98] For more details, see Articles 79, 80 and 81, ibid.
[99] Article 79(4), ibid.
[100] Article 86, ibid.
[101] Article 79(5), ibid.
[102] Article 80(2), ibid.

rejected or has not been acted upon within a reasonable time.[103] In those situations, it takes on a mediating role to settle disagreements between NCAs. It may also exercise its powers and take action against an NCA for breach of EU law.[104]

11.8 SANCTIONS

11.8.1 *Administrative and Criminal Sanctions*

Administrative sanctions need to satisfy the criteria of effectiveness, proportionality and dissuasiveness. They shall also apply to all infringements of applicable rules, even to the ones that are not specifically addressed by Article 70.[105] National laws also need to provide for liability of natural persons, such as members of the investment firms' and market operators' management body, or any other natural or legal persons who are responsible for an infringement, in the case of obligations applicable to investment firms, market operators, data reporting services providers, credit institutions related to investment services or investment activities and ancillary services.[106]

The range of administrative sanctions and measures is very wide and includes public statements, orders to cease the conduct, withdrawal or suspension of the authorization of an institution (for example, an investment firm, market operator or regulated market), temporary or permanent ban against any member of the investment firm's management body (or any other person responsible for management functions) and a temporary ban on investment firms.[107]

MiFID II has also increased the level of minimum harmonization of administrative sanctions, given the fact that MiFID I simply required effective, proportionate and dissuasive administrative sanctions and measures. Operating on the basis of 'minimum maximums', as we have seen in other areas of capital markets law in this book, the administrative pecuniary sanctions provided under Article 70(6)(f-h) are up to €5 million or 10% of the total annual turnover for legal persons and up to €5 million for natural persons. In both cases, sanctions can be up to twice the amount of the profits resulting from the breach, if such profits can be determined. Paragraph 7 of the same Article mentions that Member States can provide for higher levels of pecuniary sanctions, along with additional sanctions or measures. Therefore, it will be very interesting to see whether national laws will adhere to these new series of administrative sanctions and gradually converge in the severity, frequency and intensity of sanctions imposed.

In order to coordinate the exercise of sanctioning powers among NCAs, Article 72(2) provides a very useful guide for determining the type and level

---

[103] Article 82, ibid.
[104] Article 82(2), ibid.
[105] Article 70(3)–(5), ibid.
[106] Article 70(2), ibid.
[107] Article 70(6), ibid.

of administrative sanctions or measures.[108] Indeed, MiFID II accentuates the need for indirect harmonization in this area by focusing on the conceptual elements of sanctions and measures and by attempting to converge their perception, interpretation and implementation across NCAs. This indirect harmonization effort is, in our opinion, a positive step towards gradual uniformity in the interpretation of the three sanctions criteria required in various EU capital markets texts: efficiency, proportionality and dissuasion.

Lastly, Article 71 aims to accentuate the severity and deterrent effect of sanctions via compulsory disclosure requirements for NCAs, which are required to publish every decision on sanctions and measures, while providing information on the type and nature of the breach, as well as the identity of the natural or legal persons affected by the decision. Aware of the risks involved in increased transparency in this area, MiFID II also allows NCAs to delay such publication, to publish decisions anonymously, or even not to publish a decision at all if they believe that such an action would be disproportionate, would seriously jeopardize the stability of the financial system or an ongoing investigation, or would cause disproportionate and significant damage to related institutions or natural persons.

Mandatory disclosure of sanctions is undoubtedly a highly effective means of deterrence, as well as a strong trigger for market reaction. 'Naming and shaming' has traditionally been regarded as a social sanction that can theoretically become more serious than the sanction itself or even last longer, depending on the unpredictable cascading effects on investors, third parties and stakeholders at large. It will be challenging to see how Member States will handle all these practices in the future, especially after the increasing demand for such disclosure from the EU.

Criminal sanctions applicable to investment firms have not been harmonized. MiFID II recognizes the right for Member States to provide for and impose criminal sanctions.[109]

11.8.2 Civil Liability and Alternative Dispute Resolution

Civil liability regimes continue to vary considerably across the EU, with some national laws facilitating civil claims and others making such claims impracticable. The rationale for a civil liability regime in the area of investment firms is a sound one, taking into consideration the contractual relationship between investment firms and their clients, along with the losses possibly incurred by a firm's clients by various infringements related notably to disclosure, advisory services and execution that may be deficient. MiFID II does not introduce

---

[108] The gravity of the duration of the breach, the degree of responsibility and the financial strength of the natural or legal person, the magnitude of profits as well as the losses suffered by third parties due to the breach, the level of cooperation with the NCA, and any possible prior breaches.

[109] Article 70, ibid.

any civil liability regime but simply mentions that mechanisms should be in place to ensure that compensation may be paid or other remedial action taken, according to national law, for any financial losses or damage suffered due to an infringement of MiFID II/MiFIR.[110] Investors remain dependent on non-harmonized national rules of variable content and different layers of investor protection. Harmonization of civil liability regimes in this (as in many other) areas not only corresponds to a legitimate need for protection and compensation, but also goes hand in hand with an ever-growing cross-border operational framework for investment firms, whose deficiencies may impact various investors in different jurisdictions. It therefore remains to be seen whether the political willingness at the EU level will be determinant in the future to overcome barriers arising from different legal traditions and reticence arising from investment firms themselves whose financial exposure would significantly increase.

For the time being, alternative dispute resolution seems to be the main focus of MiFID II. Member States must ensure the setting up of efficient and effective complaints and redress procedures for the out-of-court settlement of consumer disputes concerning the provision of investment and ancillary services that investment firms provide. Existing bodies should be used where appropriate, and Member States must also ensure that all investment firms adhere to one or more bodies that implement such complaint and redress procedures. These bodies must cooperate actively with their counterparts in other Member States within the ambit of a cross-border dispute resolution framework. NCAs must notify ESMA of the complaint and redress procedures available under their jurisdiction.[111]

Alternative dispute resolution mechanisms are definitely welcome in this framework, but may not achieve the same deterrent effect as a judicial mechanism establishing civil liability. Indeed, remaining attached to a purely compensatory function of rules that seek to address investment firms' deficiencies that harm clients may not be the only recommended way forward. Reinforcing and harmonizing civil liability regimes may also award a more deterrent connotation against infringements in this area, setting the foundations of a more functional, facilitating and efficient enforcement mechanism.

11.9 Conclusion

Investment firms hold a central place in the investment chain, as they channel investments towards issuers and offer a wide range of investment services and products to their clients. Creating a regulatory framework that understands the specificities, differences and complexities of the investment firm sector by offering the necessary level of flexibility, while at the same time ensuring adherence to high-level principles, is a complicated task. The traditional preference

---

[110] Article 69, ibid.
[111] Article 75, ibid.

for principles-based regulation, broadly formulated principles and reliance on internal control mechanisms testifies to the inability of legal rules to prescribe a 'one size fits all' approach. It also denotes a regulatory preference for the facilitation of firms' activities and services instead of the restriction of their business, in the light of a hypothetically overriding investor protection principle. Notwithstanding the critiques that have been formulated against the flexibility of the current regulatory stance, this chapter has aimed to show the range of requirements that are supposed to ensure a sound relationship between investment firms and their clients.

Investment firms are subject to authorization, organizational, compliance, governance, conflicts of interest and conduct of business requirements. The mosaic of such rules risks becomes counterproductive if investment firms conceive of compliance in a one-dimensional way, by failing to adopt a more holistic approach towards business ethics. At the same time, the broad nature of rules leaves considerable space to investment firms for subjective interpretation, creative compliance and avoidance of restrictions, such restrictions aim to align their incentives with those of their clients. For example, we have seen that conflicts of interest rules still provide considerable discretion to firms for managing such conflicts, without providing the necessary safeguards to clients. More emphasis on fine-tuning, with ESMA's orientation tools, such as Guidelines, rather than multiplication of rules, may bring more tangible results in creating and maintaining a sound business culture within investment firms.

Crucial to such developments will be the role that NCAs will continue to take on, under the discreet aegis of ESMA, to supervise firms effectively and detect possible infringements. Enforcement mechanisms are also vital in this sense. Without a doubt, MiFID II has increased the minimum harmonization of the administrative sanctions and paved the way for more convergence among NCAs. Other types of enforcement have been left behind, with no tangible signs of further developments in the future. Alternative dispute resolution, as currently prescribed by MiFID II, is a satisfactory step but civil liability also needs to be facilitated, so as to enhance investor protection.

CHAPTER 12

Financial Analysts

12.1 INTRODUCTION

Financial analysts have traditionally been regarded as gatekeepers in capital markets as their task is to gather and analyse information related to issuers and to assist market actors in their future investment decisions. Their presence and importance in the market is undoubtedly due to the fact that market actors are not in a position to decipher the plethora of available information and need to rely – to some extent – on various service providers who act as intermediaries, such as financial analysts. As information intermediaries, financial analysts are expected to act in the best interests of their clients and of the market at large so as to function as an additional gatekeeper that, on the one hand, makes investors aware of investment opportunities and, on the other hand, exerts a monitoring pressure upon issuers.

Nevertheless, the gatekeeping function of financial analysts has not been unanimously observed since the industry's initial growth in the USA. Analysts have been involved in well-known corporate scandals and have been accused of fraud, conflicts of interest, collusion with issuers and deficient research.[1] Their involvement in such practices leads to issuer-related information being presented overoptimistically, channelling investment inappropriately and causing massive losses for investors. The legal response to regulating financial analysts has therefore gone hand in hand with the outbreak of scandals that necessitate a more interventionist approach to ensure proper functioning of the analyst industry. Indeed, the traditional approach was based upon self-regulation, encouraging analysts to aspire to broadly formulated best principles. The shift towards more restrictive rules in the USA sparked a similar interest in the EU that has nowadays achieved a satisfactory level for a series of requirements.

Apart from the form that legal intervention may take in this area, additional concerns have been raised due to the fact that investors may still decide to use analysts' recommendations even if they have been alerted by the press or the regulator of conflicts of interest and deficient methods of analysis. This

---

[1] For an overview of financial analysts' involvement in US scandals, see J.C. Coffee Jr., *Gatekeepers: The Professions and Corporate Governance* (OUP, 2006), 263; J.E. Fisch, 'Regulatory Responses to Investor Irrationality: The Case of the Research Analyst' (2006) 10 *Lewis and Clark Law Review* 57.

trend may be explained in light of the short-termism that is prevalent in capital markets. Indeed, financial analysts have also been viewed as an additional layer of pressure on managers to pursue short-term goals. These observations are important to understanding the wider operational framework in which analysts conduct their activities and finding the most appropriate legal response to ensure their gatekeeping function and investor protection from deficient practices.

Financial analysts are also subject to more generally applicable rules, related *inter alia* to investment firms and market abuse, which complement the regulatory framework and aim to safeguard overall market integrity and investor confidence when they can be adversely affected by illegal practices. The enforcement framework in this area is predominantly characterized by administrative sanctions that are now subject to a reinforced – but timid – harmonization process. Civil liability, for investors who have suffered losses due to deficient analyst information, is still in its nascent stages, and the hurdles to further reforms appear significant.

12.2 FINANCIAL ANALYSTS

12.2.1 Different Types of Financial Analysts

Financial analysts can be categorized as follows: buy-side, sell-side and independent financial analysts.[2] Buy-side analysts are usually employed by institutional investors. They aim to increase the performance of their various investment portfolios. Sell-side analysts are employed by brokerage firms whose role is to sell financial instruments, while at the same time providing other services to issuers (such as underwriting services). Independent analysts generally work for market actors that want to receive financial analysis services either by hiring analysts directly or by subscribing to these services together with other market actors. In doing so, these independent analysts work for sell-side firms that are not engaged in the concomitant provision of investment banking services, thus offering an operational framework more 'independent' from potential conflicts of interest.

The way these three types of analysts provide their services also raises further questions about the availability of information derived from their work and about the definition of the audience that reads their results. Buy-side analysts will only provide information for institutional investors for making future investment decisions and increasing the value of investment portfolios. Sell-side analysts will provide the information to brokerage firms for their investment clients; independent analysts will work on a subscription-type model or for certain market actors. It is clear from this brief description that analysts' work is not purported to serve the market at large since the availability of

---

[2] On these and further categories of analysts, see Forum Group, 'Financial Analysts: Best Practices in an Integrated European Financial Market', 4 September 2003, 18, at http://euroirp.com/wp-content/uploads/2016/10/EU_Forum_Group_Report_04-09-03.pdf; R. Veil (ed.), *European Capital Markets Law* (2nd edn, Hart Publishing, 2017), 524.

information is not destined to reach all market actors.[3] Indeed, widespread availability of such information would render analysts' services less attractive and less profitable.[4] Their operational methods therefore serve specific investment agendas, depending on the audiences' investment preferences, and do not aim to increase price efficiency for the whole investor community, creating an underlying different starting point in trading for the investors who can afford paying for such services.

Persons interested in financial analysis may perceive buy-side and independent analysts as a reliable information source since these analysts conduct research for the benefit of investors and aim to inform them in the best way possible. Sell-side analysts may be viewed in a more critical light given the fact that they are primarily serving the interests of sellers of financial instruments – who may also provide other services to issuers – and therefore the contact with issuers and the ensuing pressure for the emission of positive results will inevitably have a greater influence on their work.

Even though these arguments appear plausible, buy-side analysts may use sell-side analysts' services to complement their own results and to offer an even more sophisticated assessment of the information available to their clients. It is therefore erroneous to assume that these three categories of analysts are completely distinct or that conflicts of interest[5] will primarily arise within the sell-side analysts' framework. The role that financial analysts have traditionally played in capital markets is very important in both financial and social terms. Empirical evidence has shown that their reports influence stock prices,[6] and that the quantity of analyst coverage is positively correlated with price efficiency and firm value.[7] Their recommendations may be specific as to future investment decisions (for example, 'buy', 'sell' or 'hold') or more general, by making reference to broader items, such as price targets. It is inevitable that sell-side analysts will be more prone to optimistic evaluations when they recommend buying securities, compared to their recommendations to sell securities, given the larger proportion of brokerage fees at stake[8] for the acquisition of securities by potential clients. The collective spirit of enthusiasm inevitably leads to inflation of research results. This inflation then destabilizes market integrity due to the massive influence that analysts have on future investment decisions.

---

[3] Although in some jurisdictions sell-side analyst reports may be available to the public.

[4] S.J. Choi, 'Framework for the Regulation of Securities Market Intermediaries' (2004) 1(1) *Berkeley Business Law Journal* 45, 50.

[5] See 12.2.2.

[6] J.R. Graham, C.R. Harvey and S. Rajgopal, 'The Economic Implications of Corporate Financial Reporting' (2005) 40 *Journal of Accounting and Economics* 73.

[7] Amongst a vast literature, see K.H. Chung and J. Hoje, 'The Impact of Security Analysts' Monitoring and Marketing Functions on the Market Value of Firms' (1996) 31 *Journal of Financial and Quantitative Analysis* 493.

[8] On this and other facets of the financial analyst industry, see J. Payne, 'The Role of Gatekeepers' in N. Moloney, E. Ferran and J. Payne, *Oxford Handbook of Financial Regulation* (Oxford University Press, 2015), 254, 263.

Apart from the recipients of analyst reports, financial analysts themselves have a general preference for positive results, when they use them for their own work, that will further nurture their optimism. The same reaction is less likely to occur in the presence of less positive results.[9] These two layers of optimism – the first related to the willingness to generate more brokerage fees and the other to the generalized tendency to overreact to positive results – further accentuate the influence that analysts exert on investors and the market at large.

Amongst numerous empirical studies that aim to decipher financial analysts' role towards issuers, investors and markets at large, particularly enlightening are the ones that emphasize the potentially negative role that analysts play with regard to firm innovation. Indeed, it has been shown that issuers that enjoy large analyst coverage are in fact less innovative.[10] This finding may be explained by the fact that financial analysts exert short-term pressure on managers by indirectly discouraging issuers from pursuing long-term goals and greater innovation. This conclusion has also been backed by a vast quantity of empirical evidence, according to which managers have declared their willingness to prioritize short-term earnings targets over long-term value for their own career-related concerns.[11]

It is clear that financial analysts play a key role in capital markets with potentially considerable negative ramifications on price efficiency, firm innovation, long-term goals and investment trends. These consequences may be further exacerbated by the presence of conflicts of interest; our attention will now turn to this matter.

12.2.2 Potential Conflicts of Interest

Conflicts of interest in the area of financial analysis are numerous and likely to arise in various circumstances.[12] Their disclosure and appropriate management[13] are essential to safeguarding the quality of the financial analyst industry, the reliability of the services provided, their clients' confidence in their work, and market integrity as a whole. A stricter approach, prohibiting conflicts of interest and restricting interaction between issuers and brokerage multiservice firms, would be a drastic solution but would create adverse effects, especially for SMEs, which would struggle to ensure affordable research coverage.[14]

---

[9] J.C. Easterwood and S.R. Nutt, 'Inefficiency in Analysts' Earnings Forecasts: Systematic Misreaction or Systematic Optimism?' (1999) 54 *Journal of Finance* 1777.

[10] J. He and X. Tian, 'The Dark Side of Analyst Coverage: The Case of Innovation (2013) 109(3) *Journal of Financial Economics* 856.

[11] J.R. Graham, C.R. Harvey and S. Rajgopal, 'The Economic Implications of Corporate Financial Reporting' (2005) 40 *Journal of Accounting and Economics* 3.

[12] For an overview, see IOSCO, 'Report on Analyst Conflicts of Interest' (2003), at http://www.iosco.org/library/pubdocs/pdf/IOSCOPD152.pdf; see also, Coffee, above n. 1, 249; H. McVea, 'Research Analysts and Conflicts of Interest – The Financial Services Authority's Response' (2004) 4 *Journal of Corporate Law Studies* 97, 105.

[13] See Section 12.4.5.

[14] Forum Group, above n. 2, 23.

Most conflicts of interest are more likely to arise with sell-side analysts. This is due to the fact that buy-side analysts are employed by institutional investors whose interest is to maximize their investment portfolios' value. Their interests are therefore aligned with those of their employers and their clients, since the aim is the production of an objective, reliable and ultimately successful report in that the information produced leads to profitable investment decisions. Independent analysts are also less likely to be involved in conflicts of interest, since they sell their research reports to their clients and their interests are aligned with the recipients of the reports, not to mention that their reputation is a sign of their independence and their success in the industry.

First of all, as mentioned above, sell-side analysts are employed by brokerage firms and are supposed to provide information that will be used for the investment decisions of the firms' clients. The same brokerage firms are also involved in providing investment banking services to issuers, such as underwriting services or mergers and acquisitions consultancy services. It is therefore a profitable strategy for the brokerage firms to have their sell-side analysts following and analysing issuers' progress, while at the same time assisting issuers in pursuing successful capital-raising operations. Sell-side analysts are funded by brokerage firms via cross-subsidies arising from their investment banking service fees charged to issuers.[15] The concomitant provision of investment banking services and the (optimistic and positive) coverage by their analysts makes brokerage firms highly profitable and exerts ongoing pressure on their analysts to continue recommending investments or to avoid issuing negative reports related to those issuers.[16]

The use of financial analyst services by issuers also becomes a *sine qua non* in the presence of investment banking business with brokerage firms, as the full package of services is considered to be a rational strategy to maximize capital-raising operations. Issuers may be tempted to 'remind' brokerage firms the importance of the fees paid for investment banking services, so as to ensure a more positive analyst coverage. They may also take more drastic action by reducing contact with analysts or cutting back auxiliary service contracts with the brokerage firm. It is easy to understand how financial analysts are steered towards compromises in the quality of their work within this interconnected framework the aim is to maintain a lucrative income for brokerage firms out of the provision of various services to issuers.

Secondly, conflicts may arise from analyst compensation and reporting mechanisms.[17] Remuneration schemes vary among jurisdictions, but it is sufficient to

---

[15] On cross-subsidies, see J.E. Fisch and H.A. Sale, 'The Securities Analyst as Agent: Rethinking the Regulation of Analysts' (2003) 88 *Iowa Law Review* 1035, 1045.

[16] S.J. Choi, above n. 4, 50. See also A. Agrawal and M.A. Chen, 'Do Analyst Conflicts Matter? Evidence from Stock Recommendations' (2007) Robert H. Smith School Research Paper No RHS 06-38, at https://ssrn.com/abstract=654281; the authors provide empirical evidence that the level of analysts' recommendations is related to the magnitude of conflicts of interest.

[17] IOSCO, above n. 12, 10.

mention that any link between an analyst's remuneration and factors that may incentivize the release of inflationary reports is very likely to give rise to conflicts of interest. For example, a bonus component in an analyst's salary related to performance indicators (creation or facilitation of investment banking transactions managed by the brokerage firm,[18] increase in the brokerage firm's fees) or to analyst rankings (broker votes, institutional investor ratings) is bound to influence analysts in their daily work to a much greater extent than in a fixed salary scenario. Reporting mechanisms within the brokerage firm may also give rise to conflicts of interest. If financial analysts are expected to share their provisional reports with other departments in the same brokerage firm, there may be pressure to amend their results or adjust their publication dates.

Thirdly, there may be financial interests of various types in issuers covered by financial analyst reports. These interests may vary from stakes in the issuer's share capital held by persons working at the analyst's firm, to commercial relationships (for example, a loan) between brokerage firms and issuers.[19]

12.2.3 Analysts' Influence on Investors

Having examined the numerous actual and potential conflicts of interest that financial analysts face, it would be plausible to argue that, under a proper disclosure regime, the recipients of analyst reports would know about the magnitude and importance of such conflicts before they make their investment decisions. Recipients would therefore be in a position either to rely on analyst reports or to ignore them in the light of conflicts of interest that would make them less reliable and less subjective.

Experience has nevertheless shown that, even if the recipients of information are aware of such conflicts, they may still take analyst reports into account for their decision-making processes. Although investor irrationality cannot be ruled out or be tackled at any level of the investment chain by legal or other provisions, it is important to note that such irrationality goes beyond any potential legal reforms and may still have a decisive impact on the way analyst reports are used or ignored. For example, an analyst's report influenced by known conflicts of interest that aligns with the recipients' short-term agenda and issues positive price targets may become an additional layer of confidence in the decision-making process for future investment strategies notwithstanding the subjective context in which it has been produced. Under the same perspective, an objective report, exempt of conflicts of interest, may easily be ignored due to its lack of alignment with short-term investment strategies or its less optimistic content.

Extending the discussion beyond the disclosure of conflicts of interest by analysts themselves, an additional layer of protection would be the NCA's potential warning to investors about such conflicts to enable them to avoid relying on such reports. Nevertheless, according to the US experience, NCA

---

[18] See, for example, L.D. Brown, A.C. Call, M.B. Clement and N.Y. Sharp, 'Inside the "Black Box" of Sell-Side Financial Analysts' (2015) 53(1) *Journal of Accounting Research* 1, 4.
[19] IOSCO, above n. 12, 9.

warnings in the past have not been successful in preventing investors from relying on conflicted reports by analysts.[20]

Some optimistic arguments may derive from the fact that empirical evidence has suggested that analysts are unlikely to be in a position to mislead the public systematically and for a long period,[21] since investors will understand – sooner or later – the magnitude of conflicts of interest and the eventual losses arising from relying on such reports. Nevertheless, the general reliance problem remains, as it is not so much the presence of systemically misleading practices that matter, but rather the multitude of conflicts of interest that may exert an ad hoc influence on investors at any moment in time within the ambit of various analyst reports.

As far as the legal response to analyst deficiencies is concerned, and taking into account the fact that investor irrationality cannot be tackled solely under a financial analyst-related initiative, it is important to focus on provisions that aim to ensure the proper production and presentation methods for the recipients of information. Any reform in that sense, even perfectible, will safeguard the reliability of the financial analyst industry in the eyes of interested market actors and will continue to allow financial analysts to exercise their (supposed) gatekeeping function.

12.3 EU Legal Sources

Under a global legal interventionist trend and a call for more stringent rules in capital markets law, following from the US Sarbanes-Oxley Act 2002, which aimed to tackle a series of well-known corporate scandals and *inter alia* financial analysts' involvement in deficient reporting practices, EU law moved to formulate legal provisions that regulate financial analysts in 2003 with the Market Abuse Directive.[22] The 2003 MAD was further enriched by Directive 2003/125 with regard to administrative rules for the fair presentation of investment recommendations and the disclosure of conflicts of interest.[23] Nevertheless, the EU had not experienced the full range of negative ramifications of the financial analyst industry, as had been the case in the USA. Financial analyst reports did not have the same impact and deleterious effect on corporate reporting in the EU, where ownership structures – and the ensuing investor reliance upon analysts – were (and to some extent remain) quite different. From the outset, the EU reforms have shown a rather timid approach with the concomitant formation of a Forum Group on Financial Analysts that favoured disclosure, self-regulation and best practices.[24]

---

[20] Fisch, above n. 1, 59.

[21] Agrawal and Chen, above n. 16, 1.

[22] Directive 2003/6/EC of the European Parliament and of the Council of 28 January 2003 on insider dealing and market manipulation [2003] OJ L 96/16 (hereinafter 2003 MAD).

[23] Commission Directive 2003/125/EC of 22 December 2003 implementing Directive 2003/6/EC of the European Parliament and of the Council as regards the fair presentation of investment recommendations and the disclosure of conflicts of interest [2003] OJ L 339/73.

[24] Forum Group, above n. 2.

Regulation (EU) No 596/2014,[25] which replaced the 2003 MAD and Directive 2003/125, provides definitions for investment recommendations and for information recommending or suggesting an investment strategy. The Delegated Regulation 2016/958[26] provides more detailed rules applicable in this area and has mainly reproduced the regime under the 2003 MAD.

12.4 The 'Recommendations' Regime

12.4.1 The Concept of 'Recommendations'

The definitions of 'information recommending or suggesting an investment strategy' and 'investment recommendations' are provided by the 2014 MAR and are both seen as 'recommendations' by the Regulation 2016/958.[27] Information recommending or suggesting an investment strategy is interpreted as information that has been produced by a series of market actors (independent analysts, investment firms, credit institutions, other persons whose business is to produce investment recommendations and their employees) that expresses, directly or indirectly, a particular investment proposal in respect to a financial instrument or an issuer.[28] This category of actors – commonly known as 'qualified persons' – necessitates a more burdensome regulatory framework since their professional status triggers an additional interest in confidence on behalf of investors. The applicable provisions therefore apply to this category even if the information expresses an indirect proposal regarding an instrument or an issuer.

On the other hand, actors who are not 'qualified persons' and who propose a particular investment decision regarding a financial instrument are subject only to the 2014 MAR provisions (and those found in Regulation 2016/958) if they propose such decisions in a direct reference to financial instruments.

Investment recommendations relate to information recommending or suggesting an investment strategy, in an explicit or implicit way, concerning one or several financial instruments or the issuers. Such information includes any opinion regarding the present or future value or price of these instruments, purported for distribution channels or for the public.[29]

---

[25] Regulation (EU) No 596/2014 of the European Parliament and of the Council of 16 April 2014 on market abuse (market abuse regulation) and repealing Directive 2003/6/EC of the European Parliament and of the Council and Commission Directives 2003/124/EC, 2003/125/EC and 2004/72/EC [2014] OJ L 173/1 (hereinafter 2014 MAR).

[26] Commission Delegated Regulation (EU) 2016/958 of 9 March 2016 supplementing Regulation (EU) No 596/2014 of the European Parliament and of the Council with regard to regulatory technical standards for the technical arrangements for objective presentation of investment recommendations or other information recommending or suggesting an investment strategy and for disclosure of particular interests or indications of conflicts of interest [2016] OJ L 160/15.

[27] Article 2(1), ibid.

[28] Article 3(1)(34), 2014 MAR.

[29] Article 3(1)(35), ibid.

The form of recommendations includes not only written recommendations but also oral ones, such as meetings, roadshows, audio or video conferences, or radio, television or website interviews.[30]

Persons who produce investment recommendations or other information recommending or suggesting an investment strategy must clearly and prominently disclose their identity, i.e. their names and job titles. This disclosure obligation applies to all the natural or legal persons involved in such production (including those acting under contract).[31] The identity of the relevant NCA must also be disclosed when the person producing recommendations is an investment firm or a credit institution (or persons working under a contract of employment or otherwise).[32] When persons producing recommendations are subject to self-regulatory standards or codes of conduct, a reference to those standards or codes must be given.[33]

12.4.2 The Different Layers of Requirements

The general requirements[34] are imposed upon any person who produces 'information recommending or suggesting an investment strategy', as explained above, including 'qualified persons' and other persons.[35]

The additional requirements[36] are only imposed on certain categories of market actors, such as qualified persons[37] and experts. Experts are defined by Regulation 2016/958 as the persons referred to in Article 3(1)(34)(ii), 2014 MAR (non-qualified persons) who repeatedly propose investment decisions regarding financial instruments and who present themselves as having financial expertise or experience or put forward their recommendations in such a way that other persons would reasonably believe they have financial expertise or experience.[38] The justification for imposing additional requirements not only for qualified persons but also for experts lies in the reliance that the market and potential clients inevitably have shown towards market actors whose business or portrayal of their activities conveys a message of expertise or experience. Some indicators for the identification of experts may be the frequency with which they produce recommendations, the number of their followers when they propose recommendations, their work history, and the eventual transmission of their recommendations by third parties, such as the media.[39] Increased

---

[30] Article 6(4), Regulation 2016/958.
[31] Article 2(1), ibid.
[32] Article 2(2), ibid.
[33] Article 2(3), ibid.
[34] Articles 3 and 5, ibid.
[35] Article 3(1)(34), 2014 MAR.
[36] Articles 4 and 6, Regulation 2016/958.
[37] See Section 12.4.1.
[38] Article 1, Regulation 2016/958.
[39] Recital 2, ibid.

client protection in this framework is therefore necessary given the greater level of risk involved not only for investors but also for market integrity.

12.4.3 The Presentation of Recommendations

The presentation of recommendations must be objective so as to ensure their accessibility and minimize the risks of misleading their recipients. The following requirements are laid out:

- clear separation of facts from interpretations, estimates, opinions and other types of non-factual information;
- clear and prominent indication of all substantially material sources of information;
- reliability of all sources of information or, in the presence of doubt, clear indications;
- clear and prominent labelling of all projections, forecasts and price targets, as well as indications of the material assumptions made in producing or using them; and
- clear and prominent indication of the date and time when the production of the recommendation was completed.[40]

An obvious accessibility problem arises in the case of non-written recommendations containing the above-mentioned information. Persons producing recommendations are expected to state where the required information can be directly and easily accessed free of charge.[41] Persons who produce recommendations may also be expected to substantiate them upon request by NCAs.[42]

Qualified persons and experts are also subject to additional presentation requirements. Their recommendations must include the following items in a clear and prominent way:

- if applicable, a statement that the recommendation has been disclosed to the issuer to which the recommendation relates, directly or indirectly, and that it has been subsequently amended;
- a summary of any valuation basis or methodology, as well as the underlying assumptions for the evaluation of financial instruments or issuers or for the setting of a price target for financial instruments (and an indication and summary of any relevant changes);
- if proprietary models have not been used, an indication of the place where detailed information, regarding the valuation or methodology and the underlying assumptions, can be directly and easily accessed;
- if proprietary models have been used, an indication of the place where material information about these models is directly and easily accessible;

---

[40] Article 3(1), ibid.
[41] Article 3(2), ibid.
[42] Article 3(3), ibid.

- the meaning of any recommendation made ('buy', 'sell' or 'hold') and the length of time of investment to which the recommendation relates must be adequately explained. Moreover, any appropriate risk warning, including a sensitivity analysis of the assumptions, must be indicated;
- a reference to the planned frequency of updates to the recommendation;
- an indication of the relevant date and time for any price of financial instruments mentioned in the recommendation;
- in the presence of variation of a recommendation compared to previous ones produced within the preceding 12 months, the change and the date of the previous recommendations must be indicated; and
- a list of all the recommendations on any financial instrument or issuer disseminated within the preceding 12 months. The list must contain the dissemination date, the identity of all persons involved in the production of the recommendation, the price target and the relevant market price at the time of dissemination, the direction of the recommendation in the validity time period of the price target or of the recommendation.

12.4.4 Conflicts of Interest

Conflicts of interest have been dealt with in Regulation 2016/958 and contain both general and additional obligations (applicable to qualified persons and experts).

According to the general obligations, natural and legal persons who produce recommendations must disclose all relationships and circumstances that could reasonably be expected to impair the objectivity of the recommendation. This shall include interests or conflicts of interest, and must relate to any natural or legal person(s) involved in producing the recommendation regarding financial instruments or issuers that are directly or indirectly related to the recommendation.[43]

In the case of legal persons, the above-mentioned information must also include any interests or conflicts of interest of any person belonging to the same group that are known (or reasonably expected to be known) to the persons involved in the production of the recommendation or known to persons who are not involving the production of the recommendation but have or could reasonably be expected to have access to the recommendation prior to its completion.[44] In the case of natural persons, the above-mentioned information must include any interests or conflicts of interest of any person closely associated with the said natural person.[45]

According to the additional obligations, qualified persons and experts are required to include a series of information in the recommendation.[46] First of all, if they own a net long or short position exceeding the threshold of 0.5% of

---

[43] Article 5(1), ibid.
[44] Article 5(2), ibid.
[45] Article 5(3), ibid.
[46] Article 6(1), ibid.

the total issued share capital of the issuer,[47] they must release a statement to that effect, specifying whether their position is long or short. Secondly, a statement is also required if the issuer has holdings that exceed 5% of the total issued share capital of the qualified person or expert. Thirdly, qualified persons or experts (or any other person belonging to the same group as them) must disclose if they are market makers or liquidity providers in the financial instruments of the issuer, if they have been lead managers or co-managers over the previous 12 months of any publicly disclosed offer of financial instruments of the issuer, if they are party to any agreement with the issuer relating to the provision of services of investment firms[48] or to the production of the recommendation.

If the producer of the recommendation is an investment firm or a credit institution (or a natural or a legal person working for either of them under a contract), they must also include the following information:

- a description of the effective internal organizational and administrative arrangements, as well as any information barriers they may have set up for the prevention and avoidance of conflicts of interest with respect to the recommendations;
- a statement related to the fact that the remuneration of natural or legal persons, working for them and where they are involved in producing the recommendation, is directly tied to transactions in services of investment firms they perform or to trading fees they receive; and
- when natural persons, working for them, purchase shares of the issuer to which the recommendation relates, directly or indirectly, prior to a public offering of such shares, the investment firm or the credit institution must disclose the price and date of acquisition of these shares.[49]

Investing firms or credit institutions (or natural or legal persons working for them) must publish, on a quarterly basis, the proportion of all recommendations (for example, 'buy', 'sell' or 'hold') over the previous 12 months and the proportion of issuers corresponding to each of those categories to which such person has supplied material services of investment firms over the previous 12 months.[50]

12.5 DISSEMINATION OF RECOMMENDATIONS BY THIRD PARTIES

The dissemination of recommendations by third parties is a potentially risky operational framework. The recipient of recommendations may be misled and may make deficient use of the available information. Regulation 2016/958

---

[47] See Chapter 10.

[48] This statement will be made under the condition that it would not impair the disclosure of any confidential commercial information and that the agreement has been in effect over the previous 12 months or has given rise during the same period to the obligation to pay or receive compensation.

[49] Article 6(2), ibid.

[50] Article 6(3), ibid.

provides some basic safeguards to ensure the proper functioning of the dissemination channel of the available information.

Disseminators of recommendations produced by third parties must disclose their identities (in a clear and prominent manner), the relationships and circumstances that may impair the recommendation,[51] and the date and time when the recommendation is first disseminated.[52] If the disseminator is an investment firm or a credit institution (or a natural or legal person working for them), they must also communicate the identity of the relevant NCA, as well as their own interests or indication of conflicts of interest (both the general and the additional requirements as explained above). The investment firm or credit institution is nevertheless exempted from disclosing information regarding conflicts of interest if they are acting as the disseminating channel of the recommendations produced within the same group, without exercising any discretion as to the selection of the content of disseminated recommendation.[53]

These general requirements introduce a relatively 'light touch' operational framework for disseminators of recommendation, but Regulation 2016/958 also provides for additional requirements for the dissemination of summary or extracts of recommendations, given the fact that such dissemination methods may be more misleading to recipients. Indeed, disseminators of summaries or extracts of recommendations also need to ensure that such summaries or extracts are clear and not misleading, are identified as a summary or extract and that they include a clear identification of the original recommendation.[54] Information about the producer of the recommendation needs to be available either directly (in the summary or in the extract) or indirectly via a reference to the accessibility point for all recipients and free of charge.[55]

Additional risks may arise when the disseminators of recommendations have altered the latter prior to their communication to recipients. Such recommendations need to indicate clearly the substantial alteration in detail, comply with the requirements of the presentation of recommendations and of the disclosure of conflicts of interest[56] and also include a reference to the (free of charge) accessibility point of the information[57] regarding the producer of the original recommendation.

12.6 GENERALLY APPLICABLE RULES

Financial analysts are subject to more broadly applicable rules that are not designed for the financial analyst industry per se. As this chapter is focused

---

[51] Including interests or conflicts of interest concerning any financial instrument or the issuer to which the recommendation relates (directly or indirectly).
[52] Article 8(1), ibid.
[53] Article 8(2), ibid.
[54] Article 9(1), ibid.
[55] Article 9(2), ibid.
[56] Articles 2 to 5, ibid.
[57] Prepared in accordance with Articles 2 to 6, ibid.

solely on the analyst-related legal rules, it will give only a brief account of the more general provisions that relate to two broad areas: market abuse (insider dealing[58] and market manipulation[59]) and investment firms.

12.6.1 Market Abuse

As far as insider dealing is concerned, financial analysts are expected to comply with all relevant rules that aim to maintain market integrity and investor confidence. The potential risks may arise if their recommendations are based on inside information. Financial analysts can be primary insiders when they obtain inside information within the ambit of their employment.[60]

The 2014 MAR specifies that research and estimates based on publicly available data should not be regarded as inside information per se, but when the publication or distribution of information is normally expected by the market and such information provided views from a recognized market commentator or institution, the information may constitute inside information. Although the line cannot be drawn in a generalized way, since the eventual existence and use of inside information can only be judged on a case-by-case basis, it is sufficient to note that it may become problematic for the recipient of information to fully estimate the source and the nature of each informational item of a recommendation.

Financial analysts are not allowed to acquire or dispose of financial instruments, to recommend that another person engage in insider dealing (namely, most usually, the recipients of their recommendations) or to unlawfully disclose inside information.[61]

Market manipulation is another set of rules that are relevant to financial analysts, given the numerous ramifications on market integrity that may arise via manipulative strategies within this framework.

First of all, financial analysts may be engaged in the dissemination of false or misleading information via the media, including the internet, or any other means that emits false or misleading signals related to the supply, demand or price of a financial instrument or that achieves an artificial or abnormal price for that instrument.[62] The distinctive feature of this manipulation category is that intention is required as the person involved in the dissemination must have known, or is supposed to have known, that the information was false or misleading.[63] A distinction needs to be drawn between false and misleading signals in the presentation of recommendations: false signals should be based on incorrect informational items, whereas misleading signals should refer to a deficient presentation of several types of correct information or even omission of some information that misleads the recipient.

---

[58] See Chapter 8.
[59] See Chapter 9.
[60] Article 8(4)(c), 2014 MAR. For the definition of 'primary insiders', see Section 8.3.3.
[61] See Section 8.3.4.
[62] Article 12 (1)(a), ibid.
[63] Article 12(1)(c) ibid.

Secondly, financial analysts may also employ fictitious devices or any kind of deception or contrivance that may have an actual or a potential impact upon the price of a financial instrument.[64] The 2014 MAR provides a non-exhaustive list of indicators of fictitious devices or any other form of deception or contrivance: particularly relevant in the case of financial analysts are cases in which trading orders/transactions are linked to the production/dissemination of investment recommendations that are erroneous, biased or demonstrably affected by material interest.[65] Financial analysts may therefore be directly concerned by such provisions.

Thirdly, financial analysts may be voicing an opinion in any type of media about a financial instrument, while having taken a prior position on this product without disclosing the conflict of interest to the public.[66] 'Qualified persons' and 'experts', who are also subject to additional requirements under Regulation 2016/958, given their capacity to attract a wide interest from other market actors due to their professional status, can be identified with the development of such strategies.

12.6.2 Investment Firms

According to Directive 2014/65,[67] investment research and financial analysis constitute ancillary security services.[68] Investment firms that provide their main investment services together with investment research are thus obliged to comply with a broader series of organizational requirements set out in the Implementing Directive 2006/73.[69] Firms that only provide investment research services are therefore not subject to the MiFID spectrum. The research activities (e.g. investment research) covered under MiFID II as

---

[64] Article 12(1)(b), ibid.

[65] Annex I, ibid.

[66] Usually referred to as 'scalping'.

[67] Directive 2014/65/EU of the European Parliament and of the Council of 15 May 2014 on markets in financial instruments and amending Directive 2002/92/EC and Directive 2011/61/EU Text with EEA relevance [2014] OJ L 173/349 (hereinafter MiFID II).

[68] Article 4(1)(3) and Annex I Section B(5), ibid.: '[i]nvestment research and financial analysis or other forms of general recommendation relating to transactions in financial instruments.' Investment research is defined as 'research or other information recommending or suggesting an investment strategy, explicitly or implicitly, concerning one or several financial instruments or the issuers of financial instruments, including any opinion as to the present or future value or price of such instruments, intended for distribution channels or for the public': Article 24(1), Commission Directive 2006/73/EC of 10 August 2006 implementing Directive 2004/39/EC of the European Parliament and of the Council as regards organizational requirements and operating conditions for investment firms and defined terms for the purposes of that Directive [2006] OJ L 241/26.

[69] Ibid. All organizational requirements will be maintained under the Commission Delegated Regulation (EU) supplementing Directive 2014/65/EU of the European Parliament and of the Council as regards organizational requirements and operating conditions for investment firms and defined terms for the purposes of that Directive, 25 April 2016, C(2016) 2398 final: Articles 33–37.

'ancillary services' are not identical to the general financial analyst framework, as analysed above, since they constitute one fraction of 'investment recommendations',[70] as covered by the Regulation 2016/958.[71]

Firms must comply with a series of organizational requirements related to conflicts of interest so as to ensure an appropriate level of independence for all concerned persons in this area. These requirements are not specifically designed for financial analysts, since they are of a broader nature, but are expected to be implemented in relation to financial analysts by investment firms.[72]

The conflicts of interest policy contains a series of measures:

- effective procedures for the prevention or control of the exchange of information between relevant persons engaged in activities involving the risk of a conflict of interest;
- separate supervision of relevant persons acting on behalf of or providing services to clients whose interests may conflict;
- removal of any direct link between the remuneration of relevant persons engaged in one activity and the remuneration of persons engaged in another activity, in the presence of conflict of interest;
- measures for the prevention or limitation of any person from exercising inappropriate influence on other persons who carry out investment or ancillary services; and
- measures for the prevention or control of the simultaneous or sequential involvement of relevant persons in separate investment or ancillary services when such involvement may impede the proper management of conflicts of interest.[73]

Additional organizational requirements are also provided when firms produce and disseminate investment research. More specifically, investment firms are expected to implement arrangements so as to ensure that:

- financial analysts and other relevant persons cannot be involved in personal transactions or trade, on behalf of any other person (including the investment firm) in financial instruments to which the investment research relates, by knowing the likely timing or content of that investment research until its recipients have had a reasonable opportunity to act upon it;
- in other circumstances (not covered by the above point), such transactions cannot take place unless prior approval of a member of the firm's legal or compliance function has been secured;
- investment firms, financial analysts and other persons involved in the production of investment research must not accept inducements from those with a material interest in the subject matter of such research;

---

[70] Recital 28, ibid.
[71] See Section 12.4.1.
[72] Article 25(1), ibid.
[73] Article 22(3), ibid.

- investment firms, financial analysts and other persons involved in the production of the investment research must not promise issuers favourable
research coverage; and
- issuers, relevant persons other than analysts and any other persons must not
be allowed to review a draft of the investment research before its dissemination for the purpose of verifying compliance with the firm's legal obligations.[74]

12.7 ENFORCEMENT FRAMEWORK

12.7.1 Administrative Sanctions and Measures

The 2014 MAR makes administrative sanctions and measures for insider
dealing infringements stricter by enriching them in great depth and detail.[75]
This initiative is particularly welcome, especially compared with the previous
2003 MAD framework that only required 'effective, proportionate and dissuasive' administrative sanctions and measures.[76] Its most notable characteristic is
the introduction of new thresholds with regard to pecuniary sanctions. First of
all, for breaches of Article 20(1), NCAs can impose maximum administrative
pecuniary sanctions of at least three times the amount of the profits related to
the infringement, when the amount of such profits can be determined.[77] Moreover, natural and legal persons can be subject to maximum pecuniary sanctions
of at least €500,000[78] and €1 million,[79] respectively. It is also worth noting
that Member States retain the possibility of providing for higher levels of sanctions.[80] The 2014 MAR thus aims to raise the minimum levels of maximum
pecuniary sanctions, while leaving national laws the discretion to increase the
severity of sanctions if they wish. Notwithstanding the unquestionable merits
of such minimum harmonization, the introduction of minimum minimums in
pecuniary sanctions would have been even more beneficial to the increase of
their dissuasiveness across the EU.

Similarly to Article 28(c) of the Transparency Directive, as analysed in
Chapter 5, Article 31 of the 2014 MAR provides a useful guide to the elements
that must be taken into account by NCAs when determining the type and level
of administrative sanctions.[81] It is clear that this alignment with the Transparency
Directive aims indirectly to enhance a harmonization trend among NCAs that

---

[74] Article 25(2), ibid.
[75] Article 30, 2014 MAR.
[76] Article 14(1), 2003 MAD.
[77] Article 30(2h), 2014 MAR.
[78] Article 30(2)(i) and (iii), ibid.
[79] Article 30(2)(j) and (iii), ibid.
[80] Article 30(3), ibid.
[81] The gravity of the duration of the breach, the degree of responsibility and the financial
strength of the natural or legal person, the importance of profits as well as the losses suffered
by third parties due to the breach, the level of cooperation with the NCA, any eventual former
breaches and any measures taken for the prevention of repetition of the breach.

are now required to start designing, interpreting and implementing sanctions with regard to a fixed minimum of circumstances applicable at the EU level.

This is undoubtedly an encouraging step towards gradual convergence of the *modus operandi* of NCAs that may prove even more useful than formal harmonization measures, which deal with minimal penalties, insofar as it could accustom authorities to a new way of thinking and calculating the severity of sanctions, adopting a much more holistic approach that may not necessarily coincide with traditional approaches.

12.7.2 Civil Liability

Civil liability regimes vary considerably in the case of financial analysts – as in many areas of capital markets law. The 2014 MAR does not provide any clarification on this type of liability, and it therefore remains a national matter how Member States design such liability. Discussion in academic literature has been rather sparse.

In UK law, in the absence of any specific provision for the civil liability of financial analysts, the general provision of the Financial Services and Markets Act 2000 related to private right of action for any contravention shall be applicable in this framework.[82]

Civil liability of financial analysts has nevertheless been accepted in a much more straightforward way in French law in the highly publicized *LVMH* v. *Morgan Stanley* case.[83] Morgan Stanley was required to pay LVMH €30 million in damages on the basis of Article 1382 of the French civil code (the general civil liability provision). The *Tribunal de Commerce* made reference to a series of deficiencies by Morgan Stanley that caused prejudice to LVMH: lack of a clear separation between investment and financial analyst services, lack of disclosure of conflicts of interest between LVMH and Morgan Stanley, inaccurate declarations regarding the debt ratio of LVMH and denigration of Louis Vuitton's image, as well as a systematic indication of LVMH's weaknesses while at the same time favouring LVMH's rival, Gucci, in various reports. The court further emphasized the lack of loyalty, reliability, security and professional ethics of the financial analyst industry.

By establishing a causal link between the above-mentioned deficiencies and LVMH's prejudice, the court made reference to the damage caused to LVMH's image in the light of Morgan Stanley's strategy to compare LVMH with Gucci, by denigrating the former and praising the qualities of the latter. The prejudice was therefore, according to the court, a moral one and the €30 million awarded in damages were determined on the basis of the court's 'sovereign power'.

Although the court did not provide more information on the profits earned by Morgan Stanley in this case, and its 'sovereign power' was the only

---

[82] Section 150, FSMA 2000.
[83] *Tribunal de commerce, Paris, Chambre supplémentaire*, 12 January 2004, RG 2002093985.

justification for the award of such a high amount of damages, it is clear that the main motivation for the recognition of civil liability of financial analysts was the need to convey the message to the whole industry that deficiencies would not be tolerated. In fact, the court also mentioned that the opinions and financial analysis of a large bank (such as Morgan Stanley, in this case) *necessarily* have an impact on issuers, without providing any other clarification on this point. Notwithstanding the debatable character of such a broad assumption, it becomes evident how civil liability was used in this framework to accentuate the dissuasiveness of enforcement.

12.8 CONCLUSION

The area of financial analysis has been the field for an incremental but rather timid regulatory attention at the EU level. The various obstacles that interfere with the gatekeeping function that financial analysts are expected to perform have been addressed by EU law in a satisfactory way, and the applicable rules are constantly evolving towards a more sophisticated framework that aims to cast light on all the potential operational deficiencies in the way financial analysts interact with the rest of the market. The most notable obstacle relates to conflicts of interest that will inevitably arise in the investment chain and can compromise the reliability and reputation of financial analysts. It is expected that disclosure in this area will enable recipients of analysts' services to decide how and to what extent they should use analyst reports. Nevertheless, investor reliance on such reports has been observed even when alarming signs have come forward in the financial press or through regulators.

The crucial parameter for safeguarding the reliability of such services should therefore not be exclusively focused on sophisticated regulatory requirements, but also on ongoing efforts to educate investors and assist them in distinguishing between short-term and long-term goals that are served indirectly by such reports. A short-term strategy will inevitably rely on overoptimistic reports, notwithstanding alarming signs, and will further reduce the usefulness of analysts' services and the gatekeeping function that financial analysts are expected to perform.

Future regulatory steps need to take into account the fact that it is ultimately a matter of client demand and expectations (most notably in the area of sell-side analysts) that drives financial analysts to maintain their operational status quo. By increasing regulatory requirements in the area of financial analysts, the risks of making such services not only costlier but also more complicated will inevitably become greater. Maintaining sophisticated but not excessively burdensome requirements, as is currently the case, by aiming to shift the attention of both issuers and investors towards building a more objective and trustworthy relationship with financial analysts would become a more reasonable regulatory approach in the future. This would also ensure the accessibility of such services to less well-known or smaller issuers who need extensive coverage in order to maximize the potential success of their capital-raising operations.

Enforcement is another key factor for the implementation of regulatory requirements. Notwithstanding the minimum harmonization carried out in the area of administrative sanctions, it remains to be seen to what extent NCAs will exercise their powers and if such exercise will take place under a converged mentality across the EU. Civil liability regimes are at an embryonic stage, with some notable exceptions in French law, and need further attention so as to increase their dissuasiveness in the area of financial analysts.

CHAPTER 13

Credit Rating Agencies

13.1 INTRODUCTION

Credit rating agencies (hereinafter CRAs) have undoubtedly become key players in capital and financial markets due to the pivotal role of their activities for the creditworthiness of the various entities (companies, States, etc.) whose debt is subject to their evaluation.[1] The information they provide has clearly shown its impact on various market actors since they function as informational intermediaries between the rated entities and the rest of the market interested in deciphering the quality of their debt. To highlight their importance even further, we must bear in mind that in the past decades they have also functioned as providers of 'regulatory licences'[2] due to the ever-growing regulatory reliance on their ratings. Indeed, regulators chose to issue a series of criteria in order to recognize certain CRAs for regulatory purposes in an effort to discharge the inevitably complex task of constant verification of the quality of the ratings used by various market actors. This regulatory over-reliance made credit ratings even more important since the main focus was thereby shifted (unfortunately) to their regulatory accreditation – and their ensuing prestige – rather than their quality per se.

Notwithstanding their historically predominant presence in the markets and their gatekeeping function, CRAs were left without any stringent regulatory framework at the EU level. This regulatory laxity, justified by the need to maintain competitiveness and market-led discipline as well as by the regulatory over-reliance on these services, was further amplified by a common perception that the International Organization of Securities Commissions (hereinafter IOSCO) Code of Conduct was fulfilling its role in an adequate way due to CRAs' high rate of compliance.[3] This strong market and institutional support had allowed CRAs to operate in complete freedom with regard to their *modus*

---

[1] J.C. Coffee Jr., *Gatekeepers: The Professions and Corporate Governance* (Oxford University Press, 2006), 287.

[2] F. Partnoy, 'The Siskel and Ebert of Financial Markets? Two Thumbs Down for the Credit Rating Agencies' (1999) 77 *Washington University Law Quarterly* 619, 624.

[3] Based on the self-regulatory framework of the 'comply or explain' principle. See for example CESR, 'Report by CESR on Compliance of EU Based Credit Rating Agencies with the 2008 IOSCO Code of Conduct' (2009), CESR/09-417, 3, at http://www.esma.europa.eu/system/files/09_417.pdf.

operandi despite some initial and strong signs of criticism, following the Enron and Parmalat scandals in 2002.[4]

The regulatory attention and perception of CRA-related risks nevertheless changed dramatically after the global financial crisis when it gradually became apparent that CRAs were heavily involved in the overrating of structured finance products, such as mortgaged backed securities (MBSs) and collateralized debt obligations (CDOs), and were to blame for failing to evaluate credit risk at large. The political and social framework was thus very receptive for a much more interventionist approach by the European Commission, which in 2009 adopted the first Regulation in this field: Regulation (EC) No 1060/2009 (hereinafter CRA Regulation I).[5] This first phase was purported to mark decisively the first framework applicable to CRAs and to draw a perimeter on their activities, while conveying the political message that the EU was ready to set higher and more stringent regulatory standards in this field, thus endeavouring to exert influence on its international homologues during the proliferation of reform agendas around the globe.

After this initial regulatory step, the EU was ready to deepen CRA reforms by giving ESMA considerable new powers for registration, supervision and sanctioning. With the adoption of Regulation (EU) No 513/2011 (hereinafter CRA Regulation II),[6] ESMA became the central point of reference for CRAs, obtaining crucial centralized powers but maintaining its cooperation possibilities with NCAs, which would from now on assist ESMA in its ambitious regulatory programme. The last important reform in the European CRA agenda was adopted in 2013 via Regulation (EU) No 462/2013 (hereinafter CRA Regulation III).[7] This third regulatory intervention was aimed at controlling even more subtle issues related to market risks, such as, *inter alia*, the reduction of regulatory dependence on ratings, specific issues on conflicts of interest and rotation of CRAs. Most importantly, this Regulation created a civil liability regime for CRAs aiming to enhance investor and issuer confidence in their activities. The three Regulations are also accompanied by the 2013 CRA Directive,[8] a series of administrative rules, in the form of Delegated Regulations, as well as various ESMA measures.

---

[4] C.A. Hill, 'Rating Agencies Behave Badly: The Case on Enron' (2003) 35 *Connecticut Law Review* 1145.

[5] Regulation (EC) No 1060/2009 of the European Parliament and of the Council of 16 September 2009 on credit rating agencies [2009] OJ L 302/1.

[6] Regulation (EU) No 513/2011 the European Parliament and of the Council of 11 May 2011 amending Regulation (EC) No 1060/2009 on credit rating agencies [2011] OJ L 145/30.

[7] Regulation (EU) No 462/2013 the European Parliament and of the Council of 21 May 2013 amending Regulation (EC) No 1060/2009 on credit rating agencies [2013] OJ L 146/1.

[8] Directive 2013/14/EU of the European Parliament and of the Council of 21 May 2013 amending Directive 2003/41/EC on the activities and supervision of institutions for occupational retirement provision, Directive 2009/65/EC on the coordination of laws, regulations and administrative provisions relating to undertakings for collective investment in transferable securities (UCITS) and Directive 2011/61/EU on Alternative Investment Funds Managers in respect of over-reliance on credit ratings [2013] OJ L 145/1.

This chapter will aim to critically challenge all these reform waves at the EU level and will argue that, notwithstanding the key benefits of centralization of powers and harmonization of requirements for the functioning and supervision of CRAs, there is still considerable room for improvement. More specifically, although the focus of the EU regulatory framework is mainly expressed through a series of rules aiming to enhance the operational efficiency of ratings, ensuring an optimal quality of ratings may need a different approach. Moreover, efforts to minimize regulatory dependence clearly show positive signs of a more mature regulatory conception of the importance of ratings, but the EU framework has yet to tackle the more delicate issue of providing incentives or, more generally, encouraging investors in a tangible way to reduce their own over-reliance on the same services. ESMA will definitely have a very important role to play in the future, in terms of both engaging with CRAs in a fruitful dialogue for the improvement of their operational methods and emitting signals to the market with regard to the credibility of CRAs and ensuring compliance with the EU framework when it exercises its supervisory and sanctioning powers. The chapter will also examine the CRA civil liability regime, which may have the allure of an accountability mechanism, but still needs further reform to be able to function as an efficient and persuasive deterrence tool.

13.2 Regulatory Framework Applicable to the Issuance of Ratings

13.2.1 Credit Ratings and Ratings Outlooks

The entire set of EU rules is applicable to credit ratings issued by CRAs registered in the EU and publicly disclosed or distributed by subscription.[9] A rating, in this framework, is an 'opinion regarding the creditworthiness of an entity, a debt or financial obligation, debt security, preferred share or other financial instrument, or of an issuer of such a debt or financial obligation, debt security, preferred share or other financial instrument, issued using an established and defined ranking system of rating categories'.[10] Ratings are usually the result of a contract between an issuer and a CRA whereby the latter evaluates the former's credit quality, in whichever form it may arise as seen above. Rating may also be the result of a unilateral decision made by the CRA.

In both cases, of paramount importance is the influence of a rating on other market participants' perception of an issuer or a financial instrument that is relevant to its activities The EU framework is constantly attempting to decipher

---

[9] Article 2(1), Regulation (EC) No 1060/2009. Paragraph 2 of the same Article enumerates the various ratings which do not fall under the ambit of the Regulation, such as private credit ratings, credit scores as well as ratings produced by export credit agencies and central banks: Article 2(2), ibid.

[10] Article 3(1), ibid.

the implications of ratings and to enlarge its application spectrum. Therefore, CRA Regulation III – quite wisely so – extended its regulatory perimeter to 'rating outlooks'. These are defined as opinions regarding the likely direction of a rating over the short and medium terms.[11] The Regulation emphasizes their importance as equivalent to that of credit ratings and hence all its requirements with regard to the accuracy, transparency and the avoidance of conflicts of interest must be equally applicable to rating outlooks. This reform certainly testifies to the ongoing trend towards an intrusive regulatory approach that seeks to protect the market from any possible amplification of 'contagion effects' from collective reliance on different types of ratings.

13.2.2 Registration Process

Registration of CRAs has been debated for a long time with regard to its usefulness and its contribution to the quality of ratings issued. On the one hand, the choice for an EU registration process presents a series of advantages pertaining to the organization of the CRA sector, the increase in CRAs' credibility for those that obtain registration status and the maintenance of market actors' confidence in the reliability of the regulatory framework.[12] On the other hand, various views have been expressed with regard to the innate inability of regulators to ensure rating quality via the registration process due to the thin line between formal compliance with registration criteria and potential deficiencies in the substance of rating activities that are difficult to identify at the regulatory level.[13]

Moreover, concerns have been formulated in relation to the risks arising from an extremely rigorous registration process that can create entry barriers to the CRA sector and freeze competition and innovation.[14] Notwithstanding these potential risks, the EU political agenda was quite keen on creating a very robust regulatory framework, partly to address public concern about CRA involvement in the financial crisis and partly to ensure access to rating services in the EU along with compliance to rigorous standards. Therefore, the current framework should be seen as an imperative need for control of the CRA sector and for the establishment and maintenance of adequate entry standards to strengthen, if not the rating quality, then at least the reliability of ratings to the markets and the public at large.

---

[11] See for example Article 6(1), Article 7(5), Article 8(2) and Article 10(1) (2) and (2)(a), ibid.

[12] F. Partnoy, 'Rethinking Regulation of Credit Rating Agencies: An Institutional Investor Perspective' (April 2009) Council of Institutional Investors, at http://ssrn.com/abstract=1430608.

[13] S. Rousseau, 'Agences de notation de crédit et crise financière: quel rôle pour la régulation financière?' in A. Couret and C. Malecki (eds), The Current Challenges of Financial Law (LGDJ 2010), 293, 315.

[14] S. Pei Woo, 'Stress Before Consumption: A Proposal to Reform Agency Ratings' (2012) 18(1) European Law Journal 62.

The EU regulatory framework provides for a centralized and mandatory registration process under the ambit of ESMA. This framework was initially introduced with CRA Regulation II in 2011 after careful consideration of the unnecessary delays and costs associated with NCAs becoming involved in the registration process.[15] ESMA needed to ensure a wide operational spectrum in order to conduct its activities as efficiently as possible, and the centralization of the registration process facilitates this task considerably and provides unrestricted access to the EU area for CRAs once the registration comes into effect.

Articles 14 to 20 elaborate – in a considerable amount of detail – the whole registration process with details regarding the information that must be included in the application,[16] the language in which the application must be drafted,[17] the time frames for ESMA's assessment of the complete character of a registration application and the notification of the decision to register or refuse registration.[18] To ensure ESMA's accountability and the transparency of its operational framework, the European authority also needs to communicate to the European Commission, the EBA, the EIOPA and the NCAs as well as sectoral competent authorities, any decision related to registration or withdrawal of registration of CRAs. Moreover, it must publish and regularly update a list of registered CRAs on its website.[19]

ESMA also retains the right to withdraw the registration of a CRA for a series of reasons included in Article 20, such as the absence of credit ratings for six months, the provision of false statements or the adoption of any other irregular means to obtain registration, and the failure to meet the conditions of registration.

13.2.3 Ratings Issued by a Third Country

Taking into account practical implications and international elements in CRA operations, this EU framework is endeavouring to adopt an inclusive approach towards third countries by allowing ratings issued by CRAs in these countries to be endorsed by EU-registered CRAs and by certifying third country CRAs in order for their ratings to be disseminated in the EU. This regulatory openness towards third countries testifies to the need to facilitate activities while allowing third country actors to develop their services in the EU, but also to make the EU regulatory framework a point of reference for

---

[15] More generally on centralization trends at EU level: E. Wymeersch, 'The Institutional Reforms of the European Financial Supervisory System, an Interim Report' (2010) Financial Law Institute, Universiteit Gent, Working Paper No 2010-01, at http://ssrn.com/abstract=1541968.

[16] Annex II, Regulation (EC) No 1060/2009.

[17] Article 15(3), ibid.

[18] Twenty working days to assess whether the application is complete and notify the CRA, 45 working days for a CRA or 55 working days in the case of a group of CRAs (with a potential extension of 15 working days) following the notification to examine the application and to reach a decision: Article 15(4), Article 16(1) and (2), Article 17(1) and (2), ibid.

[19] Article 18, ibid.

third country CRAs, via the requirements for adherence to standards similar to the EU ones, as well as a point of influence for the international regulatory agenda.[20]

A CRA that is registered in the EU may endorse ratings issued by a third country CRA under the following conditions: both agencies belong to the same group, the third country is able to show that it is subject to requirements related to conflicts of interest, disclosure requirements and outsourcing guarantees, similar to those found in Articles 6–12 of the EU Regulation, ESMA retains the right to assess and monitor the compliance of the third country CRA and cooperates with the third country regulator and, lastly, the third country CRA is in a position to provide all necessary information to ESMA for its effective supervision.[21]

The certification process[22] is also very important as it allows for dissemination of ratings issued by third country CRAs in the EU, and it is subject to the fulfilment of the following conditions: the third country CRA is authorized or registered as well as supervised in that third country, the European Commission has already adopted an equivalence decision in respect of the legal and the supervisory framework of that third country, appropriate cooperation arrangements and mechanisms have been established between ESMA and the third country regulator and, lastly, the ratings issued by the third country CRA are not of systemic importance to the financial stability or integrity of the financial markets of one or more Member States.[23]

So far, both the endorsement and the certification procedures have proven to be successful and ESMA's approach has shown tolerance of other jurisdictions, thus marking the need for regulatory openness and facilitation of rating activities beyond EU borders.

13.2.4 Issuing Principles and Methodologies

EU law has tried to adopt an intrusive approach with regard to the principles and methodologies that are used by CRAs for the issuance of ratings. In doing so, the regulatory framework expects to ensure credit rating quality and methodological consistency across the sector. Although such a goal is laudable, it is highly doubtful whether an increasing prescription of a series of criteria and

---

[20] N. Moloney, 'Reform or Revolution? The Financial Crisis, EU Financial Markets Law, and the European Securities and Markets Authority' (2011) 60(2) *International and Comparative Law Quarterly* 521, 525–528; K. St. Charles, 'Regulatory Imperialism: The Worldwide Export of European Regulatory Principles on Credit Rating Agencies' (2010) *Minnesota Journal of International Law* 399.

[21] Article 4(3), Regulation (EC) No 1060/2009.

[22] The application needs to be submitted in accordance with the provisions for the registration process outlined in Article 15: Article 5(2), ibid.

[23] Article 5(1), ibid.

the expectation that these principles will be unanimously applied in the pre-paratory phase of credit ratings will be in a position to actually ensure credit rating quality.[24]

The Regulation provides, under Article 7, that CRAs are expected to ensure that the rating analysts, employees and any other person related to credit rating activities dispose of the appropriate knowledge and experience for their duties. Moreover, CRAs should not allow the above-mentioned persons to be involved in any negotiations regarding fees or payments with third parties or rated entities.[25] The Regulation also provides for a rotation mechanism for rating analysts and persons who approve credit ratings, and forbids their compensation to be linked to the amount of revenue that the CRA receives from rated entities or third parties.[26]

With regard to the methodologies adopted, CRAs are required to disclose publicly their methodologies, models and key rating assumptions (defined in Annex I, Section E, Part I, point 5). They are also expected to ensure, via the adoption, implementation and enforcement of adequate measures, that all ratings and rating outlooks issued are based on and relevant to a thorough analysis of all information which also needs to be of sufficient quality and collected from reliable sources. The main problem with the requirement to proceed to a thorough analysis of information is that it is not accompanied by an express duty of diligence which would additionally oblige CRAs to ensure that the information is comprehensive or, more generally, to verify its veracity.[27] This absence of duty may be seen as a compromise between the adoption of an intrusive regulatory stance and the need of the CRA sector for flexibility and less exposure to litigation. Nevertheless, in our opinion, such a duty should be imposed to increase the rating quality, as it will become an efficient measure for a more profound analysis of the available information for the issuance of ratings.

Adding to the overly vague wording of the Regulation, rating methodolo-gies must satisfy the criteria of rigour, systematicity and continuity, and they must also be subject to validation against historical data. These three concepts can be interpreted variably by CRAs, and hence it remains to be seen how rating quality will actually be affected by these criteria.[28] Following the intro-duction of a civil liability regime, CRA Regulation III amended Article 8(2) by providing that CRAs need to stipulate that the rating is the agency's opinion

---

[24] The rating quality may also derive from other factors, such as the emergence of a more demanding and sophisticated investor community which is, currently, unlikely to develop independent critical thinking since the increasing amount of regulation risks exacerbating the dependence on ratings. This is particularly true since the investor community will increasingly rely on ratings given the presence of a much more detailed and burdensome regulatory framework and the illusion of an efficient safeguard against inappropriate practices given the amount of intrusion at the EU level.

[25] Article 7(2) Regulation (EC) No 1060/2009.

[26] Article 7(4)(5), ibid.

[27] M. Andenas and I. H-Y. Chiu, *The Foundations and Future of Financial Regulation: Governance for Responsibility* (Routledge, 2013), 212.

[28] On these three concepts as well as the practical interpretative difficulties arising in this context, see Andenas and Chiu, ibid., 213–215.

and that reliance should be of a limited degree, mirroring the concerns for litigation exposure mentioned above.[29]

Amongst the numerous other requirements on methodologies, it would be useful to mention the requirement for monitoring credit ratings, as well as for constant (or at least annual) review of ratings and methodologies, especially when material changes take place and may have a potential impact on a rating.[30] CRA Regulation III requires that sovereign ratings must be reviewed at least every six months, following the considerable amount of criticism from various Member States with regard to rating methodologies that affected their sovereign debt negatively.[31]

In the presence of intended changes to methodologies, models or rating assumptions, CRAs are required to engage in a very detailed procedure: they must first publish the proposed material changes or rating methodologies on their website by inviting stakeholders to express their comments for a month; disclose the spectrum of ratings potentially affected by such changes; inform immediately ESMA and publish on their website the consultation results, the responses to the consultation and the new methodologies, to put these ratings under observation; and review them as well as to eventually re-rate them if they finally assess that they have been affected by these changes.[32]

Trying to further safeguard the reliability of ratings as well as any parties that may be affected from potential errors in rating methodologies, the Regulation requires CRAs to notify immediately ESMA of these errors and all affected rated entities, to publish the errors that have an impact on their ratings on their websites and to correct these errors in the rating methodologies.[33]

13.2.5 Comparability of Ratings

Comparability of ratings has become one of the main concerns of the EU regulatory agenda, trying to ensure convergence of publication methods in various areas of information disclosed to the market at large. Article 11(2) provides for CRAs to make available in a centralized database, established by ESMA (Central Rating Repository, hereinafter CEREP), information pertaining to their historical performance data following a standardized form provided by ESMA, which then publishes the information on its website. Adding to the comparability regulatory impetus, ESMA proposed a European standard for credit ratings that can consolidate all ratings, but then decided to maintain it for purely supervisory purposes (SOCRAT), namely non-public CRA disclosures.

Although CEREP enhances comparability and allows both regulators and investors to better absorb information related to CRA activities, concerns have been expressed with regard to the proposal for a European Rating Index (EURIX), based on the SOCRAT standard, since this would risk eliminating divergent

---

[29] Article 8(1-3), ibid. See also Section 13.5.4.
[30] Article 8(5), ibid.
[31] Ibid.
[32] Article 8(6), ibid.
[33] Article 8(7), ibid.

opinions that could theoretically enhance rating accuracy. Indeed, forced standardization of presentation methods considerably reduces investors' capacity to critically evaluate and challenge ratings as they can become accustomed to relying on the proposed EU rating scale and developing a mechanistic interpretation of the available data.[34] Furthermore, MacNeil argues that transparency provisions may not be able to position investors at an equal level to CRAs given the fact that the latter may have access to issuer-related 'inside information'[35] and that these kinds of privileges will continue to nurture an over-reliance trend, making CRAs more important and 'informationally efficient' in the eyes of the investor community.[36]

By standardizing all information available, ESMA will inevitably increase comparability of ratings, which is currently needed and should be welcomed as an initiative, but it may fail in the broader goal of empowering investors with better analytical skills in the long term. Therefore, the current framework cannot be seen as the ultimate goal for enhancing accessibility of information, and it needs to be accompanied by other reforms to enhance investors' governance role and better prepare them for evaluating standardized information in an optimal way.

13.3 MAJOR REGULATORY CHALLENGES

13.3.1 Conflicts of Interest

Conflicts of interest have been at the forefront of various debates over the exercise of activities of various market actors, and the EU applicable rules provide a very detailed framework with regard to the avoidance of such conflicts for CRA employees. Inevitably, operating in a complicated and interconnected market spectrum, credit rating analysts and other employees may frequently be faced with such conflicts. This is why it is of pivotal importance to ensure that they conduct their activities without being affected by such conflicts.[37]

Moreover, the 'issuer pays' model,[38] which emerged in the 1970s after abandoning the 'investor pays' model,[39] has traditionally created delicate situations

---

[34] Andenas and Chiu, above n. 27, 230.

[35] According to Article 17(8) MAR permitting issuers to disclose inside information to a third party under a duty of confidentiality.

[36] I. MacNeil, 'Credit Rating Agencies: Regulation and Financial Stability' in T. Cottier, R.M. Lastra, C. Tietje and L. Satragno (eds), *The Rule of Law in Monetary Affairs* (Cambridge University Press, 2014), 178, 201.

[37] Such conflicts may refer to personal or business relations with an issuer, the provision of consultancy services to the same issuer, as well as to the remuneration of a person that may be linked with business arising from issuers.

[38] MacNeil, above n. 36, 181; L. Bai, 'On Regulating Conflict of Interests in the Credit Rating Industry' (2010) 13 *New York University Journal of Legislation and Public Policy* 253.

[39] The 'investor pays' model was abandoned due to the increasing complexity of CRA activities and the popular trend of democratization of information for the benefit of the entire investor community and not only of investors who were in a position to remunerate CRAs to evaluate credit quality and help them with their investment decisions: M. Pagano and P. Volpin, 'Credit Ratings Failures: Causes and Policy Options' in M. Dewatripont, X. Freixas and R. Portes (eds), 'Macroeconomic Stability and Financial Regulation: Key Issues for the G20' (2009), 129, at http://www.voxeu.org/index.php?q=node/3167.

for CRAs due to the remuneration fees received when issuers choose a CRA to evaluate their credit quality.[40] The concomitant provision of consultancy services can also jeopardize the independent judgement of CRA employees, who may be tempted to adopt a more favourable position on the evaluation being conducted, resulting in the emergence of a sort of 'negotiation'[41] between the issuer and the CRA for the rating outcome.

Last but not least, issuers may be under pressure to contract the services of a CRA following the publication of an unsolicited very prudent and potentially negative rating due to the lack of a series of information which would only be available had the issuer signed a contract with the CRA giving full access to information regarding its entity.[42] This type of pressure may also be exercised more strategically by CRAs when they intentionally choose to be very prudent to trigger an increased demand from the issuer community for the provision of rating services.[43]

Under a general perspective, it is useful to question the potential efficiency of 'conflicts of interest-related' measures that pertain to ensuring and maintaining rating quality.[44] Two diverging doctrinal trends aim to highlight, on the one hand, the irrelevance of conflicts of interest to the increase of rating accuracy,[45] and on the other, the necessity to insist on measures ensuring the avoidance of such conflicts to improve rating quality.[46] The debate is irresolvable as there is no empirical evidence of a clear correlation between the avoidance of conflict of interest and the efficiency of the rating exercise. It is therefore laudable to argue that, notwithstanding the absence of such evidence, it is legitimate for a regulatory framework to target such conflicts that may exacerbate the presence and maintenance of an 'issuer-friendly' and inflationary mindset

---

[40] Alternative remuneration arrangements have been put forward to alleviate these distorted effects: for example, upfront fees paid to CRAs independently from that of the issuance of ratings and in association with a 'credit shopping' prohibition. For a critical approach, see MacNeil, above n. 36, 194. It should be also borne in mind that other proposals have seen the light in the USA arguing in favour of the creation of a board, under the supervision of SEC, with the authority to assign CRAs to issue ratings (Franken amendment) were finally abandoned: A. Darbellay, *Regulating Credit Rating Agencies* (Edward Elgar, 2013), 88–89. This proposal could have reduced significantly conflicts of interest in this area as it would have prevented issuers from choosing CRAs for the provision of ratings.

[41] H. McVea, 'Credit Rating Agencies, the Subprime Mortgage Debacle and Global Governance: The EU Strikes Back' (2010) 59 *International and Comparative Law Quarterly* 701, 712.

[42] S. Rousseau, 'Enhancing the Accountability of Credit Rating Agencies: The Case for a Disclosure-based Approach' (2006) 51 *McGill Law Journal* 617, 637.

[43] F. Partnoy, 'How and Why Credit Rating Agencies Are Not Like Other Gatekeepers' in Y. Fuchita and R.E. Litan (eds.), *Financial Gatekeepers: Can They Protect Investors?* (Brookings Institution Press, 2006), 71.

[44] Andenas and Chiu, above n. 27, 205.

[45] See for example, N.B. Neuman, 'A "Sarbanes-Oxley" for Credit Rating Agencies? A Comparison of the Roles Auditors' and Credit Rating Agencies' Conflicts of Interests Played in Recent Financial Crises' (2010) 12 *University of Pennsylvania Journal of Business Law* 921.

[46] B.J. Kormos, 'Quis Custodiet Ipsos Custodes? Revisiting Rating Agency Regulation' (2008) 4 *International Business Law Journal* 569.

on behalf of CRAs. Even if an increase in rating accuracy cannot be guaranteed by imposing such measures, it is preferable from a regulatory point of view to impose a series of restrictions on CRAs to further delineate their operational spectrum and make sure that well-known practices will not be repeated in the future, risking to create a systemic reaction, as seen in the case of structured finance products during the global financial crisis.

Unfortunately, the regulatory responsiveness in this field testifies to a rather 'over-prudent' approach, with some requirements creating a fairly burdensome operational framework. Nevertheless, this plethora of rules should be perceived more as an over-reaction, driven partially by political agendas (as shown above) to dubious rating practices rather than as a sophisticated regulatory approach that is in a position to understand and evaluate *ex ante* all the risks involved. Indeed, the difficulties in regulating such a complicated sector make the EU rules and ESMA more prone to 'over-reaction' to safeguard market stability. It is believed that that the EU framework may shift towards a more relaxed approach, although in the distant future, once – and if – ESMA develops a much more targeted and sophisticated supervisory capacity.[47]

Therefore, in the current framework, the Regulation treats rating quality as dependent on the compliance with various prescriptive (detailed) and some broader (more principle-based) requirements with regard to conflicts of inter- est, targeting their existence with a 'variably intrusive' regulatory approach. The more detailed rules aim to create a compliance culture with specific requirements that are easy to monitor, and the broader meta-regulatory provi- sions aim to encourage CRAs to aspire optimal operational and organizational standards, the detailed prescription of which would be a rather impossible task for the regulator.[48]

13.3.1.1 Prescriptive Rules
The prescriptive rules apply to a vast series of persons involved in CRA activities, such as shareholders, managers, rating analysts, employees and other persons who may be linked to or offer services related to a CRA.[49] CRAs are required to take all necessary measures to ensure that credit ratings or rating outlooks are not affected by any existing or potential conflict of interest involving them- selves or any other person from the above-mentioned list. A series of further requirements is included in Article 7; these aim to ensure that these persons

---

[47] See for example the recommendations by the European Court of Auditors with regard to the perfectible supervision of certain types of conflict of interest by ESMA: European Court of Auditors, 'EU supervision of credit rating agencies – well established but not yet fully effective' (2015) No 22, 35, at http://www.eca.europa.eu/Lists/ECADocuments/SR15_22/ SR_ESMA_EN.pdf.

[48] CRAs may ask to be exempted from certain requirements when, being able to demonstrate the disproportionate character of these requirements, they have fewer than 50 employees or have implemented their own measures and procedures ensuring compliance with the objectives of the regulatory framework: Article 6(3), ibid.

[49] Article 6(1), Regulation (EC) No 1060/2009.

will be subject to restrictions with regard to their participation in negotiation regarding fees or payments, to an appropriate rotation mechanism (applicable to analysts, lead analysts and approvers of ratings),[50] to the dissociation of their remuneration from the CRA's revenues and to a series of other requirements contained in Annex I, Section C of the Regulation.[51]

CRAs are also expected to introduce and maintain an effective internal control structure with regard to the procedures for the prevention and mitigation of conflicts of interest, along with ensuring the independence of ratings and the persons mentioned above. It is further hoped that the establishment and periodic review of standard operating procedures, related to corporate governance, organizational and management features of conflicts of interest, will strengthen rating accuracy and quality.[52]

For example, with regard to corporate governance requirements, one notable requirement is the presence of an administrative or supervisory board with senior management that is tasked with ensuring the independence of rating activities, the compliance of the agency with all the requirements of the Regulation, and the identification, management and disclosure of conflicts of interest. Furthermore, the Regulation prescribes the presence of independent directors with clear monitoring powers over rating policies, internal quality control systems, conflicts of interest related measures and procedures, as well as compliance of governance processes.[53] Although the goal of ensuring rating quality is laudable, it is highly doubtful whether these corporate governance requirements will provide further assurance of meeting this goal, especially taking into consideration the deficiencies of similar requirements applicable to companies, along with the difficulties that independent directors constantly face in effectively monitoring an entity's activities.[54]

CRAs are expected to establish and maintain an independent compliance function department. This department's role is to monitor and to report on compliance issues of the agency and its employees with regard to the EU Regulation's provisions. Its role has an advisory and assistance component as well towards all persons targeted by the EU provisions to ensure compliance. In order for such a department to function in an optimal way, CRAs need to empower it with the necessary resources, expertise and access as well as to appoint a compliance officer who will be responsible for the compliance function.[55]

---

[50] Rotation of analysts, lead analysts and approvers of ratings every five, four and seven years, respectively, during which they are allowed to be involved in rating activities related to the same rated entity: Annex I, Section C(8), ibid.

[51] Among others, the following requirements are notable: prohibition from having investments that are or may be related to the rated entity, having a previous relationship with the rated entity, and receiving gifts or favours from anyone who is involved with the CRA.

[52] Article 6(4), ibid.

[53] Annex I, Section A(1-2), ibid.

[54] See for example, A. Johnston, 'Corporate Governance is the Problem not the Solution: A Critical Appraisal of the European Regulation on Credit Rating Agencies' (2011) 11 *Journal of Corporate Law Studies* 395.

[55] Annex I, Section A(5-6), Regulation (EC) No 1060/2009.

Shareholders have also been under regulatory scrutiny with CRA Regulation III since, in 2013, the new Article 6(a) dealt with conflicts of interest with regard to investments in CRAs. More specifically, shareholders or members of a CRA, holding at least 5%[56] of the capital or the voting rights in that agency or in a connected company, are prohibited from holding similar capital participation and exercising similar voting rights or control in any other CRA, having the right to decide upon the appointment or removal of members of the administrative or supervisory board of any other CRA, or even being themselves a member of these boards.

13.3.1.2 Broader Rules

The second series of requirements with regard to the avoidance of conflicts of interest focuses on broader organizational and operational issues included in Annex I, Section A and B of the Regulation. The broader organizational and operational requirements are meta-regulatory in essence since they do not prescribe excessively the expected methods that need to be adopted but only provide a general framework with desired outcomes that each CRA is expected to achieve. These measures are considered to be the best way forward in an area where a prescriptive framework would be unfeasible and would result in an attempt to micromanage CRA activities.[57]

With regard to the organizational requirements, the most noteworthy issues are the adoption of adequate policies and procedures for compliance purposes with the Regulation as well as of sound administrative, accounting, internal control and risk assessment procedures. Moreover, CRAs are required to establish appropriate and effective organizational and administrative arrangements for the prevention, identification and elimination, or management and disclosure, of any conflicts of interest. Lastly, they are expected to establish appropriate systems, resources and procedures for the maintenance of continuity and regularity in the performance of their activities, as well as a review function for the periodic review of the appropriateness of their rating methodologies, assumptions and models.[58]

The meta-regulatory operational requirements focus on arrangements for adequate records of rating activities that must include a series of information.[59] The remaining operational requirements are more prescriptive in nature; these refer to various restrictions on actual or potential conflicts of interest and the

---

[56] The 5% threshold is in accordance with other EU texts, for example the Transparency Directive, as explained in Chapter 5, and seen as an important threshold which should trigger further restrictions on shareholders. Therefore, it is hoped that by constraining these actors to obtain an even bigger power, which may allow them to exercise a dominant influence over various CRAs, conflicts of interest and the compromise of the rating quality overall can be minimized.

[57] Andenas and Chiu, above n. 27, 208.

[58] Annex I, Section A, Regulation (EC) No 1060/2009.

[59] Annex I, Section B(7), ibid.

obligation to disclose to the public of the names of revenue sources (if they represent more than 5% of the CRA's annual income).[60]

As a general observation and critical appraisal of meta-regulatory provisions, it remains to be seen whether CRAs will actually engage with these goals to fully implement the spirit of the Regulation or whether the interpretation of broad terms, such as 'sound', 'adequate', 'appropriate', 'effective', will serve as an excuse for the furtherance of strategies that aim to accommodate CRA needs for operational flexibility. Taking into account the coexistence of these broad measures with the previously mentioned prescriptive provisions, which require a rather 'clear-cut' responsiveness to detailed rules, it will be particularly interesting to assess the overall attitude of CRAs with regard to the adoption of a harmonious approach that will be able to satisfy both extremely detailed provisions and more 'principle-based' ones.

Adding to these concerns, it will be challenging for ESMA to effectively supervise the compliance with these meta-regulatory provisions due to the variety of structures and internal systems that CRAs will develop individually for the same compliance purposes. The inherent difficulty in supervising these areas leaves doubts as to whether the entirety of provisions will be able to enhance rating quality and convince CRAs to adopt a truly engaging behaviour with regard to the regulatory framework.[61]

13.3.2 *Reducing the Over-Reliance on Credit Ratings*

CRAs had traditionally acquired a 'quasi-regulatory' status since various financial institutions as well as European authorities, seeking an auxiliary 'safety valve' in their limited evaluation capacity, relied on their ratings to better assess the credit quality of the various entities. This reality also had severe ramifications for the shaping of issuer behaviour since it is well known that rated entities started being more focused on creating securities in a way that would

---

[60] Annex I, Section B(1–6), ibid. Special mention needs to be made with regard to the prohibition of the concomitant provision of consultancy or advisory services to a rated entity, depicting the well-known concerns arising from such phenomena during the financial crisis: Annex I, Section B(4), *ibid*. See also Iain MacNeil, who argues that the underlying conflict of interest in these cases is of a different nature (compared to the other conflicts mentioned above) and 'not capable of resolution by disclosure, internal management or regulatory rules': MacNeil, above n. 36, 184. According to Annex I, Section B(4), ibid., CRAs may provide services other than issue of credit ratings (ancillary services). Ancillary services include market forecasts, estimates of economic trends, pricing analysis and other general data analysis as well as related distribution services. Cash opines that the above-mentioned prohibition should also cover ancillary services; CRAs should be given the right to choose the provision of credit rating services only or ancillary services only – but not both – and they should have a maximum of two calendar years from the date of enactment of such reform to divest the declined business entirely: Daniel Cash, *Regulation and the Credit Rating Agencies: Restraining Ancillary Services* (Routledge 2018).
[61] Andenas and Chiu, above n. 27, 209.

ensure high ratings, disregarding the quality of their financial products.[62] The creation of distorted incentives for the furtherance of these practices clearly showed its limits since rated entities were planning their activities depending on rating criteria and regulators continued to confer a pivotal role to CRAs by nurturing a pro-cyclical reliance trend among all market actors.

Following the debacle in the use of ratings by various institutions and the facilitation of certain operations based on 'regulatory licences' that were partially to blame for the sub-prime crisis,[63] the EU framework has decided to detoxify institutions that were depending mechanistically or solely on ratings for regulatory purposes by 2020. This task of course will prove to be very difficult since appropriate alternatives to credit risk evaluation need to be identified and implemented at EU level. Indeed, the first step was taken with the commissioning of a study to examine the feasibility of the development of a European creditworthiness assessment for sovereign debt. The report issued by the Commission nevertheless expressed some concerns, shared with the Financial Stability Board,[64] with regard to pro-cyclicality risks in this area.[65] Indeed, replacing private ratings with alternative ones will most probably shift the investors' attention to another informational source without resolving the over-reliance trend.[66]

For the time being, CRA Regulation III has inserted Articles 5(a), 5(b) and 5(c) aiming to provide an initial framework to tackle over-reliance on ratings by financial institutions, European authorities and, generally, in EU law. More specifically, financial institutions are required to make their own credit risk assessment while avoiding relying solely or mechanistically on ratings. Moreover, the sectoral competent authorities that supervise these institutions are expected to assist the latter in this goal by monitoring the adequacy of their credit risk assessment processes and encouraging them to mitigate the impact of such references.[67] EBA, EIOPA, ESRB and ESMA are expected not to refer

---

[62] Darbellay, above n. 40, 57.

[63] Partnoy, above n. 2, 624. See also, more generally, A. Kern, 'The Risk of Ratings in Bank Capital Regulation' (2014) 25(2) *European Business Law Review* 295.

[64] Financial Stability Board, 'Thematic Review on FSB Principles for Reducing Reliance on CRA Ratings', 12 May 2014, 2, at http://www.financialstabilityboard.org/wp-content/uploads/r_140512.pdf.

[65] Commission, 'Report from the Commission to the European Parliament and the Council on the Appropriateness of the Development of a European Creditworthiness Assessment for Sovereign Debt', 23 October 2015, Brussels, COM(2015) 515 final, 18, at https://ec.europa.eu/transparency/regdoc/rep/1/2015/EN/1-2015-515-EN-F1-1.PDF.

[66] The report concludes that, for the time being, such a creditworthiness assessment for sovereign debt does not seem proportionate or appropriate with regard to the aim to eliminate over-reliance on external ratings: 18, ibid. Of course, also bearing in mind the investor community, a further distinction needs to be made with regard to institutional and retail investors. The first category will usually dispose of other informational sources that can be used in comparison with credit ratings and also has a more sophisticated analytical capacity for investment decisions. The second category has far fewer information sources (due to limited resources and expertise) and is much more likely to continue relying on credit ratings in the absence of other alternatives.

[67] Article 5(a), ibid.

to credit ratings in their guidelines, recommendations and technical standards when such references can possibly trigger sole or mechanistic reliance on ratings. The EU Regulation also prescribed the removal, where appropriate, of such references by the end of 2013 in already existing guidelines and recommendations to accelerate the reform wave in this area.[68]

The current trend for reduction of over-reliance on ratings is, undoubtedly, the right regulatory choice that will convey the message for a more autonomous and sophisticated stance from the investor community with regard to the use of credit ratings. The 2013 CRA Directive took a first step in that direction by amending a series of directives dealing with IORPs, UCITS and AIFs.[69] Nevertheless, as mentioned above, the path towards more education and sophistication will inevitably prove to be rather long and difficult. Alternative and trustworthy evaluation methods, which will not trigger similar over-reliance trends, need to be put in place in order for market actors to debunk the idea that credit ratings are absolutely irreplaceable and to start using them as one auxiliary opinion regarding an entity's creditworthiness.[70]

13.3.3 CRA Rotation

CRA Regulation III was also notable for the rotation mechanism introduced for the specific category of re-securitizations. Under Article 6(b), CRAs are prohibited from issuing ratings on new re-securitizations, which have underlying assets from the same originator, for a period exceeding four years. CRAs are also expected to request issuers to provide information with regard to other rating agencies that have a contractual relationship for the same matter and the percentage of outstanding rated re-securitizations that these contracts cover.[71] This disclosure framework increases the transparency in this field and prevents both issuers and rating agencies from developing overfamiliar contractual relationships. The Regulation also provides for a cooling off period, equal to the duration of the expired contract and without exceeding four years, during which a CRA is prohibited from entering into a new contract for rating re-securitizations with assets from the same originator.[72]

Conscious of the need to preserve competition among CRAs of different sizes at the EU level, the CRA Regulation provides for a series of exemptions

---

[68] Article 5(b), ibid.

[69] Directive 2013/14/EU, above n. 8.

[70] For example, it has been suggested that market prices and measures (despite their imperfections during volatility periods) could constitute a viable alternative to the use of investors and regulators: F. Partnoy, 'Overdependence on Credit Ratings was a Primary Cause of the Crisis', San Diego Legal Studies Paper No 09-015, 15, at http://ssrn.com/abstract=1430653. For other alternatives, such as multi-factor models, and their critical assessment, see A. Horsch and J. Kleinow, 'Regulation by Ratings: An Economic Point of View' (2014) 25(2) European Business Law Review 249, 264–266.

[71] Article 6(b)(2), Regulation (EC) No 1060/2009.

[72] Article 6(b)(3), ibid.

from the above-mentioned limitations. An exception from the four-year rotation mechanism is provided when at least four CRAs each rate more than 10% of the outstanding re-securitizations,[73] and a wide exception from the entire Article 6(b) is provided when a CRA has fewer than 50 employees, or annual turnover less than €10 million, at group level.[74]

The debate on the usefulness of rotation mechanisms is ongoing as the European Commission presented in 2016 a report, *inter alia*, on periods for rotation with regard to the rating of different instruments. In this report it announced that a potential extension of the mandatory rotation mechanism to other financial products would be premature given the lack of sufficient data available that would allow the analysis of the impact of such reforms on rating practices.[75] It has also ensured that it will keep on monitoring market developments in the future. The definite advantage of rotation mechanisms is the opportunity given to smaller-sized CRAs to participate more actively in the rating market and to start building a larger clientele as well as their own expertise with regard to rating activities. Nevertheless, concerns have been raised with regard to the fact that forcing smaller-sized CRAs to actively participate at this level while undertaking higher profile clients may not necessarily result in the provision of ratings of the highest quality, especially in the beginning, due to their inexperience.[76] Bearing these potential limitations in mind, which should not – in our opinion – become an obstacle for more competition, it is undoubtedly positive that there is a clear willingness to proceed with rotation mechanisms at the EU level in order to increase competition among CRAs.

Under a broader perspective, CRA Regulation III also invites issuers who intend to appoint at least two CRAs for the rating of the same issuance or entity to consider appointing at least one CRA that does not have more than 10% of the total market share (subject to availability).[77] The appointment of the second CRA that does not satisfy this criterion shall be documented. Therefore, this provision aims to foster competition by including smaller-sized CRAs in rating activities but it ultimately depends on the issuer to involve them in such cases. The flexibility offered to issuers may well just serve as an excuse not to respond to this regulatory incentive. This is why the future regulatory

---

[73] Article 6(b)(2), ibid.

[74] Article 6(b)(5), ibid.

[75] Commission, 'Report from the Commission to the European Parliament and the Council on Alternative Tools to External Credit Ratings, the State of the Credit Rating Market, Competition and Governance in the Credit Rating Industry, the State of the Structured Finance Instruments Rating Market and on the Feasibility of a European Credit Rating Agency' (2016) Brussels, COM(2016) 664 final, 19, at https://ec.europa.eu/transparency/regdoc/rep/1/2016/EN/1-2016-664-EN-F1-1.PDF.

[76] B. Masters and A. Barkers, 'Regulators Warn Against Ratings Plan' *Financial Times* (London, 29 February 2012).

[77] Article 8(d)(1), Regulation (EC) No 1060/2009. ESMA is also expected to publish on its website a list on an annual basis including all CRAs with their total market share and the types of ratings that they issue, which may serve as an initial point for such a choice by issuers: Article 8(d)(2), ibid.

framework could re-examine this flexibility, subject to the absence of evidence of the practical impact or benefits of the current provision, and proceed with a mandatory provision for the second appointment of smaller-sized CRAs.[78]

These initiatives will be able to bring tangible benefits to market actors who use ratings in their activities[79] on the condition that CRAs are given the chance, and the time, to develop equally sophisticated methodologies in order to offer services of equal quality to their clients and to the public at large. The above-mentioned measures thus serve this goal, and it ultimately depends on issuers to start using other CRAs with a different mindset, escaping from a traditional perception of the usefulness of the well-known Big Three which, benefiting from the oligopoly in this area,[80] may severely compromise rating quality due to the lack of competition and the absence of a serious threat to their predominance in the CRA industry.[81]

13.3.4 Sovereign Ratings

Sovereign ratings have become extremely important especially after highly publicized cases involving downgrades of sovereign debt from CRAs (France, Greece, etc.) which sparked political outrage and an urgent desire to accelerate reforms at the EU level. These can be defined as ratings of States or of regional or local authorities of a State, of a debt or financial obligation or other financial instrument whose issuer may be one of the above-mentioned entities or even an international financial institution, composed by two or more States, which is involved in the mobilization of funding and provision of financial assistance for one of the members of that institution.[82] ESMA has decisively conveyed the message of increased public scrutiny over sovereign ratings, especially after the investigation conducted in 2013 that formulated severe criticism of some methods used by CRAs in this area.[83]

CRA Regulation III moved towards a very detailed framework for sovereign ratings addressing these political concerns as well as criticism of rating methods by inserting Article 8(a). CRAs are expected to issue sovereign ratings while

---

[78] See, also in this sense, T. M.J. Möllers and C. Nierdorf, 'Regulation and Liability of Credit Rating Agencies – a More Efficient European Law?' (2014) 3 *European Company and Financial Law Review* 333, 362.

[79] S. Rousseau, 'A Question of Credibility: Enhancing the Accountability and Effectiveness of Credit Rating Agencies' (2012) Institut C.D. Howe, Commentary No 356, 15, at http://ssrn.com/abstract=2130806.

[80] Moody's, Standard & Poor's and Fitch share 95 percent of the global rating market.

[81] J. Mathis, J.J. Mcandrews and J-C. Rochet, 'Rating the Raters: Are Reputation Concerns Powerful enough to Discipline Rating Agencies?' (2009) 56(5) *Journal of Monetary Economics* 657.

[82] Article 3(1)(iv), Regulation (EC) No 1060/2009.

[83] ESMA, 'Credit Rating Agencies: Sovereign Ratings Investigation' (2 December 2013) ESMA/2013/1775, at http://www.esma.europa.eu/system/files/20131780_esma_identifies_deficiencies_in_cras_sovereign_ratings_processes.pdf. See also N. Gaillard, 'How and Why Credit Rating Agencies Missed the Eurozone Debt Crisis' (2014) 9(2) *Capital Markets Law Journal* 121, 132.

taking into consideration the individual characteristics of a State. This is a very welcome reform, as CRAs have traditionally been criticized for not taking into consideration individual characteristics of States, not just in the EU but also at the global level, as was shown in the case of the 1990s Asian financial crisis.[84] Generic statements containing revisions of groups of countries are also prohibited if not supplemented by individual country reports that must be made publicly available.[85]

The Regulation seeks to prevent unpredictable public communications, which are based upon information not disclosed with the consent of the rated entity and that may have a rapid effect on sovereign ratings, by requiring CRAs to proceed to such communications only when they hold information generally available or when there are no reasons for which the rated entity would not give its consent to such disclosure.[86]

Another important reform concerns the calendar by which sovereign ratings can be published. CRAs are expected to publish on their website and to submit annually to ESMA a calendar at the end of December which will predetermine the dates for the publication of both unsolicited (maximum three dates for the following 12 months) and solicited sovereign ratings and related rating outlooks. Any deviation from the calendar should be accompanied with a detailed explanation and does not exempt CRAs from their obligations under Article 8(2), Article 10(1) and Article 11(1).[87] It does not come as a surprise that this provision was inserted in the EU regulatory framework in 2013, following a series of incidents where CRAs were disclosing solicited and unsolicited ratings on an ad hoc basis, triggering market reactions and increasing the volatility of markets at large. The calendar should thus be welcomed as a measure that seeks to stabilize the adverse effects of unpredictable disclosure events on sovereign ratings and to measure the expectations of the users of such ratings.

Lastly, the Regulation provides for a periodic review of sovereign ratings at least every six months.[88] This provision aims to enhance the reliability of sovereign ratings and to ensure their regular updating.

13.3.5 Structured Finance Instruments

Following the debacle of CRAs in their dubious involvement in ratings of structured finance instruments, CRA Regulation III aims to increase transparency by requiring from the issuer, the originator and the sponsor of a structured finance instrument to publish jointly on a website, created by ESMA specifically for this purpose, a series of information.[89] The information shall

---

[84] See for example, H. Reisen, 'Ratings since the Asian Crisis' (2003) OECD Development Centre, Working Paper No 214, at http://www.oecd.org/dev/pgd/1934625.pdf.

[85] Article 8(a)(1), Regulation (EC) No 1060/2009.

[86] Article 8(a)(2), ibid.

[87] Article 8(a)(3) (4), ibid.

[88] Article 8(5), ibid.

[89] Article 8(b)(1), ibid.

pertain to the credit quality and performance of the underlying assets of the instrument, the structure of the securitization transaction, the cash flows and any other collateral that supports a securitization exposure. The information must also include any relevant matter for conducting stress tests on the cash flows and collateral values related to the underlying exposures.

Aiming to decrease overfamiliarity and the undesirable effects of conflicts of interest that became evident in the area of structured finance instruments, the Regulation requires the appointment of at least two CRAs for the provision of independent ratings on this kind of instrument.[90] The two CRAs must not belong to the same group, must not be related to the other CRA under various scenarios (as shareholders or members, via voting rights, a right to appoint or remove members of the board, members sitting on both boards of the two CRAs, control or dominant influence). This measure will undoubtedly prove useful and will decrease the potential risks of overfamiliarity, although the well-known 'group thinking' problem among the most high-profile CRAs could also become a problem when there is a common perception as to the methods that should be followed to rate structured finance instruments and, hence, the overall result might be very similar despite the formal independence criteria being respected. The provision is therefore a first step towards the diversification of evaluations received, but much more needs to be done to ensure true independence of CRAs.

13.4 THE CRA SUPERVISORY FRAMEWORK

13.4.1 ESMA's Supervisory Competence

The shaping of the supervisory framework at the EU level was undoubtedly a crucial step towards the creation of an efficient monitoring scheme for CRAs. ESMA needed a vast array of powers and operational means to be able to perform its very ambitious role with regard to the CRA industry. As an overall assessment, it can certainly be argued that the supervisory framework is designed in a refined way, balancing ESMA's operational impetus with the well-known concerns of the *Meroni* doctrine,[91] following a rather delicate debate around this issue.[92] ESMA is in charge not only of the CRA supervision per se, but also of the issuance of guidelines and, most importantly, of the coordination of its cooperation with NCAs. This supervisory structure is justified due to the relatively small section that CRAs occupy in the market (compared to other industries), the considerable cross-border activities that they have traditionally developed, as well as the transnational character of their impact that may affect investment decisions.

---

[90] Article 8(c)(1), ibid.

[91] Case 9/56 *Meroni* v. *High Authority* [1957 and 1958] ECR 133.

[92] See for example Commission, 'Impact Assessment Board: Proposal for Amending Regulation 1060/2009 on Credit Rating Agencies', 20 April 2010, D(2010), Brussels, Ref. Ares (2010)205437, 2, at http://ec.europa.eu/smart-regulation/impact/ia_carried_out/docs/ia_2010/sec_2010_0680_en_resub.pdf.

The ongoing supervision of CRAs has been made much easier thanks to the implementation of periodic disclosure obligations and the creation of a public website called the European rating platform (hereinafter ERP). CRAs are expected to notify ESMA periodically on a series of issues, as indicated in Article 9 of Delegated Regulation (EU) No 2/2015;[93] the information provided should then be made available, among other types of information, via the ERP.

13.4.2 Supervisory Powers

ESMA may require all the information needed to perform its duties in this framework from a vast range of actors (persons involved in rating activities, third parties and rated entities and other persons who are otherwise closely and substantially related or connected to CRAs). This may be done either by simple request (non-binding) or by decision (binding). Article 23(b) enumerates the procedural aspect of both simple requests and decisions that need to be followed by ESMA when it decides to communicate them to the persons concerned.

Moreover, Article 23(c) provides for general investigative powers of the same series of actors. Such investigations may be conducted by officials or other persons authorized by ESMA (examination of various materials, obtaining certified copies of such materials, summons of concerned persons, interviews of other natural or legal persons for the collection of information, and request of telephone and data traffic records). To further enrich its investigative powers, Article 23(d) specifies the procedure for on-site inspections that may be carried out on business premises, with or without prior announcement.

The legitimacy of relevant procedures with regard to supervisory measures (and the ensuing levying of fines) is strengthened with the appointment of an independent investigating officer in cases where ESMA believes that there are serious indications of the potential existence of facts constituting various infringements (listed in Annex III of the Regulation). The investigating officer has to meet independence criteria and follow a procedure for the accomplishment of her tasks, as defined in Article 23(e), and then must submit the file with her findings to ESMA's Board of Supervisors. In turn, the Board will decide whether an infringement has been committed and proceed with the adoption of supervisory measures and the levying of fines.

13.4.3 ESMA and NCAs

Another important issue that can guarantee the optimal use of supervisory measures as well as the implementation of an efficient supervisory framework at the EU level is the fruitful cooperation between ESMA and the NCAs. With

---

[93] Delegated Regulation (EU) No 2/2015 of 30 September 2014 supplementing Regulation (EC) No 1060/2009 of the European Parliament and of the Council with regard to regulatory technical standards for the presentation of the information that credit rating agencies make available to the European Securities and Markets Authority [2014] OJ L 2/24.

the transfer of a considerable amount of powers to the European authority, EU law needed to ensure the maintenance of important links with the national authorities which will seek to facilitate ESMA's operations. The CRA Regulation has a series of provisions ensuring a considerable level of cooperation although it remains to be seen whether NCAs will be able to keep pace with ESMA's growing regulatory maturity with regard to that CRA sector and, therefore, accomplish their role as ancillary monitoring points of reference.

Without analysing all the provisions of the CRA Regulation in detail, it would be useful, for the purposes of this chapter, to mention that the overall framework provides for exchange of information between ESMA, NCAs and the sectoral competent authorities, transmission of information from ESMA to various monetary and other public authorities responsible for payment and settlement systems and vice versa.[94] ESMA can also cooperate with supervisory authorities of third countries with regard to the exchange of information[95] and may also disclose information received from these authorities with their consent.[96]

The other component of an efficient cooperation framework relies on ESMA delegating a series of tasks to NCAs. These tasks may involve the power to request information and to conduct investigations and on-site inspections, as explained above and in accordance with Articles 23(b) and 23(d)(6). Any delegation of tasks does not limit ESMA's capacity to conduct and monitor these tasks on its own account.[97] Most importantly, the CRA Regulation expects NCAs to notify ESMA of any acts contrary to the Regulation taking, or having taken, place in their territory or in a territory of another Member State, to suggest to ESMA that it should use the powers to request information and to conduct investigations and, lastly, to suggest to ESMA that it uses its powers with regard to the suspension of use of ratings for regulatory purposes.[98]

As an overall impression with regard to this cooperation framework, the CRA Regulation undoubtedly provides a sufficient framework for national authorities to assist ESMA, in various ways, in its role. Nevertheless, the efficiency of any future cooperation will ultimately depend on the level of sophistication of national authorities which will determine their prompt reactiveness to any acts contrary to the Regulation as well as the full exercise of their 'regulatory know-how' with regard to CRAs. It is therefore essential to ensure further convergence among national authorities in terms of expertise, supervisory skills as well as the availability of sufficient resources in order to empower them to exercise their role in a way that truly serves the Regulation's purposes. This task will be particularly difficult to achieve, especially considering that ESMA faces the same challenges in terms of expertise and resources, as we have already seen.

---

[94] Article 27, ibid.
[95] Article 34, ibid.
[96] Article 35, ibid.
[97] Article 30, ibid.
[98] Article 31, ibid.

13.5 THE ENFORCEMENT FRAMEWORK

13.5.1 General Observations

Article 36 of the CRA Regulation provides that Member States will establish rules on penalties for infringements of Article 4(1). These penalties must satisfy the criteria of effectiveness, proportionality and dissuasiveness. The sectoral competent authority must also disclose to the public all penalties imposed for the same infringements with the constraint of potentially serious risk for the financial markets or disproportionate damage for the parties involved, as previously mentioned.[99] For all other infringements, ESMA is taking the lead on enforcement with a series of measures and considerable discretion, as we shall see later on, but with a series of procedural guarantees and restrictions that aim to enhance its sanctioning legitimacy.

Contractual issues that may arise in this area are not included in the CRA Regulation, which leaves Member States with the discretion to apply their general principles of contract law. More generally, civil liability has become one of the most hotly debated issues, and an issuer will have to overcome the obstacle of contractual clauses aiming to exclude CRA liability and which are found frequently in this kind of contract.[100] The Regulation only specifies that civil liability can be limited in advance when such limitation is reasonable and proportionate, as well as permissible by the applicable national framework.[101] Therefore, it will be very interesting to see how national legal systems will evolve around the existence of contractual clauses seeking to exclude CRA liability and how they will interpret reasonableness and proportionality in this framework with regard to clauses that seek to limit civil liability.

13.5.2 ESMA Non-pecuniary Sanctions

ESMA's non-pecuniary enforcement measures are vast and they can include the withdrawal of registration, the temporary prohibition of a CRA from issuing ratings, the suspension of the use of ratings for regulatory purposes, the requirement for the CRA to end the infringement, and the issuance of public notices.[102] Although ESMA theoretically has the right to intervene with various

---

[99] The CRA Regulation I had already attempted to coordinate indirectly the rigour of sanctions imposed at the national level, without further harmonizing their framework at the EU level, by asking Member States to notify the European Commission of their national provisions applicable to this area. To date, there has been a significant discrepancy in national provisions with regard to various types of sanctions. The current divergence therefore highlights the necessity to envisage further reforms in order to harmonize sanctions and offer adequate protection to all affected parties from various types of infringements at the EU level.
[100] French law that seeks to protect the weak party in this framework by forbidding and deeming such clauses unwritten provides an interesting example, as it has opted for a clear prohibition which does not leave room for manoeuvre: Article 544-6, *Code monétaire et financier*.
[101] Article 35(a)(3), Regulation (EC) No 1060/2009.
[102] Article 24(1), Regulation (EC) No 1060/2009.

measures, up to now, it has only issued public notices and this paucity of other measures raises questions about both the delicacy of the cases arising from CRA practices and the reluctance of ESMA to take on the risks, in the early stages of its existence, for its decisions to be frequently reviewed by the CJEU which would inevitably create further legitimacy concerns over its decision-making processes.

In an attempt to increase the sophistication of ESMA's operational methods with regard to the adoption of supervisory measures, Article 24(2) lists a series of factors that should be taken into account by the Board of Supervisors with regard to the nature and seriousness of an infringement: its duration and frequency, any potential series or systemic procedural weaknesses, any connection of the infringement with financial crimes, and lastly, the intentional or negligent character of the infringement.

The Regulation also ensures a transparent procedure for the notification of CRAs and their right to appeal the decision, as well as their right of defence.[103] These procedural safeguards aim, once again, to strengthen ESMA's legitimacy in adopting various measures in this field.

13.5.3 ESMA Pecuniary Sanctions

CRA Regulation II triggered a substantial reform in the area of fines that can be imposed by ESMA's Board of Supervisors in the presence of an intentional or negligent infringement. The Regulation provides a series of amounts applicable to different types of infringements with minimum and maximum levels.[104] ESMA is also given further guidance with regard to the calculation of the fines and, more specifically, is expected to take into consideration the CRA's annual turnover in the preceding business year. Moreover, in order for the fines to target the infringement in an optimal way, ESMA is expected to calculate the final amount based on aggravating factors (for example, repeated commission of the infringement, duration of infringement for more than six months, revelation of systemic weaknesses of the CRA, etc.) or mitigating ones (for example, commission of infringement for less than ten working days, adoption of measures to avoid similar infringements in the future, coefficients, etc.).[105] ESMA's Board of Supervisors may also impose periodic penalty payments in order to constrain a CRA to put an end to an infringement, to force a person to supply complete information in the ambit of a similar request, or to compel a person to cooperate in an investigation or an on-site inspection.[106]

All fines and periodic penalty payments must be disclosed to the public unless such disclosure would create a disproportionate damage the parties

---

[103] Article 24(5), Article 25, Regulation (EC) No 1060/2009.
[104] See Article 36(a)(2) for a full list, ibid.
[105] See Annex IV for a full list, ibid.
[106] Article 36(b), ibid.

involved or would significantly expose at risk the financial markets.[107] The willingness of the Regulation to insist on 'name and shame' practices is welcomed since it will strengthen ESMA's profile in the future, conveying to the market that ESMA is effectively protecting investors and other parties potentially affected by ratings. It thus remains to be seen to what extent ESMA will make use of the alternative option of non-disclosure for the reasons mentioned above. All decisions on the levying of a fine or a periodic penalty payment are subject to review by the CJEU, which can annul, reduce or increase these fines and penalties.[108]

In a critical appraisal of the current regime, ESMA has unsurprisingly developed a much more cooperative rather than sanctioning approach related to questionable practices by CRAs, as the immediate levying of high fines would risk chilling the industry.[109] Indeed, in various reports, it can be seen that ESMA is trying to develop a rather discursive rhetoric on the current deficiencies of some methodologies and on the benefits of adhering to the spirit of the EU Regulation. This choice is wise, from a regulatory point of view, since it can help the CRA industry gradually enhance its practices and be encouraged to join a 'race to the top' compliance trend. Nevertheless, the available sanctions also need to be used often to convey a stronger message with regard to ESMA's power and capacity to detect and sanction inappropriate practices.[110]

There is no doubt that the emerging civil liability, to which our chapter will turn below, may create a sense of outsourcing the 'redressing function' to the private sector, after the occurrence of losses, and hence may weaken ESMA's sanctioning power in the eyes of the public. Be that as it may, the coexistence of regulatory intervention with private enforcement is well-known in other areas of capital markets law, as shown in previous chapters, and it will be challenging to see the evolution of both frameworks striving to achieve adequate dissuasive and redressing powers on the CRA industry.

---

[107] Article 36(d), ibid.
[108] Article 36(e), ibid.
[109] See for example the public notice issued in the case of an erroneous release of an email alert to the subscribers of Standard and Poor's which denoted failure to meet a series of organizational requirements: ESMA, 'Decision to Adopt a Supervisory Measure Taking the Form of a Public Notice in Accordance with Articles 23(e)(5) and 24 of Regulation (EC) No 1060/2009 of the European Parliament and of the Council of 16 September 2009 on Credit Rating Agencies', 20 May 2014, ESMA/2014/544, at https://www.esma.europa.eu/sites/default/files/library/2015/11/2014-544_-_decision_supervisory_measure_articles_23e_and_24_of_regulation_1060-2009.pdf.
[110] ESMA has so far imposed a €30,000 fine on DBRS Ratings Limited for the negligent commission of infringement related to the arrangements for keeping adequate records: ESMA, 'Decision to Adopt a Supervisory Measure Taking the Form of a Public Notice and to Impose a Fine in Accordance with Article 23e(5), 24, 36a and 36c of Regulation (EC) No 1060/2009 of the European Parliament and of the Council of 16 September 2009 on credit rating agencies' (2015), ESMA/2015/1048, at https://www.esma.europa.eu/sites/default/files/library/2015/11/2015-1048.pdf.

13.5.4 Civil Liability

More recently, one of the most-debated topics involving the EU framework applicable to CRAs has been the civil liability regime that was introduced by CRA Regulation III. Civil liability did not come as a surprise in 2013 to all Member States since some of them had already introduced a comparable regime for CRAs and even established much stricter rules (this was notably the case in France).[111] This new regime seeks to complement the sanctions framework at the EU level and to subject CRAs to a wider spectrum of enforcement methods. Inevitably, academic opinions vary considerably as to the appropriateness of such a regime, which may discourage new CRAs from entering the EU market.[112] We believe that these concerns should not be overstated due to the fact that the regime, as it currently stands, does not present any significant exposure danger for CRAs given the considerable amount of obstacles that claimants will have to overcome, as we shall see later on in this chapter. On the contrary, it is the author's opinion that the current regime should be further facilitated and reformed so that CRA civil liability serves as a true deterrent against inappropriate practices, while offering compensation to claimants and safeguarding the markets from harmful practices by exercising its dissuasive force.

Article 35(a) of the CRA Regulation provides that an investor or issuer may claim damages from a CRA that has committed, intentionally or through gross negligence, an infringement that has an impact on a credit rating and has caused damage to the claimant. The same Article further analyses the conditions upon which investors and issuers may claim damages. An investor must establish a reasonable reliance on a credit rating in order to decide to invest, hold or divest from a financial instrument covered by the rating, a potentially insurmountable obstacle, especially for institutional investors.[113] The Commission unfortunately backtracked on this issue, as the reliance element was

---

[111] Article L. 544-5 *Code monétaire et financier.* French law only required (apart from damage and causal link) showing an infringement of the EU framework, putting aside further distinctions between gross or simple negligence and so on.

[112] B. Haar, 'Civil Liability of Credit Rating Agencies – Regulatory All-or-Nothing Approaches between Immunity and Over-Deterrence', (2013) University of Oslo Faculty of Law Legal Studies Research Paper Series No 2013-02, 11, at http://ssrn.com/abstract=2198293; N.S. Ellis, L.M. Fairchild and F. D'Souza, 'Is Imposing Liability on Credit Rating Agencies a Good Idea: Credit Rating Agency Reform in the Aftermath of the Global Financial Crisis' (2011–2012) 17 *Stanford Journal of Law Business & Finance* 175, 211–217.

[113] Institutional investors – mentioned in Article 4(1) – are expected, according to Article 5a, to make their own credit risk assessment and cannot rely exclusively or mechanistically on credit ratings. It will therefore prove to be extremely difficult to show that they complied with this duty while ultimately choosing to rely on a credit rating. This is because if both assessments (their own and the CRA's one) are similar, they won't be able to show the required reliance. If the assessments are different and they still choose to rely upon the credit rating, they will probably not have complied with their own duty provided in Article 4(1): Möllers and Nierdorf, above n. 78, 347.

introduced only after its initial proposal.[114] An issuer must show that the rating covers its financial instrument(s), as well as the fact that the infringement was not due to misleading or inaccurate information provided by the issuer to the CRA, either directly or indirectly from publicly disclosed information.

Moreover, according to paragraph 2 of the same Article, the claimant bears the burden of proof to show, with accurate and detailed information, that the CRA has committed an infringement[115] as well as the latter's impact on the rating issued. It is important to note that the Regulation does not provide a definition of 'accurate and detailed information' as it leaves the assessment of these terms to national courts that will also have to take into account that claimants may not be in a position to access information available only to the CRA.

Moreover, the Regulation does not provide definitions for terms such as 'damage', 'intention', 'gross negligence', 'reasonably relied', 'due care', 'impact', 'reasonable' and 'proportionate' as they should be the object of interpretation and application depending on the respective national legal framework. Lastly, remaining issues in the civil liability framework but which are not covered by the Regulation as well as further civil liability claims, which may be available in some national laws, will keep on being determined and applied in accordance with national provisions.[116]

The civil liability regime, especially compared to other legal frameworks,[117] undoubtedly constitutes a first experimental step towards broadening the variety of legal claims potentially brought against CRAs that have been involved in infringements in order – apart from compensating harmed parties – to exert further dissuasive pressure against the committing of infringements.[118] Nevertheless, the current framework needs to be seen under a more critical perspective due to the various obstacles that it puts for a successful claim to take place. As it has been shown, claimants will have to go through various interpretation conundrums to succeed in their claim. These difficulties make the current framework deficient because it does not ensure the presence of a dissuasive mechanism against CRA infringements, nor does it provide an accessible away for claimants to obtain compensation for damages they have suffered.

---

[114] Commission, Proposal for a Regulation of the European Parliament and of the Council Amending Regulation (EC) No 1060/2009 on Credit Rating Agencies, 15 November 2011, Brussels, COM(2011) 747 final, 33, at http://ec.europa.eu/internal_market/securities/docs/agencies/COM_2011_747_en.pdf.

[115] Another point on which the Commission backtracked from its initial position which was much more considerate of claimants' inherent difficulty in deciphering rating procedures – due to lack of expertise and necessary information – since it was reversing the burden of proof: Commission, ibid., 21.

[116] Article 35(a)(4) and (5) Regulation (EC) No 1060/2009.

[117] For an interesting comparative analysis, see Möllers and Nierdorf, above n. 78, 354–361; M. Lehmann, 'Civil Liability of Rating Agencies– An Insipid Sprout from Brussels' (2016) 11(1) *Capital Markets Law Journal* 60, 68–72.

[118] Lehmann (2016) 62, ibid.

13.6 Towards A Refinement of the Current EU Framework

13.6.1 'Systemic-Risk' Sensitive Regulatory Approaches and Investors' Role

One matter of pivotal importance is the refinement of the current EU regulatory framework to obtain a more sophisticated approach in the area of systemic dimensions that credit ratings may present.[119] As previously discussed, both regulators and investors have traditionally been over-dependent on credit ratings by reinforcing their systemic risk importance. Information originating with CRAs has obtained its own symbolic connotation in the eyes of the regulatory and investor community up to an extent that it has distinguished itself entirely from the information related to the rated entity. Indeed, market actors will react instantly to ratings not only because the latter reflect a positive or negative shift in the rated entity's creditworthiness, but also because they are aware of their systemic importance to other actors and financial markets at large.[120]

What is even more preoccupying, the CRA oligopolistic market has made disclosed information homogeneous in the sense that divergence in ratings has become less and less frequent due to the predominance of the Big Three, the ensuing reduced competition for smaller CRAs, and the regulatory over-dependence on ratings. The efforts to reduce regulatory over-reliance and to increase competition among CRAs, as explained above, are therefore very positive signs for the creation of a variable informational framework which that would allow the recipients of information to become more critical when they evaluate it, having at their disposal different opinions about the same entities.[121]

The homogenization of information, also due to the public availability of ratings in conjunction with the 'issuer pays' model and regulatory rules dependent on ratings, has therefore made ratings systemically important. This in turn raises concerns about their predominance at the global level. Even though it would be premature to predict a gradual abandonment of the 'issuer pays' model and a return to the 'investor pays' one, the author opines that the reduction of oligopoly in the CRA industry, in association with a cautious approach to the standardization of rating information, is what will most probably become the decisive factor for fostering investors' governance role in this area.[122] The above-mentioned EU convergence efforts towards greater

---

[119] For a detailed discussion of these risks, see MacNeil, above n. 36, 192–193.

[120] C.A. Hill, 'Regulating the Rating Agencies' (2004) 82 *Washington University Law Quarterly* 4, 68.

[121] Darbellay, above n. 40, 181–183.

[122] Bearing of course in mind that increasing competition alone may not be able to achieve the same result since the maintenance of the 'issuer pays' model will continue to exert pressure for high ratings without focusing on rating quality. It has been even argued that increased competition in this framework may also lead to detrimental effects: H. Gilderhaus, 'The Rating Agency Oligopoly and its Consequences for European Competition Law' (2012) 3 *European Law Review* 269, 292. See also MacNeil, above n. 36, 195 citing an empirical study which showed that the quality of ratings issued by Moody's and Standard and Poor's deteriorated following increased competition from Fitch: Bo Becker and Todd Milbourn, 'How Did Increased Competition Affect Credit Ratings?' (2010) NBER Working Paper 16404, September 2010, at http://www.nber.org/papers/w16404.pdf.

standardization of disclosed information therefore need to take into account the necessity of preserving divergence in opinions, as well as avoiding transforming a future harmonized framework into a 'key reference' for market actors. This development would only maintain investor dependence on ratings and would not allow market actors to move towards adopting a more active behavioural stance.

Although the ongoing intrusive EU approach can be explained in the light of the willingness to increase the control of CRA activities and ensure their reliability, it would be more preferable to adjust the level of intervention slightly and to focus on a series of issues, such as systemic risk monitoring, which are much more critical to the credit trading quality but not currently under increased regulatory scrutiny.[123] This would also complement ESMA's macro-prudential supervisory role and would enhance its assistance role in the European Systemic Risk Board regarding the exchange of information on systemic financial stability risks.

All the above-mentioned proposals therefore aim to gradually create a more 'systemic-risk' sensitive EU regulatory approach by reducing some of the systemic elements of ratings, enhancing the monitoring focus on the pertinent system issues and, lastly, providing an informational framework to market actors that enables them to become more critically challenging and active when evaluating the quality and the reliability of ratings.[124] It is under this last objective that regulators can realistically expect both issuers and investors to exert a governance function not only *ex ante* when they use ratings in their strategies, but also *ex post* when they seek to initiate civil proceedings against CRAs. It is towards the latter aspect that our analysis will now turn.

13.6.2 The Feasibility of a More Meaningful Enforcement Framework

Although the coexistence of ESMA's sanctioning powers with the civil liability regime initiated by issuers or investors may give the impression of a contradictory framework, divided between the expectation for the regulator's supervisory efficiency and the market actors' activism, it is our opinion that the overall pressure on CRAs, stemming from these two areas, will ultimately depend on the facilitation of the sanctioning tools.

With regard to ESMA's sanctioning powers, as mentioned above, it is crucial that ESMA should adopt a cautious approach, as has been the case so far, to avoid seeing its wide authority being challenged by the CRA industry.

---

[123] Andenas and Chiu, above n. 27, 235.

[124] Bearing of course in mind that efforts to convince investors to conduct more due diligence will inevitably incur costs and may also testify to a certain 'irony in resolving the problem of over-reliance by requiring market participants to rely less on a better informed agent, which has specialized expertise, and more on their own judgement': MacNeil, above n. 36, 202.
Be that as it may, encouraging more due diligence can certainly lay the foundations for the shaping of a more active community in the future.

The discursive and pedagogic approach that has been observed in its public notices has the potential to function as a first experimental approach to further enhance dialogue with CRAs regarding regulatory expectations. Nevertheless, ESMA's sanctioning role can be developed further by enriching its structure with more staff, offering more 'CRA industry-specific' expertise. While it is plausible to argue that supervisory costs would be increased in this case, it would be reasonable to suggest that unless it enhances its expertise in dealing with complex CRA strategies, ESMA will not be in a position to fully detect all infringements of EU rules. In this perspective, pecuniary sanctions should then follow to convey the appropriate dissuasive message to CRAs.

Facing the above-mentioned obstacles, EU law should give space to market actors' activism and allow them to exert pressure on CRAs in the presence of alleged losses suffered due to infringements. It is therefore essential to secure a full range of dissuasive tools for potential claimants in the ambit of the civil liability regime. It is only under this perspective that market actors will be able to fully exercise their engagement strategies. While reiterating our belief that facilitation of the element of reliance on credit ratings and the burden of proof of an infringement should become part of a future reform agenda of the civil liability regime,[125] it is crucial for the time being to ensure an efficient implementation of the very broadly formulated EU rules into national laws. Indeed, the first impression is rather disappointing since Member States will continue to follow their own legal traditions with regard to civil liability, offering once again forum shopping opportunities for claimants and legal uncertainty for CRAs.[126]

13.7 CONCLUSION

The *prima facie* signs arising from the frequency and intensity of EU reforms in the area of CRAs are undoubtedly promising, since they testify to a much more robust regulatory stance, especially compared to the former self-regulatory framework that failed to convince CRAs to adhere to a rigorous operational framework. Nevertheless, the way in which EU law has attempted to address and control the activities of CRAs may not be the most efficient. This is particularly true for the accentuation of operational standards that dictate, in theory, a sounder procedural framework for the issuance of ratings but are not, by any means, adapted to ensuring the reliability and quality of ratings.

Moreover, although EU law is beginning to show signs of regulatory maturity, especially with regard to the reduction of dependence on ratings, it has so far failed to provide a framework that would allow market participants to develop a much more active role in order to base their decisions on alternative methods as well as to evaluate credit ratings in a better way. The 'systemic-risk'

---

[125] Reviving the Commission's initial proposal in 2011: Commission, above n. 114.

[126] As has wisely been mentioned, '[l]ike a Trojan horse, the introduction of the reference to national law has eroded the proposal from the inside': Lehmann, above n. 117, 78.

elements of ratings therefore need to be taken into consideration very carefully when reforming the regulatory framework, in terms of both monitoring and reducing oligopolistic CRA trends and market over-reliance on homogenized information. Last but not least, the civil liability regime, despite its ambition to strengthen the accountability of CRAs, might create a series of obstacles to potential claimants and lead to a rather unsatisfactory accountability frame-work. In the author's opinion, further flexibility in tackling these obstacles will be key to the enhancement of the *ex post* governance role that market actors should play in the future.

CHAPTER 14

Proxy Advisors

14.1 INTRODUCTION

The important role that proxy advisors have already developed in the USA (Institutional Shareholder Services, Glass Lewis, etc.) and even more recently in Europe (Ethos, Proxinvest, European Corporate Governance Service, etc.) seems to be an inevitable effect of the extreme difficulty that institutional investors face when seeking to ascertain and decipher complex corporate governance strategies.[1] Several resolutions submitted for a shareholders' vote attest to the need for shareholders to fully understand business opportunities, sophisticated management decisions, and the overall impact of their vote on both a company's financial position and the performance of their portfolio investment. Given the current investment framework, marked by the ever-increasing emergence of institutional shareholders and transnational investment strategies, it has become essential to rely on proxy advisors in order to evaluate resolutions and vote accordingly in an accelerated and cost-saving framework.[2]

Proxy advisory firms are in charge of advising institutional investors and exercising the voting rights of the latter, who most often delegate these powers to such firms in an accelerating cost-saving framework.[3] The ever-growing influence of proxy advisors on institutional investors has triggered the need for the introduction of disclosure obligations in order to provide the necessary information to existing and potential clients on how they intend to exercise their activities and therefore allow these clients, as well as other market participants and regulators, to better understand proxy advisors' role and evaluate them in an adequate way.

Proxy advisory firms have thus emerged to satisfy their clients' need for rapid, efficient corporate scrutiny and subsequent voting recommendations, apart from other services such as proxy voting. Although the service provided

---

[1] P.E. Masouros, 'Is the EU Taking Shareholder Rights Seriously? An Essay on the Impotence of Shareholdership in Corporate Europe' (2010) 7 *European Company Law* 195, 199.

[2] P. Rose, 'The Corporate Governance Industry' (2007) 32 *Journal of Corporation Law* 887, 897.

[3] Taking into consideration investors' lack of expertise in deciphering complex corporate decisions and their lack of funds for thorough research of companies' profiles but, most importantly, the constant pressure on many asset managers and institutional shareholder groups to deliver short-term benefits to their clients, the need for proxy services has become indisputable in the modern investment era: Rose, above n. 2, 897.

in this framework is unquestionably legitimate, the overall way in which it is provided, as well as its degree of influence on investors, must be addressed transparently at the EU level. Ensuring a high-quality service, along with a sophisticated approach when this service is actually used, are two objectives that require considerable attention if the common goal of creating a better investment environment is to be achieved.

A certain degree of regulatory intervention is necessary to eliminate any remaining preoccupying issues in the investment chain, and thus to fulfil these objectives. Indeed, investors tend to be overly reliant on the service provided by their proxy advisors, thus refraining from exercising their own independent judgement when invited to vote on resolutions.[4] This problematic situation has indirectly driven the debate towards the need for greater transparency in the proxy advisory industry in order to ensure such services maintain high-quality standards.

14.2 BACKGROUND

In the Green Paper on corporate governance,[5] the Commission initially mentioned the possibility of regulatory intervention in this field, a statement that was recently followed by the amended Shareholder Rights Directive.[6] The period between these two stages is highly interesting: the feedback from stakeholders on the appropriateness of such an agenda as explained in the Green Paper was very positive, showing a clear preference for more transparency. ESMA subsequently began its own consultation period with various stakeholders, and in February 2013, published its Final Report[7] on the results of the consultation and planning the introduction of an EU Code of Conduct, prepared by the Best Practice Principles Group (BPPG), an industry committee made up of proxy advisory firm representatives.[8] As we can observe, the regulatory choice for a Code of Conduct and the preparation of the Best Practice

---

[4] D.M. Gallagher, 'Remarks Before the Corporate Directors Forum' (2013), at http://www.sec.gov/news/speech/2013/spch012913dmg.htm. However, according to some empirical studies, the influence of voting recommendations is not that apparent: see, for example, S.J. Choi, J.E. Fisch and M. Kahan, 'The Power of Proxy Advisors: Myth or Reality?' (2010) 59 *Emory Law Journal* 869.

[5] Commission, 'Green Paper: the EU Governance Framework', Brussels (2011) COM (2011) 164 final, 14, at http://ec.europa.eu/internal_market/company/docs/modern/com2011-164_en.pdf#page=2; P-H. Conac, 'L'amélioration des règles applicables aux conseillers en vote' (2013) 7/8 *Revue des Sociétés* 404.

[6] Directive (EU) 2017/828 of the European Parliament and of the Council of 17 May 2017 amending Directive 2007/36/EC as regards the encouragement of long-term shareholder engagement [2017] OJ L 132/1.

[7] ESMA, 'Final Report: Feedback Statement on the Consultation Regarding the Role of the Proxy Advisory Industry', ESMA/2013/84, 19 February 2013, at http://www.esma.europa.eu/content/Feedback-statement-consultation-regarding-role-proxy-advisory-industry.

[8] GBPP, 'The Best Practice Principles for Shareholder Voting Research 2014' (2014), at http://bppgrp.info/wp-content/uploads/2014/03/BPP-ShareholderVoting-Research-2014.pdf.

Principles for Shareholder Voting Research by an industry committee testified to the need for maximum flexibility as this was the first approach for the introduction of a disclosure framework at the EU level, with very few examples of similar attempts in EU Member States.

Subsequently, ESMA issued a Report in 2015 related to the evaluation of the development of Best Practice Principles (BPP) and its outcome was broadly positive. The Commission followed with a rather different approach in the proposal for the amendment of the Shareholder Rights Directive, by proposing that proxy advisory firms publicly disclose a series of information on an annual basis with regard to the preparation of their voting recommendations without any recourse to the 'comply or explain' principle. That stance was in sharp contrast with the soft law framework of BPP and was finally slightly softened with the final version of the Shareholder Rights Directive, as we will see below. The new EU regulatory framework is still unclear and its future relationship with the BPP needs further examination. In order to highlight what the future disclosure framework could look like at the EU level, our attention will shift to two jurisdictions so as to show that persistent national differences in the area of proxy advisors will be of relevance for any future regulatory initiative.

14.3 THE UK AND FRENCH APPROACHES

A comparative analysis of the UK and French frameworks will make the argument for more transparency at the EU level even more interesting since various national frameworks currently in place provide different disclosure spectrums and show the reason why flexibility may need to be maintained, at least for the time being, in the proxy advisory industry's disclosure obligations. The argument for more flexibility focuses mainly on the fact that proxy advisory firms have not been previously subject to any disclosure obligations at the EU level, including in some EU Member States. It would therefore be only utopic to assume that the Shareholder Rights Directive will secure a uniform and widely applicable regulatory approach and bring substantial results in terms of transparency and comparability between different practices experienced at the EU level.

The UK Stewardship Code includes the proxy advisory industry in a general way in its spectrum, expecting such firms to become voluntary signatories and to abide by its principles.[9] Conversely, the French competent authority (*Autorité des Marchés Financiers*, hereinafter AMF) adopted in 2011 a recommendation that, although it does not have binding force, takes a rather stricter approach than the UK one.[10]

---

[9] Financial Reporting Council (FRC), 'The UK Stewardship Code' (2012), 9, at http://www. frc. org.uk/getattachment/e2db042e-120b-4e4e-bdc7-d540923533a6/UK-Stewardship-Code-September-2012.aspx.

[10] *Autorité des Marchés Financiers*, 'Recommandation AMF n° 2011-06 sur les agences de conseil en vote', 18 March 2011, 3, at http://www.amf-france.org/documents/general/9900_1.pdf.

For example, acknowledging the risk of conflicts of interest when providing various services, the AMF recommendation asks proxy advisory firms to mention any possible ties to the company whose resolutions they are evaluating, to shareholders who have proposed resolutions at the general meeting for which the proxy advisors have provided a report for their clients, and lastly, to any persons who might control directly or indirectly the public company or majority shareholdings as mentioned above. On the contrary, the UK Stewardship Code contains a rather general obligation to publicly disclose the robust policy on managing conflict of interest that its signatories should develop.

Moreover, with regard to engagement with investee companies, the UK Stewardship Code leaves the signatory parties to determine the framework for this type of engagement, while providing some very general recommendations. Principle 6 of the Code states, for example, that '[i]nstitutional investors should disclose the use made, if any, of proxy voting or other voting advisory services. They should describe the scope of such services, identify the providers and disclose the extent to which they follow, rely upon or use recommendations made by such services.'[11] Nevertheless, the AMF recommends that 'the proxy advisor submit its draft report to the relevant company for review, failing which the proxy advisor shall clearly state in its analysis report that the draft was not submitted for review and explain the reasons why'.[12]

Moreover, under the condition that the company has informed the proxy advisory firm of its resolutions, the board's reports and any other documents, at least 35 days before the general meeting, it has at least 24 hours to communicate any eventual remarks or comments. The firm has to include in its analysis report, upon the company's request, its comments on its voting recommendations, under the condition that those comments are precise, enlighten the shareholders on the draft resolutions and do not discuss the general voting policy. If applicable, the firm corrects any material mistakes detected in its analysis report and previously noted by the company concerned, and ensures disclosure to the investors as quickly as possible.[13]

This comparative analysis aims to highlight the different mentalities around the level and quality of interventionism in the proxy advisory industry. The UK Stewardship Code, following a much more flexible approach with very general guidelines applicable to a broad series of market participants, creates a satisfactory framework for proxy advisory firms, leaving them the freedom to operate in the market and disclose their practices accordingly. On the other hand, the French recommendation – albeit not binding – aims to shape a much more stringent framework which has not been unanimously accepted, taking into consideration the criticism from some respondents to the ESMA report that this recommendation has already created an unfavourable environment for some proxy advisory firms in comparison with other legal advisors or

---

[11] FRC, above n. 9, 9.
[12] AMF, above n. 10, 3.
[13] 3, ibid.

non-European firms.[14] This probably shows that the industry is not yet ready, in its entirety, to accept a stringent framework and instead prefers maximum operational flexibility and the subsequent malleability of applicable rules. Different regulatory approaches to shaping and suggesting a possible engagement with issuers make it even more arduous to achieve a meaningful EU consensus on this matter.

14.4 THE BEST PRACTICE PRINCIPLES

In 2013 a BBPG was formed by proxy advisory firms that aimed to formulate their own Principles within a soft law framework. In 2014, an EU Code of Conduct was launched.[15] It comes as no surprise that proxy advisory firms are not required to follow the Code's BBP but are merely encouraged to become signatories, and concomitantly to that assumption, are expected to disclose compliance with (or deviation from) the Principles based upon the 'comply or explain' principle. The relatively new disclosure imperatives in this area necessitate for these market actors, similar to disclosure deriving from institutional investors and asset managers, a certain degree of flexibility.

BPPG has issued three main Principles, accompanied by guidance notes recommending how the Principles should be applied. The three Principles refer to the service quality (provision of services delivered in accordance with agreed client specifications and disclosure of research methodologies and, if applicable, 'house' voting policies), the management of conflicts of interest (disclosure of a related policy that details the procedures for addressing potential or actual conflict of interest that may arise with regard to the provision of proxy services) and, lastly, the communications policy (disclosure of the policy for communication with issuers, shareholder proponents, other stakeholders, media and the public). It is also important to emphasize the very flexible nature and vague wording of some crucial provisions of this Code of Conduct which, coupled with the flexibility of the 'comply or explain' principle, give substantial leeway to proxy advisory firms to continue to determine the way in which they conduct their business without necessarily avoiding some delicate issues for which they have been already criticized, the management of conflicts of interest being the most notable.

In their statements of compliance, proxy advisory firms should describe in a meaningful way how they apply the Principles and related guidance, disclose any specific information set out in the guidance, and in cases in which they do not comply with either the Principles or the relevant information, they should provide a reasoned explanation for their 'non-compliance'.[16]

---

[14] ESMA, above n. 7, 18.

[15] BBPG, 'Best Practice Principles for Providers of Shareholder Voting Research & Analysis', March 2014, at http://bppgrp.info/wp-content/uploads/2014/03/BPP-ShareholderVoting-Research-2014.pdf.

[16] On this last issue, see L. Klöhn and P. Schwarz, 'The Regulation of Proxy Advisors', (2013) 8(1) *Capital Markets Law Journal* 90.

ESMA issued a Report in 2015 related to the evaluation of the development of BBP and its outcome was broadly positive, notwithstanding some key issues that need further improvement, such as the content of the explanations for non-compliance and the different approaches taken with regard to disclosure of conflicts of interest as well as of the relationship of voting policies and guidelines with voting recommendations.[17]

BBPG launched in October 2017 a review of the operation of BBPs to ensure they achieve their objectives and to examine any areas that might need reform. This development is inevitably influenced by the new disclosure obligations, applicable to proxy advisory firms, introduced by the Shareholder Rights Directive, to which our attention will now turn.

14.5 THE SHAREHOLDER RIGHTS DIRECTIVE

Since 2012 the Commission had in its plans to reinforce rules applicable to proxy advisors.[18] Indeed, with the initial proposal for the amendment of the Shareholder Rights Directive, the Commission moved in a rather surprising direction when it chose to require Member States to ensure that proxy advisory firms adopt and implement adequate measures, so as to safeguard the accuracy and reliability of their voting recommendations, without any recourse to the 'comply or explain' principle. This principle, as mentioned above, is vital for disclosure obligations at an embryonic stage specifically for proxy advisory firms. According to that same proposal, such firms were also expected to publicly disclose a series of information annually related to the preparation of their voting recommendations (again without any mention of the 'comply or explain' principle).

In its final version, the Shareholder Rights Directive has shaped disclosure obligations applicable to proxy advisors in the following (different) fashion:

(1) Firstly, Member States shall ensure that proxy advisors disclose publicly a reference to a code of conduct that they apply and also need to report on the application of that code. The 'comply or explain' principle has now been introduced so as to allow them to explain why they have chosen not to apply a code of conduct or they have decided to depart from some of its parts (if they apply one). The information provided needs to be updated on an annual basis and made publicly available.[19] The reference to a code of conduct in the Shareholder Rights Directive, accompanied by the 'comply or explain' principle, testify to a discreet approximation of the EU regulatory framework to the proxy advisory industry and its

---

[17] ESMA, 'Report: Follow-up on the Development of the Best Practice Principles for Providers of Shareholder Voting Research and Analysis' (2015) 18 December 2015, ESMA/2015/1887, at https://www.esma.europa.eu/sites/default/files/library/2015-1887.pdf.

[18] Commission, 'Action Plan: European Company Law and Corporate Governance – A Modern Legal Framework for More Engaged Shareholders and Sustainable Companies', Strasbourg, 12 December 2012, COM(2012) 740 final, 11, at http://eur-lex.europa.eu/LexUriServ/LexUriServ.do?uri=COM:2012:0740:FIN:EN:PDF.

[19] Article 3(j)(1), Directive (EU) 2017/828.

national or EU efforts[20] to promote its own principles and norms. Such disclosure also paves the way for encouraging more proxy advisory firms to adhere to a code of conduct across the EU and start reporting on its application. The Shareholder Rights Directive does not specify the contents of the report of such application, diminishing therefore the clarity, enforceability and usefulness of the new rule.

(2) Secondly, Member States shall ensure that proxy advisors disclose publicly on an annual basis at least the following information in relation to their research, advice and voting recommendations:
- the essential features of applied methodologies and models
- the main information sources used
- the applicable procedures for the safeguard of the quality of research, advice and recommendations as well as the qualifications of the involved staff
- whether and, if so, how do market, legal, regulatory and company-specific conditions are taken into account
- the essential elements of voting policies for each market
- whether dialogue with companies, falling within their activities' spectrum, as well as with the stakeholders of the company takes place and, if so, their extent and nature and, lastly,
- the applicable policies for the prevention and management of potential conflicts of interests.[21]

It should also be noted that such disclosure obligations are publicly disclosed but meant to inform adequately proxy advisors' clients about the accuracy and reliability of their activities. The emphasis upon these firms' clients aims to highlight the conceptual mindset within which such disclosure needs to take place and will inevitably influence the informational content provided to the public.

(3) Thirdly, Member States shall ensure that proxy advisors identify and disclose to their clients any actual or potential conflicts of interest (or business relationships) that may exert an influence on their services, as well as the actions that they have taken to eliminate, mitigate or manage this type of conflict.[22]

The first impression from the Directive's framework is that it creates a rather inconsistent framework with the EU Code of Conduct. This is due to the fact that, while very flexible, the Code of Conduct covers a considerable range of issues that, if combined with the related guidance, gives the market the chance to receive a considerable amount of information on proxy advisory firms. On the contrary, the Commission seems to have opted for disclosure of a minimum of

---

[20] See 2.4.3 and 2.4.4.

[21] Article 3(j)(2), Directive (EU) 2017/828.

[22] Article 3(j)(3), ibid. It should be also noted that the possibility to manage such conflicts was absent from the initial proposal of the Shareholder Rights Directive, which was exclusively focused upon the elimination or mitigation of such conflicts.

issues in a binding framework. Moreover, the 'comply or explain' principle is used for reference to a code of conduct, under 3(j)(1), but sits rather uncomfortably with the other hard law disclosure requirements under 3(j)(2) and (3).[23]

14.6 CONCLUSION

As a general conclusion, we firmly believe that it would have been preferable to coordinate private and public efforts in a better way so as to shape an initial regulatory framework for proxy advisory firms and to avoid further confusion and inconsistencies between different sources of rulemaking both at the national and EU levels. The main concern about the Directive's framework is that, by leaving it to Member States to require proxy advisors to disclose information on a specific series of issues, national frameworks will inevitably move towards this informational minimum without necessarily making the effort to trigger further reforms and create a more sophisticated and elaborate informational spectrum for the benefit of the rest of the market. At the same time, the BPP issued by BPPG will continue to exist at the EU level as a private-sector initiative and as a non-binding document that invites proxy advisory firms to become signatories and follow its principles.

The rather unfortunate result will therefore be that proxy advisory firms will be required to follow a minimum of binding disclosure requirements at the national level, with variable outcomes, while maintaining the discretion to adhere to (and probably not sufficiently engage with) a broader non-binding set of principles at the EU Code of Conduct level.

The main concern about this inconsistency is that it will become rather burdensome for the rest of the market to understand the information disclosed according to the regulatory framework at both the national and EU levels. Although it is rather premature to predict the outcomes of these different regulatory initiatives, the EU agenda needs to take into serious consideration potential sources of informational inconsistency and confusion that will make the overall disclosure exercise somewhat burdensome and – ultimately – of little use to market participants. A pertinent example in this sense is that the French framework is the only one in the EU that currently provides rules for the relationship between proxy advisory firms and issuers.[24] This and other national specificities will inevitably create discrepancies among Member States and will impede transparency in this area for the recipients of information.

It is hoped that the review of BPP may bring the private and the public sectors even closer to the creation of a more coordinated disclosure framework. This result will benefit both proxy advisory firms, who will avoid extra costs, and investors as well as stakeholders who will be able to find the information they need in a more concentrated manner.

---

[23] It should be also borne in mind that the use of 'whether' in two of these hard law informational requirements may create further confusion as to their nature and content, creating a multi-layered legal order (semi-hard and hard) and differentiation among proxy advisor statements: Article 3(j)(2), ibid.

[24] See 2.4.3.

BIBLIOGRAPHY

M. Andenas and I. H-Y. Chiu, *The Foundations and Future of Financial Regulation: Governance for Responsibility* (Routledge, 2013).

J. Armour, 'Who Should Make Corporate Law: EC Legislation versus Regulatory Competition' (2005) 48 *Current Legal Problems* 369.

J. Armour, D. Awrey, P. Davies, L. Enriques, J. Gordon, C. Mayer and J. Payne, *Principles of Financial Regulation* (Oxford University Press, 2016).

J. Armour, B.S. Black, B.R. Cheffins and R. Nolan, 'Private Enforcement of Corporate Law: An Empirical Comparison of the UK and US' (2009) 6 *Journal of Empirical Legal Studies* 687.

E. Avgouleas, *The Mechanics and Regulation of Market Abuse* (Oxford University Press, 2005).

E. Avgouleas, 'A New Framework for the Global Regulation of Short Sales: Why Prohibition is Inefficient and Disclosure Insufficient' (2010) 15 *Stanford Journal of Law Business and Finance* 376.

E. Avgouleas, *Governance of Global Financial Markets: The Law, the Economics, the Politics* (Cambridge University Press, 2012).

E. Avgouleas and G. Ferrarini, 'The Future of ESMA and A Single Listing Authority and Securities Regulator for the CMU' in E. Avgouleas, D. Busch and G. Ferrarini (eds), *European Capital Markets Union* (Oxford University Press, 2018).

M. Bianchi, C. Di Noia and M. Gargantini, 'The EU Securities Law Framework for SMEs: Can Firms and Investors Meet?' in Colin Mayer, Stefano Micossi, Marco Onado, Marco Pagano and Andrea Polo (eds), *Finance and Investment: The European Case* (Oxford University Press, 2018) 253.

H. Søndergaard Birkmose, 'European Challenges for Institutional Investor Engagement – Is Mandatory Disclosure the Way Forward' (2014) 2 *European Company and Financial Law Review* 214.

H. Søndergaard Birkmose (ed.), *Shareholders' Duties* (Kluwer Law International, 2017).

B.S. Black, 'The Legal and Institutional Preconditions for Strong Securities Markets' (2001) 48 *UCLA Law Review* 781.

B.R. Cheffins, *Corporate Ownership and Control: British Business Transformed* (Oxford University Press, 2008).

I. H-Y. Chiu, *Regulatory Convergence in EU Securities Regulation* (Kluwer Law International, 2008).

I. H-Y. Chiu, 'Turning Institutional Investors into "Stewards": Exploring the Meaning and Objectives of "Stewardship"' (2013) 66 *Current Legal Problems* 443.

I. H-Y. Chiu, *Regulating (from) the Inside: The Legal Framework for Internal Control in Banks and Financial Institutions* (Hart Publishing, 2015).

I. H-Y. Chiu, 'Corporate Governance and Risk Management in Banks and Financial Institutions' in I. H-Y. Chiu (ed.), *The Law on Corporate Governance in Banks* (Edward Elgar, 2015), 169.

B. Clarke, 'The Takeovers Directive – Is a Little Regulation Better Than No Regulation?' (2009) 15(2) *European Law Journal* 174.

B. Clarke, 'Reinforcing the Market for Corporate Control' (2011) 22 *European Business Law Review* 517.

J.C. Coffee Jr., 'Market Failure and the Economic Case for a Mandatory Disclosure System' (1984) 70 *Virginia Law Review* 717.

J.C. Coffee Jr., 'Racing Towards the Top? The Impact of Cross-Listings and Stock Market Competition on International Corporate Governance' (2002) 102 *Columbia Law Review* 1757.

J.C. Coffee Jr., *Gatekeepers: The Professions and Corporate Governance* (Oxford University Press, 2006).

P-H. Conac, 'Cash-Settled Derivatives as a Takeover Instrument and the Reform of the EU Transparency Directive', in H. Søndergaard Birkmose, M. Neville and K. Engsig Sørensen (eds), *The European Financial Market in Transition* (Kluwer Law International, 2012) 49.

P. Davies, 'Liability for Misstatements to the Market: Some Reflections' (2009) 9 *Journal of Corporate Law Studies* 295.

C. Di Noia and M. Gargantini, 'Issuers at Midstream: Disclosure of Multistage Events in the Current and in the Proposed EU Market Abuse Regime' (2012) 9(4) *European Company and Financial Law Review* 484.

C. Di Noia and M. Gargantini, 'Unleashing the European Securities and Markets Authority: Governance and Accountability after the ECJ Decision on the Short Selling Regulation (Case C-270/12)' (2014) 15 *European Business Organization Law Review* 1.

F.H. Easterbrook and D.R. Fischel, 'Mandatory Disclosure and the Protection of Investors' (1984) 70 *Virginia Law Review* 669.

L. Enriques, 'Regulators' Response to the Current Crisis and the Upcoming Reregulation of Financial Markets: One Reluctant Regulator's View' (2009) 30(4) *University of Pennsylvania Journal of International Law* 1147.

L. Enriques and M. Gatti, 'Is There a Uniform EU Securities Law After the Financial Services Action Plan?' (2008) 14(1) *Stanford Journal of Law Business and Finance* 43.

L. Enriques and S. Gilotta, 'Disclosure and Financial Market Regulation' in N. Moloney, E. Ferran and J. Payne (eds), *The Oxford Handbook on Financial Regulation* (Oxford University Press, 2015), 511.

E. Ferran, 'Understanding the New Institutional Architecture of EU Financial Market Supervision' in G. Ferrarini, K.J. Hopt and E. Wymeersch, *Rethinking Financial Regulation and Supervision in Times of Crisis* (Oxford University Press, 2012).

E. Ferran, N. Moloney, J.G. Hill, and J.C. Coffee Jr., *The Regulatory Aftermath of the Global Financial Crisis* (Cambridge University Press, 2012).

G. Ferrarini and P. Giudici, 'Financial Scandals and the Role of Private Enforcement: The Parmalat Case' (2005) ECGI – Law Working Paper No. 40/2005, 42, at http://ssrn.com/ abstract=730403

L. Gullifer and J. Payne, *Corporate Finance Law: Principles and Policy* (2nd edn, Hart Publishing, 2015).

K.J. Hopt, 'Better Governance of Financial Institutions' in G. Ferrarini, K.J. Hopt and E. Wymeersch (eds), *Financial Regulation and Supervision. A Post-Crisis Analysis* (Oxford University Press, 2012), 337.

M.C. Jensen and W.H. Meckling, 'Theory of the Firm: Managerial Behaviour, Agency Costs and Ownership Structure' (1976) 3 *Journal of Financial Economics* 305.

A.R. Keay, 'Comply or Explain in Corporate Governance Codes: In Need of Greater Regulatory Oversight?' (2014) 34(2) *Legal Studies* 279.

D.C. Langevoort, 'Taming the Animal Spirits of the Stock Markets: A Behavioral Approach to Securities Regulation' (2002) 97 *Northwestern University Law Review* 135.

I. MacNeil, *An Introduction to the Law on Financial Investment* (2nd edn, Hart Publishing, 2012).

I. MacNeil, 'Credit Rating Agencies: Regulation and Financial Stability' in T. Cottier, R.M. Lastra, C. Tietje and L. Satragno (eds), *The Rule of Law in Monetary Affairs* (Cambridge University Press, 2014), 178.

I. MacNeil, 'Rethinking Conduct Regulation' (2015) 30(7) *Butterworths Journal of International Banking and Financial Law* 413.

I. MacNeil, 'Enforcement and Sanctioning' in N. Moloney, E. Ferran and J. Payne (eds), *The Oxford Handbook on Financial Regulation* (Oxford University Press, 2015), 280.

I. MacNeil and X. Li, 'Comply or Explain: Market Discipline and Non-Compliance with the Combined Code' (2006) 14(5) *Corporate Governance: An International Review* 486.

N. Moloney, 'Confidence and Competence: The Conundrum of EC Capital Markets Law' (2004) 4 *Journal of Corporate Law Studies* 1.

N. Moloney, *How to Protect Investors: Lessons from the EC and the UK* (Cambridge University Press, 2010).

N. Moloney, 'Reform or Revolution? The Financial Crisis, EU Financial Markets Law, and the European Securities and Markets Authority' (2011) 60(2) *International and Comparative Law Quarterly* 521.

N. Moloney, 'The Investor Model Underlying the EU's Investor Protection Regime: Consumers or Investors? (2012) 13 *European Business Organization Law Review* 169.

N. Moloney, *EU Securities and Financial Markets Regulation* (3rd edn, Oxford University Press, 2014).

M.T. Moore, 'The Evolving Contours of the Board's Risk Management Function in UK Corporate Governance' (2010) 10 *Journal of Corporate Law Studies* 279.

M.T. Moore, *Corporate Governance in the Shadow of the State* (Hart Publishing, 2013).

M.T. Moore and E. Walker-Arnott, 'A Fresh Look at Stock Market Short-Termism' (2014) 41(3) *Journal of Law and Society* 416.

M. Neville and K. Engsig Sørensen, 'Suspension of the Exercise of Voting Rights – A Step Towards Deterrent and Consistent Sanctioning of EU Transparency Requirements?' (2017) Nordic & European Company Law Working Paper No 16-25, at https://ssrn.com/abstract=2958677

J. Payne, 'The Regulation of Short Selling and Its Reform in Europe' (2012) 13 *European Business Organization Law Review* 413.

J. Payne, 'The Role of Gatekeepers' in N. Moloney, E. Ferran and J. Payne, *Oxford Handbook of Financial Regulation* (Oxford University Press, 2015), 254.

M.C. Schouten and M. Siems, 'The Evolution of Ownership Disclosure Rules Across Countries' (2010) 10(2) *Journal of Corporate Law Studies* 451.

K. Sergakis, 'Deconstruction and Reconstruction of the "Comply or Explain" Principle in EU Capital Markets' (2015) 5(3) *Accounting, Economics and Law: A Convivium* 233.

M. Siems and A. De Cesari, 'The Law and Finance of Share Repurchases in Europe' (2012) 12 *Journal of Corporate Law Studies* 33.

M. Siems and M. Nelemans, 'The Reform of the EU Market Abuse Law: Revolution or Evolution?' (2012) 19 *The Maastricht Journal of European and Comparative Law* 195.

K. Engsig Sørensen, 'Shareholders' Duty to Disclose' in H. Søndergaard Birkmose (ed.), *Shareholders Duties* (Kluwer Law International, 2017), 319.

V. Tountopoulos, 'Market Abuse and Private Enforcement' (2014) 3 *European Company and Financial Law Review* 297.

C. Van der Elst and A. Lafarre, 'Bringing the AGM to the 21st Century: Blockchain and Smart Contracting Tech for Shareholder Involvement' (2017) ECGI – Law Working Paper No. 358/2017, at https://ssrn.com/abstract=2992804

R. Veil (ed.), *European Capital Markets Law* (2nd edn, Hart Publishing, 2017).

C. Villiers, *Corporate Reporting and Company Law* (Cambridge University Press, 2005).

E. Wymeersch, 'The Institutional Reforms of the European Financial Supervisory System, an Interim Report' (2010) Financial Law Institute, Universiteit Gent, Working Paper No 2010-01, at http://ssrn.com/abstract=1541968

INDEX